# Contemporary
# Western Europe

This book, part of a college-level audio/print course in international studies, was developed by the Global Understanding Project at National Public Radio in cooperation with the Institute on Western Europe at Columbia University and National Media Programs, University Extension, University of California, San Diego. Funds for the preparation of print and audio materials were provided by the Annenberg/CPB Project, which was established in 1981 by a grant to the Corporation for Public Broadcasting from the Annenberg School of Communication.

 An Annenberg CPB/Project

# CONTEMPORARY WESTERN EUROPE

## Problems and Responses

Edited by

**Glenda G. Rosenthal**

and

**Elliot Zupnick**

**PRAEGER**

PRAEGER SPECIAL STUDIES • PRAEGER SCIENTIFIC

New York • Philadelphia • Eastbourne, UK
Toronto • Hong Kong • Tokyo • Sydney

**Library of Congress Cataloging in Publication Data**
Main entry under title:

Contemporary Western Europe.

  Edited collection of pieces from the Columbia University Institute on Western Europe and the text element of a 4-part audio course.
  Bibliography: p.
  Includes index.
  1. Europe—Politics and government—1945–     —Addresses, essays, lectures.   2. Europe—Economic conditions —1945–     —Addresses, essays, lectures.   3. Europe— Social conditions—20th century—Addresses, essays, lectures.   I. Rosenthal, Glenda G. (Glenda Goldstone) II. Zupnick, Elliot, 1923–

JN94.AzC66   1984          940.55          84-6835
ISBN 0-03-071792-2 (alk. paper)
ISBN 0-03-071793-0 (pbk.  :  alk. paper)

Copyright credits and permissions have been collated in the acknowledgments section of the front matter.

Published in 1984 by Praeger Publishers
CBS Educational and Professional Publishing
a Division of CBS Inc.
521 Fifth Avenue, New York, NY 10175 USA
© 1984 by The Corporation for Public Broadcasting and The Regents of the University of California.

456789 052 987654321

Printed in the United States of America
on acid-free paper

# Acknowledgments

## Unit I

John E. Rodes, "Another Postwar Period." From *A Short History of the Western World*. Copyright © 1970 John E. Rodes. Reprinted with the permission of Charles Scribner's Sons.

Charles L. Robertson, "Toward European Unity." From *International Politics Since World War II*. Copyright © 1975 by John Wiley & Sons, Inc. Reprinted by permission of John Wiley & Sons, Inc.

"Europe Divided." From *An Encyclopedia of World History* by William L. Langer. Copyright 1940, 1948, 1952, and © 1968, 1972 by Houghton Mifflin Company. Copyright © renewed 1969 by William L. Langer. Reprinted by permission of Houghton Mifflin Company.

Walter Laqueur, "European Politics, 1970–1978." Excerpted from *A Continent Astray: Europe, 1970–1978* by Walter Laqueur. Copyright © 1979 by Walter Laqueur. Reprinted by permission of the Oxford University Press, Inc.

William H. Overholt, "Update Spring '83." From William H. Overholt, Editor, *Global Political Assessment* Number 15, October 1982–April 1983. Copyright © 1983 by the Research Institute on International Change, Columbia University.

## Unit II

Harry K. Girvetz, "The Welfare State." From "Welfare State" by Harry K. Girvetz. Portions of this article are reprinted by permission of the publisher from the *International Encyclopedia of the Social Sciences*, David L. Sills, Editor, Volume 16, pages 512–521. Copyright © 1968 by Crowell Collier and Macmillan, Inc.

Milton Friedman, "The Role of Government in a Free Society." Reprinted from *Capitalism and Freedom*, Chapter 11, pages 22–36, by Milton Friedman by permission of The University of Chicago Press. © 1962 by The University of Chicago. All rights reserved.

## Unit III

T. Alexander Smith, "An Overview of Political Institutions." Reprinted from *The Comparative Policy Process* by T. Alexander Smith by permission of ABC-Clio, Inc. Copyright © 1975 by T. Alexander Smith.

## Unit IV

## Unit V

## Unit VI

B. Guy Peters, "Politics in Britain: How Power Is Used." From *Comparative Politics* by Dan N. Jacobs, David P. Conradt, B. Guy Peters, and William Safran. Copyright © 1983 by Chatham House Publishers, Inc. Also available in *European Politics* by David P. Conradt, M. Donald Hancock, B. Guy Peters, William Safran, and Raphael Zariski (Chatham, N.J.: Chatham House Publishers, 1984). Reprinted by permission.

P.A. Allum, "Italy's Executive and Legislature." From *Italy—Republic Without Government?* by P.A. Allum. Reprinted by permission of W.W. Norton & Company, Inc. and George Weidenfeld and Nicolson Limited, London. Copyright © 1973 by P.A. Allum.

William Safran, "Politics in France: How Power Is Used." From *Comparative Politics* by Dan N. Jacobs, David P. Conradt, B. Guy Peters, and William Safran. Copyright © 1983 by Chatham House Publishers, Inc. Also available in *European Politics* by David P. Conradt, M. Donald Hancock, B. Guy Peters, William Safran, and Raphael Zariski (Chatham, N.J.: Chatham House Publishers, 1984). Reprinted by permission.

## Unit VII

Karl W. Deutsch and D. Brent Smith, "Social Structure in Contemporary West Germany." From Karl W. Deutsch, D. Brent Smith, pp. 241–246, "Social Structures, Interest Groups and Elites," in *Modern Political Systems: Europe*, 4th Ed., Roy C. Macridis, Ed., © 1978. Reprinted by permission of Prentice-Hall, Inc., Englewood Cliffs, N.J.

Francis G. Castles, "Scandinavia's Changing Political Culture." From Francis G. Castles, pp. 430–432, 437–438, 444–447, "Scandinavia: The Politics of Stability," in *Modern Political Systems: Europe*, 4th Ed., Roy C. Macridis, Ed., © 1978. Reprinted by permission of Prentice-Hall, Inc., Englewood Cliffs, N.J.

William Safran, "French Politics: The Economic and Social Context." Abridged from *The French Polity*, First Edition, by William Safran. Copyright © 1977 by Longman Inc. Reproduced by permission of Longman Inc., New York.

A.H. Birch, "British Government: The Society and the People." From *The British System of Government*. Copyright © 1967, 1968, 1973 by George Allen & Unwin Ltd. Reprinted by permission of George Allen & Unwin (Publishers) Ltd.

R.M. Punnett, "The Social Context of British Politics." From *British Government and Politics* by R.M. Punnett, Fourth Edition, London, Heinemann Educational Books Ltd., 1980. Reproduced by permission of the publisher. Second Edition, by permission of W.W. Norton & Company, Inc. Copyright © 1971, 1970, 1968 by R.M. Punnett.

## Unit VIII

"Economic Trends, 1960–1980." From the Organisation for Economic Co-operation and Development, *Historical Statistics, 1960–1980*. Copyright 1982 by the OECD, Paris, France. Reprinted by permission.

Sir Geoffrey Howe, "Speech Introducing the 1979 Budget Resolution." Excerpted from pages 235–263, *Parliamentary Debates (Hansard)*, Fifth Series, Volume 968, House of Commons Official Report, 1979. Reproduced by permission of Her Majesty's Stationery Office, London.

Steven Rattner, "Report Card on Thatcherism." © 1983 by The New York Times Company. Reprinted by permission.

"France: New Government, New Strategy." Excerpted from the *OECD Observer*, no. 115, March 1982. Copyright 1982 by the *OECD Observer*. Reprinted by permission.

Janice McCormick, "Thorns Among the Roses: A Year of the Socialist Experiment in France." From *West European Politics*, Volume 6, Number 1, January 1983. Reprinted by permission of Frank Cass & Co. Ltd.

"Ten-Point Program of Action." Adapted from "Ten-Point Plan to Restore Trade Balance," prepared by the Press and Information Service of the French Embassy, March 1983. Reprinted by permission of the French Embassy Press and Information Service.

## Unit IX

Organisation for Economic Co-operation and Development, "The New Interventionism." From *Positive Adjustment Policies: Managing Structural Change*. Copyright © 1983 by OECD. Reprinted by permission of OECD. (Note: OECD publications may be obtained from the OECD Publications and Information Center, Suite 1207, 1750 Pennsylvania Ave. N.W., Washington, D.C. 20006.)

Wyn Grant, "A Typology of Policy Alternatives." From *The Political Economy of Industrial Policy* by Wyn Grant. Copyright © 1982 by Butterworth & Co (Publishers) Ltd. Reprinted by permission of the publisher.

Wyn Grant, "Industrial Policy: The British Case." From *The Political Economy of Industrial Policy* by Wyn Grant. Copyright © 1982 by Butterworth & Co (Publishers) Ltd. Reprinted by permission of the publisher.

Organisation for Economic Co-operation and Development, "France: New Strategies in Industrial Policy." From *OECD Economic Surveys, 1982–1983: France*. Copyright © 1983 by OECD. Reprinted by permission of OECD.

Juergen B. Donges, "Industrial Policies in West Germany's Not So Market-Oriented Economy." Extracted, with permission, from "Industrial Policies in

West Germany's Not So Market-Oriented Economy" which appeared in the September 1980 number of *The World Economy*, the quarterly journal of the Trade Policy Research Centre, London. Copyright © 1980 by Elsevier Science Publishers B.V. Reprinted by permission of *The World Economy* and Elsevier Science Publishers, B.V.

Wyn Grant, "The European Community and Industrial Policy." From *The Political Economy of Industrial Policy.* Copyright © 1982 by Butterworth & Co (Publishers) Ltd. Reprinted by permission of the publisher.

Organisation for Economic Co-operation and Development, "The New Protectionism." From *Positive Adjustment Policies: Managing Structural Change.* Copyright © 1983 by OECD. Reprinted by permission of OECD.

## Unit X

Elliot Zupnick, "Social Welfare and Politics." Original material written for the book.

Peter Flora and Jens Alber, "The Development of Welfare States in Europe." Published by permission of Transaction, Inc. from *The Development of the Welfare States in Europe and America*, edited by Peter Flora and Arnold J. Heidenheimer. Copyright © 1981 by Transaction Books.

Jürgen Kohl, "Trends and Problems in Postwar Public Expenditure Development." Published by permission of Transaction, Inc. from *The Development of the Welfare States in Europe and America*, edited by Peter Flora and Arnold J. Heidenheimer. Copyright © 1981 by Transaction Books.

David Brand, "Generosity's Price: Social Welfare Costs in the Netherlands." Reprinted by permission of *The Wall Street Journal*, © Dow Jones & Company, Inc. 1983. All Rights Reserved.

Barnaby J. Feder, "Sweden's Welfare State Under Stress." © 1983 by The New York Times Company. Reprinted by permission.

## Unit XI

Commission of the European Communities, "The European Community and the Energy Problem." Excerpted from *The European Community and the Energy Problem*, European Documentation Collection, published by the Commission of the European Communities, 1983. Reprinted by permission of the Office for Official Publications of the European Communities.

The Swedish Institute, "Energy and Energy Policy in Sweden." From *Fact Sheets on Sweden*, November 1983. Reprinted by permission of The Swedish Institute, Stockholm.

Commission of the European Communities, "Review of Member States' Energy Policy Programs." From "Review of Member States' Energy Policy

## Unit XII

## Unit XIII

Karl Kaiser, Winston Lord, Thierry de Montbrial, and David Watt, "Western Security: What Has Changed? What Should Be Done?" Excerpted from *Western Security: What Has Changed? What Should Be Done?* by Karl Kaiser et al. Copyright 1981 by the Council on Foreign Relations, Inc., and the Royal Institute of International Affairs. Used by permission.

"The Theater Nuclear Weapons Debate." From *The New York Times*, January 23, 1983. © 1983 by The New York Times Company. Reprinted by permission.

Stanley Hoffmann, "NATO and Nuclear Weapons: Reasons and Unreason." Excerpted by permission of *Foreign Affairs*, Winter 1981–82. Copyright 1981 by the Council on Foreign Relations, Inc.

## Unit XIV

Howard Bliss, "The Schuman Declaration." From *The Political Development of the European Community* edited by Howard Bliss, © Copyright, 1970, Xerox Corporation. Used by permission of Ginn and Company (Xerox Corporation).

Richard Mayne, "Europe Responds: The ECSC." Reprinted from *The Community of Europe* by Richard Mayne, by permission of W. W. Norton & Company, Inc. and Victor Gollancz Ltd., London. Copyright © 1962 by Richard Mayne.

Howard Bliss, "The Messina Resolution." From *The Political Development of the European Community* edited by Howard Bliss, © Copyright, 1970, Xerox Corporation. Used by permission of Ginn and Company (Xerox Corporation).

"The European Community System." Excerpted from three publications of the Commission of the European Communities: "The Institutions of the European Community," *European File*, March 1982; "Relaunching Europe: Agricultural Policy, Target 1988," *European File*, February 1982; and "The Institutions of the European Community," *Working Together: The Institutions of the European Community*, 1982. Reprinted by permission of the Commission of the European Communities. Also excerpted from *European Community Facts*, courtesy of the European Community Information Service, Washington, D.C.

Baudouin I, King of the Belgians, "Europe 25 Years After." From *Europe 25 Years After the Signature of the Treaties of Rome: Speeches Made at the Official Celebration at the Palais des Académies in Brussels on 29 March 1982*. Reprinted by permission of the Council of the European Communities.

Commission of the European Communities, "Towards European Union? A Public Opinion Poll." Excerpts from "Public Opinion and Europe," *European File*, May 1982. Reprinted by permission of the Commission of the European Communities.

## Unit XV

# Development Team

## Academic Project Coordinators

**Elliot Zupnick, Ph.D.**
Director, Institute on Western Europe
Columbia University

**Mary L. Walshok, Ph.D.**
Dean, University Extension
University of California, San Diego

## Chief Academic Consultant

**Glenda G. Rosenthal, Ph.D.**
Assistant Professor of Political Science
Columbia University

## Chief Research Associate

**Ritva Poom**
Columbia University

## Editorial Director

**Linda Wood**
National Media Programs
University of California, San Diego

## Associate Editor

**Helen Hawkins, Ph.D.**
National Media Programs
University of California, San Diego

## Project Manager

**Lynn Fontana, Ph.D.**
International Studies
National Public Radio

## Project Coordinator

**Yvonne Hancher**
National Media Programs
University of California, San Diego

## Research Assistants

Oksana Dackiw
Kevin Kennedy

## Editorial Assistants

Barbara Rose
Phil Muilenburg

# Advisory Committee
# Global Understanding Project

**Dr. Rose L. Hayden**
Executive Director
National Council on Foreign
Languages and International Studies

**Mr. James R. Mahoney**
Director, International Services
American Association of
Community and Junior Colleges

**Ms. Carol Katzki**
Associate Director
National University Continuing
Education Association

**Dr. Sheilah Mann**
Director, Educational Affairs
American Political Sciences
Association

**Dr. F. Stephen Larrabee**
Professor,
Department of Government
Cornell University

**Mr. Timothy Plummer**
Director,
Education and Communications
Asia Society

**Dr. Frank Wolf**
Associate Dean,
School of General Studies
Columbia University

# Contents

# Preface

*Contemporary Western Europe: Problems and Responses* is a key component of the audio/print course, "Contemporary Western Europe," developed by the Global Understanding Project at National Public Radio. The book was edited by Dr. Glenda G. Rosenthal and Dr. Elliot Zupnick of the Institute on Western Europe at Columbia University, with assistance from Linda Wood and Dr. Helen Hawkins, in association with National Media Programs, University Extension, University of California, San Diego.

The primary goal of the Global Understanding Project is to provide adult learners with opportunities to explore and better understand some of the more pressing global political issues of our time. The course materials developed for "Contemporary Western Europe" include a blend of audio and print components. The audio component consists of fifteen hour-long audio programs, which were produced on location in Western Europe. Each program features commentaries by authorities on foreign affairs as well as interviews with European policymakers, scholars, and people on the street who provide insights into problems and concerns that are shared by Europeans and Americans alike. The print component includes this anthology, as well as a study guide and a faculty/administrative manual. This book, produced by the combined efforts of two leading Western Europe scholars, is designed to complement the audio programs. In its presentation of excerpts from the writings of prominent individuals in the field of European affairs, along with supportive documents culled from a variety of scholarly, popular, and government sources, the book sheds light on some of the major policy problems facing Europeans today and shows how the different countries of Western Europe are attempting to cope with these problems. The study guide and faculty/administrative manual are designed to assist students and educators in making the most constructive use of the materials. A special feature of the course is a twenty-minute audio program designed to help students improve their listening skills.

The Global Understanding Project has also produced a second course, titled "The Challenge of China and Japan," as well as a series of audio/print resource modules for use in traditional political science classrooms. The issues explored—economics, arms control/security, bureaucracies, social welfare, and political parties—are presented in an international context. Each module includes an audio program, an essay written by a scholar in the field, and an instructor's guide.

The Global Understanding Project was funded by the Annenberg/ CPB Project, which was established in 1981 by a grant to the Corporation for Public Broadcasting from the Annenberg School of Communication. The two major goals of the Project are 1) to demonstrate the use of telecommunications systems for addressing unique problems of higher education and 2) to create one or more significant collections of innovative, high-quality, college-level materials.

# Introduction

The readings included in *Contemporary Western Europe: Problems and Responses* have been carefully selected to give the reader a broad understanding of the various types of governing processes prevalent in Western Europe today as well as an insight into the major policy problems currently being faced by the different Western European governments. While the book views each European country as having its own historical, cultural, and social heritage, a major focus is the wide range of responses to common problems found among the different Western European countries today. How are the individual Western European governments, with all their historical and cultural diversity, dealing with such issues as inflation, unemployment, declining industries, immigration, energy supply and demand, and national security? For our purposes in attempting to answer these questions, governance can be viewed as a complex interweaving of historical and contemporary forces that have a profound influence on both national and Europe-wide responses to important policy problems.

Another important focus of the book is the growing connectedness among the Western European nations, particularly among those of the advanced industrialized world. Indeed, it is becoming increasingly apparent that many of the problems facing Europeans, and other peoples of the world as well, can no longer be solved by individual countries alone. In the closing decades of the twentieth century, global interdependence has become a vivid economic and political reality. The question is, how well can we adapt to this new interdependence and more important, how quickly? Are our present systems of government prepared to take the important steps toward mutual cooperation that may ultimately determine the quality of life in future decades? The book explores these and related questions.

To provide the reader with the historical background needed to understand political life in contemporary Western Europe, Unit I presents a brief overview of some of the key historical developments since the end of World War II that have contributed to the shaping of present-day European politics. Units II through VI examine the various institutions and agents of government found in Western Europe in order to shed light on the different processes of policy formulation, decision making, and policy implementation that are characteristic of the different European countries. Unit VII makes the transition from the discussion of the institutions and processes of government presented in the first half of the book to a treatment of some of the more pressing contemporary problems. The social factors discussed in this unit are critical elements of Western European society and are bound up in some of the most important concerns of public policy formation in many European countries. Units VIII through XIV focus on specific issues that are of critical concern to European policymakers today. The final unit, Unit XV, examines the ways in which the political choices and decisions made by Europeans in dealing with the salient issues of the day affect their relationships with other parts of the world.

# Unit I

# The Historical Background

Our study of political life in contemporary Western Europe begins with a look at some of the recent historical developments that have contributed to the shaping of present-day European politics. At the end of World War II, the nations of Western Europe were faced with a new world political structure in which the United States and the Soviet Union emerged as competing giants in a power struggle made more ominous by the existence of nuclear weapons. Much of Western Europe had suffered extensive physical damage as well as other losses as a result of the war, and by the time Germany surrendered in May 1945 the economy of Western Europe was a shambles. With financial assistance from the United States, however, it was possible for the war-torn European democracies to carry out the difficult tasks of reconstruction.

Countries varied considerably in their rate of recovery. In some areas, reconstruction efforts were complicated by divisive ideological rivalry that was spearheaded by the United States and the Soviet Union and that eventually resulted in the separation of Europe into East and West blocs and of Germany into two nations. But despite these divisive forces, there was a strong impulse toward federalism among the nations of Western Europe. A sense of individual weakness, the threat of communist gains, American inducements, and a desire to regain pre-war economic and political status provided the original impetus for Western Europe's cooperative movement toward mutual development, which culminated in 1958 in the formation of the European Economic Community (EEC or "Common Market").* Although American influence remained strong in Western Europe until the 1970s, European dependence on the United States has gradually decreased over

the years as the Western democracies have prospered economically and regained self-confidence.

This unit provides an overview of key developments in
Western Europe since the end of World War II. As John E. Rodes
outlines in "Another Postwar Period," the countries of Western Europe varied in their rate of recovery, in their particular
postwar problems, and in their political responses to them.
Nations that had been reduced to second-rank status by the
war, after having been world colonial powers for a century or
more, faced serious political adjustments. Several Western
European countries shaped new constitutions or new party
structures. Many received American economic assistance as
the two new superpowers competed for influence in the region. Nearly all joined with the United States in the North
Atlantic Treaty Organization (NATO), a mutual defense alliance. In "Toward European Unity," Charles L. Robertson describes the series of cooperative organizations which culminated in the creation of the European Economic Community.

A map of Europe in the 1970s, "Europe Divided," reveals
that the basic alignments of countries in the East-West bloc
have remained virtually unchanged since 1949, when Germany was split into two separate countries. Walter Laqueur,
in "European Politics, 1970–1978," shows how the economic
crises of the 1970s challenged governments' ability to respond, unleashed feelings of impotence and a desire for
change, and put new strains on the already-troubled Atlantic
Alliance. William H. Overholt evaluates the current economic situation in "Update Spring '83," the final reading in
this unit, and shows how political uncertainty and economic
tensions have led to a widespread swing toward conservatism
throughout much of Western Europe.

---

*The European Economic Community (EEC) is also referred to as the "Eu-
ropean Community," although that term more generally applies to the collection of institutions that includes the EEC along with the European Coal and
Steel Community (ECSC) and the European Atomic Energy Community (Euratom or EURATOM). (See Unit XIV.)

# 1

# Another Postwar Period

John E. Rodes

In these excerpts from a chapter in *A Short History of the Western World*, Rodes outlines the responses of the major Western European countries to conditions following the Second World War and examines the new roles the United States and the Soviet Union assumed in world affairs.

In modern war, distinctions between victor and vanquished have become increasingly blurred. Russia, France, and China, for example, emerged on the side of the victors in World War II, yet they suffered more devastation than some of the defeated states. Similarly, no correlation existed between being on the winning side and the speed of postwar recovery. West Germany's economy, for instance, recovered rapidly, whereas economic reconstruction of France took much longer. Although different factors affected the progress of recovery in each area, two general inferences are possible: most countries received outside aid, particularly from the United States; and reconstruction in most instances was complicated by ideological rivalry between Marxism and anti-Marxism, coupled with the power struggle between Russia and America that emerged at the end of the war.

In July 1945, the Allied Big Three (Stalin, Truman, and Attlee) met at Potsdam near Berlin to establish directives for the occupation of Germany. The resultant Potsdam Agreements, although intended as temporary measures, gradually assumed long-range importance, since the Allies could not agree on a formal peace treaty for Germany. According to the Potsdam Agreements, Germany was given her 1937 boundaries in the West, except for the coal-rich Saar, which was temporarily placed under French administration. . . .

The defeated nation was divided into four zones, governed respectively by Russian, English, American, and French zone commanders who theoretically acted under the supervision of an Allied Control Authority (ACA). Similarly, the city of Berlin, deep inside the Russian zone, was split into four Allied sectors.

At Potsdam it was furthermore stipulated that Germany be demilitarized and de-Nazified, and that democratic ideals be encouraged. Reparations were to be paid by the removal of factories and industrial equipment, by the seizure of foreign assets, and by deliveries from current production. Ethnic Germans residing in Poland, Czechoslovakia, and Hungary were to be transferred to Germany. Moreover, German industry was placed under strict economic controls to prevent the manufacture of war materiel, to decartelize her industrial complexes, and to limit her level of production. No central German government was to be established until democratic institutions had been developed at the local level. However, Germany as a whole was to be treated as an economic unit, with a free flow of goods from one occupation zone to another, and "so far as . . . practicable," there was to be "uniformity of treatment of the German population throughout Germany."

Acting like a provisional legislature for all of Germany, the Allied Control Authority, representing the four occupying powers, passed ordinances to implement the Potsdam Agreements. Yet, wide differences soon developed between the four zones, since execution of such directives depended on the four zone commanders and their respective governments. Both France and Russia were interested in keeping Germany impotent. The French sought this end by pressing for a loose confederation of states, whereas the Russians favored a centralized state, which they hoped would be dominated by Socialist or Communist parties. Great Britain desired a unitary German state with some reserved local powers, and America called for a federal system. . . .

Mounting tension between the three Western occupiers and the Soviet Union prevented agreement on reparations deliveries to Russia, on badly needed financial and economic reforms for Germany, and on an all-German peace treaty. Hence Great Britain and the United States, with the reluctant consent of France, merged their zones and proceeded with plans for the creation of a federal government for the three Western zones. By the spring of 1948, all four-power cooperation on the Potsdam model had ceased. The stalemate was soon climaxed with a total land blockade of Berlin by the Russians, who hoped to force the Western powers to lift their ban on reparations deliveries to Russia from the Western zones. The West successfully countered Russia's gambit with a dramatic eleven-month airlift of food and supplies for the Western sectors of Berlin. After the failure of this Berlin blockade, Russia and the West, even more than before, each went their own way in administering their respective areas of occupied Germany. Germany and the city of Berlin thus became divided into two states.

In the fall of 1948, the United States, England, and France author-ized the election of a convention for their three zones to draft a provi-sional constitution, with the understanding that the Russian zone could join in at any time. Dominated by the new Christian Democratic Union and the Social Democratic party and guided by Allied advice, this constitutional convention eventually produced the so-called Basic Law, a provisional constitution for the Federal Republic of Germany. Subject to a special Occupation Statute and separate provisions for the industrial Ruhr region, Western Germany, with Konrad Adenauer as Chancellor, was then given conditional self-government by the Western Allies on September 21, 1949. Two weeks later, the Russians trans-formed their zone into the German Democratic Republic, controlled by Walter Ulbricht's Socialist Unity party, a combination of Communists and Socialists.

Economic reconstruction had initially been hindered by zonal divi-sions, by the lack of a sound currency, by the influx of refugees and the uncertainty of Germany's political future. The currency reform of 1948 and the establishment of a stable government in 1949 quickly initiated a remarkable industrial resurgence in Western Germany. With Ameri-can support in the form of the Marshall Plan and other aid programs, with new industrial equipment replacing that destroyed by bombing or dismantled as reparations, with a highly cooperative and skilled labor force, and with no expenses for rearmament, the West German econ-omy revitalized itself miraculously. By 1955, West Germany had over-come severe agricultural shortages and assumed the third place among the world's industrial powers. . . .

As the cold war intensified and led to armed confrontation in Korea (1950), the two Germanies became increasingly absorbed into the op-posing camps. The United States, in particular, sought the creation of a West German army that could contribute toward the defense of Western Europe against a possible Soviet attack. Despite strong misgivings among many Germans and serious reservations in France and Great Britain, the Bonn government of West Germany finally agreed to remili-tarize. In return for building a new conventional army and joining the North Atlantic Treaty Organization, the Federal Republic was granted its sovereignty in May, 1955, just ten years after Germany's surrender to the Allies. In response, Russia stepped up the remilitarization of East Germany and incorporated her economic and military resources into the communist bloc of Eastern Europe. The division of Germany thus became frozen into the antagonism between the Western and the Com-munist camps. . . .

Postwar recovery among the lesser ex-Axis states was slower than in Germany and Japan. Austria, for example—although immediately permitted to form a central government, which prevented the kind of splintering that occurred in Germany—was unable to recuperate while under foreign occupation. Effective economic rehabilitation began only after 1955, when the first thaw in the cold war after Stalin's death led to agreement on a treaty for Austria. . . .

Italy's postwar status was ambiguous, since she was both a defeated Axis power and a co-belligerent of the Allies. Large-scale destruction, lack of food and raw materials, inexperience with democratic processes, and distrust between former Fascists and ex-partisan fighters complicated the reshaping of Italy's political and economic life. After a popular referendum abolished the discredited monarchy, a new constitution, conservative in tenor and favorable to the Catholic Church, was promulgated in 1948. The subsequent elections were crucial for the future of Italy. A large Communist party, supported by left-wing Socialists, contended against Alcide de Gasperi's conservative Christian Democrats and turned Italy's polls into a battlefield of the cold war. American promises of aid vied with communist charges of "American imperialism." When the electorate endorsed de Gasperi, Italy turned firmly to the West and eventually joined the North Atlantic Treaty Organization (NATO). Despite economic progress, however, political stability continued to be jeopardized by the weakness of the moderates in contrast to the strength of the Communist party, the largest outside the communist bloc countries.

Although not an avowed belligerent in World War II, Franco's Spain had flirted with Hitler and sent a Spanish division to fight against Russia. Hence the United Nations, in 1946, barred Spain from all U.N. organizations. . . . As in the case of Germany and Japan, the Korean War changed America's attitude. Spain was granted diplomatic recognition and economic aid and made a partner of America's overseas military establishment. Thereafter, the Western Europeans reluctantly admitted the dictatorial Franco regime into the world community. With Spain's economy slowly improving, Franco gradually loosened his dictatorship, although until the late 1960s, he retained full personal control of the government of Spain.

As in 1918, Great Britain and France emerged from a World War on the victorious side, but this time facing the painful acknowledgment that they no longer ranked among the first powers of the world. To be sure, most citizens were primarily concerned with the immediate problem of their material existence; also, the numerous socialists in both countries, traditionally international in outlook, were less worried about national prestige than were the more empire-minded conservatives. Yet, the morale of the British and the French depended to some extent on the skill of their governments in offering compensatory satisfactions at home as substitutes for the lost glory and the colonial empires that were slipping from their control.

England's Labor government under Clement Attlee concentrated its efforts on raising the standard of living of the lower classes. It passed legislation to grant more power to labor unions, to provide free medical service for everyone, and to nationalize, among others, the Bank of England, the coal and electric power industries, and the transport and communications facilities. Nationalization of basic enterprises resulted not only from the socialist dogma that such industries should be run in the interest of *all* the people. The Labor ministry also argued that only the government had sufficient funds to effect needed modernization and to increase productive capacity. . . .

Although Great Britain felt compelled gradually to dismantle her empire, first in Asia and then in Africa, and although she reluctantly recognized that in world decisions she carried only a secondary voice behind America and Russia, she attempted to safeguard a measure of world-wide influence through skillful diplomacy and military preparedness. She retained the sympathetic support of most members of the former empire and maintained a military presence through a far-flung chain of naval bases. Despite the cost, which she could ill afford, she temporarily continued to develop her navy and air force, instituted a peacetime draft, and built her own hydrogen bombs. Although acting at times as mediator between Russia and America, she in fact established extraordinarily close ties with the United States, a relationship decried as tutelage by the left-wing members of the Labor Party. Toward Continental Europe, however, her attitude remained ambivalent. She joined various defensive agreements and other cooperative arrangements with non-Communist Europe, and Churchill, while not in power, eloquently supported attempts at European unification. Yet Britain long remained reluctant to abandon her isolation and to tie her economy to that of Western Europe.

With the decline of the Liberal party, the English drifted toward a two-party system. Elections in 1951 returned the Conservatives to power for thirteen years, until the Labor party in turn regained control of the government. Since the Laborites gradually substituted pragmatic measures for doctrinaire socialism, and the Conservatives acquiesced in the basic ideals of the welfare state and recognized the necessity to continue the dismantling of the empire, these governmental changes produced few essential alterations in policy.

French postwar problems differed from those of Great Britain. In World War II, France had suffered more destruction, and she had undergone the humiliation of foreign occupation as well as quasi-civil war among Nazi collaborators, Vichy French, Communists, the French underground, ànd [Charles] de Gaulle's Free French. Furthermore, Britain still enjoyed a workable political system and cohesion through loyalty to a popular monarchy, whereas France, having scuttled the Third Republic in favor of Vichy's fascist regime, faced the task of writing a new constitution and constructing a viable political framework. De Gaulle, who acted as provisional President, favored the creation of a strong executive ànd resigned when his advice was not heeded. The new constitution, which the feuding parties and a bewildered electorate finally adopted in 1946 as basis for France's Fourth Republic, retained the strong legislature that had characterized the Third Republic. Once again ministerial instability, caused by bickering among numerous political parties, marked the French political scene.

The weak French coalition governments, succeeding one another in a rapid ministerial merry-go-round, could not solve the nation's financial, economic, and imperial problems. Postwar recovery continued to be hampered by inflation, lagging industrial production, an inequitable tax imposition, a poor tax-collection system, and an inefficient, entrenched bureaucracy.

Attempts to transform her colonial empire into a French Union similar to the British Commonwealth proved only a temporary expedient as a step toward colonial independence. The North African possessions, Morocco, Tunisia, and Algeria, agitated restlessly against French domination, even though Algeria was officially considered an integral part of France. In Indo-China—consisting of Laos, Cambodia, Cochin-China, Tonkin, and Annam—where nationalistic feelings had grown steadily during the Japanese occupation, the French sought unsuccessfully to regain their former control through a mixture of force and concessions. . . .

The United States, and to some extent Russia, emerged from the war with problems largely the reverse of those of England and France. Whereas the war had toppled the latter from first-power status, it had catapulted America and the Soviet Union to control over vast areas of the globe. Whether reluctantly or by imperialistic design, the two giant powers soon found themselves sharing in the responsibility for patrolling the world, a task previously exercised by Western Europe's colonial powers. Furthermore, unlike Britain and France, the United States exported considerably more than she imported and hence was the major creditor and financier of the world. The United States dollar had supplanted the British pound sterling as the preferred international currency (except for gold), a position it was to retain until the mid-1960s. . . .

. . . America assumed firm political and military commitments on a global scale. Besides joining the United Nations, she occupied the forefront in various international cooperative organizations and entered into an array of military pacts. The Truman Doctrine of 1947, specifically aimed at bolstering the troubled governments of Greece and Turkey, summed up the new stand "that it must be the policy of the United States to support peoples who are resisting attempted subjugation by armed minorities or by outside pressure."

---

# 2

## Toward European Unity

Charles L. Robertson

The political unification of Western Europe has long eluded its proponents, but some significant progress has been made in establishing cooperative organizations for mutual benefit among various nations. Here, Charles L. Robertson traces important milestones on the road which led to the "Common Market" and analyzes related political events, particularly in France under Charles de Gaulle.

. . . The reluctance to accept the division of the world into two blocs—a widely evident view among groups not in power, but shared by those in power—gave impetus to the move for European unity. The movement for some kind of unification had a long history and took various forms. The combination of individual weakness, Russian pressures, American inducements, and the desire to be more than merely part of the American bloc brought it to fruition.

American initiatives, largely inspired by the idea of containment, led to the creation of the Organization for European Economic Cooperation [OEEC] and the European Payments Union [EPU]—both fruit of the Marshall Plan. . . . But there were purely European moves that reflected different aims.

Earliest of these was the Benelux Customs Union of Belgium, the Netherlands, and Luxemburg. . . .

On the political front, Winston Churchill's call for a "kind of United States of Europe," delivered at Zurich University on September 19, 1946, helped to inspire the work of a host of new organizations devoted to the idea. Their own activities, Cold War developments, and popular response led to the signing, on May 5, 1949, of the Statute of the Council of Europe. It received sufficient ratifications to come into force in August.

The Council of Europe and the accompanying Committee of Ministers were essentially cooperative rather than supranational organs, reflecting the reluctance of all the governments concerned to surrender any of their powers. . . .

The Council's basic purpose was to suggest ways of effecting European integration. Since it could only recommend, while governments disposed, a split rapidly developed between the Council and the Committee of Ministers: the Council charged that the Committee kept it from doing any useful work. Within the Council itself another split occurred between "federalists" and "functionalists"—those who wanted to develop a set of viable political institutions first, and those who wanted to build "from the bottom" and thus create forms of economic cooperation, common institutions with limited functions, all of which would eventually serve as the foundations for political organs.

Further developments hinged on Franco-German relations. . . .

. . . German reconstruction proceeded so fast that to accommodate it French Foreign Minister [Robert] Schuman had to do even more. He devised a scheme—the Schuman Plan—that would allow for German reconstruction and yet guarantee that it would pose no threat to France. The German and French coal and iron and steel industries would be pooled under the control of a high authority. Removed from the sovereignty of existing governments, the steel industry would no longer provide the foundation for military aggression of one against the other. . . . But on June 13, 1950, before the actual negotiations got under way, it produced an event that would have long-lasting repercussions: the British Labour Party stated it could not participate: "European peoples do not want a supranational authority to impose agreements." The European movement was now split. On the security level it comprised an Atlantic Community; on the political level it included Western Europe as a whole. But on the economic level, although cooperation among all the Western countries was guaranteed through the OEEC and EPU, the little Europe of the Six began to emerge. . . .

From 1945 to 1956 no Western state could contest American supremacy. In these years a smaller but viable Europe re-emerged from the ashes of World War II; yet American opposition to the 1956 Suez adventure,* appeared to define the limits of European independence. Europeans no longer depended upon American economic aid, but a major part of their trade was with the United States. They had rebuilt and reequipped their own armies, but the presence of 350,000 American

---

*Ed. note: After invading Egypt to prevent nationalization of the Suez Canal, Britain and France were forced to withdraw when U.S. President Dwight Eisenhower made clear his opposition to the use of force in settling international disputes and the Soviet Union threatened to intervene.

troops and American control of atomic weapons demonstrated that NATO, under United States leadership, was still the guardian of European security. Despite anger over Suez, mistrust of [John Foster] Dulles, misgivings about American foreign policy generally, and years of often effective Communist propaganda, America retained an unassailable position and role; young people in Europe still named it as the country in which they would most like to live. American leaders and the American people thought of themselves as the leaders in the fight against both colonialism and totalitarian tyranny.

The next 15 years brought a startling change. Stimulated rather than dejected by the defeat of the proposed European Defense and Political Communities in 1954 and by the Suez disaster of 1956, European leaders gave the idea of unity a new lease on life, and produced the European Economic Community (EEC) or Common Market. . . .

. . . [T]he signature in Rome on March 25, 1957 of the treaties creating the European Economic Community and Euratom may be used to mark another major development of the postwar period: the emergence of a prosperous and self-confident Europe after 40 years of wars, depression, and social and political chaos. The new European prosperity was more widely shared than in the past; Western European countries had by and large divested themselves of empire, and the eastern boundaries of the new Europe were far to the west of where they once had been. German division continued to plague the continent, and the nuclear threat shadowed everything. But for the first time in over half a century—and in spite of much questioning of the established order—Europeans again believed in a future.

The European Economic Community included only six nations: France, Germany, Italy, Belgium, Luxemburg, and the Netherlands. Prosperity, with all its attendant difficulties began in the early 1950s, long before the formation of the EEC. Nevertheless, the establishment of the EEC so soon after the collapse of the European Defense Community and the proposed Political Community in 1954 was an extraordinary political step, testifying to the ingenuity and energy of all those men who rallied from the earlier defeat to bring to fruition the new proposals.

What they planned, in short, was a broad customs union—an association of states in which trade barriers among them would be eliminated and a common tariff to the outside world established around them. Britain declined to participate in the negotiations, pleading its Commonwealth and Atlantic commitments. The French, in early 1957, still attempting to integrate Algeria into France and trying to forge a new set of relationships with their other African territories, almost halted the negotiations with their demand that some kind of associated status be arranged for overseas territories. In the end, the other countries paid the French price to get the Common Market: overseas territories would have access to the Common Market without having to pay the common tariff. They could, however, maintain their own external tariffs against the rest of the world, and their developing industries could retain some protection against European products that would not be allowed to regular Common Market members. The price also included establishment of a Common Market development fund to be channeled to the associated territories (including the Belgian Congo and Ruanda-Urundi). But other states also received concessions: the Common Market included a bank to channel funds to low-income areas within the Market—which meant, in practice, southern Italy.

The planners of the Common Market hoped for one thing: that the stages of growth through which it was to pass would lead to eventual political unity. They reasoned that establishment of a common customs boundary around a free-trade area would mean that the countries involved would eventually have to bring into harmony their social security laws, tax systems and fiscal policies, and policies on investment. The planners hoped that as each stage was reached, with the concomitant necessity for further harmonization of domestic policies, the countries' governments would find that the easiest way to bring policies into line was through handing them over to the central organs of the Common Market.

But people who were not particularly interested in such political integration supported the Common Market on the basis of economics alone. They could believe its aim—the creation of a huge internal market—could be achieved through cooperation rather than unity. Full achievement of the Market would take 12 to 15 years, so that events might well modify some of the later stages and escape clauses could be invoked. In other words, people with a variety of views were able to support the proposed Common Market, and ratification proceeded with relatively few difficulties. The treaty and the companion one establishing a European Atomic Energy Community* took effect on January 1, 1958. The Market members soon began cutting their internal tariffs and modifying other internal restrictions—quotas, subsidies, discriminatory transport charges, and so on.

Ten years later, and despite various crises, internal tariffs disappeared completely and the common external ones came into effect. In the meantime the various Councils of Ministers and Commissions of the Common Market and Euratom and of the earlier Coal and Steel

---

*Ed. note: Popularly known as Euratom.

community merged, while all came to share a Parliament, Court of Justice, and legal, statistical, and information services. . . .

"Europe" . . . had come far. France, as always, remained the key element in the fluctuations. . . . In good part, these fluctuations were a consequence of the views and the rise and decline of one towering figure, General Charles de Gaulle.

De Gaulle came to power in 1958 when military insurrection threatened the weak and vacillating government of the Fourth Republic. France had never been more prosperous. But the officers of an army that had fought long and bitterly in Indochina only to withdraw in 1955 felt they had been sabotaged by governmental weakness at home. The army had gone into Suez in 1956, and a weak government had capitulated to foreign pressure and withdrawn from it. In 1958 four to five hundred thousand French troops were in Algeria, attempting to quell a nationalist insurrection. A million French Algerians insisted that Algeria remain French, and discovery of oil deposits that might lessen French dependence upon the unstable Middle East led to increased pressures to hold onto Algeria. Yet the rebellion persisted. . . . Once more, behind a determined Army, the government wavered. De Gaulle and his supporters had long held that the only solution to France's perennial governmental instability lay in elimination of Parliamentary supremacy and the party system; in May 1958 they and Algerian settlers found the army ready to act. Officers seized power in the North African territory, and other officers in France refused the government's demand to order them to relinquish it. Under threat of paratroop attack upon the mainland, the Parliament and President bowed, and de Gaulle, the army's choice, was invested as Prime Minister.

In short order, and with Parliamentary sanction, a Gaullist Constitution was produced, submitted to public referendum where it won acceptance by a 4 to 1 vote, and de Gaulle became President of the new Fifth Republic. The Constitution drastically curtailed the powers of Parliament while increasing those of the President. Subsequent changes approved by referenda further strengthened the office. . . .

The stability was misleading. . . . European industry in general and French in particular had little of the dynamism of American industry, allocated far less of its funds to research and, in fact, faced its fastest-growing competition not abroad, but in American-owned industry in Europe. Moreover, the almost unbelievable growth of Japanese industry in the 1960s was producing a new competitor, just when French industry found itself being opened up to more and more competition from its EEC partners, as the Common Market internal tariffs crumbled. Unnoticed by all but financiers, speculators, and some few government officials, another development posed a further threat: the growing American balance-of-payments deficit. The United States could correct the excess outflow of American dollars in several ways; almost any one of them would involve reduced sales or exports to the United States. This alone, was bound to hurt European economies. But even more, it would lead the Japanese, limited in terms of what they could sell to America, to further penetration of the European market.

So it was, in May 1968, when French students joined in a world-wide movement of student protest, and triggered a general strike by laborers whose expectations and dissatisfactions increased as the affluence of the surrounding society increased, the whole Gaullist edifice toppled. . . . His prestige gravely diminished, vulnerable on other fronts as well, de Gaulle weathered the 1968 crisis but resigned on April 28, 1969 over subsequent defeat in a referendum on a relatively minor matter of governmental reform. . . .

# 3

# Europe Divided

## William L. Langer

The alignment of the European nations into East and West blocs has remained essentially unchanged since 1949, when Germany was split into what eventually were to be two separate countries and the NATO alliance was created. Greece and Turkey were already within the Western sphere of influence, although they did not become members of NATO until 1952. Germany's admission to NATO in 1955 spurred the immediate formalization of the Warsaw Pact, a mutual defense treaty which established an alliance between the U.S.S.R. and the Eastern European countries under Soviet influence, which included East Germany, Albania, Czechoslovakia, Bulgaria, Hungary, Poland, and Roumania. Albania withdrew from the Warsaw Pact in 1968. Since this map was made, steps have been taken to admit Spain to NATO membership.

Europe in 1970. Reprinted by permission from William L. Langer, *An Encyclopedia of World History* (1972).

# 4

# European Politics, 1970–1978

## Walter Laqueur

The impact of economic conditions on political events is usually more clearly felt in bad times than in good. In the following selection, Laqueur examines the series of economic crises that hit Europe in the 1970s and asks whether the countries of Western Europe were, in fact, becoming ungovernable.

European history during the 1970s is largely about a sequence of economic emergencies and the ways in which governments, parliaments, and experts tried to cope with such problems as inflation and unemployment and crises in balances of payments and investments. . . .

Unemployment and inflation constituted serious problems. . . . But even at a time of recession the great majority of Europeans had enough money to buy non-essential goods, and . . . , by and large, they were better off than at any other period in the past, and of course, still much wealthier than the rest of the world with the exception of the U.S., Canada, and a few oil-producing countries.

And yet there was a feeling of gloom and doom, of the center coming apart, of an end of stability, of the bankruptcy of the system . . . It is certainly true that measured against the expectations of the 1950s and 1960s, of steady growth and constantly rising living standards, the feeling in the 1970s was one of disappointment. Elsewhere, as in Britain, there was dejection because the country had been doing badly in comparison with others. . . . No country remained immune to the revolution of expectations, and the more the consumers' mentality spread in the societies of Western Europe, the greater the importance attributed to the production and distribution of goods. . . . What made the recession appear so formidable was not however its magnitude but a feeling of impotence. Yet even such serious problems as youth unemployment or the energy crisis were by no means intractable. The know-how, the technical means to cope with the issues existed. But the political will to deal with them, the solidarity, the leadership, were in short supply and consequently there was a fear that the countries of Europe were becoming, or had already become, ungovernable. . . .

A great many causes have been adduced to explain the European crisis of the 1970s. Yet in the final analysis the basic roots were not hidden. Firstly, the weakness of the political system, unable to resist the conflicting demands of various sections of society, and secondly, the clash between the urge for more freedom on one hand and the need for more order on the other. . . .

This . . . is the background to the crisis facing the countries of Western Europe. . . . The basic problems were remarkably similar, but there was still a great deal of variation in their respective misfortunes, and this will now be examined. . . .

## GREAT BRITAIN

During the 1970s Britain became the "sick man of Europe." . . . Britain in foreign eyes was the most striking case of the sad decline that a mixture of bad luck and incompetence had visited upon a once powerful, self-confident, forward-looking nation. . . . Britain had become one of the poorest nations of Europe and also one of the least productive. . . .

. . . [S]terling had steadily fallen, and prices had risen; in 1973, a boom year, British industrial production had risen by 7%, but the overall record of the British economy was still bad. A great many reasons have been adduced to explain this; lack of professionalism in management and the cult of the amateur, inept bureaucratic involvement, inadequate investment, industrial conflict produced by a multiplicity of craft unions, overmanning, resistance to technological progress by trade unions, and unwillingness on the part of the management to learn from the example of others. Above all perhaps, the proportion of work force employed in manufacture declined far more rapidly in Britain than in any other major industrial country. The service sector rose more sharply (from 47% to 55% between 1960 and 1974), without however improving the quality or the extent of the services. There were, in short, fewer people to generate greater income.

The industrial climate deteriorated very badly; if some two million work days were lost in 1964, the figure had risen to 24 million in 1972— not to count the work-to-rule, ban-of-overtime, and go-slow strikes. British productivity became a topic of greater interest to humorists and gag writers than to economists and statisticians, let alone foreign buyers. . . .

## FRANCE

General de Gaulle had called a referendum on regional reform which took place in April 1969. . . . [W]hen it appeared that de Gaulle had been defeated, he announced his immediate resignation in the briefest of communiques. . . . De Gaulle was succeeded by a man who was not scheduled to be his heir, though he had served for six years as his prime minister. . . .

[Georges] Pompidou was a shrewd politician. . . .

During its first three years the reputation of Pompidou's government soared on a wave of success and some foreign observers predicted a glorious future for France. Economic progress continued, the left was split, and the regime faced no major challenges. But even before the full effects of the economic recession were felt in 1973, public support began to vanish. . . . The country sank into an economic recession and the political effects soon followed. France was divided into two camps of more or less equal strength; as the left moved towards unity, and the center and right towards division, and as the party in power got the blame for the deteriorating economic situation, the ruling coalition's base of popular support continued to shrink. Giscard d'Estaing, who became the new president of the republic after Pompidou's death, scraped through by a mere 300,000 votes in the elections of May 1974.

The obvious economic grievances apart, the basic complaints against Pompidou's administration and that of his successor focused on the absence of change, and this at a time when the demand for change was no longer confined to revolutionaries on the left. France, it was argued, was a blocked society, it was ruled by a bureaucracy, octopus-like . . . , ineffective, and out of touch with the people. Technocracy, it was said, was no answer to social and political ills, and people had no feeling of active participation, the rigid social structure did not correspond with the exigencies of a modern society. The government did not dare to do away with the archaic procedures, prerogatives, and privileges (sometimes of medieval origin) of small groups. These complaints were by no means groundless, and it was also true that differences in income were greater in France than in almost any other advanced society, that taxation was often ineffective. When Giscard tried to push through a modest capital gains tax, he encountered stiff resistance from the rich. The French right, which had never been distinguished for its social consciousness and far-sightedness, was clearly in no mood for concessions, and as a result all the latent conflicts became even more acute. Lastly, there was the growing complaint that successive governments, sold on the idea of economic growth, had neglected the quality of life. . . .

Giscard introduced a new style, partly on the Kennedy pattern, and there was a great deal of idealistic speech-making during the early days of his rule about a new society and a new democracy. . . .

Of Giscard's promised reforms only a few materialized. . . .

. . . France remained deeply divided into two more or less equally strong camps, and the long term survival of the government coalition still depended on its ability to overcome its internal splits and the paralysis of will it had shown in the previous years. . . .

## GERMANY

When the Social Democrats took over the reins of government in 1969 almost a quarter of a century had passed since the end of the Second World War and Germany had emerged as the richest and most stable country in Western Europe. Germany's post-war economic recovery had been one of the miracles of the century. . . .

True, the Social Democratic-Liberal coalition had only a tiny majority. . . . But by and large the left-liberal coalition justified the hopes of the electorate. This was the period when relations with the Soviet Union and the other East European countries were normalized and when massive trade surpluses continued. In the general elections of November 1972 the Social Democrats became the strongest party in the land; the future of the coalition seemed assured for an indefinite period. . . .

Germany's economic woes were not remotely comparable to those facing the other European nations. Its inflationary rate—about 6% in 1975—was the envy of all other countries. . . . If there were reasons for concern these were long-term rather than immediate. . . .

Post-war German recovery had been so spectacularly successful because it had been based on consensus politics, on the realization that a common effort was needed. . . . By the middle seventies, however, the German consensus came under severe strain. The unions were no longer willing to give priority to investment; they became more insistent on getting their rewards here and now. At the same time there was renewed trouble in the universities: the number of students had trebled within a decade, and as in so many other countries there was a danger, indeed a near certainty, of academic unemployment. . . .

The terrorist campaign of the 1970s preoccupied German society far beyond its intrinsic importance. Perhaps it was only natural in view of the German longing for perfection and their apparent inability to live with a modicum of disorder, something other, more fortunate nations seemed to relish. Some observers argued that Germany faced a civil war-like situation. . . . Some felt inclined to brand everyone as a "sympathizer" who was not altogether happy with the status quo in Germany. . . .

German prosperity and stability did not necessarily make for popularity among her neighbors. . . . There was envy that Germany should weather the economic storms better than the other European countries and that its institutions seemed more stable. . . .

## ITALY

Italy's time of adversity began with the mass strikes of the hot autumn of 1969 and has continued ever since. The underlying reasons have not been in dispute: the "imperfect two party system," the intricate spoils system which undermined confidence in the state, the presence of an inflated bureaucracy and ineffective state sector in the national economy, the unpleasant social consequences of the stormy economic growth of the 1960s. . . . [E]conomic mismanagement resulted in an inflationary rate which at the depth of the recession was even higher than Britain's as well as 1.7 million unemployed. . . . Italy had a trade deficit of eight billion dollars in 1974, and it managed to survive only by means of credits from the IMF [International Monetary Fund] and Germany. . . . In Italy, . . . one has to turn from the economic to the political aspects of the crisis to understand its apparent intractability. . . .

. . . [A]fter three decades of uninterrupted rule the Christian Democrats were no longer capable of governing and there was no democratic alternative. . . . The conviction gained ground that Italy could not be ruled without the Communists, but there was equally no conviction that it could be done with them. Still, as the economic recession deepened, as student unrest, wildcat strikes, and terrorism from left and right threatened a total breakdown of public order, some arrangement with the PCI (Italian Communist party), tacit or open, became an apparent necessity, and the history of Italy in recent years has been the story of the gradual emergence of ad hoc compromises rather than the great "historical" compromise about which everyone talked. . . .

Some aspects of the Italian situation resembled the state of affairs that had prevailed in the country in the years before the rise of fascism. Terrorist gangs, some of them recipients of foreign help, roamed the streets. . . . [P]olitical opponents were attacked or intimidated, newspaper offices were bombed, "reactionary" and "right-wing" judges and journalists were shot. . . .

The situation in the universities was quite chaotic: Rome University, built for some 10–15,000 students had grown to 165,000, following an "open admission" policy. This was an extreme, but by no means altogether untypical case. Officially the universities continued to function, but in practice whole departments no longer provided systematic tuition, standards fell abysmally, and many of the graduates could not find work commensurate with their expectations. They joined the ranks of the demonstrators for whatever cause was put on the political agenda. . . .

. . . [I]n Italy. . . there was no political outlet for many of the country's discontents. Nowhere among advanced industrial societies was the feeling so widespread that the citizen had no means of expressing his views and desires and that the whole system had ceased to function. . . . [I]n March 1978 the Communists received equal footing with the other parties in shaping government policies. In exchange it was agreed that the Communists would vote for the government and not just abstain. The Communists dropped their original demand for cabinet posts (December 1977) and promised support for a national unity emergency government "to get Italy out of the depth of the crisis." . . .

## SPAIN

When General [Francisco] Franco died in November 1975 he had been in power longer than any other chief of government or head of state in Europe. . . . [H]ardly anyone had believed that the transition from authoritarian to democratic rule would be relatively short and painless. . . . Important changes had taken place well before Franco's death: economic development had been strong; per capita income had risen tenfold from $248 to $2,865 between 1960 and 1975; and even if the cost-of-living had risen by almost 400 per cent during that period this was commensurate with a very considerable increase in living standards. Spanish export earnings and the number of cars in use, to provide two more examples, had grown at a similar rate. Six million foreign tourists had visited Spain in 1960; fifteen years later their number had risen to thirty million, the largest in Europe. During the same period some five million Spaniards had moved from the countryside to the towns, and several million had gone to work outside Spain. On the surface, Spain had changed more during the last two decades than any other European country.

But there was also political change side by side with the repression that continued through the early seventies. . . . Towards the end of its existence, the Franco regime was no more than a loose coalition of a variety of factions and interest groups jockeying for position. It no longer inspired awe, fear, or hate, except perhaps among national minorities. Spain was not a time bomb about to explode, and while the great majority of Spaniards, as it was soon to appear, wanted far-reaching change, they were in no mood for a revolution, let alone a new civil war.

King Juan Carlos, who had been appointed by Franco as his successor, appointed Adolfo Suarez as prime minister, and the two, much to the surprise of left-wing critics, pushed a Political Reform Act through Parliament which within the span of a year was to transform radically the Spanish political landscape. After some hesitation even the Communist party was made legal (April 1977). There was an enormous upsurge in political (as in cultural) activity. In preparation for Spain's first free elections in forty years some two hundred political parties emerged. In view of such internal division there were serious doubts whether Spain was ready for democracy. Yet again, the sceptics were confounded: two-thirds of the votes went to the two major parties—the Union of the Democratic Center (35 per cent) and the Socialist Workers party (29 per cent). Both the Communists (9 per cent) and the right (8 per cent) fared much less well than their well-wishers and many outside observers had assumed; perhaps even more significant was the fact that the Spanish Communists were the most liberal in Europe, and that the right . . . was also willing to abide by the democratic rules. During the election campaign and after, the party leaders showed a measure of maturity and responsibility that no one had expected in the light of Spain's previous experiments with democracy. . . .

Thus the first stage of the transition period was passed without any major upheavals. . . .

## PORTUGAL AND GREECE

When freedom returned to Portugal in April 1974 the country had been under dictatorial rule for a period even longer than neighboring Spain, and the prospects seemed even less promising. The coup was carried out by a group of officers who had been demoralized (and radicalized) by the colonial wars in Africa in which they were not defeated but which, they had learned by bitter experience, the country could no longer afford. . . . During the first year after the revolution, effective control was in the hands of . . . several hundred middle rank officers. . . .

. . . It was only after the democratic forces inside the junta had asserted themselves that notice was taken of the popular will. . . .

By late 1975 the struggle for freedom seemed to have been won; [Mario] Soares the Socialist became prime minister. But the fight was by no means over; the difficulties facing Soares were formidable. . . . Unlike Spain, the Portuguese dictatorship had not laid the foundation for a modern economy, and the heritage of the post-liberation inter-regnum in which enormous wage increases had been given while pro-ductivity was declining had further undermined the Portuguese econ-omy. Lastly, the army of the unemployed was swelled by the hundreds of thousands of repatriates from Africa. . . . Only through foreign loans was the Soares government able to keep the country afloat. . . .

Unlike the Portuguese dictatorship, the Greek military junta was not overthrown, it crumbled and disappeared in late July 1974. This had been preceded by a struggle for power inside the junta and a wave of protest demonstrations. . . . On the domestic scene the transition to democracy went smoothly. [T]he new government received an over-whelming vote of confidence (54 per cent) in the elections of November 1974. There was an even greater majority for the abolition of the monar-chy in the plebiscite the month after. . . . Greece faced the same eco-nomic problems as the rest of Europe. . . . The main political issue was the instability among the political parties, the constant splits and shifts with new parties appearing, aligning or realigning themselves, or disin-tegrating rapidly and with monotonous regularity. . . .

# 5

# Update Spring '83

## William H. Overholt

In these excerpts from an article published in spring 1983, the author surveys the current economic situation in Western Europe and points out that the greater success of the more conservative governments in achieving economic recovery has led to a widespread swing toward conservatism throughout Western Europe, even in countries that have traditionally relied on socialist strategies to solve their economic problems. He warns that unless tensions within the European Community are resolved, Western Europe may face "a very difficult time ahead" in its efforts to sustain economic recovery and achieve fuller employment.

. . . The advent of the world economic recovery was generally recognized by Western Europeans by early spring [1983]. Greater success in countries with more conservative governments, and hope that recovery will give governments greater ability to address pressing social problems, has enhanced a widespread swing toward more conservative governments and policies in much of Western Europe. Even in those countries, like Sweden, Spain, Portugal, and Greece, where the trend has apparently been in the opposite direction, the governments have been proceeding with extreme caution in implementing "socialist" programs. France, Europe's most active socialist government, has set an example of the failure of traditional socialist and social democratic economic policy.

However, doubts remain as to whether the recovery will be sufficiently enduring, strong, or well-coordinated to ensure much progress toward fuller employment and industrial adjustment. Recent tensions within the European Community (EEC), notably between France and Germany over monetary and trade policy, vividly illustrated the seriousness of the divisions within Western Europe which, if the recovery is not sustained, could quickly recur and threaten a fundamental fracture in the common market of a kind that was narrowly averted during the recession. Likewise, domestic protests in the prospective host countries for the U.S. Pershing II and ground-launched cruise missiles (GLCMs) are likely to intensify during the year as the time of first deployments approaches. However, there was little doubt that the deployments would proceed on schedule in West Germany, Britain, and Italy barring an unexpected breakthrough in the Soviet-American negotiations in Geneva, and the peace movement may well wane after the deployments get underway.

In West Germany, the political uncertainty created by the fall of the Social Democrat/Free Democrat (SPD/FDP) coalition in September and the succession of the Christian Democrat (CDU) dominated coalition under Helmut Kohl was resolved by elections in early March. The election confirmed the new coalition in office and reaffirmed the essential role of the FDP, which had at one time seemed likely to lose representation in parliament. The CDU/FDP coalition could dominate German politics for the rest of the decade. . . . On the left, the future is more uncertain. . . . [T]he SPD received the lowest vote since 1961 and is torn between the center-left exponents of the Schmidt tradition and those who wish to move party policies more to the left in the hopes of siphoning off the 5.6 percent support that went to the Greens (environmental/anti-nuclear parties). . . .

In France, the Socialist government of President Francois Mitterrand and Prime Minister Pierre Mauroy found itself presented during the winter with the heavy bills for its precipitous expansionary measures of 1981–1982. As a result the government faced difficult decisions concerning internal austerity measures, further devaluation of the franc (and possibly even leaving the European Monetary System (EMS), and protectionist measures. By March, with substantial government losses in the municipal elections, President Mitterrand was forced to act. Economically, the government opted to resist the temptation of massive protectionism and to exploit this choice to pressure West Germany into bearing the greater part of the burden of currency realignments within the EMS. At the same time, stringent internal deflationary measures, which West Germany demanded, and tight exchange control restrictions were imposed in an attempt to prevent further weakening of France's external economic position. . . .

In Britain, economic recovery contributed to Mrs. Thatcher's decision about the date of the General Election, due before May 1984. A June date was chosen because of signs that the government's control of public expenditure was weakening and fears that inflation, running at under 4 percent in April, would rise; fears that the Labour Party would finally emerge from its internal divisions by the summer and present a more attractive prospect to the electorate, notably by capitalizing on its opposition to the nuclear missile deployment in Britain; a parallel fear that the Social Democrat/Liberal Alliance might recover strength after its recent slump in the polls; concern that the unprecedentedly low rate of strikes would increase with recovery; and a general feeling that, even though unemployment remains high, the recovery created favorable conditions for the Conservatives [who achieved a decisive victory]. . . .

In northern Europe, the most important political and economic question has been whether the recently formed center-right coalitions would be able to consolidate their positions. By and large they have been successful, while in Sweden the Social Democratic government of Prime Minister Olof Palme has been openly stating its determination not to make the mistakes that the French Socialist government made in 1981–82 and has had some success in obtaining trade union cooperation in a strict economic policy. . . .

In European Community affairs, the threat to Franco-German co-operation, which has always been the foundation of stability and progress in the EEC resulted in a period of tense and often acrimonious wrangling. The crisis in the EMS, leading to the mid-March currency realignments, was the major event of the period. . . . [O]ther issues dividing the major nations were agricultural policy and the budget. . . . These problems basically pit West Germany against one or more of its partners, since they mostly boil down to claims by the less economically successful nations against the largest and most prosperous economy. . . . At best, the Community faces a very difficult time ahead. . . .

# Unit II

# Governance

Most contemporary Europeans would agree that responsibility for such vital national concerns as foreign relations, military defense, and the maintenance of law and order properly belongs to government. Not everyone would agree, however, that government should assume equal responsibility for social welfare. Nonetheless, Europeans' demands for economic security and social services have grown at such a steady rate since World War II that expenditures for social welfare now constitute a large and increasing percentage of total government outlays in Western Europe. Today, programs designed to protect citizens from economic adversity and to provide them with an economic "cushion" from cradle to grave abound in almost every advanced industrialized Western European society, albeit against a backdrop of public debate that raises questions about the basic assumptions on which the welfare state is founded and that challenges government's ability to respond to its citizenry's expectations.

Given the prevalence of social welfare programs in these countries, it is not surprising that many Europeans have come to depend on the various benefits and "safety nets" such programs provide. Yet countermovements in opposition to the welfare state have continued to spring up all over Western Europe as economic growth has slowed and sources of funds for social welfare programs have dwindled. Advocates of the welfare state argue that social welfare programs should be extended and made more comprehensive while critics warn that the fiscal burden of these programs, most of them already in place, will ultimately lead to economic breakdown and the collapse of the whole system of governance. Clearly, the issues raised in this debate have important implications for governance in Western Europe as well as for the future of the welfare state.

In addition to having quite different opinions concerning the value of social welfare, the types of reforms that are needed, and the amount of taxes that should be required to offset the costs of a welfare state, Europeans also disagree about the functions that government should perform in carrying out these programs and effecting the necessary changes. Not surprisingly, these conflicting expectations and opinions have played a central role in shaping governance in Western Europe, and thus the debate that currently surrounds them may be seen as a mirror of present-day Western European politics. This is not to deny the equally important roles that other issues have played in the choice of governance in Western Europe. Rather, the issues of social welfare simply offer particularly good insights into the structure, functions, and problems of governance in these countries.

The purpose of this unit is to explore the underlying rationale of arguments both for and against the welfare state. The readings focus on two strikingly different points of view and were selected in part for how well they represent opposite ends of the spectrum in the debate over the welfare state. In "The Welfare State," Harry K. Girvetz traces the history of welfare legislation in Europe and sets out the arguments in favor of modern governments assuming even greater responsibility for maintaining their citizens' well-being. American economist Milton Friedman, the leading exponent of the anti-welfare state position presents the opposite point of view in "The Role of Government in a Free Society." Although the examples Friedman cites are drawn from the American political experience, the issues he raises have general applicability to Western Europe as well, where his views are widely espoused by welfare state opponents.

# 6

## The Welfare State

Harry K. Girvetz

In this article from the *International Encyclopedia of the Social Sciences,* Harry Girvetz traces the history of welfare legislation in Western Europe, describes the policies pursued by the modern welfare states, and presents the arguments commonly offered in support of governments assuming greater responsibility for citizens' social welfare.

The welfare state is the institutional outcome of the assumption by a society of legal and therefore formal and explicit responsibility for the basic well-being of all of its members. Such a state emerges when a society or its decision-making groups become convinced that the welfare of the individual (beyond such provisions as may be made "to preserve order and provide for the common defense") is too important to be left to custom or to informal arrangements and private understandings and is therefore a concern of government. In a complex society such assistance may be given to the individual directly or, just as often, to the economic interest most immediately affecting his welfare. The rubric is a relatively recent one not to be found in the traditional political lexicons, so that the point at which a state, in expanding social services to its citizens, earns this label is imprecise and controversial. The terms "basic security" or "well-being" have been and will be construed variously, and the interpretation of welfare is in flux—especially in the United States. In short, an account of the welfare state must struggle with a large legacy of ambiguity.

Every society, preliterate no less than literate, makes some provision for those of its members who find themselves in distress. In the case of aborigines such provision is almost exclusively assumed by so-called primary groups: the family or other kinship groups, or neighbors rallying spontaneously to aid the victims of calamity. Among primitive peoples, aid to the needy may be a by-product of other institutional arrangements, but it is often related to well-defined ideals of generosity and charity. Thus, among the Eskimos, although the hunter enjoys an absolute right to the game he kills, it is taken for granted that he will share it with his needy neighbors. Among the Australian aborigines, on the other hand, sharing the quarry is not left to the discretion of the hunter but is governed by rigid kinship rules which give elder relatives an inviolable claim to a portion of the kill. In a study of the east African Baganda, John Roscoe said that "no one ever went hungry. . . because everyone was welcome to share a meal with his equals," and he observed, possibly with some exaggeration, that among nonliterate peoples existing on the subsistence margin "it is generally the rule that when there is not enough, all hunger alike; when there is plenty, all participate."

As society becomes more complex, responsibility for helping the distressed may be assumed by the ruling authority, if only as when the government of Rome pacified the rabble with "bread and circuses," or by ecclesiastical agencies, as in the case of the Roman Catholic church during the Middle Ages, or by guilds, fraternities, and similar associations. For many centuries, the church in Europe, heeding the words of Jesus and the earlier words of Amos in praise of charity and kindness to the poor, assumed a major responsibility for the relief of human suffering. It established hospitals, orphanages, and (to a lesser extent) poorhouses, sometimes made outright gifts and loans, and even sheltered travelers. The work of such orders as the Alexian Brothers, who buried the poor, the Order of St. Lazarus, whose members cared for lepers, and the Knights Hospitalers, who supervised hospitals, was typical. In England, the dispossession of the monasteries and the breakup of the manors forced the state to assume the burden. Thus, a law of 1572 provided for collectors and overseers to compel heretofore voluntary payments for poor relief. Subsequently, the famous Elizabethan "Old Poor Law" of 1601 definitely accepted the principle of state responsibility for care of the needy, frugal though the provision may have been. Also, it levied a specific tax for poor relief and established categories of need. Even so, throughout this period the real burden of responsibility continued to fall on the family and the village community until the industrial revolution and the developments associated with it drastically transformed the prevailing pattern throughout Europe and America. England in the last decades of the eighteenth and the start of the nineteenth century provides the classic example.

## THE INDUSTRIAL REVOLUTION

Industrialization and the shift of population from the countryside to the city, hastened in England by the enclosure acts, greatly weakened primary groups. Many functions such as food preparation, recreation, and education, once exclusively performed by the family, were increasingly taken over in industrialized urban areas by other agencies. Today, in the city, almost everything used by the family is made outside the home. It has become increasingly difficult for elders and children to contribute to the support of the family group, as was the case in a rural agrarian society. At the same time the growth of a secular outlook has undermined traditional notions governing separation and divorce and has resulted in the breakup of an increasingly larger proportion of marriages. Accordingly, the enduring patriarchal family of tradition, often embracing three generations and assorted collateral kin, has become a two- and more often a single-generation group, when it has not broken up altogether. During the very period when the number of aged has rapidly multiplied, the family has become less and less available for their maintenance, not to mention the problem of care of the handicapped and of the casualties of broken homes. Meanwhile, the same period that has witnessed a declining role for the family has also seen the increased mobility and impersonality of city life loosening the once-close ties binding neighbors together.

[In addition,] the industrial revolution brought into new prominence the class of so-called "able-bodied poor." Whether in the Soviet Union and Communist China today or in England and America in the nineteenth century, capital accumulation on a scale necessary to generate rapid and continuing industrialization can be achieved only at the expense of the level of living of the average worker-consumer. If worker-consumers are incapable of effective resistance, either politically through the exercise of meaningful suffrage or economically through strong labor unions, the sheer pace of industrialization is bound to produce widespread poverty. . . .

At the same time the industrial system exacerbated the kind of dependency that results from enforced idleness. . . . Unlike earlier societies in which distress was brought about by crop failures and other unavoidable disasters, or by chronic shortage of resources, distress was now caused by institutional arrangements that conspired to keep people from using their creative energies and conjoined depressed wages with a rising level of expectations. It was in such fertile soil that the welfare state germinated. . . .

## BIRTH OF THE WELFARE STATE

[In] the philosophy of the welfare state, poverty and dependence are no longer regarded as evidence of personal failure. Quite apart from the physically disabled, workers who are underpaid and unemployed or intermittently employed are considered to be impoverished through no fault of their own. Where the supply of labor nearly always exceeds the demand and opportunity is unevenly distributed, it is held that the free market fails in a vast number of cases to proportion reward to merit. As the wealth created by modern industry increases it is contended that there is enough to assure everyone, including the physically and mentally handicapped, of adequate support without unfairly penalizing or impairing the initiative of the talented and enterprising. An income large enough to provide the basic necessities of life in adequate measure is regarded as the right of every member of society. If anyone's income falls short, it should be supplemented not as an act of charity but as an act of social justice.

. . . Finally, advocates of the welfare state contend that the price of widespread deprivation in an era of rising expectations is social instability on a scale unknown to preindustrial societies, where poverty was inescapable and therefore taken for granted; and they argue that such expectations can be frustrated, if at all, only by jettisoning democracy itself.

Such is the general orientation of what has also been called the social service state. However, the welfare state was not transferred fully delineated from the blueprints of social architects to the soil of England, continental Europe, and the United States. Its career varies with each country.

In England it was born of efforts to curb the abuses of the factory system and to improve penal institutions and outdoor relief. But efforts to humanize the factory system and to liberalize the provisions of the Poor Law of 1834 seemed increasingly like mere tinkering with particular grievances. A new age of humanitarianism was dawning, more sensitive to human suffering than its predecessors. Enfranchised and increasingly well-organized workers clamored for substantive reform. Historic surveys such as Charles Booth's *Life and Labour of the People in London* (see Booth et al. 1889–1891) and B. S. Rowntree's *Poverty: A Study of Town Life* (1901) documented the presence of dire poverty on a vast scale in the "workshop of the world." Finally, in 1905, prodded by widespread unemployment, Britain undertook a comprehensive examination of the administration of its poor laws. The Royal Commission on Poor Laws and Relief of Distress set up to make the investigation is famous for the report of its minority, led by Beatrice Webb. Among other things, this report proposed the abolition of Britain's archaic poor laws and the substitution of a comprehensive program of social insurance (1909). This recommendation, along with his own impression of the new German program of social insurance, contributed to David Lloyd George's historic decision to sponsor the program of unemployment and health insurance subsequently contained in the National Insurance

Act of 1911. This legislation, prepared in large part by William H. Beveridge, chief architect of the welfare state in the English-speaking world, embarked Great Britain on the program which has since been expanded to provide insurance for all its people "from the cradle to the grave." The famous Beveridge report of 1942 and the National Health Service and National Insurance acts of 1946 were milestones on the way. Today, in Australia and New Zealand as well as in Great Britain, a basic program of social security is taken for granted by all parties, and, apart from details, is no longer subject to debate.

The evils of industrialism were felt more tardily in Germany and the remedies applied more promptly. A national system of social insurance was instituted by Bismarck as early as the 1880s. Intent on combating the appeal of Marxian socialism, perceiving that a healthy, contented working class would make for a stronger Germany, and anxious that German workers identify themselves with the state, the Iron Chancellor, appropriating the ideas of economists like Adolf Wagner and Gustav von Schmoller, introduced the compulsory feature into social insurance and applied it to the whole German nation. The program was expanded after World War I to include unemployment as well as old age and health insurance. Austria, the Scandinavian countries, the Low Countries, and, finally, France and Italy all followed suit.

By the 1930s only the United States, among the nations involved in the industrial revolution, was without a comprehensive program of social security. Its great wealth, its polyglot population, its expanding frontier which provided a built-in safety valve, and a governmental system of checks and balances that discourages decisive social action except during periods of emergency all conspired to defer basic reform. It required the great depression, which forced millions of willing workers into prolonged idleness and posed the glaring paradox of mass deprivation in the midst of potential abundance, to goad the country into action.

The resulting program, devleoped over a period of years, has been directed in the United States, as elsewhere, at the major causes of insecurity: *(a)* inadequate income for those who work; *(b)* disabilities resulting from accident, sickness, youth, old age, widowhood, and motherhood; and *(c)* unemployment.

## PROGRAM OF THE WELFARE STATE

### Raising Worker Income

Improvement of income may be brought about either by increasing the amount of goods produced or by a more equitable distribution of the available supply of goods. Given glaring inequalities of income, the first concern of the welfare state in its initial phase has been to achieve distributive justice. Government action may accomplish this (1) by expanding the number of public services; (2) by a progressive tax system and a variety of taxes levied on employers for the benefit of their employees; (3) by facilitating the growth of a strong labor movement enabling workers to bargain on equal terms with their employers and a consumer movement enabling buyers to bargain more effectively with sellers; (4) by means of minimum-wage legislation.

### Expansion of Public Services

Obviously, real income is increased when society provides free services such as education, recreation, and housing to those who would otherwise not have access to them. . . . It must be emphasized that where a direct transfer of real values is involved, the philosophy of the welfare state construes distributive justice not merely as dictating such a transfer but as requiring it without reference to the income of the recipients and as the fulfillment of a social obligation. Means tests are anathema to the welfare state. The United States is the only industrialized country which fails to include one of the most basic services, namely, medical care, among those provided for on this basis. . . .

### Progressive Tax Systems

One of the earlier devices for effecting a redistribution of income was the use of a progressive tax system. . . .

Although adoption of a progressive tax is in principle a major modification of the traditional system of property rights, clearly it must have rigorous and consistent application to be meaningful. Such application is most closely approximated in the Scandinavian countries and Great Britain, less so in the United States, and even less so in Italy—which may well be a significant factor in the popularity of communism south of the Alps.

### Labor and Consumer Legislation

Legislation encouraging collective bargaining as a factor in influencing the distribution of income consisted initially of removing the legal bans and disabilities imposed on labor unions during the period of *Hochkapitalismus* and, later, as in the United States, of requiring employers (engaged in interstate commerce) to bargain collectively with employees through unions of their own choosing. . . .

### Minimum-Wage Legislation

Perhaps the most drastic departure from traditional economic practice has been the adoption of minimum-wage legislation. Certainly, the

Fair Labor Standards Act of 1938, since amended to include virtually all American workers and to raise the hourly minimum, took the United States a long way in the direction of the welfare state.

## The Productivity Debate

When all such devices have been enumerated it must be made clear that the limiting factor in any redistribution of incomes is the point at which initiative and enterprise are discouraged with resulting loss in productivity. The point at which such discouragement occurs is a subject of vigorous debate between partisans and opponents of the welfare state. That there is such a point, varying with each historical situation, will readily be granted; but advocates of the welfare state will argue that there is no constant called "human nature" by reference to which the issue can be settled. . . .

The issue is relevant because it directs attention to productivity as a variable in determining adequate compensation. Advocates of the welfare state have come to give far more attention than heretofore to the question of productivity potentiality. . . and . . . the need for measures to expand production, since the social implications of such measures are likely to be far less explosive than a redistribution of incomes.


## Aid to the Disabled

The measures taken to provide more adequately for those who work are only partly applicable to those who are unable to work by virtue of physical disability. The disabled fall into two major groups: those who are too handicapped ever to have earned a livelihood, such as children, the mentally disturbed and defective, the blind; and those who, although disabled, have had a record of earned income.

The welfare state provides direct grants for the adequate care and support of the first group and, where appropriate, stresses rehabilitation—as earlier programs did not. Categories of need are carefully distinguished and programs of help systematically differentiated according to category—a striking contrast to the days when the mentally disturbed were thrown together with the old, the sick, the blind and lame, and even mothers and young children, in the same institution. . . .

The second group, those disabled people with a record of earnings, must face the double threat of the loss of earning power and the cost of care, in the event of old age, accident (occupational or other), and illness. Compulsory social insurance has become the classical means for meeting their needs. This device applies the principle that society must set aside, and require its members to set aside during the periods when they are gainfully employed, small sums of money to provide against expected or unexpected future disability. Payments and benefits usually vary, at least up to a point, with the amount of earnings of the insured. In some cases the provision is for the cost of care (as with the victims of illness or industrial accident), in others for the loss of earnings (as in the case of federal help to the aged in the United States). A mature welfare state would provide for both. . . .

## Unemployment and the Welfare State

The welfare state concerns itself not only with securing an equitable income for those who are employed and with caring for those who are incapable of employment: it also addresses itself to the problem of those who are able to work but prevented from doing so by forces over which they have no control. In such cases it is customary to distinguish between frictional unemployment and cyclical unemployment. When cyclical unemployment becomes acute it is generally called mass unemployment.

*Frictional unemployment* was defined by William Beveridge as "unemployment caused by the individuals who make up the labour supply not being completely interchangeable and mobile units, so that, though there is an unsatisfied demand for labour, the unemployed workers are not of the right sort or in the right place to meet that demand." Workers may be displaced by a labor-saving device or a device they are not trained to use, because of climatic conditions or seasonal fluctuations in the market (seasonal unemployment), because of a disagreement with the employer concerning the conditions of work, because of the failure of the enterprise in which they are employed, or because they are in transit from one job to another. They are victims of frictional unemployment. Such unemployment, although it can be reduced to a bare minimum, . . . is unavoidable and may involve about 2 per cent of the work force. In a populous society. . . , this can involve a great many people.

In the prewelfare period the victims of frictional unemployment were largely left to their own devices or forced to seek public or private charity. Today, in every economically developed country, since Bismarck introduced "socialism from above" in Germany, the problem of frictional unemployment is in the main met by compulsory unemployment insurance. . . .

However, as has often been pointed out, while unemployment payments may solve the problem of want, the problem of enforced idleness with all of its demoralizing consequences remains. Measures must therefore be taken to facilitate the re-employment of displaced workers by retraining them for work suited to their abilities, by providing adequate counseling services, and by setting up unemployment offices. All these are part of the armory of the welfare state.

Traditionally, frictional unemployment has been regarded as unemployment of short duration. Recently, increasing attention has been given to "hardcore" or "prosperity" unemployment, sometimes described as prolonged frictional unemployment and more technically called "structural." *Structural unemployment* involves workers who are made jobless not as a result of recessions or depressions but by large-scale changes in technology, shifts in consumer taste, and the development of new products. It may also refer to changes in the composition of the labor force: large-scale additions of younger workers, resulting from continuing population growth; of older workers, resulting from an extension of the life span; of female workers; or of previously excluded members of minority groups. Such structural unemployment is not associated with fluctuations in the business cycle and is therefore called "secular." However, to the extent that it is not only more prolonged but potentially much more widespread than frictional unemployment, structural unemployment must be regarded as a form of mass unemployment, so that, like *cyclical unemployment*, it must ultimately exhaust the resources of even the most generous unemployment insurance system.

Beyond this, advocates of the philosophy underlying the welfare state contend that the etiology of structural unemployment is more akin to cyclical than to frictional unemployment. Frictional unemployment is largely unavoidable and we can only palliate its consequences. On the other hand, the structurally unemployed are out of work for the same reason that the cyclically unemployed are without work: not because they are intrinsically unemployable but because there is not enough effective demand for their services; the economy does not function at a sufficiently high level to utilize all its manpower. . . .

For [this] reason and because neither direct relief, nor insurance benefits, nor any welfare program thus far cited can cope with the effects of mass unemployment, whether it be secular (structural) or cyclical, advocates of the welfare state have taken the position that, in the words of Beveridge's now famous *Full Employment in a Free Society,* "It must be a function of the State . . . to protect its citizens against mass unemployment, as definitely as it is now the function of the State to defend the citizens against attack from abroad and against robbery and violence at home. . . ."

## NEW DIRECTIONS

Such are the outlines of the welfare philosophy inspired by the crudities of primitive capitalism and the agonies of the interbellum depression. But that philosophy is not a fixed one, and in the mid-1960s new emphases were already discernible.

. . . [T]he welfare state in its present outline bears the mark of its origins in the needs of the poor and oppressed. . . . The energies of reformers were absorbed in finding remedies for mass deprivation and mass unemployment. . . .

As welfare programs, new and old, mitigate the more extreme forms of suffering, architects of the welfare state are increasingly thinking in terms of the acute problems directly threatening society as a whole—the prosperous as well as the poor, whites as well as Negroes, the native born as well as the immigrant. . . .

In the 1930s Keynes, preoccupied with increasing production, could write that he saw no reason to suppose that the existing system "seriously mis-employs the factors of production." It seems likely that the welfare philosophy of tomorrow (if not of today) will charge that, on this score, Keynes falls short. Such a philosophy, if it is also democratic, will categorically reject the idea that a few elected officials may compel others to spend their incomes in one way rather than another; it will simply insist that conditions be provided which enable consumers when they make purchases, and citizens when they vote taxes, to make more rational decisions. Such conditions would no doubt include a commission on national goals having access to the most expert opinion and empowered to hold hearings and sponsor conferences at all levels, national, regional, and local. It would also be empowered to use the formidable resources of television (including prime time) on a grand scale to acquaint citizens en masse with the condition of their schools, hospitals, housing, parks, streams, etc., and with the economic as well as the social cost of neglecting them, not to mention the cost of overburdening and underpaying teachers, probation officers, hospital attendants, and others. Additional conditions might include better controls over advertising and, in the political sphere, a reorganization of the legislative branches of the government at all levels, which might prevent small, strategically placed committees from obstructing the will of large legislative majorities.

Clearly, these are concerns far removed from the humiliations of the almshouse and the degradations of the early factory system, against which the welfare state in its first phases was an institutionalized protest. That is to say, these conditions are removed from the exclusive preoccupation with minimal security that has largely dominated the welfare state. But they appeal to the same kind of social conscience and enlist the same sense of social justice.

The welfare state, whether as thus prefigured or in its present form, invites widely differing appraisals. . . . Its critics regard it as the omni-competent state, pre-empting the private efforts through which individuals achieve moral stature by helping each other; sapping initiative; coddling the inferior; and ultimately regimenting everyone. The Soviet Union provides security and all the social services for its citizens; it is also a barracks state. So runs the argument.

Apologists for the welfare state in the free world, less optimistic about the possibilities of achieving utopia than nineteenth-century reformers and more alert to the hazards of statism since the rise of modern totalitarianism, insist that the welfare state not only leaves ample room for self-help and for what businessmen in the United States call "welfare capitalism": it ultimately encourages creative initiative and promotes freedom by banishing fear, by minimizing suffering, and by reducing class and other antagonisms. They argue also that the welfare state is quite compatible with an economic system in which free enterprise plays a central role, although they may differ among themselves concerning whether the welfare state should limit itself to compensating for the imbalances and minimizing the frictions to which a free economy is inevitably subject, or seek positively to advance general prosperity and happiness.

Meanwhile history has rendered a verdict concerning the tendencies of the welfare state, partial (in a double sense) though historical verdicts always are. That verdict may be found by looking to the Soviet Union and its regimented people. But it may also be found by turning to the Scandinavian countries, to Great Britain, to West Germany, to Australia and New Zealand, and to the United States. It would be difficult to charge that the peoples of these countries are regimented or that private enterprise does not enjoy a flourishing life of its own even in the most "socialistic" of them. In any event, there are no signs, outside of marginal groups mostly centered in the United States, of a disposition to curb the welfare state. It rides the wave of the future.

# 7

# The Role of Government in a Free Society

## Milton Friedman

Nobel prize-winning economist Milton Friedman is one of the foremost champions of the free-market, or "liberal," philosophy of government. In the following selection, Friedman discusses the advantages of allowing market forces to resolve as many issues as possible. He then identifies the narrow range of functions which he considers beyond the scope of market operations and which therefore should constitute the only legitimate concerns of government. His references to American examples are equally applicable to European welfare states.

A common objection to totalitarian societies is that they regard the end as justifying the means. Taken literally, this objection is clearly illogical. If the end does not justify the means, what does? But this easy answer does not dispose of the objection; it simply shows that the objection is not well put. To deny that the end justifies the means is indirectly to assert that the end in question is not the ultimate end, that the ultimate end is itself the use of the proper means. Desirable or not, any end that can be attained only by the use of bad means must give way to the more basic end of the use of acceptable means.

To the liberal, the appropriate means are free discussion and voluntary co-operation, which implies that any form of coercion is inappropriate. The ideal is unanimity among responsible individuals achieved on the basis of free and full discussion. This is another way of expressing the goal of freedom. . . .

From this standpoint, the role of the market . . . is that it permits unanimity without conformity; that it is a system of effectively proportional representation. On the other hand, the characteristic feature of action through explicitly political channels is that it tends to require or to enforce substantial conformity. The typical issue must be decided "yes" or "no"; at most, provision can be made for a fairly limited number of alternatives. Even the use of proportional representation in its explicitly political form does not alter this conclusion. The number of separate groups that can in fact be represented is narrowly limited, enormously so by comparison with the proportional representation of the market. More important, the fact that the final outcome generally must be a law applicable to all groups, rather than separate legislative enactments for each "party" represented, means that proportional representation in its political version, far from permitting unanimity without conformity, tends toward ineffectiveness and fragmentation. It thereby operates to destroy any consensus on which unanimity with conformity can rest.

There are clearly some matters with respect to which effective proportional representation is impossible. I cannot get the amount of national defense I want and you, a different amount. With respect to such indivisible matters we can discuss, and argue, and vote. But having decided, we must conform. It is precisely the existence of such indivisible matters—protection of the individual and the nation from coercion are clearly the most basic—that prevents exclusive reliance on individual action through the market. If we are to use some of our resources for such indivisible items, we must employ political channels to reconcile differences.

The use of political channels, while inevitable, tends to strain the social cohesion essential for a stable society. The strain is least if agreement for joint action need be reached only on a limited range of issues on which people in any event have common views. Every extension of the range of issues for which explicit agreement is sought strains further the delicate threads that hold society together. If it goes so far as to touch an issue on which men feel deeply yet differently, it may well disrupt the society. Fundamental differences in basic values can seldom if ever be resolved at the ballot box; ultimately they can only be decided, though not resolved, by conflict. The religious and civil wars of history are a bloody testament to this judgment.

The widespread use of the market reduces the strain on the social fabric by rendering conformity unnecessary with respect to any activities it encompasses. The wider the range of activities covered by the market, the fewer are the issues on which explicitly political decisions are required and hence on which it is necessary to achieve agreement. In turn, the fewer the issues on which agreement is necessary, the greater is the likelihood of getting agreement while maintaining a free society.

Unanimity is, of course, an ideal. In practice, we can afford neither the time nor the effort that would be required to achieve complete unanimity on every issue. We must perforce accept something less. We are thus led to accept majority rule in one form or another as an expedient. That majority rule is an expedient rather than itself a basic principle is clearly shown by the fact that our willingness to resort to majority rule, and the size of the majority we require, themselves depend on the seriousness of the issue involved. If the matter is of little moment and the minority has no strong feelings about being overruled, a bare plurality will suffice. On the other hand, if the minority feels strongly about the issue involved, even a bare majority will not do. Few of us would be willing to have issues of free speech, for example, decided by a bare majority. Our legal structure is full of such distinctions among kinds of issues that require different kinds of majorities. At the extreme are those issues embodied in the Constitution. These are the principles that are so important that we are willing to make minimal concessions to expediency. Something like essential consensus was achieved initially in accepting them, and we require something like essential consensus for a change in them.

The self-denying ordinance to refrain from majority rule on certain kinds of issues that is embodied in our Constitution and in similar written or unwritten constitutions elsewhere, and the specific provisions in these constitutions or their equivalents prohibiting coercion of individuals, are themselves to be regarded as reached by free discussion and as reflecting essential unanimity about means.

I turn now to consider more specifically, though still in very broad terms, what the areas are that cannot be handled through the market at all, or can be handled only at so great a cost that the use of political channels may be preferable.

## GOVERNMENT AS RULE-MAKER AND UMPIRE

It is important to distinguish the day-to-day activities of people from the general customary and legal framework within which these take place. The day-to-day activities are like the actions of the participants in a game when they are playing it; the framework, like the rules of the game they play. And just as a good game requires acceptance by the players both of the rules and of the umpire to interpret and enforce them, so a good society requires that its members agree on the general conditions that will govern relations among them, on some means of arbitrating different interpretations of these conditions, and on some device for enforcing compliance with the generally accepted rules. As in games, so also in society, most of the general conditions are the unintended outcome of custom, accepted unthinkingly. At most, we consider explicitly only minor modifications in them, though the cumulative effect of a series of minor modifications may be a drastic alteration in the character of the game or of the society. In both games and society also, no set of rules can prevail unless most participants most of the time conform to them without external sanctions; unless that is, there is a broad underlying social consensus. But we cannot rely on custom or on this consensus alone to interpret and to enforce the rules; we need an umpire. These then are the basic roles of government in a free society:

to provide a means whereby we can modify the rules, to mediate differences among us on the meaning of the rules, and to enforce compliance with the rules on the part of those few who would otherwise not play the game.

The need for government in these respects arises because absolute freedom is impossible. However attractive anarchy may be as a philosophy, it is not feasible in a world of imperfect men. Men's freedoms can conflict, and when they do, one man's freedom must be limited to reserve another's—as a Supreme Court Justice once put it, "My freedom to move my fist must be limited by the proximity of your chin."

The major problem in deciding the appropriate activities of government is how to resolve such conflicts among the freedoms of different individuals. In some cases, the answer is easy. There is little difficulty in attaining near unanimity to the proposition that one man's freedom to murder his neighbor must be sacrificed to preserve the freedom of the other man to live. In other cases, the answer is difficult. In the economic area, a major problem arises in respect of the conflict between freedom to combine and freedom to compete. What meaning is to be attributed to "free" as modifying "enterprise"? In the United States, "free" has been understood to mean that anyone is free to set up an enterprise, which means that existing enterprises are not free to keep out competitors except by selling a better product at the same price or the same product at a lower price. In the continental tradition, on the other hand, the meaning has generally been that enterprises are free to do what they want, including the fixing of prices, division of markets, and the adoption of other techniques to keep out potential competitors. Perhaps the most difficult specific problem in this area arises with respect to combinations among laborers, where the problem of freedom to combine and freedom to compete is particularly acute. . . .

Another economic area that raises particularly difficult problems is the monetary system. Government responsibility for the monetary system has long been recognized. It is explicitly provided for in the constitutional provision which gives Congress the power "to coin money, regulate the value thereof, and of foreign coin." There is probably no other area of economic activity with respect to which government action has been so uniformly accepted. This habitual and by now almost unthinking acceptance of governmental responsibility makes thorough understanding of the grounds for such responsibility all the more necessary, since it enhances the danger that the scope of government will spread from activities that are, to those that are not, appropriate in a free society, from providing a monetary framework to determining the allocation of resources among individuals. . . .

In summary, the organization of economic activity through voluntary exchange presumes that we have provided, through government, for the maintenance of law and order to prevent coercion of one individual by another, the enforcement of contracts voluntarily entered into, the definition of the meaning of property rights, the interpretation and enforcement of such rights, and the provision of a monetary framework.

## ACTION THROUGH GOVERNMENT ON GROUNDS OF TECHNICAL MONOPOLY AND NEIGHBORHOOD EFFECTS

The role of government just considered is to do something that the market cannot do for itself, namely, to determine, arbitrate, and enforce the rules of the game. We may also want to do through government some things that might conceivably be done through the market but that technical or similar conditions render it difficult to do in that way. These all reduce to cases in which strictly voluntary exchange is either exceedingly costly or practically impossible. There are two general classes of such cases: monopoly and similar market imperfections, and neighborhood effects.

Exchange is truly voluntary only when nearly equivalent alternatives exist. Monopoly implies the absence of alternatives and thereby inhibits effective freedom of exchange. In practice, monopoly frequently, if not generally, arises from government support or from collusive agreements among individuals. With respect to these, the problem is either to avoid governmental fostering of monopoly or to stimulate the effective enforcement of rules such as those embodied in our antitrust laws. However, monopoly may also arise because it is technically efficient to have a single producer or enterprise. I venture to suggest that such cases are more limited than is supposed but they unquestionably do arise. A simple example is perhaps the provision of telephone services within a community. I shall refer to such cases as "technical" monopoly.

When technical conditions make a monopoly the natural outcome of competitive market forces, there are only three alternatives that seem available: private monopoly, public monopoly, or public regulation. All three are bad so we must choose among evils. Henry Simons, observing public regulation of monopoly in the United States, found the results so distasteful that he concluded public monopoly would be a lesser evil. Walter Eucken, a noted German liberal, observing public monopoly in German railroads, found the results so distasteful that he concluded public regulation would be a lesser evil. Having learned from both, I reluctantly conclude that, if tolerable, private monopoly may be the least of the evils.

If society were static so that the conditions which give rise to a technical monopoly were sure to remain, I would have little confidence in this solution. In a rapidly changing society, however, the conditions making for technical monopoly frequently change and I suspect that both public regulation and public monopoly are likely to be less responsive to such changes in conditions, to be less readily capable of elimination, than private monopoly.

Railroads in the United States are an excellent example. A large degree of monopoly in railroads was perhaps inevitable on technical grounds in the nineteenth century. This was the justification for the Interstate Commerce Commission. But conditions have changed. The emergence of road and air transport has reduced the monopoly element in railroads to negligible proportions. Yet we have not eliminated the ICC. On the contrary, the ICC, which started out as an agency to protect the public from exploitation by the railroads, has become an agency to protect railroads from competition by trucks and other means of transport, and more recently even to protect existing truck companies from competition by new entrants. Similarly, in England, when the railroads were nationalized, trucking was at first brought into the state monopoly. If railroads had never been subjected to regulation in the United States, it is nearly certain that by now transportation, including railroads, would be a highly competitive industry with little or no remaining monopoly elements.

The choice between the evils of private monopoly, public monopoly, and public regulation cannot, however, be made once and for all, independently of the factual circumstances. If the technical monopoly is of a service or commodity that is regarded as essential and if its monopoly power is sizable, even the short-run effects of private unregulated monopoly may not be tolerable, and either public regulation or ownership may be a lesser evil.

Technical monopoly may on occasion justify a *de facto* public monopoly. It cannot by itself justify a public monopoly achieved by making it illegal for anyone else to compete. For example, there is no way to justify our present public monopoly of the post office. It may be argued that the carrying of mail is a technical monopoly and that a government monopoly is the least of evils. Along these lines, one could perhaps justify a government post office but not the present law, which makes it illegal for anybody else to carry mail. If the delivery of mail is a technical monopoly, no one will be able to succeed in competition with the government. If it is not, there is no reason why the government should be engaged in it. The only way to find out is to leave other people free to enter.

The historical reason why we have a post office monopoly is because the Pony Express did such a good job of carrying the mail across the continent that, when the government introduced transcontinental service, it couldn't compete effectively and lost money. The result was a law making it illegal for anybody else to carry the mail. That is why the Adams Express Company is an investment trust today instead of an operating company. I conjecture that if entry into the mail-carrying business were open to all, there would be a large number of firms entering it and this archaic industry would become revolutionized in short order.

A second general class of cases in which strictly voluntary exchange is impossible arises when actions of individuals have effects on other individuals for which it is not feasible to charge or recompense them. This is the problem of "neighborhood effects". An obvious example is the pollution of a stream. The man who pollutes a stream is in effect forcing others to exchange good water for bad. These others might be willing to make the exchange at a price. But it is not feasible for them, acting individually, to avoid the exchange or to enforce appropriate compensation.

A less obvious example is the provision of highways. In this case, it is technically possible to identify and hence charge individuals for their use of the roads and so to have private operation. However, for general access roads, involving many points of entry and exit, the costs of collection would be extremely high if a charge were to be made for the specific services received by each individual, because of the necessity of establishing toll booths or the equivalent at all entrances. The gasoline tax is a much cheaper method of charging individuals roughly in proportion to their use of the roads. This method, however, is one in which the particular payment cannot be identified closely with the particular use. Hence, it is hardly feasible to have private enterprise provide the service and collect the charge without establishing extensive private monopoly.

These considerations do not apply to long-distance turnpikes with high density of traffic and limited access. For these, the costs of collection are small and in many cases are now being paid, and there are often numerous alternatives, so that there is no serious monopoly problem. Hence, there is every reason why these should be privately owned and operated. If so owned and operated, the enterprise running the highway should receive the gasoline taxes paid on account of travel on it.

Parks are an interesting example because they illustrate the difference between cases that can and cases that cannot be justified by neighborhood effects, and because almost everyone at first sight regards the conduct of National Parks as obviously a valid function of government. In fact, however, neighborhood effects may justify a city park; they do not justify a national park, like Yellowstone National Park or the Grand Canyon. What is the fundamental difference between the two? For the city park, it is extremely difficult to identify the people who benefit from it and to charge them for the benefits which they receive. If there is a park in the middle of the city, the houses on all sides get the benefit of the open space, and people who walk through it or by it also benefit. To maintain toll collectors at the gates or to impose annual charges per window overlooking the park would be very expensive and difficult. The entrances to a national park like Yellowstone, on the other hand, are few; most of the people who come stay for a considerable period of time and it is perfectly feasible to set up toll gates and collect admission charges. This is indeed now done, though the charges do not cover the whole costs. If the public wants this kind of an activity enough to pay for it, private enterprises will have every incentive to provide such parks. And, of course, there are many private enterprises of this nature now in existence. I cannot myself conjure up any neighborhood effects or important monopoly effects that would justify governmental activity in this area.

Considerations like those I have treated under the heading of neighborhood effects have been used to rationalize almost every conceivable intervention. In many instances, however, this rationalization is special pleading rather than a legitimate application of the concept of neighborhood effects. Neighborhood effects cut both ways. They can be a reason for limiting the activities of government as well as for expanding them. Neighborhood effects impede voluntary exchange because it is difficult to identify the effects on third parties and to measure their magnitude; but this difficulty is present in governmental activity as well. It is hard to know when neighborhood effects are sufficiently large to justify particular costs in overcoming them and even harder to distribute the costs in an appropriate fashion. Consequently, when government engages in activities to overcome neighborhood effects, it will in part introduce an additional set of neighborhood effects by failing to charge or to compensate individuals properly. Whether the original or the new neighborhood effects are the more serious can only be judged by the facts of the individual case, and even then, only very approximately. Furthermore, the use of government to overcome neighborhood effects itself has an extremely important neighborhood effect which is unrelated to the particular occasion for government action. Every act of government intervention limits the area of individual freedom directly and threatens the preservation of freedom indirectly for reasons elaborated in the first chapter.

Our principles offer no hard and fast line how far it is appropriate to use government to accomplish jointly what it is difficult or impossible for us to accomplish separately through strictly voluntary exchange. In any particular case of proposed intervention, we must make up a balance sheet, listing separately the advantages and disadvantages. Our principles tell us what items to put on the one side and what items on the other and they give us some basis for attaching importance to the different items. In particular, we shall always want to enter on the liability side of any proposed government intervention, its neighborhood effect in threatening freedom, and give this effect considerable weight. Just how much weight to give to it, as to other items, depends upon the circumstances. If, for example, existing government intervention is minor, we shall attach a smaller weight to the negative effects of additional government intervention. This is an important reason why many earlier liberals, like Henry Simons, writing at a time when government was small by today's standards, were willing to have government undertake activities that today's liberals would not accept now that government has become so overgrown.

## ACTION THROUGH GOVERNMENT ON PATERNALISTIC GROUNDS

Freedom is a tenable objective only for responsible individuals. We do not believe in freedom for madmen or children. The necessity of drawing a line between responsible individuals and others is inescapable, yet it means that there is an essential ambiguity in our ultimate objective of freedom. Paternalism is inescapable for those whom we designate as not responsible.

The clearest case, perhaps, is that of madmen. We are willing neither to permit them freedom nor to shoot them. It would be nice if we could rely on voluntary activities of individuals to house and care for the madmen. But I think we cannot rule out the possibility that such charitable activities will be inadequate, if only because of the neighborhood effect involved in the fact that I benefit if another man contributes to the care of the insane. For this reason, we may be willing to arrange for their care through government.

Children offer a more difficult case. The ultimate operative unit in our society is the family, not the individual. Yet the acceptance of the family as the unit rests in considerable part on expediency rather than principle. We believe that parents are generally best able to protect their children and to provide for their development into responsible individuals for whom freedom is appropriate. But we do not believe in the freedom of parents to do what they will with other people. The children are responsible individuals in embryo, and a believer in freedom believes in protecting their ultimate rights.

To put this in a different and what may seem a more callous way, children are at one and the same time consumer goods and potentially responsible members of society. The freedom of individuals to use their economic resources as they want includes the freedom to use them to have children—to buy, as it were, the services of children as a particular form of consumption. But once this choice is exercised, the children have a value in and of themselves and have a freedom of their own that is not simply an extension of the freedom of the parents.

The paternalistic ground for governmental activity is in many ways the most troublesome to a liberal; for it involves the acceptance of a principle—that some shall decide for others—which he finds objectionable in most applications and which he rightly regards as a hall-mark of his chief intellectual opponents, the proponents of collectivism in one or another of its guises, whether it be communism, socialism, or a welfare state. Yet there is no use pretending that problems are simpler than in fact they are. There is no avoiding the need for some measure of paternalism. As Dicey wrote in 1914 about an act for the protection of mental defectives, "The Mental Deficiency Act is the first step along a path on which no sane man can decline to enter, but which, if too far pursued, will bring statesmen across difficulties hard to meet without considerable interference with individual liberty." There is no formula that can tell us where to stop. We must rely on our fallible judgment and, having reached a judgment, on our ability to persuade our fellow men that it is a correct judgment, or their ability to persuade us to modify our views. We must put our faith, here as elsewhere, in a consensus reached by imperfect and biased men through free discussion and trial and error.

## CONCLUSION

A government which maintained law and order, defined property rights, served as a means whereby we could modify property rights and other rules of the economic game, adjudicated disputes about the interpretation of the rules, enforced contracts, promoted competition, provided a monetary framework, engaged in activities to counter technical monopolies and to overcome neighborhood effects widely regarded as sufficiently important to justify government intervention, and which supplemented private charity and the private family in protecting the irresponsible, whether madman or child—such a government would clearly have important functions to perform. The consistent liberal is not an anarchist.

Yet it is also true that such a government would have clearly limited functions and would refrain from a host of activities that are now undertaken by federal and state governments in the United States, and their counterparts in other Western countries. . . . [I]t may help to give a sense of proportion about the role that a liberal would assign government simply to list . . . some activities currently undertaken by government in the U.S., that cannot, so far as I can see, validly be justified in terms of the principles outlined above:

1.   Parity price support programs for agriculture.

2.   Tariffs on imports or restrictions on exports, such as current oil import quotas, sugar quotas, etc.

3.   Governmental control of output, such as through the farm program, or through prorationing of oil as is done by the Texas Railroad Commission.

4. Rent control, such as is still practiced in New York, or more general price and wage controls such as were imposed during and just after World War II.

5. Legal minimum wage rates, or legal maximum prices, such as the legal maximum of zero on the rate of interest that can be paid on demand deposits by commercial banks, or the legally fixed maximum rates that can be paid on savings and time deposits.

6. Detailed regulation of industries, such as the regulation of transportation by the Interstate Commerce Commission. This had some justification on technical monopoly grounds when initially introduced for railroads; it has none now for any means of transport. Another example is detailed regulation of banking.

7. A similar example, but one which deserves special mention because of its implicit censorship and violation of free speech, is the control of radio and television by the Federal Communications Commission.

8. Present social security programs, especially the old-age and retirement programs compelling people in effect (a) to spend a specified fraction of their income on the purchase of retirement annuity, (b) to buy the annuity from a publicly operated enterprise.

9. Licensure provisions in various cities and states which restrict particular enterprises or occupations or professions to people who have a license, where the license is more than a receipt for a tax which anyone wishes to enter the activity may pay.

10. So-called "public-housing" and the host of other subsidy programs directed at fostering residential construction such as F.H.A. [Federal Housing Authority] and V.A. [Veterans Administration] guarantee of mortgage, and the like.

11. Conscription to man the military services in peacetime. The appropriate free market arrangement is volunteer military forces; which is to say, hiring men to serve. There is no justification for not paying whatever price is necessary to attract the required number of men. Present arrangements are inequitable and arbitrary, seriously interfere with the freedom of young men to shape their lives, and probably are even more costly than the market alternative. (Universal military training to provide a reserve for war time is a different problem and may be justified on liberal grounds.)

12. National parks, as noted above.

13. The legal prohibition on the carrying of mail for profit.

14. Publicly owned and operated toll roads, as noted above.

This list is far from comprehensive.

# Unit III

# Constitutions and Parliaments

Every contemporary Western European nation adheres to some form of political democracy, but this is not to suggest that all Western European governments are alike. In fact, the various systems of government within Western Europe differ from one another in rather striking ways. For example, some, such as West Germany, are based on detailed, written constitutions while others, like Great Britain, eschew written sets of laws and rely instead on fundamental principles of governance. Some are constitutional monarchies; others are republics. In some, the head of state, usually the president, exercises wide powers while in others the majority of power resides in a parliamentary assembly. Generally speaking, governmental structures in Western Europe may be ranged along a continuum according to how they delegate power. At one end are the parliamentary systems, in which the legislature is the supreme governing power, and at the other end are the presidential systems, in which the greatest power resides with the executive. In between are systems in which power is shared between the legislature and the executive. Furthermore, in contrast to the United States where there is a distinct separation of legislative, executive, and judicial powers, in Western Europe the functions of the various branches of government often overlap.

This unit suggests the wide variety of democratic systems found in present-day Western Europe and examines the many different features that characterize them. In "An Overview of Political Institutions," T. Alexander Smith compares the political systems of three major Western European countries—Great Britain, West Germany, and France. Detailing the differences between Britain's parliamentary system and the presidential systems popular in West Germany and France, Smith identifies the characteristics of Britain's government that have contributed to its greater stability over the long term. Lawrence C. Mayer and John H. Burnett, in "Policymaking Structures in Western Europe's Parliamentary Democracies," examine the various functions of both written and unwritten constitutions in a number of Western European political systems. The authors then go on to analyze the processes inherent in Western Europe's different forms of representative assemblies and the roles played by the various chiefs of state, contrasting in particular the differences between constitutional monarchies and republics. Comparisons are also made between Western European political systems and the American political system.

# 8

# An Overview of Political Institutions

T. Alexander Smith

This comparison of the strengths and weaknesses of three major political institutions contrasts the long-term stability and continuity of Britain's two-party parliamentary system to the impermanence of Germany and France's pre-World War II multiparty governments.

. . . Although a major aim of comparative politics is to achieve ever higher levels of generality in explaining political phenomena, this task is exceedingly difficult without a grounding in the experiences of particular nations and governments. . . .

. . . For example, a few have developed a relatively high degree of political consensus, while others have traditionally experienced deep ideological and social cleavages. Similarly, some possess two-party systems and hence the ability to form governments based on majorities, whereas others have been characterized by multiparties and coalition government. Again, certain nations differ markedly in executive-legislative relationships; that is, both parliamentary and presidential types of government are included as well as a somewhat mixed variation (Fifth Republic, France). All in all, there are rather sharp divergences in experience and practice among Western [European] nations.

## GREAT BRITAIN

The British form of government has long had its share of scholarly admirers in the United States. . . . Supporters of the British system have delighted in its coherence and ability to govern, particularly as evidenced by the concept of government responsibility before Parliament. The British cabinet stands or falls as a collective body. In the highly unlikely event that the House of Commons votes it out of office, the prime minister has two choices. He may submit his resignation; in all probability, however, he will dissolve the House and call upon the populace to resolve the issue. Responsibility is therefore assured, for the sovereign voter theoretically knows whom to credit with either troubles or satisfaction he may derive from the current government.

The clear lines of responsibility and accountability running from government to voter are undoubtedly facilitated by the British two-party system. Unlike many nations on the Continent, Great Britain has been blessed with cabinets composed entirely of Labour or Conservative party members. Consequently, it has been unnecessary to include several parties in each cabinet, thereby blurring the lines of accountability. And unlike the American two-party system, Britain's does not experience those periodic deadlocks between president and Congress which too often result from being controlled by different parties representing different constituency interests.

From the British standpoint, the United States and such Continental nations as Italy and France (at least in the Third and Fourth Republics) confuse or avoid responsibility because they divide power among the legislative and executive branches or because government coalitions, which may include small, centrist parties, are unlikely to reflect dominant feelings in the country. Neither America nor the Continental multiparty systems . . . "buckle" legislative and executive branches in a meaningful, harmonious relationship. But in Great Britain, Parliament and cabinet are securely welded through common party ties and party discipline, the cabinet being the leadership of the parliamentary majority party. Major decisions are made within cabinet or parliamentary caucus with ultimate decisions binding all members of the majority.

The prime minister, furthermore, is the true leader of his party and government. With many patronage prerogatives, controls over parliamentary agenda and debate, and the right of dissolution, he occupies an exalted position of authority within Parliament. Unlike his executive counterparts in many other nations, he has little need to worry about powerful legislative committees emasculating his program, since rigorous discipline usually keeps his followers in line.

Of course, there are periodic denunciations of cabinet government as little more than disguised dictatorship. The prime minister's imposing powers of patronage through his right to appoint his fellow cabinet ministers, ministers of state, parliamentary secretaries, and external party organization leadership and shadow governments (in the case of the Conservatives) are certainly clear evidence of his strong position. True, in making selections, he must carefully consider the wishes of powerful factional leaders, and to this extent his freedom of choice is limited. Nevertheless, as many as one-fifth of the majority's parliamentary membership may receive some sort of patronage dispensation from the leader. Similarly, as head of a disciplined party, the prime minister can count upon the loyal support of his backbenchers. As a result, the right of the legislature to bring a government to its knees through a vote of no confidence is largely a dead issue in present-day Britain, since no party is likely to vote against its own leadership and risk facing the opposition with a divided majority at election time.

The fear of disguised dictatorship, unresponsive to the wishes of the people and its representatives in the legislature, is directed toward other aspects of cabinet government as well. Although many thinkers question the growing powers of the prime minister and his cabinet at the expense of Parliament, more fear the enhanced role in policy making of the permanent higher civil service. Unlike its American counterpart, the British bureaucracy is protected from undue pressure. Each minister can place himself between high civil servants and the elected members of Parliament since a minister assumes personal responsibility for his own ministry. For both bureaucrat and minister, of course, there are advantages. The bureaucrat retains anonymity, integrity, a reputation for impartiality, and, in general, a prestigious position as servant of the Crown. He also finds it simple to remain aloof from partisan warfare. The minister, on the other hand, gains loyalty from the higher civil servant and security from the knowledge that he is getting advice unencumbered by partisan loyalties.

Although it has been argued that question time in Parliament provides an excellent way to air criticisms of administrative malfeasance, the British legislature has few of those checks upon the bureaucracy available to its American counterpart: the investigatory power, the practically unlimited ability to bring administrators before congressional committees, and the practice of continual oversight. Such checks are shunned on the grounds that they endanger cabinet responsibility before Parliament and, ultimately, the people.

While one need not conclude that the British political system is in any way undemocratic in essentials—after all, its rulers are subject to periodic elections—it is clearly a centralized democracy in terms of executive decision making. Because much policy is certainly forged behind the scenes by ministers, bureaucrats, and the interest groups, Parliament tends to resemble a mere ratifying body. In this sense, it seems most tame when compared to the rambunctious American Congress.

Ordinary parliamentary backbencher initiatives occur less frequently in Great Britain than in the United States because Great Britain's doctrine of collective responsibility, a disciplined party system, and a well-developed executive committee structure place a damper on backbencher independence. Hence, the British MPs do not find it a simple matter to vote their personal convictions or those of their individual constituencies. As a result, the more open system of bargaining and coalition building, a part of life in the American Congress, is much less blatant in the House of Commons; but the fundamental process itself is surely evident. . . .

## WEST GERMANY

[Great Britain is] considered [a] highly stable democrac[y], unencumbered for the most part by traditions of political oppositions which threaten the constitutional order. This cannot be said for West Germany and France. Each of these nations has been faced historically with grave threats from extremists on left and right. Germany has been especially subject to political division and turmoil. Unification of most German-speaking peoples came only in the latter part of the nineteenth century; prior to 1871 Germans had been divided into many different kinds of political orders. Little other than the church and the Holy Roman Empire held these diverse states together in feudal times. But even that fragile unity was cut asunder by Martin Luther's revolt against the church and the subsequent growth of Protestantism in the northern areas. Thus, the divisions of religion were superimposed upon prior political divisions. Later, following the French Revolution of 1789, Napoleon's invasion of the German states did result in the imposition of some unity, but the major consequence was more to awaken the fires of German nationalism than to sow the seeds of liberalism as implied in the ideas of the French Revolution.

When German unity did finally take place in the latter half of the nineteenth century, it was achieved not under more Westernized Austria but rather under the hegemony of more Eastern-oriented Prussia; and Prussia was geared to nationalism, militarism, and a centralized and bureaucratic Germany, not to an emerging bourgeois liberalism already pressing for major political and social change throughout Europe. Led by an arrogant *Junker* aristocracy which manned the key military and civil service positions, by 1871 Prussia had unified most German-speaking peoples under its leadership.

Furthermore, Prussia was not wedded to free market concepts on the order of the British model. An emphasis upon military power and national might led its leaders to support cartels and in general to engage in monopolistic practices; in return a protected German industry supplied the leaders with the tools of war. In Great Britain and France, an independent, politically confident bourgeoisie made its influence increasingly felt. In Germany, however, industry, particularly prior to 1933, was led by men who reflected the status needs and hierarchical relationships of older, more traditional values. As a result, industrialization did not change German society; more accurately, it was fused with, and shaped by, preindustrial values.

World War I ended Prussian hegemony. The new Weimar Republic established in its place a democratic constitution which was supported by more liberal forces, especially the Social Democrats. But democracy was never really given a chance to operate. When harsh reparations were demanded from the victorious Allies following the German defeat in World War I and democratic elites, not the authoritarians of Wilhelmenian Germany, were forced to pay the bill, opposition propaganda utilized this humiliating treatment as a pretext to struggle against the regime. In addition, the gravest inflation and the worst depression in memory hardly gave the Weimar Republic an opportunity to gain legitimacy. And out of this humiliation and turmoil arose a political movement of the extreme right, the National Socialist party (Nazis). The extreme left as represented by the Communist party gained in popularity. These parties made parliamentary democracy unworkable because their strong representation in the legislature enabled them to shake the various coalition governments to their foundations. The fragility of coalitions in turn led to a belief among many Germans that democracy as a system was simply unworkable.

That the Weimar Republic would fall under such conditions is hardly surprising. In 1933, Nazi Adolf Hitler was designated chancellor by an aging President Paul von Hindenburg. Utilizing emergency powers handed over to him by the president, Hitler quickly destroyed his political opposition and soon created what can only be called a totalitarian political system in which basic freedoms were ruthlessly suppressed. His policies of expansion in foreign affairs finally led to World War II and another German defeat. Once again the dream of unity had been shattered, for postwar Germany was divided into Western and Eastern zones, one side controlled by the American, British, and French occupation forces, the other side by the Soviet Union. Out of this partition arose two regimes, the democratic Federal Republic of Germany and the Russian Communist-led German Democratic Republic.

### The Federal (Bonn) Republic

Following World War II, in September 1948, a constituent assembly met once again to attempt the creation of a viable German democracy.

Undoubtedly, the turbulent political history of Germany weighed heavily upon the delegates. With the Weimar experience planted firmly in their minds, many delegates were determined that the new attempt at democracy would not only assure the democratic forms but that it would also create a government sufficiently strong to ward off the threats of extreme right and left alike. To insure these ends, the Bonn constitution, while recognizing the role of political parties in politics, reduced the power of the two strongest Weimar institutions, the president and *Bundestag* (lower house), and strengthened the position of the chancellor. The latter, however, remained constitutionally responsible to the lower house. The notorious Article 48 of the Weimar constitution, which had allowed President Hindenburg to rule by emergency decree and to delegate power to the chancellor to suspend civil liberties and to govern without the support of a parliamentary majority, was eliminated. (In 1968, however, new emergency laws were added to the constitution under which civil liberties could be restricted in certain circumstances.) In addition, the Bonn constitution deprived the president of an independent political base, since he was to be indirectly elected for no more than two five-year terms by a special convention composed of members of the *Bundestag* and an equal number of representatives of the state legislatures.

It was felt that a major reason for government instability in Weimar lay in an unholy alliance of the extremist parties in the legislature which were unable to come to an agreement among themselves, but could easily vote more moderate governments out of office. Thus, just as the founders of the French Fifth Republic would do some ten years later, the Bonn framers sought to legislate political stability into existence. Their solution to the problem of instability was the "constructive vote of no confidence" by which no chancellor could be overthrown until his opposition could come up with an alternative chancellor of its own.

Indeed, not only was the chancellor strengthened at the expense of the president, but the role of a traditional institution, the *Bundesrat* (upper house), was enhanced. Composed of representatives of the *Land* (state) governments in proportion to population, the *Bundesrat* is essentially a congress of appointed state ministers who vote on instructions from their governments. As such, it is designed to represent states rather than parties, since each state casts its votes as a unit. The constitutional powers of the *Bundesrat* reflect traditional notions of German federalism which emphasize direct participation by the provincial governments in national policy making and administration rather than distinctly separate powers for each jurisdictional level of government. . . .

**FRANCE**

Unlike the United States, Great Britain, or even Canada, France has faced a chronic problem of political instability. . . .

Despite the undeniable fact that its social and economic structures have been greatly modernized since the end of World War II, France still seems susceptible to large-scale social conflicts such as the explosion in May 1968 between students and workers on one side and middle-class Gaullists and their supporters on the other. . . .

. . . [S]ocial and political tensions within the French polity have led to periodic alterations in the constitutional order. . . .

## The Third Republic (1875–1940)

Although the Third Republic had a relatively long life by French standards, it was still characterized by political instability. Executive authority was made weak almost from the beginning because presidents were allowed small constitutional scope within which to operate. Their principal duties involved ceremonies, appointments, and nominations. The nominating function was especially noteworthy, since the president was called upon to nominate a potential prime minister who in turn would be acceptable to a majority of deputies in the lower house of the legislature. In this sense, then, the system functioned somewhat as an hereditary monarchy, minus the security of heredity and status, of course.

Despite its rather formidable constitutional powers, the presidency was soon placed in a position subordinate to that of the legislature. Following an 1877 electoral contest a conservative president, Marshal Marie Edmé Patrice MacMahon, dissolved the Chamber of Deputies in a dispute with its radical membership and he was forced to resign (1879). Thereafter, the president lacked the power of dissolution and the lower house assumed a growing importance. But this weakening of the presidency did not lead to a strengthening of the cabinets and premiers. Third Republic governments were usually of short duration, perpetually threatened with overthrow by hostile groups of deputies. Whereas cabinets in present-day Britain, West Germany, or the Fifth Republic have generally retained disciplined majority support in their legislatures, tight controls over legislation throughout the initiation and committee stages and therefore dominance of agenda and debate and resistance to interpolation, Third Republic governments enjoyed none of these advantages of security or authority.

Since there were so many parties in the Chamber of Deputies, the role of the small center groups became crucial in the formation of governments. But since the cabinets were created from these small and diverse parties, and since the resulting majorities had so few permanent links binding them together, any disagreement was easily translated into a government crisis. Indeed, . . . during the 70 years of the Third Republic, some 50 prime ministers and 500 different cabinet ministers took part in the exercise of governmental power. Under such changing conditions, governments lacked authority, much less decisiveness. As a result power passed to disparate groups of deputies and to the standing committees, each of which was dominated by highly particularistic interests. Important and innovative government bills therefore either died in the Chamber of Deputies or were emasculated in committee or on the floor. . . .

A basic problem for the stability of the Third Republic resulted from the total absence of a majority party during the life of the regime. Indeed, it could be argued that the weak presidency, premier and cabinet flowed from this inability to find a majority in the legislature. . . .

## The Fourth Republic (1945–58)

Established immediately following World War II, the Fourth Republic continued in the tradition of its immediate predecessor with multipartyism, legislative dominance, and a weak executive. Not surprisingly, it was unable to cope with certain postwar difficulties which would have made life uncomfortable for even the strongest of governments. A rampant inflation, the growth of rebellion in the French colonies, and a Communist party more popular than ever because of its role in the Resistance were sufficient in themselves to encourage political instability. The leader of the Resistance forces and first premier of the new republic, General Charles de Gaulle, had hoped to create a strong executive independent of the lower house and the parties; but the traditional groupings, now aided by the growth of new parties, quickly asserted themselves following the end of hostilities. In disgust de Gaulle resigned as premier in January 1946, and went into temporary political exile. In 1947, however, he sought to return to power through the creation of a new political party, the Rally of the French People (RPF).

It is hard to imagine a higher degree of instability than that of the Fourth Republic in terms of executive leadership. The system was nominally a parliamentary one, but far removed from the stable parliamentary governments found in the other nations discussed here. None of the parties was strong enough to command a majority in the all-powerful National Assembly; and two groups, the French Communist party and the Gaullist RPF, were committed for very different reasons to the destruction of the system itself. Together they had enough votes to make life quite uncomfortable for the various governments of the day. The result was government by a number of small centrist-oriented parties, each jealous of its own prerogatives, and all too eager to bring down any cabinet which failed to do its bidding.

Indeed, the average life span for each of these cabinets was only about five months, although most of them fell not by a vote of no confidence, but rather because some angry coalition partner decided to leave. Ironically, the unending stream of new governments produced a much less profound change than might appear at first glance, since all too often many of the same ministers in a fallen cabinet returned to power in the succeeding one. These returns occurred because the various center parties, due to their narrow and tenuous majorities, had little room to maneuver between the large Communist and Gaullist parliamentary groups; hence, there were simply not many different possibilities open to forge a new coalition. As a result, and despite apparent instability, some governmental continuity was nevertheless achieved. . . .

## The Fifth Republic (1958–   )

When General de Gaulle and his followers returned to power in May 1958, following a revolt in Algeria by settler and army insurgents against the discredited Fourth Republic, they were determined to restore the power of the state so that France might once again assume its place among the powerful nations of the world. The Gaullists quite naturally blamed the weakness and corruption of the Fourth Republic upon the dominant position of the National Assembly, an institution which seemed to create and destroy governments at will.

General de Gaulle's remedy for France's ills lay in the creation of a new constitution which had as its basis a strong executive to contain a rambunctious legislature. To the Gaullists, Fourth Republic instability was not caused so much by the views and behavior of ordinary Frenchmen, or even by French politicians, as by institutional arrangements which gave the lower house (the National Assembly) the right to vote governments up and down at will. Thus, since the problem was deemed as a legal one, the remedy as well was a legal one.

General de Gaulle had set forth the outlines for a new constitution as early as 1946 in his famous speech at Bayeux, when he called for a strong president independent of the whims of the parliament. In 1958, with his trusted disciple and constitutional expert, Michel Debré, he put his wishes into practice. Therefore, according to the new Fifth Republic constitution, a president, as the physical embodiment of the state and "arbiter," was given extensive powers, including the right to negotiate treaties, to dissolve the National Assembly, to submit bills to national referenda, to appoint the prime minister (and on his recommendation, the members of the government), and to suspend the constitution itself for a limited period in the event of a national emergency. Imagine an American president with the power to dissolve Congress and call for new elections or with the prerogative of overriding a recalcitrant Senate and House by submitting his proposals to the public for ratification. Indeed, the one area in which the French president may have been in a weaker position than his American counterpart lay in his indirect election by an electoral college of notables. Even this potential limitation—potential because de Gaulle's authority and prestige hardly required constitutional justification—was rectified in October 1962, when the general, acting on what may only be termed unconstitutional grounds, submitted to referendum a bill allowing henceforth for the direct election of the president of the republic.

An aggrandizement of the presidency was not the only way by which the National Assembly was reduced in stature in the Fifth Republic. To ensure that the Assembly remained more docile than in the past, the upper house, the Senate, was given the power to veto and amend legislation emanating from the lower house. Senators were elected indirectly by deputies, general councillors, and municipal council delegates. Each one was to serve for nine years, and the terms were staggered. In the case of division between the two houses, however, the government position was paramount, for it had the right to resolve the dispute according to its own discretion. Finally, the new constitution declared the incompatibility of ministerial portfolio and National Assembly membership. Thus, upon assuming a government position, the individual deputy was required to resign his seat. Gaullists had long argued that such a reform would discourage potential ministers from conspiring against cabinets.

The Fifth Republic constitution was not designed so much to give power to the president as to make him something of a modern Caesar. In fact, there is strong evidence that Michel Debré, the principal author of the new constitution and first prime minister in the Fifth Republic, believed that General de Gaulle wished mainly to observe the political wars from Olympian heights as an "arbiter," intervening only intermittently in the decision-making realm of domestic politics. Indeed, it was expected that de Gaulle's interests lay for the most part with the great concerns of foreign policy. Consequently, what can only be called parliamentary government was expected to take care of the more mundane concerns of day-by-day government.

That parliamentary government was what Debré had in mind may be suggested from Article 20 of the constitution. There it plainly states that the prime minister "directs the policy of the nation." Apparently Debré expected the parliamentary aspects of the regime to become predominant once de Gaulle lost himself in foreign policy concerns or departed from the scene. However, when the general opted for a nationally elected president in 1962, Debré dutifully fell into line in support of a presidential regime.

At any rate, the de Gaulle-Debré creation is a hydra-headed executive with built-in potential for conflict between president and prime minister. . . .

# 9

# Policymaking Structures in Western Europe's Parliamentary Democracies

## Lawrence C. Mayer with John H. Burnett

This selection from a comparative study titled *Politics in Industrial Societies* examines the functions of various types of constitutions in terms of such concepts as fundamental principles, legitimation of cultural norms, sovereignty, and accountability. Against this background, it then goes on to analyze the processes inherent in Western Europe's different forms of representative assemblies and the roles played by the various chiefs of state, contrasting in particular the differences between constitutional monarchies and republics.

## CONSTITUTIONS AND CONSTITUTIONALISM

. . . The term *constitution* is used in two quite distinct senses. Americans tend to use it in its more familiar sense to refer to a set of fundamental written laws that designate the format of government. These laws are fundamental in the sense that they override ordinary acts of the legislature. Normally, these laws are more difficult to change than ordinary legislation. Fundamental laws do have legal sanction, however. Alleged violations of the laws are dealt with through the judicial processes.

The meaning of the term *constitution* is not exhausted by this legal conception. The British political system, for example, has no such set of fundamental written laws, but scholars do speak of the English or British constitution.

### Constitutions as Fundamental Principles

The term in a broader sense refers to those procedures for making decisions and choosing decision makers that are fundamental to the essential nature of the system. The term *fundamental* means that which cannot be altered without changing the essential character of the system. For example, if a British cabinet should resist the pressure to resign in the face of an unambiguous expression of no-confidence by the legislature . . . , the entire structure of accountability of the cabinet to society through the intermediary agency of Parliament would no longer pertain. [It has been argued that] it is this particular structure of accountability that defines parliamentary democracy. The structure of accountability of the governors to the governed is perhaps the most fundamental set of procedures for any system.

Other procedures are alterable without altering the fundamental essence of the system. . . . We are distinguishing between what is fundamental and what pertains to the circumstances of a particular time, presuming that some things ought to be easier to change than others. The purpose in making a constitution harder to change than ordinary legislation is that the rules inherent in the character of a system ought to be harder to change than the resolution of issues that pertain to the circumstances of the moment. Presumably, the constitution would confine itself to the former class of rules while the latter type of rules would be reflected in ordinary legislation.

This concept of fundamental principles enables us to speak of a British constitution in the absence of a set of fundamental written laws for that system. The British constitution is comprised of four basic elements, only the first two of which possess legal sanction: common law, acts of Parliament, landmark documents, and convention. . . .

In systems lacking a long evolutionary development, especially in systems emanating from a revolution, legitimacy must be created overnight for the new set of institutions. Only legal sanctions can impart such instant legitimacy. That is why written constitutions are the rule and unwritten ones the exception.

Thus, one of the functions of a written constitution is to legitimate the consensus of fundamentals that has already evolved in a society. It is doubtful that a constitution can create such a consensus.

Yet, even in the case of a written constitution, we can discen constitutional significance in rules beyond those in the written constitution. . . .

Sweden possesses four legal documents that are generally recognized as comprising its formal constitution. . . . Several specific substantive rules have been included in some of these documents. There is a difficulty in placing what is fundamental and enduring with what is relevant to current issues. Policy—substantive decisions regarding who gets how much of what—must be changeable or the system cannot adapt or respond to input from its context. To make the fundamental equally easy to alter would render the character of the system vulnerable to the passions of a point in time.

Despite their incorporation of numerous substantive matters, Sweden's constitutional documents are relatively hard to amend. Apparently, the substantive matters are not of such importance as to affect the flexibility of the system. . . .

## The Intermingling of the Fundamental and the Circumstantial

Clearly, the "true constitution" . . . is rarely completely coterminous with the fundamental written law. To varying degrees, fundamental and circumstantial rules tend to be found intermingled in the same source, whether that source be a written document or the customs of a community. The capacity to make the distinction between what is fundamental and what is not is an important criterion for political stability and adaptability. This capacity is not a function of the nature of the constitution. The Americans, with a short, general, written constitution, the British, with an unwritten constitution, and the Swedes, with a longer, more substantive and detailed written document, all seem to possess that capacity. The answer to the question of why a nation is not disposed to tinker with its procedural fundamentals is not that they are formally more difficult to change than its circumstantial rules. Instead, the answer is that procedural fundamentals have acquired greater legitimacy in some systems than in others. . . .

## Functions of Constitutions: Legitimacy and Forms

A constitution can only legitimate the norms of a society insofar as it reflects them. A set of constitutionally imposed norms in conflict with the norms of the society in which it operates will not be viable. . . . The classic case for the absence of such congruence is the Weimar Constitution [Germany, 1919–1933], which was based on highly egalitarian authority relations imposed on a society with very deferential or even submissive attitudes toward authority. It is psychologically difficult to condition oneself always to defer to authority at home, school, work, and all other aspects of one's life and suddenly regard oneself as an equal in political wisdom to one's political authorities. Such incompatibility between perceptions of one's roles produces psychological strain. A constitution cannot create freedom or democracy. It can only reflect, explicate, and legitimate an existing cultural disposition in that direction. . . .

## Functions of Constitutions: The Transfer of Power

We have suggested that one major function of a constitution is the legitimation of cultural norms, a process that is essential for the peaceful transfer of power. The transfer of power is an inescapable problem of all political systems. Political leadership can never be perpetual; even lifetime monarchs are mortal. Peaceful transfer of power has historically been the exception rather than the rule. The resolution of the divisive questions of when power will be transferred and which of several competing claimants shall be the new power wielder is made acceptable to all concerned by the legitimation of a set of rules by which these questions are resolved.

Not all constitutions have managed to legitimate a set of procedures for the transfer of power. Frequently, authoritarian systems fail to specify such a set of procedures, a failure that precipitates recurring power struggles. After all, a distinguishing characteristic of systems is that tendency to base the policymaking process on the will of the ruler or oligarchic elite rather than on the rule of law. The rule of law refers to a system in which the will of the elite is subordinate to the legitimated procedures of the society. Of course, these procedures may dictate deferring to the will of the ruler; hence, the distinction between will and the rule of law may not always be clear in practice.

The problem in transferring power stems from the fact that competition for political power seems inevitable. Democratic constitutions institutionalize this competition in the form of open elections and of provisions for a regular or emergency transfer. . . .

## SOVEREIGNTY

One of the fundamental elements of a constitution is the locus of sovereignty. Sovereignty. . . refers to the final or ultimate authority to make and enforce law. In the United States, we have a system of "popular sovereignty"—the concept that sovereignty resides in "the people" (presumably referring to the aggregate of citizens) and is delegated to the elite. From this concept is derived the notion of the social contract—the idea that the legitimate authority of the decision makers must be delegated by the governed. The idea of the social contract goes well back in the history of political philosophy. Among others, it is explicitly associated with the writings of John Locke, the nineteenth-century English philosopher whose writings so strongly influenced the American Declaration of Independence. This conception of popular sovereignty was also explicit in the writings of a number of eighteenth-century French philosophers, such as Rousseau. Popular sovereignty is a fundamental tenent of French and American constitutional theory.

Although Locke and other contract theorists such as Hobbes were Englishmen, English constitutional theory is not based on popular sovereignty. Instead, sovereignty in Britain resides in the concept of the crown. In fact, the concept of the crown is virtually synonymous with the locus of sovereignty. The crown is not simply the monarch. At one time the monarch exercised most of the powers of the crown. Through the course of British political history, nearly all of these powers have passed from the hands of the monarch to ministers acting in his or her name. The decisions of judges, acts of Parliament, etc., are made in the name of the monarch, who in turn *legally* (but not in fact) still exercises the powers of the crown. Thus, even though both houses of Parliament pass a bill proposed by the cabinet, the bill does not become law until the monarch (or a person speaking for the monarch) "wills it."

The significance of crown power is that it entails the proposition that somewhere in the government there is the capacity to respond to any public need or demand. Government under the concept of crown power does not legally have to receive an explicit or implicit delegation of power from the people in order to act. . . .

It should be recognized that the locus of sovereignty, an essentially legal matter, is not the same as the question of whether a government is accountable or responsive to the electorate, an essentially political matter. The locus of sovereignty in the crown does not preclude political democracy through structural accountability of the decision makers.

## THE LOGIC OF PARLIAMENTARY DEMOCRACY

With the exception of the United States, Fifth Republic France, and Sweden, the industrial democracies have all been variations on the basic parliamentary theme. While the De Gaulle constitution has retained some of the forms of parliamentary government . . . , the basic structure of accountability in that system is much closer to the presidential format of the United States than to the parliamentary format. . . .

### The Structure of Accountability

Accountability refers to stable, recurring patterns of interaction, procedures that provide instruments for holding those who make au-

GREAT BRITAIN

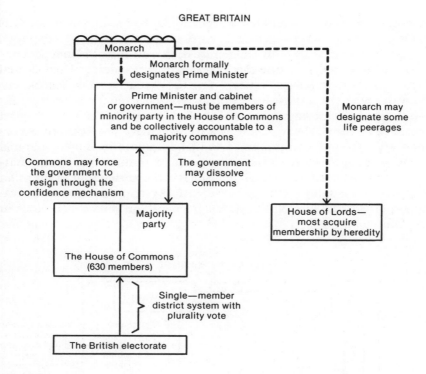

Figure 9.1.

thoritative decisions for a society accountable to that society for the consequences of the decisions. Accountability may be structured through the instrument of the direct popular election of the political executive as in the case of the French and American presidents. . . . By contrast, the political executive in parliamentary democracies is indirectly accountable to the electorate, at least in a formal sense. The direct accountability of political executives in parliamentary systems is to the lower house of the legislature. (Clearly, upper houses fall outside the logic of the system as the proverbial fifth wheel on a wagon. Perhaps the general decline in the power and significance of upper houses in parliamentary democracies may be partially understood in the light of this lack of an obvious role for them in the structure of accountability.)

Specifically, the tenure of the political executive in parliamentary systems is contingent on the executive retaining at least the passive support of the majority of the lower house. A loss of support may be expressed in either of two ways: the house refuses to pass a major piece of legislation initiated by the executive or the house approves of a motion of censure or no confidence. When a lack of confidence is so expressed, the executive is generally expected to resign. . . .

In presidential systems the tenure of the executive is independent of the will of the legislature (for example, the presidents of the United States and Fifth Republic France). Here the executive must reach compromises with the legislature in order to govern, even though the executive's tenure is autonomous of that body. The difference is that in the presence of legislative discontent with executive programs in parliamentary systems, compromises and adjustments in those programs must be reached before the formal expression of that legislative dissatisfaction in a legislative vote or decision. In the presence of an intransigent executive or legislature, a presidential system may produce political stalemate and immobility, as has happened on several occasions in the United States. . . .

THE FIFTH FRENCH REPUBLIC

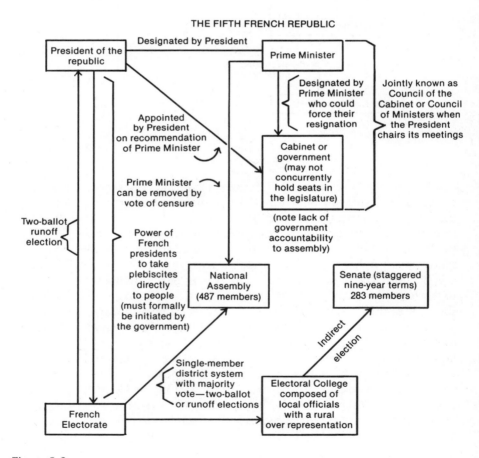

Figure 9.2.

# THE ROLE OF REPRESENTATIVE ASSEMBLIES

The word *legislature* can be misleading if it is taken to imply that the national representative assembly formulates public policy. Policy in industrial societies originates with the political executive to an overwhelming extent. In the United States and Great Britain over 90 percent of all legislation originates with the executive. This is true despite the fact that the American presidency does not exercise the control over the legislative process exercised by the British cabinet . . .

The executive in industrial societies tends to formulate alternatives, but the formulations are implicitly presented to the legislature in the form of whether this cabinet proposal shall be adopted or not. Although legislatures are incapable of effectively formulating comprehensive policy, they are capable of compelling substantial revision of the policies formulated by the government. . . .

In stable parliamentary democracies, legislatures rarely formally say no to major policy proposals of the executive, for that would bring down the government and in most cases force new elections, placing the jobs of the legislators as well as those of the executive on the line. Instead, because of this understood capacity of parliaments to withdraw "confidence" from the executive, executives generally determine the existence of strongly held objections to their policy formulations in the legislature prior to a confrontation on a formal vote and adjust their policy formulations accordingly. In this way, in those systems characterized by a disposition to bargain and compromise, the confidence mechanism serves its check-and-balance function without generating cabinet instability.

The legislature is structurally suited to use its deliberative function to check and balance the governing function of the executive because it is in the legislature that the "outs" (opposition) are accorded an input in the policymaking process. It is in the legislative deliberations that minorities get to confront the majority. Thus, excluding the variable political role of the courts (which is nowhere else as great as in the United States), the legislature is the only structure where the government is continuously confronted with another point of view. It is a forum in which non governmental parties can mobilize that antiincumbent support that renders democratic political systems competitive.

## The Representative Function

Legislatures, in addition to limiting the discretion of the executive in their check-and-balance role, may be argued to perform a representative function. Two questions arise from such a conception: who is being represented and what is entailed by the concept of representation?

The first question asks if the legislators' primary duty is to the interests of those in their constituencies who voted for them, of their constituencies as a whole, or of the political system at large (that is, the nation). Edmund Burke, the British political philosopher and statesman of the late eighteenth century, in a now classic speech to the voters in his constituency at Bristol, said that when the interests of his constituents conflict with those of the nation at large, the duty of the legislator is to protect the national interests. . . . Alternatively, the role of the members of a legislature could be conceptualized as that of speaking for the perceived interests and demands of their hometown constituents. . . .

## Upper Houses in Parliamentary Systems

In federal systems, the tendency is for the political subsystems to be at least formally represented in an upper house. American readers will be familiar with the equal representation of each state in the Senate. The West German *Lander* are not only represented in the Bundesrat of the Federal Republic (in strength roughly proportionate to their respective populations), but the respective *Land* governments equal appoint their Bundesrat representatives, instruct them on how to vote, and may remove them. Because the delegations of each *Land* in the Bundesrat vote as a bloc on instruction from their *Land* government, the party affiliation of the individual delegate has no impact on his or her vote. The vote is instead a function of the political complexion of the *Land* government. . . .

With the exception of Germany and Switzerland, this representation of political subdivisions in the upper house is more of a formal than a genuine phenomenon in democratic systems. . . . As long as the responsibility of the government is to the lower house, upper houses in parliamentary systems appear to be structures in search of a logical role in the system. Members of the government are overwhelmingly, if not exclusively, members of the lower house. . . . Because the challenges to government policy occur in the questions and general debate in the lower house of the countries under consideration, it is desirable if not imperative for members of the government to be present to defend their policies and to supply information about them. . . . A further factor contributing to the decline in the impact of upper houses on the national decision-making process in parliamentary democracies is their tendency toward a nonrepresentative character. The British House of Lords is, of course, the classic example. Peopled in theory by all members of the hereditary aristocracy and life peers (1062 by August 1968), in practice fewer than 300 ever show up and considerably fewer than that attend regularly. . . .

## The Meaning of Representation

What does it mean to represent someone? One possible answer is that representatives should ascertain and follow their constituents' wishes as closely as possible on as many issues as possible. . . . Burke's answer, by contrast, . . . was that the MP owes his constituents not only his presence but his reasoned judgment. The representative is, by this conception of his role, a full-time student of public affairs whose judgments about affairs ought to carry more weight than the uninformed judgments of the average constituents. . . .

## Parliamentary Debate

It has been argued . . . that the parliamentary function of control of the executive entails "criticism" rather than "obstruction." This distinction entails the idea that, except in extreme circumstances, the legislature ought not to prevent the executive's program from being enacted. "Control" consists of publicizing and trying to persuade the public of the weak points in the government's position. By this conception, the debate preceding a . . . vote is a more significant part of Parliament's function than the vote itself.

Given the significance of the debating function, the variation in the character of debate in the nations under consideration is worth noting. The concept of debate normally entails an exchange of ideas, a situation in which a proposition is critiqued or answered with a counterproposal. This conception of debate may be distinguished from a series of more or less unrelated speeches. Speechmaking has been the rule in industrial democracies; debate has been the exception.

The British Parliament is frequently held up as epitomizing what debate ought to be in a legislature. Nowhere is a process of extemporaneous give and take more pronounced. The pros and cons of issues are delineated; rarely does a controversial assertion go unanswered. This may be seen in contrast to the succession of speeches found in other chambers such as in France, West Germany, or the United States—speeches often seemingly unaffected by any preceding remarks.

When debate occurs in Britain or elsewhere, it tends to take the form of criticism or defense of government-formulated policy. . . . Debate in the Swedish Riksdag, although less extensive than in Britain, is similarly structured into a "proposition" and "counterproposition" upon the introduction of the annual budget. The most likely debate occurs on general policy propositions at this time. Specific "bread-and-butter" compromises are hammered out in committee hearings. By contrast, most other Continental assemblies are characterized by a series of speeches that often ramble without really doing much to clarify the issues and without the give and take of debate. . . .

In competitive party systems . . . debate and criticism are essential in the process of attempting to mobilize support for or against a government's position. When debate is replaced by a series of speeches, this function is poorly served. Although fulfilling this function of debating the organization of support and opposition, debate in the British House of Commons has no effect on impending divisions, which are along party lines. The real impact of debate in Britain and similar systems is the cumulative support of or opposition to the overall performance of the government as determined at the next general election. This is, of course, the basic mechanism of accountability in a centralized cabinet system. . . .

## EXECUTIVE ROLES

Parliamentary systems divide their executive functions among two distinct roles: the political role (head of government) and the symbolic role (head of state). These correspond to what Walter Bagehot, in his classic commentary on *The English Constitution*, called the "efficient" and "dignified" aspects of the constitution, respectively. In the former role is concentrated the ultimate responsibility for policy formulation functions and adminstrative functions. The latter role concerns itself with ceremonial functions and, as the symbol of unity for the concept of the nation, integrative functions.

Presidential formats combine these two roles in one person. Thus, American presidents function both as the symbol of unity for the entire nation and, at the same time, the political and hence partisan representative of particular philosophies and interests. By effectively combining these two roles, the president can mobilize support through the role of head of state for partisan purposes.

General De Gaulle effectively did this in France. Aided and abetted by his enormous charisma, De Gaulle's power became institutionalized to the point where the successors of the general have had similarly great power.

The Fifth Republic has been called quasi-presidential because under the terms of the constitution the office of prime minister is at least partially accountable to the Assembly. However, the capacity of the Assembly to censure any prime minister having the support of the president of the republic is severely circumscribed by the political reality that the president could and almost certainly would immediately dissolve the Assembly. He can dissolve the Assembly up to once a year for any reason. Moreover, the prime minister is designated by the president, and thus far he has been designated according to the criterion of conformity to the views of the president. The prime minister is not required to secure the approval of the Assembly; hence, unlike "true" parliamentary regimes, the identity of the prime minister is not a function of the views of the legislature. Prime ministers in the Fifth Republic have tended to act in the role of deputies to the president, liaisons aiding the president in keeping the Assembly in line, and potential heirs to the presidency. Prime ministers in the Fifth Republic have not established an autonomy from the president, as British prime ministers have established their autonomy from the will of the monarch. These facts, combined with the extraordinary political powers of the French president, render the word *quasi* in the term *quasi-presidential regime* without significance. The French president is as much the head of government as the American president, if not more so. . . .

. . . Like American presidents, French presidents have broad appointive power, head the armed forces, and formulate most policy. Moreover, the French president exercises major control over the agenda of the legislature. The president has the power to raise questions of constitutionality to be brought before the Constitutional Council, the court that decides these issues in France.

As in the American system, the direct election of the French president gives that official a political base of support possessed by no other institution in the system. Because no other chief of state exists to compete for the support that normally adheres to the occupier of that role in a reasonably well-integrated society, the president of the republic is capable of mobilizing much support for his partisan political purposes out of the patriotic effect that normally adheres to his concurrent role of chief of state.

## Chiefs of State

Elsewhere, the role of chief of state is separated from that of head of government. In the remaining constitutional monarchies, the monarch fulfills that role. Among the nations we are considering, Belgium, Britain, Denmark, the Netherlands, Norway, and Sweden remain as constitutional monarchies. . . .

The Dutch monarchy has lost much prestige in recent years due to the marital and religious activities of the royal family. The Italian monarch was deposed at the end of the Second World War as a result of his collaboration with Mussolini and fascism. Similarly, the wartime behavior of the Belgian King Leopold III resulted in his abdication in favor of his son, King Baudouin. This "royal question" reinforced the cultural question, as the Flemish and Walloons divided for and against Leopold. This politicization of the monarchy, especially when involved with the divisive cultural cleavage, did nothing to enhance the prestige of that institution.

By contrast, Britain has been fortunate in the character of the individuals that have occupied its throne in the twentieth century. Men such as wartime monarch George VI displayed genuine leadership qualities and enhanced the prestige of the monarchy. While Elizabeth II seems to lack the leadership qualities of her predecessor, she has done nothing to diminish seriously the prestige of the institution. Despite some criticism from the political left, the British monarchy probably remains the most prestigious of the world's declining number of monarchies. . . .

The effectiveness of a monarch in fulfilling the functions of chief of state depends on the prestige of the institution and the character of the royal family. Monarchs have a certain advantage in fulfilling these functions over political leaders such as the French and American presidents. First, despite the political advantages in combining the two roles, the integrating force of the symbolic role should be enhanced when the chief of state is politically neutral. Second, the pomp that naturally accrues to royalty can add to the integrative effectiveness of this role. Pomp often seems out of place with presidents and prime ministers. . . . Third, freed from the burdens of political leadership, the chief of state can devote more time and attention to symbolic and ceremonial duties.

Depending on the prestige and leadership qualities of the occupant of the throne, the monarch in a parliamentary system may still exercise some political influence. In the first place, the tenure of the monarch usually vastly exceeds that of any given prime minister or head of government. Consequently, a monarch may offer a longer-term perspective. Second, this perspective is not likely to be distorted by considerations of political accountability and partisan attachment. Therefore, as Bagehot once said, the monarch has three "rights—the right to be consulted, the right to encourage, the right to warn." These "rights" adhere in proportion to the force of the monarch's personality, the prestige of the monarchy itself, and the weakness of the political head of government.

In the third place, the monarch officially designates the prime minister. When one disciplined party has a majority of the legislative seats or a clearly dominant plurality of the seats, the choice of the monarch is obviously limited to the head of the dominant party. This is normally the case among most of the nations we are considering, as aggregated party systems become the rule rather than the exception.

In some systems, however, elections are occasionally inconclusive. In Third and Fourth Republic France this was normally the case. It has been the case in the Netherlands on several occasions. When the nonlabor or nonsocialist coalitions take over in Scandinavian nations, it is not entirely clear which party dominates the coalitions. A forceful monarch, in a supposedly neutral role as arbitrator in the bargaining process among parties to form a government, may exercise some influence in that selection. . . .

## Presidents as Chiefs of State

In those parliamentary systems that are republics, a president occupies the role of chief of state. This role has often been filled by what may be termed an "elder statesman." . . .

As veteran politicians, some presidents (as in Italy, West Germany, or Fourth and Third Republic France) may retain a certain residue of political skill and an inclination to wield power. . . . In these cases, presidents, whose tenure generally exceeds that of their prime ministers, may exercise some political impact in much the same way as monarchs. Whatever impact these heads of state possess tends to be concentrated in the selection of a government—the prime minister and the cabinet.

In the case of the Italian president, the norms of political neutrality are not as strong as in the case of British, Scandinavian, or Low Country monarchs. The bounds of expectation (or the customary part of the constitution, broadly defined) permit the president to speak out on controversial questions, and Italian presidents have in fact done so. This would be unthinkable for one of the aforementioned monarchs. Similarly, the president of the Federal Republic of Germany is constitutionally prohibited from engaging in partisan activities. These same bounds of expectation in Italy permit the president to use his legal power of returning a piece of legislation to Parliament for reconsideration. This has been done on numerous occasions but never on a major piece of legislation. . . .

## The Heads of Government

In parliamentary systems, the government consists of a prime minister and the cabinet. The role of prime minister occasionally appears under other titles: in Italy, it is officially the president of the Council of Ministers; in Fourth Republic France it was premier. . . .

The cabinet consists of the heads of the governmental administrative departments—called ministers—and several policy advisors or "generalists" without administrative responsibilities. Not all ministers are necessarily part of the cabinet. In Britain certain less significant ministers are omitted from the cabinet. The generalists are called "ministers without portfolio"—that is, ministers without a department to run. . . .

The nations under consideration differ in the extent that their cabinets function as a coherent body. In a fragmented party system such as Italy's, with coalition governments composed of several parties, the cabinet is not coherent. In Britain the cabinet appears to be quite coherent. All members of British cabinets are members of the same disciplined party and owe their place in the cabinet to the prime minister. In Italy, cabinet members are often designated by the parliamentary groups irrespective of the will of the prime minister as the price for support of the government. In Italy, Fourth Republic France, and Norway, the fall of a government requires the resignation only of the prime minister. It does not preclude the cabinet members from retaining their posts or even moving to a higher (more prestigious or powerful) post in a new government. . . .

In Britain . . . the cabinet is collectively responsible to the parliament. The Belgian cabinet is also in theory collectively responsible. This means that if a government should fall, the entire cabinet would be compelled to resign. . . .

In general, the principle of collective responsibility also applies to the Low Countries, although, as in Britain, a single minister within the Dutch cabinet may be forced to resign. . . .

Cabinet responsibility works somewhat differently in the case of Italy. The entire cabinet must resign in the face of a vote of no confidence; however, most of the ministers are reappointed to the same positions in succeeding cabinets. This is in contrast to the British system, where a single party controls the entire government. Here, a transfer of power at the level of prime minister necessarily entails a total reconstitution of cabinet personnel.

Thus, in highly aggregated party systems, in which the leadership of the dominant party in effect picks the cabinet, each member of that government has a direct political interest in its survival. Except in extraordinary circumstances, to force the resignation of the prime minister would be tantamount to driving oneself out of the government. Inasmuch as a genuine impact on the official policymaking process is almost exclusively concentrated in the cabinet in these systems . . . to force the resignation of a government of which one is a part would in effect condemn oneself to the political wilderness. . . .

# Unit IV

## ———— Political Parties ————

Western Europe's political parties represent a wide variety of political philosophies and often their names bear little relation to their actual position on the ideological spectrum. Moreover, even parties called by the same name may, in different countries, represent quite different political philosophies. Thus, nowhere throughout Western Europe may a political party's official name be employed as a useful guide to its ideological orientation or current political philosophy.

Political parties play a central role in the electoral processes in Western Europe and thus have a direct impact on the formation of governments. In contrast to the United States where they tend to be alliances of different interest groups, political parties in Western Europe are more ideological in nature, with each party representing a different body of doctrine and a different cultural and political plan. Since these differences in political ideology are taken very seriously in Western Europe, it is not surprising that in choosing political leaders individual personalities are less important than they are in the United States. Instead, Europeans, by and large, tend to be drawn to one party or another primarily because of the strength of the party's ideological appeal.

In most Western European countries, governments are made up of representatives of more than one party—that is, of several parties in coalition. Currently, Great Britain is the only country in Western Europe that closely resembles the United States in having a political system that comprises two major political parties. Just as there is considerable diversity in political ideology and in governmental structure in Western Europe, so there is wide diversity in the rules governing the structure of parliamentary elections. These range from

Britain's relatively simple plurality system, in which the candidate who gets the most votes wins the seat, to the often highly complicated proportional representation systems common in West Germany, Belgium, and many other Western European countries.

Within the overwhelming diversity of Western Europe's political parties and electoral processes, the importance of political ideology is the one common thread. Indeed, it is political ideology that shapes the policies a party pursues, affects the way different parties compete for power, and ultimately determines how and what types of governments nations form.

This unit examines the structures, functions, and ideologies of Western Europe's political parties, the electoral systems that underlie them, and changing patterns in present-day party politics. In "Political Parties in Western Europe," Roy C. Macridis and Robert E. Ward examine the role of the political party in combining or "aggregating" as many interests as possible in order to effectively represent those interests in government. The authors also contrast two-party and multiparty systems, showing how functions differ in each. In "Western European Party Systems," Lawrence C. Mayer and John H. Burnett describe variations in two-party and multiparty systems and survey several of the various parties that make up the ideological political spectrum. "Electoral Systems of Representation and How They Work" presents in table form the variations, advantages, and disadvantages in plural, preferential, and proportional representation systems.

The unit concludes with three selections that examine how party structures have changed in recent years as a result of shifts in popular support. In "The Future of Britain's Political Parties," Tim Robinson assesses future prospects for the British two-party system as the Liberals and the Social Democrats challenge the declining Labour Party for status as the major party in opposition to the Conservatives. "Europe's Socialists Are Losing Their Taste for Power" examines the various forces that have been at work as socialist governments have lost or gained power in different Western European countries. The author points to increased difficulties in coalition building as a major factor in the gradual decline of the social-ist parties' strength since the mid-1970s. Finally, Sylvia Pog-gioli reports in "Italian Voters Repelled by Political Parties" that Italians' growing discontent with their government's per-vasive and costly system of favoritism is steadily undermin-ing the country's national party structure and may well even be threatening Italy's entire democratic process.

# 10

## Political Parties in Western Europe

_____ **Roy C. Macridis and Robert E. Ward** _____

This selection provides a general overview of the roles parties play in the political process in Western Europe and the means they employ to combine, clarify, and carry out the objectives of the many interests which they serve.

---

. . . Political scientists and sociologists provide us with an impressive listing of the functions of political parties. . . . [A]mong the functions most commonly given we find the following: _representation (and brokerage), conversion and aggregation; integration (participation, socialization, and mobilization); persuasion, repression, recruitment and choice of leaders, deliberation, policy formulation, control of the government._ . . .

. . . With the disappearance of the old status groups, or at least with the significant erosion of their position, power has shifted to those who receive support. With the growth and diversification of interests in an industrial society, no single interest has the remotest chance of providing singly the needed support. The use of force is very uneconomical, and persuasion appears to be the most acceptable channel. Thus interests must unite, and must convince as many persons and groups as possible about the validity of their demands. This has become the most general form of political activity. . . .

The party represents interest, aggregates it, mobilizes it, provides for possibilities of compromise among competing ones, converts it into policy, and, finally, recruits the political leaders who, by assuming control of governmental offices translate it into governmental action. The party is like a train—interests and demands feed its engine; it converts it into energy and drives the government to a predetermined place. The analogy, like all analogies, must, of course, be taken with a grain of salt—very often the place where the party wants to go to is not so definite as Grand Central Station, and quite frequently the party leader takes liberties with the program of the party that no self-respecting conductor would or can afford to take, with regard to the destination of the train.

## REPRESENTATION OF INTEREST

To exert influence, interests must make the government act or not act; they must either control it or greatly influence it. To do this, they must find a way to make the people vote for the candidates for government positions likely to be most in tune with them. To select such a government they must "appeal to the public" and spread their net as wide as possible and persuade as many people as possible that the particular candidates for governmental position are the best possible candidates for the country as a whole. It is at this stage that the party steps in. The party men become a critically important link between the government and the interests—solidly planted in both, or at least carefully looking in both directions; it bridges the two. The party assumes the function of a spokesman for one, or rather, for many interests—the farmers, the trade unions, the pacifists, the veterans, etc. It speaks for each of them, but in order to be fairly successful, it must also speak for many of them. Thus the representative function is not to be construed in literal terms—otherwise there would be a party for every interest and a single interest for every party.

## AGGREGATION AND BROKERAGE

The party attempts to bring together and represent as many interests as possible—but it is not a mere piling up or juxtaposition of interests. It would be hard, for instance, for the party to advocate at one and the same time racial equality (as a spokesman of the blacks) and racial supremacy (as a spokesman of the Southern or perhaps the suburban white). It would be hard for the British Labour party to speak for both free enterprise and welfare benefits for all workers. It would be also difficult for a party that wishes to win popular support to take a very rigid ideological position on any given issue. . . . The party must find an area—as large as possible—where there is a congruence of interests: better housing, higher wages, urban renewal, improved education, increased welfare benefits, for instance. The party, in other words, must compromise in order to represent. It acts as a broker. It takes more from one and less from another to give each as much as possible without alienating any. It not only aggregates, but synthesizes the various interests and demands into one product that the greatest possible number of consumers will buy at the political supermarket—the election. The product is the program, a set of promises of what the government will do and what the government will not do.

## MOBILIZATION

But interest, at least in the narrow sense of the term (economic interest), is not always as aggressive as people think. And interest in its broadest sense (purpose) may slumber for a long time. The party, under the appropriate conditions and circumstances, mobilizes and awakens both. Interest and purpose, thanks to the party, move from a state of latency into actualization. . . . [T]he party plays a creative role: it evokes response to demands or goals that have not as yet fully developed. In so doing, the party also restructures support and invites new forms of governmental action.

## CLARIFICATION OF ISSUES AND SELECTION
## OF THE GOVERNMENT

It is the platform that provides the ultimate synthesis and evokes participation and support. But this depends upon the party system. Under a multiparty system like the French one, the platform appeared often as an ideological statement rather than a careful compromise among interests. Under two-party systems, the parties appear to be more pragmatic and more comprehensive. The differences stem in part from the underlying motives for which popular support is sought. In a two-party system, like the British one, while clarification of issues is important, perhaps even more important is the election of a government—and at times of one man. An intensely ideological and partisan position will make victory difficult; a comprehensive and pragmatic one will make it easier to produce a larger and more attractive package. In a multiparty system, on the other hand, an election often amounts to selecting only representatives who will in turn attempt, on the basis of their own compromises and agreements, to form a cabinet—i.e., nominate the government. The parties in a multiparty situation, therefore, try to maintain their electoral clientele by the specific appeal to specific interests and ideologies. This was the case with many of the parties in France under the Fourth Republic . . . .

. . . The more the parties are involved in the direct selection of the president or a government . . . the more comprehensive is their appeal, and progressively the less ideological are they bound to be over a given period of time. (Occasional ideological flareups cannot, of course, be avoided—in England or in the United States.) In contrast, the greater the preoccupation of the parties with securing a representation in the legislature in order to participate with others in the formation of a government, the greater is their commitment to special electoral clientele, and the greater their propensity toward ideological orthodoxy.

## RECRUITMENT

The same is true for recruitment. The two-party system trains its members over a long period of time for governmental tasks. From the moment the "backbencher" (the party member with little status and influence) enters the House of Commons, his eye is set upon the Treasury bench—the place reserved for the prime minister and the cabinet members. His performance, his loyalty to the party, his ability to gain the support of his associates, will slowly bring him closer to it. Every member of Parliament is preoccupied with what the government does. Legislation is taken for granted, and deliberation is relatively unimportant. The important thing is to govern, and for the opposition party to replace the government. The Soviet Communist party recruits for the same ultimate purpose. The rules and the criteria of performance differ, but the purpose is to make room for, and finally to select, the men who will gain the top decision-making jobs and govern under the scrutiny of the party.

The same concern with recruitment does not apply to the multi-party systems, notably with France [until 1958]—first, because it was and continues to be unlikely for one party to gain a majority and thus make it possible for its leaders to govern; secondly, because the party leader was not allowed to gain ascendency within the party; and thirdly because the legislatures distrusted government leadership, and through rules and procedures not only discouraged but discredited it as well.

*The parties of the two-party system recruit and train leaders and finally make it possible for them to gain popular support and govern. In the multiparty system, emphasis is put on representation and deliberation, and not on government.*

# 11

## Western European Party Systems

### Lawrence C. Mayer with John H. Burnett

This detailed analysis describes two-party and multi-party systems; the spectrum of parties according to their ideology, program, and electoral base; and the differences in the ways parties attain organization, discipline, and cohesion.

### THE TWO-PARTY SYSTEM AND ITS VARIANTS

. . . The classic model of democracy, derived . . . from the experience of Great Britain in recent centuries and the United States, involves a two-party system, where two parties alternate in possession of the office of the chief executive. . . .

All democratic nations actually have more than two parties. . . . The question is whether the lesser parties can control enough electoral support to deny the winner a majority of seats in the legislature. . . . When the cooperation of more than two autonomous parties is required to maintain a government in office, the probability of instability is increased. . . . Thus, coalition governments face a higher probability of breaking up at some point short of the next scheduled election than do majority governments. This probability would seem to increase in close correlation with the number of parties required to compromise the governing coalition.

Much of Europe seems to be moving perceptibly in the direction of the two-party model in the sense we have discussed it—the alternation of two political forces. However, this generalization, like most generalizations, begs and overlooks numerous qualifications. Although the trend is to fewer parties, the party with a plurality of seats seldom gets a majority of seats. . . .

### DOMINANT MULTIPARTY SYSTEMS

The alternative to the two-party model in competitive party systems is a multiparty system. Like the two-party concept, it is not entirely clear exactly what multiparty systems are. . . . [T]hree or more parties do not necessarily preclude one party from obtaining a majority of seats in the lower house of the legislature. This has frequently been the case in the Scandinavian democracies. In both Norway and Sweden, a single party has dominated the government until recently almost without interruption since the Great Depression. More often than not the governing party has had a majority of seats in the legislature and has remained free from coalition entanglements or has been so close to a majority that the weaker coalition party was considerably weaker than the dominant party.

The Scandinavian experience suggests a third type: the dominant multiparty system where one party in a governing coalition is overwhelmingly stronger than its partner or partners. This is a very different thing from a coalition between a number of parties of relatively equal strength. In the former case, the weaker partners, unable to bargain effectively with the dominant party, are less likely to threaten the stability of the coalition. After all, it is generally impossible to form a government without the dominant party. The minor party has nowhere else to go but out of power. Because the Labour Party in Norway and the Social Democratic Party in Sweden have retained a majority or near majority of seats for the period of their dominance, it does not matter how fragmented the opposition may be. Insofar as cabinet stability is concerned, the key issue is the cohesiveness of the government, not of the opposition. . . .

## THE FRAGMENTED MULTIPARTY SYSTEM

Since the demise of the Fourth French Republic, a classic multiparty system has been absent from the European picture. During the Fourth Republic, no single party could command more than about a quarter of the seats. Furthermore, the strongest party was the French Communist Party—an antisystem party effectively excluded from the government. Consequently, coalitions were formed by a number of parties of relatively equal strengths. No single party in these French governments possessed sufficient strength to exercise coercive pressure on the other parties in coalitions. Persuasion alone did not prove sufficient to hold several autonomous parties in line over a range of the kind of divisive issues that have plagued France. It is therefore not surprising that French cabinets fell with almost ludicrous frequency. . . . For the sake of convenience, we refer to the systems in which governments are made up of numerous parties of relatively equal strength as fragmented multiparty systems to distinguish them from the Swedish pattern. . . .

## PARTY PROGRAM, IDEOLOGY, AND
## BASE OF ELECTORAL SUPPORT

[Scholars have drawn a] distinction between parties of expediency and programmatic parties or parties of principle. The raison d'être of the former is the maximization of votes and achievement of the widest possible appeal. The content and specificity of the platform and promises of parties will be pragmatically adjusted to that goal.

Parties of program or principle, on the other hand, exist to achieve certain substantive goals. These goals, whether the overthrow of the system or the passage of certain legislation, are the reasons why parties enter the political arena. They do not seek power, in other words, for its own sake. Instead, they are willing to sacrifice breadth of support to maintain purity of program or principle. . . .

## SOCIALISM, SOCIAL DEMOCRACY, AND
## THE DEMOCRATIC LEFT

Parties of the democratic left can be found throughout Europe. . . .

. . . [W]ith the exception of the Social Democratic Party of Germany, those parties of the left that emphasized doctrine and principle (the Austrian Socialists, the Italian Socialists, the French SFIO) by and large still do so, while those parties of the left that have broader, more pragmatic policies (the British, Australian, Norwegian, and Dutch Labour Parties; the Swedish, Swiss, and Danish Social Democrats; the Belgian Socialists) appear to have always eschewed an espousal of Marxist or even explicit socialist principles as their primary appeal. . . .

. . . [S]ocialism is not the same as Stalinist communism. The former term connotes government ownership of the major (but not all) means of production, distribution, and exchange. It is an economic variable. Democracy, it will be recalled, entails a political system involving regular competitive elections as a means of choosing between the elite and some structural limitations on the discretion of an incumbent elite—that is, some system of checks and balances. There is no logical reason why a government so chosen and so accountable cannot own the major means of production, distribution, and exchange.

Stalinism, on the other hand, entails a set of political characteristics as well as economic ones. . . . [It refers] to the nearly total absence of accountability or restraints on the political elite. This is a separate issue from who owns the means of production. . . .

. . . [T]he Social Democratic Party of Germany, . . . [t]he original Marxist Party in Europe, . . . in 1959 adopted a program that . . . asserts that only "liberal methods" can secure economic growth and full employment. Such methods are spelled out as follows: ". . . free choice of consumer goods, free choice of employment, free competition and free initiative on the part of employers are the essential foundations of a liberal economic policy. When it exceeds a certain degree, immediate interference by the state in the economy. . . does away the economic freedom." Such words, from what was originally Marx's own party, constitute an about-face. . . .

## CHRISTIAN DEMOCRACY

The center right in most industrial democracies is represented by parties with a confessional base; that is, the parties espouse the principles of a religion and direct their appeal to religious people. . . .

Most of the parties in this center-right religious pattern are of a type that is commonly called Christian democracy parties. They largely rely on a Roman Catholic base of electoral support. The exceptions are the Norwegian and Danish parties and the two Protestant parties in the Netherlands. . . .

## THE SECULAR RIGHT

Several conservative or center-right parties in Europe do not have a confessional base. Perhaps the most famous of these is the Union for New Republic (UNR) of France, the Gaullist Party. This party. . . had as its basic raison d'être support on a personal level for General De Gaulle and his political aspirations. . . .

. . . [T]he British Conservative Party, sometimes referred to as the Tories, is also free from explicit church affiliation. . . .

In Scandinavia, non-Christian conservative parties dominate the business-oriented and -supported right. This is probably due to the secular nature of Scandinavian society, which does not afford the social base for a flourishing Christian democracy. Norway, Sweden, and Denmark all have a conservative party.

By contrast, in those nations in which religion is a highly salient political force, the conservative party, if any, tends to be overshadowed by the party of Christian democracy. The Republican Party in Italy is an example of a conservative party in the shadow of Christian democracy. . . .

## PARTIES OF CLASSIC LIBERALISM

If a trend exists for European parties to lose their principled base, this trend may be most explicitly apparent in the case of European liberal parties. We are here using *liberal* in the classic nineteenth-century sense of the term. Liberalism refers to an emphasis on the value of the individual relative to the value of institutions (including the institution of the state). It refers to a minimization of restraints on human choice. It may be thought of as stressing *freedom from*, not *freedom to*. It entails opposition to the perpetuation of aristocratic and other ascribed privileges. It seeks political equality and does not concern itself with social and economic equality. Specific policy entailments of nineteenth-century liberalism included manhood suffrage, anticlericalism and laissez-faire. . . .

Ironically, liberal parties have acquired a conservative image in recent decades. Their defense of property and laissez-faire lines them up with conservative or Christian democratic parties on domestic issues. . . .

Like Christian democracy, liberalism represents a philosophic pattern represented in most European democracies by parties bearing a variety of names. Unlike the Christian parties, European liberal parties have everywhere been sharply declining in political importance (as measured by parliamentary representation), especially since the Second World War. . . .

The options for liberals appear to be twofold. In a fragmented party system or with a vacuum on the right, they may attain a measure of political success (defined by participation in governments) by acquiring the image of a domestically conservative party (defined as opposition to state socialism or extension of social welfare policies). But they may be able to operate as a balance-of-power force exercising a parliamentary influence far out of proportion to their minuscule representation. . . .

## ANTISYSTEM PARTIES

Several European nations possess a significant ideological tradition that is difficult for most Anglo-Americans to comprehend: opposition to the existing political system. . . . On the right, for example, there is a highly nationalistic party in the Federal Republic of Germany called the National Democratic Party. . . . The German NDP has been characterized as neo-Nazi. . . .

Similarly, the Italian Social Movement . . . has been labeled a neofascist party, although it denies any intention of setting up a fascist dictatorship. But Italians who were associated with or who espouse enthusiasm for Italy's Mussolini period tend to support this party. . . . Recent events have shown some of its members ready to seek attainment of political goals through violent means. . . .

The two strongest European communist parties outside of the Soviet bloc are in Italy [PCI] and France, in that order (as measured by the average percentage of national vote in postwar elections). The Italian communist party leader, Palmiro Togliatti, coined the phrase *polycentrism* to mean it is possible to have numerous centers of power in the communist world. This amounted to a declaration of autonomy for the PCI from Kremlin (or Peking) control. The PCI has been consciously engaged in the effort to play electoral politics, to appeal to sentiments and interest of patriotic Italians, and to assuage fears that PCI control of the Italian government would render Italy a satellite of the Kremlin. Accordingly, the PCI has supported many Catholic legislative demands, such as a ban on divorce, and publicly censured the Soviet invasion of Czechoslovakia in 1968. This stance of quasi-respectability has enabled the PCI to remain as the second strongest party in the country, garnering about [30] percent of the vote in the 19[83] general election.

The base of support of the PCI is clearly that of Italy's have-nots. Eighty-six percent of the PCI vote in the 1958 election came from industrial workers, tenant farmers, and agricultural workers. The PCI draws only 13 percent of its voters from the lower-middle class, and its support from the higher strata in the socioeconomic hierarchy is virtually nil. It appears that the intense efforts of the PCI to attract Catholic and middle-class votes has made little impact on those segments of the population. The fact that only about two-fifths of the industrial working class voted communist in 1958 and 48 percent of them voted either communist or socialist (PSI or PSDI) is undoubtedly because of the conflicting pull of the Catholicism of Italian workers.

[The failure of the dominant Christian Democrats] to cope with Italy's massive social and economic problems appears to [have] enhanc[ed] the legitimacy of the PCI as the only plausible alternative. . . . It seems that many Italians are able to overlook the party's name and do not regard it as antisystem. . . .

The French Communist Party has also attained a degree of legitimacy, especially among the industrial class from whence it draws about 70 percent of its votes. . . . In both France and Italy, many communist votes are votes of protest against the status quo, not votes for revolution or a Stalinist police state. . . .

## PARTY ORGANIZATION

The basic organizational [distinction is between] cadre parties and mass parties. The criterion for the distinction is the formality of the connection of party members to the party. In the United States, when a person is a member of either the Republican or Democratic Party he or she is simply more likely to vote for that party's candidates for national office than the candidates of the opposition party, when and if he or she votes at all. In short, by *party member*, most Americans really mean *party supporter*. Between elections, participation in party activities is by and large limited to very small coteries of party activists or leaders (the "pols" or "pros," in the jargon of American journalists). This is called a cadre party, and the organizational form typifies most middle-class parties elsewhere in the democratic world.

A mass party is one in which the typical rank-and-file citizen who identifies as a member of the party performs formal acts of commitment beyond voting such as paying dues and attending meetings. Membership may be direct, indirect through membership in an affiliated organization, or some combination of the two. . . .

. . . Most membership parties use a combination of direct and indirect membership. The British Labour Party, for example, has some directly affiliated members in its constituency associations. However, the majority of its members are indirectly associated through their membership in affiliated trade unions or socialist or cooperative societies. Members of affiliated unions are automatically enrolled in the party, and their dues are deducted from their paychecks unless they formally request otherwise in writing (a process known as "contract out"). Under this system, passive individuals become party members. A Conservative government in 1927 changed the system to "contract in," where the individual union member had to join the party actively in order to belong. Under this system, party membership dropped precipitously from 3.2 million to 2 million. A subsequent Labour government in 1946 reinstalled "contract out," and Labour Party climbed back to 4 million. We must conclude that around half of the Labour Party membership is due to inertia—that tendency to take the option that requires no action. The present membership of the Labour Party is around 7 million, with about 6 million of this figure attributable to indirect trade union membership.

A question is raised about the relationship between membership and voting behavior. Fragmentary evidence suggests that members are no more likely to support the party in the voting booth than nonmembers. The primary purpose in party membership appears to be the financial base it affords the party. Party members may also provide campaign workers. . . .

## PARTY DISCIPLINE AND PARTY COHESION

Related to the variable of the leader-follower relationship in parliamentary parties is the degree of party cohesion on legislative voting. This refers to the extent to which members of a given party vote as a bloc on a legislative vote or, put otherwise, the extent to which knowledge of the position of party leaders on a given legislative issue enables one to predict the vote of other legislators of the same party label. Party cohesion is one of the imperatives of cabinet stability in parliamentary regimes.

Because governments (prime ministers and their cabinets) govern in parliamentary regimes at the sufferance of a majority of the lower house of the legislature, cabinet stability depends on the stability of that majority. Where individual legislators are left to make up their own minds as to how to vote on each given issue, the probability that a large enough number of individuals to form a majority of the legislature would spontaneously come to a meeting of minds over a wide range of issues is obviously remote. Consequently, a mechanism is needed to compel those individual legislators upon whom the government relies for support to continue to vote the government's position even if they may personally disagree with that position on one or more specific issues. This mechanism is party discipline.

Clearly, party discipline cannot be applied absolutely—that is, with the requirement that each legislator votes to support the party's position no matter what it is. If party discipline were applied that absolutely, legislative voting would become totally redundant, and an important mechanism of governmental accountability would be destroyed. Normally, the effect of party discipline is to broaden the bounds of discretion of the government within which they can still count on party support. The individual legislator will not choose to suffer the penalties of breaking party discipline for a minor disagreement with the party; however, a major conflict between the party position and the fundamental principles of the individual legislator would presumably result in a break in party discipline.

One mechanism of enforcing party discipline is ultimate control of the nominating process. That is, while constituency organizations may retain the right to nominate their candidates to represent that constituency in the national legislature, national party organizations may reserve the right to veto locally determined choices. Thus, unless the individual member of the legislature is acceptable to national party leadership, he or she loses the right to campaign under that party label. To the extent that a party system is relatively aggregated, one's probability of electoral success without the label of a major party becomes increasingly remote. In some countries, expulsion from a party would probably end a potential political career. In Great Britain, for example, Winston Churchill was the only modern politician to leave the ranks of a major party without descending into the ranks of political obscurity. (Churchill's career ran from being a Conservative to a Liberal to an independent and back to a Conservative. Churchill's personal charisma was, however, unique.)

# 12

## Electoral Systems of Representation and How They Work

*The Economist*

As in all democracies, the political parties in the nations of Western Europe must operate within the particular country's system—that is, in accordance with the prescribed rules governing how legislators in that country are elected. These tables explain the intricacies of three basic electoral systems and their several variations.

**TABLE 12.1   Three Kinds of Electoral Systems**

| Plural | Preferential | Proportional (PR) |
|---|---|---|
| Candidate(s) with most votes wins(win), whether or not he has (they have) a majority of the vote. | Voter has chance to express second choice, either in the same or another ballot, if no candidate(s) has (have) absolute majority on the first count. | Seats shared by all parties' candidates according to their share of the vote. |
| Examples | | |
| Single-member first-past-the-post—eg, USA, UK. | Alternative vote (AV)—eg, Australia; second ballot—eg, France. | Single transferable vote (STV)—eg, Ireland; list systems—eg, most EEC. |
| Refinements | | |
| Semi-proportional complications: cumulative vote; limited vote; points system. | Further ballots. | Different methods of calculating quotas and remainders for allotting seats; cut-off points eliminating small parties; pool systems to make constituency results more proportional nationally. |

Advantages

Simple; short ballot paper; single-member seats possible; usually ensures one party has paliamentary majority.

Relatively simple; short ballot paper; single-member seats possible; candidates can stand without fear of splitting vote for right or left and so letting in minority opponent.

Fewer wasted votes; composition of legislature reflects voting figures; minorities represented. STV gives most choice of MP to voters and so loosens party grip on elections; list system simpler.

Disadvantages

Minorities under-represented (unless geographically concentrated); composition of legislature does not reflect national voting figures; party may have parliamentary majority with only small minority of the vote. When used for multi-member seats, deficiencies exacerbated if party grip is strong.

Chance whether results more or less disproportionate than plural system; minorities still squeezed. AV requires voting by numbers; second ballot, two trips to the polls, and final result may depend on party bargaining.

Results depend somewhat on different formulae for allotting seats; constituencies have to be large and so do ballot papers (although PR can be grafted on to single-member plural system, as in West German mix). One-party majority in parliament unlikely. STV requires long ballot paper and voting by numbers; list systems mean larger constituencies and strong party control.

**TABLE 12.2  How They Work**

| | |
|---|---|
| British | Voter marks X against name of only one candidate. Candidate with most Xs wins. |
| AV | Voter marks 1 against name of favourite candidate; 2 against next favourite, etc. If no candidate achieves 50% of 1 votes, candidate with fewest 1 votes eliminated, and his supporters' 2 votes distributed—and so on, until one candidate achieves an absolute majority. Possible, but complicated, for multi-member seats too. |
| Constituency PR | Voter marks X against favourite party's list; seats for each constituency distributed (by various formulae for dealing with acknowledged vote distribution) according to parties' share of total constituency vote. If, eg, party allotted two seats, top two candidates on its list elected, and so on. Voters sometimes permitted to express preferences within party lists; results sometimes "topped-up" with pool candidates to increase proportionality in legislature. |
| STV | Voter numbers candidates in order of preference. Electoral quota (ie, number of votes entitling candidate to one of the constituency's seats) calculated. Candidates with more than quota elected, and their "surplus" votes transferred (ie, the correct proportion of their supporters' second choices distributed); votes "wasted" on least popular candidates similarly transferred; and so on, until required number of candidates achieves quota. |
| West Germany | Voter has double ballot paper, and marks one X for a candidate for a simple plural election and one X for a party list. Half legislature elected as in Britain; other half elected off lists, to make *total* party strengths reflect list votes—ie, to correct disproportionality in plural elections. |

# 13

## The Future of Britain's Political Parties

### Tim Robinson

Recent election results called into question the British Labour Party's standing as one of the two major parties in Britain's traditional two-party system. Robinson discusses here the factors which may determine whether the Labour Party will indeed be replaced and, if so, by which challenger—the Liberals, the new Social Democrats, or the Alliance that has formed between them, which attracted significant numbers of votes in the 1983 general election.

In May [1983], when British Prime Minister Margaret Thatcher announced her intention to hold general elections, a senior Labour party leader confessed publicly that he and his comrades were unprepared to face the challenge of a political contest. The results of the elections on June 9 have borne out his worst fears. Thatcher and her Conservative colleagues scored a landslide victory largely because of the weakness of their opposition. The key question now . . . is what will become of the traditional political party system that supposedly made Britain one of the most stable nations in the world.

Britain, like the United States, has for decades had a clearcut two-party structure. Since 1945, governments have shifted back and forth from Conservative to Labour, with each party in office about the same length of time. A third party, the Liberals, consistently polled millions of votes, but gained very few seats in Parliament because its candidates could not capture first place in their constituencies.

Two years ago, however, Britain's political anatomy changed when dissident Labour moderates formed the Social Democratic party. The new party, which joined the Liberals to run in the latest elections as the Alliance, has reflected fresh political sentiments here. Though the Conservatives won only 42 percent of the popular vote, they took 397 seats in Parliament. By contrast, Labour gained 209 seats with 28 percent of the vote, while the Alliance won only 23 seats with 25 percent of the vote. Alliance leaders were correct to call the electoral system that favors the two major parties "a scandal, a travesty and a disgrace." But looking beyond the numbers, it is plain that British political opinion has altered in ways that may have a bearing on the future of the parties.

Despite its failure to win more seats in Parliament, the Alliance demonstrated its attraction for voters. More precisely, its appeal stemmed largely from the fact that numbers of voters abandoned the Labour party to support the Social Democrats. So, while the outcome of the contest was a display of confidence in Thatcher, it also represented a resounding rejection of the Labour party, which may very well be heading toward disintegration.

Founded around the turn of the century, the Labour party steadily increased its share of the vote until, following World War II, it swept into power with 48.1 percent of the electorate endorsing its programs. Labour support held at more or less that level until the mid-1960s, when the party was guided by moderates like Harold Wilson and James Callaghan. In the latest elections, however, it fell back to its level of the 1920s.

Many of Labour's problems can be attributed to internal wrangling. Though it claims to operate along democratic lines, the party was taken over in recent years by its radical faction, which proceeded to promote extreme left-wing platforms. Among its other planks, the Labour platform for the recent elections called for unilateral nuclear disarmament and the removal of American bases from Britain, massive nationalization of banking and industry, and big boosts in public spending.

Consonant with its manifesto, the party chose as its leader Michael Foot, an aged radical who revels in old-fashioned left-wing oratory and dresses so sloppily that satirists dubbed him Worzel Gummidge, a scarecrow in a children's book. Foot and his colleagues ignored the fact that British workers, despite record unemployment, are no longer certain that socialism is the answer to their difficulties.

In Great Britain, as in the United States, industrial workers are increasingly less interested in class warfare than in buying cars and acquiring their own homes. Nor are they enthused by leftist denunciations of America. Thus the survival of the Labour party will depend on its renovation. But it is bound to be torn by further internecine disputes between its radical and moderate factions.

The Liberals and Social Democrats may not necessarily be the immediate beneficiaries of Labour's decline. Two prominent Social Democratic leaders, Shirley Williams and William Rodgers, lost their seats, leaving the party in the hands of Roy Jenkins, who lacks the common touch.

On the positive side, however, the Alliance can point to the fact that its ability to poll 7.6 million votes, the highest total won by a third party in this century, has given it a strong place on the political scene. But the scene is sure to be dominated by Margaret Thatcher. She has shown dramatically that unemployment and other economic difficulties can be overcome by promises of a brighter future—which she has yet to deliver.

---

# *14*

---

## Europe's Socialists Are Losing Their Taste for Power

*The Economist*

In this report published in *The Economist* in August 1982, the author points to difficulties in coalition building, along with diminished voter support, to account for the relative decline in the strength of Western Europe's socialist parties since the mid-1970s. He also notes the wide variation from one country to another in voter response to socialist parties, a finding further evidenced by the fact that since this report first appeared, socialist governments were put out of power in West Germany and returned to power in Sweden, as our footnotes explain.

---

[In the mid-1970s,] *The Economist* published a survey of long-term electoral trends in Europe. This showed that Socialists had been remarkably successful in establishing themselves as the main government party in a clear majority of west European states. Some 54.1% of cabinet ministers in the 15 countries shown on our map which have enjoyed democratic rule ever since 1945, were Socialist (or Social Democratic or Labour). This was a considerable achievement, since these parties had polled no more than 31.2% of the votes cast in the most recent elections in the same 15 countries.

Since then the predominance of Socialists in the governments of Europe has been heavily eroded, despite the Socialists' landslide victory in France last year. The proportion of Socialists among cabinet ministers is well down, to 36.4%. Whereas in 1975 there were more than twice as many Socialist ministers as the combined total of Christian Democratic and Conservative ministers, there are now slightly fewer— 94 compared with 97. The era of Socialist strength seems to be passing. Why?

It is only partly a question of declining electoral support. Despite the large swing to the Socialists in France, there has been an overall drop in Socialist support across Europe. Yet for the most part this has

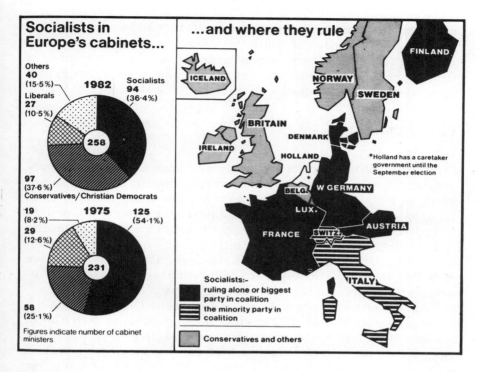

Figure 14.1.

been marginal, and far from uniform (in nine countries the Socialist vote has gone down, but in six it has increased). In some countries Socialists have clearly left government at the behest of the voters (Sweden in 1976, Britain in 1979, Norway in 1981, arguably Luxembourg in 1979). But in several countries they have been excluded (or have excluded themselves) from coalitions which would have commanded a firm basis of electoral support (notably Belgium and Holland).

In two countries—Ireland and West Germany—Socialists have not actually excluded themselves from government, but they have put their future as reliable coalition partners in doubt. The Irish Labour party was split on whether to continue its coalition with Fine Gael if the two parties had together won a majority in February's general election. The party is still divided on this issue, so for the moment there is no credible alternative to Mr. Charles Haughey's Fianna Fail government. Fine Gael has never won an overall majority on its own.

In West Germany it is only the prestige of Mr. Helmut Schmidt that has so far prevented his Social Democrats' coalition partners, the Free Democratic party, abandoning ship and combining with the opposition

Christian Democrats. The Social Democrats have become highly unat-
tractive coalition partners, partly because of their unpopularity but
mainly because of their left-wing party activists, who oppose many of
the present coalition's policies. The party is almost certain to go into
opposition before, or immediately after, the 1984 election.*

## COUNT CRAXI IN

The Socialists have not become less government-minded in every
country. In Italy, Socialists re-entered government, after a five-year
break, in 1980, and they are likely to stay there whatever the result of
the election expected soon. Nobody following the career of Mr. Bettino
Craxi, the leader of the Socialist party, can doubt his personal appetite
to hold office, preferably as prime minister. And in two Nordic countries—Denmark and Finland—it is the Social Democrats who have
shouldered the major responsibility of government in splintered multiparty parliaments. But these are the exceptions to the rule.

In Sweden and Norway, long Europe's Social Democratic strong-
holds, Socialists have adopted an all-or-nothing approach, preferring to
see minority governments formed by weaker right-wing parties rather
than explore the centre ground themselves for coalition partners. It is
arguable that exploration would have been fruitless in the past few
years, despite the fact that the Liberals—who now govern Sweden—are
nearer to the Social Democrats in their ideology than to the Conservatives, and that in Norway the Labour party has some common ground
with both the Centre (farmers') and the Christian People's parties.
These three parties together have more seats than the Conservatives
who now rule the country. Yet not only have no feelers been put out; the
possibility seems hardly to have been considered.

It was not always so. The Swedish social Democrats twice formed
coalitions with the Agrarian (now the Centre) party, in 1936–39 and
1951–57. In Norway minority Labour governments have often been
sustained by the votes of the smaller parties. In both countries, however, the Socialists no longer seem willing to engage in the compromises necessary for coalition government.

In Sweden, Mr. Olof Palme's Social Democrats hope to resume
power in the general election on September 19th [1982] after six unac-

---

*Ed. note: The Free Democrats left the coalition in September 1982, forc-
ing the resignation of Chancellor Schmidt and a general election in March 1983
in which the Christian Democrats were returned to power.

customed years in opposition. But although they have a good lead in the polls, they will probably need the support of the Communists to form a government. And the polls suggest that the Communists may not pass the 4% threshold needed to win seats in parliament. The Social Democrats do not seem prepared to consider a coalition with anybody else.*

## ANOTHER DUTCH DISEASE

Some compromises should, of course, be avoided like the plague; but a self-righteous refusal to accept any compromise is incompatible with democratic principles. Apart from the left-lurching British Labour party (which is a particular, and very sick, case), it is the Dutch Labour party which is the worst offender in this respect. The roots of its present dilemma go back to the late 1960s, which saw the beginnings of a long process of radicalisation of its leaders and its activists.

Increasingly, power and influence were assumed by younger party members who, by virtue of their jobs (typically as educational administrators, civil servants, welfare workers, academics and journalists), were able to devote the greater part of their time to political activity. Yet because none of them worked in business or in trade unions, their knowledge of the economic facts of life was minimal. This generation abandoned the traditional socialist belief in research, and substituted sloganising for analysis.

The policies adopted by these young Dutch left-wingers were based on giving more to the electors (particularly to public-sector employees and welfare beneficiaries who, together with their families, are rapidly becoming a majority of the electorate). The left-wingers called for higher social benefits, a higher minimum wage, a shorter working week, ambitious job-creation programmes and more public spending all round.

Admirable, and just about believable, so long as the Dutch economy was roaring ahead, fuelled by seemingly inexhaustible reserves of natural gas. Yet in the economic doldrums of the late 1970s the programme began to look impractical, even to its authors.

Small wonder that, rather than being shown up as having advocated policies that would not work, the Dutch Socialists have preferred

---

*Ed. note: The Social Democrats received 45.6 percent of the popular vote in the September 1982 election and obtained 166 seats (out of 349) in Parliament as opposed to the 163 obtained by the non-socialists. The party was thus freed from its traditional dependence on communist support.

to stand aside and let their opponents deal with low growth and the public-spending problem. Mr. Joop Den Uyl, the Dutch Labour leader, has struggled against the prevailing trend in his party, but he has been unable to halt it, or to prevent the party sliding in a few years from firm support of NATO into a quasi-neutralist position.

In the Dutch general election on September 8th, the Labour party is expected to do much worse than its main rival, the Christian Democrats (although it has recovered a little ground after its disastrous performance in the provincial elections in March, when it fell into third place behind the Liberals). As a result the odds are that the next Dutch government will be a centre-right coalition between the Christian Democrats and the Liberals. The Labour party has now acquired a reputation for being an awkward partner in coalitions, and none of the other Dutch parties is keen to co-operate with it.*

### FAIR-WEATHER SAILORS

The message which Dutch Socialists are now unwittingly sending to their electors is that they are essentially politicians for the good times. When the going gets rough, they no longer have the appetite to face the harsh decisions which need to be taken. Some other European Socialist parties—in neighbouring Belgium, for example—have been travelling down the same road as their Dutch comrades, though they have not yet gone so far. The Belgian Socialist party has been in opposition since the end of 1981, after a long spell in successive coalition governments.

If this process is not soon reversed, the consequences could be serious—and not just for the Socialist parties themselves. Most European countries have a system of proportional representation which cannot function properly unless there is a responsible left-of-centre party ready and willing to take its share in governing the country. If these parties opt out, the result is likely to be either prolonged instability or lopsided governments pursuing policies which do not truly reflect the wishes of their electorates.

---

*Ed. note: The Labour party did in fact emerge as the strongest party in the September 1982 elections, winning 47 seats (as opposed to 45 in the 1981 election) in Parliament. However, the center-left Democrats-66, who might have governed with Labour, were crushed in the election, dropping from 17 to 6 seats. A center-right coalition government was thus formed.

## 15

# Italian Voters Repelled by Political Parties

Sylvia Poggioli

The corruption-prone patronage system in Italy has become increasingly extensive and institutionalized. In this International Writers Service report released in June 1983, Poggioli describes the growing discontent among voters with this "spoils system" and shows how it has not only weakened the party structure but now imperils the very fabric of Italy's democracy.

Italy has had 43 governments over the past 37 years, with prime ministers and their cabinets changing as often as the seasons. This phenomenon has served to bolster the patronage system. The political parties, instead of ruling, tend to use their short terms in office to furnish their supporters with various favors, ranging from jobs to tax advantages. It is this "spoils system" run wild that has antagonized a large segment of the electorate.

Despite the recession, Italian governments continue to spend lavishly, since cuts would annoy the pressure groups that back the parties. As a result, the public-sector deficit last year equalled 15.6 percent of the gross national product, compared to 3 or 4 percent in most industrial countries. The state treasury underwrites unprofitable nationalized industries to the tune of several billion dollars per year. About one-fourth of the labor force; numbering some 5 million people, receives disability pensions. Social programs amount to roughly 40 percent of public spending, thus making labor costs here the most expensive in Western Europe. The state deficit, meanwhile, is aggravated by widespread tax evasion.

The two leading parties are the Christian Democrats, who control the national government, and the Communists, whose authority is strong in the localities. They and other parties have effectively divided up the spoils. Under a cozy arrangement designed to placate the factions, bureaucrats and employees in state-owned banks and companies are hired according to a quota sytem devised by the parties. The practice is known as "lottizzazione," or allotment. The patronage system has become increasingly extensive and institutionalized to include the directors of state theaters and the administrators of health care centers. Even the news media participate, since the government runs the television networks.

One consequence of this system has been a rise in corruption. To acquire positions of power, people must necessarily perform favors and make payoffs to those who have helped them. The emphasis on gaining power for its own sake has also led to a decline in managerial skills, so that many state-owned companies are directed by incompetents. A "black market" economy is flourishing, which deprives the state of revenues.

A salutary effect of all this has been a stronger focus on community approaches to problems. More and more Italians are rediscovering their old "village spirit," and are simply disregarding the national government as they work together. At the national level, however, a voter rebellion could lead to a vacuum of power as the political parties are weakened. . . .

Many political specialists here fear that a weaker party structure might pave the way for extremists. The Catholic Church has warned that Italy's democracy may be imperiled. The parties, only recently awakened to the growing disaffection, have been trying to rebuild their popularity by selecting candidates from among the business, art, movie and literary worlds. The Communists are going for the youth vote by promoting peace campaigns. But these efforts may not be enough to reassure voters, who plainly want a change in the structure—even if the change is not much better than what exists.

# Unit V

# National Leadership

Government in Western Europe, as in most societies in the world, is profoundly influenced by select groups or members of society known as elites. Although the political, social, and economic character of these elites varies widely from one country to another, every Western European country, without exception, draws its political leadership from one elite sector or another. This unit focuses on the creation and political impact of elites in four countries—France, West Germany, Britain, and Italy—to illustrate the different patterns of leadership and influence that are prevalent in Western Europe today.

In "France's State-Created Elites," Ezra N. Suleiman describes how, in France, access to economic and social elites, as well as to the state bureaucracy and political structure, is clearly tied to the nation's parallel system of higher education. Key positions in all sectors of society are dominated by those who are most successful in making their way through the highly selective state educational system. Suleiman shows how the arrangement perpetuates itself, with the *grandes écoles* training the elites, whose organizations reciprocate by supporting the educational institutions. For a different perspective, Lewis J. Edinger, in "Getting to the Top in West German Politics," points out that in some Western European countries political leadership roles are now more open than they were in the past, restricted neither to graduates of a few elite universities nor to members of aristocratic families, a military caste, or a "master race." Moreover, wealth is not so valuable a political asset as it is in the United States. Edinger's study of political leaders in West Germany indicates that the advantage goes rather to members of the male sex with sufficient education, experience, skill, and affiliation with a ruling party. He suggests, however, that a new generation of leaders is emerging in West Germany which may have a significant impact on present patterns of elite collaboration.

Social class and education have been, and continue to be, highly significant in British politics and society. In "The British MP: Educational and Occupational Background," Colin Mellors summarizes the results of a study of Parliament over the past thirty years and describes how Britain's two-party system has traditionally been polarized on socioeconomic grounds. Mellors shows that the Conservative Party has drawn its parliamentary candidates and political leaders almost exclusively from the upper and upper-middle classes and from those who have attended a high-ranking "public school" (private school) and who have graduated from Oxford or Cambridge universities. In contrast to this essentially homogeneous membership of the Conservative Party, the Labour Party is characterized by considerable diversity, drawing its parliamentary recruits from a wide range of class and occupational backgrounds. While a continuing process of "embourgeoisement," or rise to the middle classes, among the Labour Party politicians has in recent years reduced the educational differences between the two parties, the important distinctions based on class origins remains characteristic of British politics.

P.A. Allum, in "The Catholic Church in Italian Politics," examines the influence of the Catholic Church in contemporary Italian politics, and shows how the Church's organization runs through all aspects of Italian political, social, and economic life. The second part of the selection focuses on interest-group activity in Italy, particularly on the activities of the so-called economic groups, which were formed specifically to promote and defend the interests of such economic groupings as businessmen and industrialists, shopkeepers and farmers, artisans, and workers.

# 16

## France's State-Created Elites

Ezra N. Suleiman

Suleiman describes how a highly selective national education system monopolizes leadership throughout France, creating access not only to government service but to key positions in all sectors of society.

A distinction needs to be drawn between societies that possess elite-creating mechanisms and societies that make no institutional provisions for the creation of their elites. The more established the mechanisms are, the more likely are the elites to be characterized by or grouped into a series of small circles, as well as by a well-regulated system of networks among these circles. Moreover, the offices which these elites occupy are likely to be endowed with considerable prestige, even with a certain degree of charisma.

France has one of the most clearly established mechanisms for the creation of its elites of any Western society. This is principally due to the fact that the state takes it upon itself to form the nation's elites. The state has thus devised a system that is complex and elaborate, tying as it does the professional training of the elites to their corporate organizations. . . .

I have chosen to refer to these elites as *state* elites because they are trained by the state and destined for state service. Had they confined themselves to state service, that function alone would have ensured them a remarkable influence. The importance of these elites, however, transcends the public sector, for their members today dominate—in some instances, monopolize—the key positions in the administrative, political, industrial, financial, and even educational sectors. We are dealing therefore with what can be called state-created elites who are trained, promoted, and legitimized by a highly selective educational system and who use state education and state service as a base from which to launch themselves into other careers. The result of this practice has been to concentrate the key posts in the major sectors of society in the hands of those who are able to make their way through these institutions.

## BASIS FOR STATE MONOPOLY

The development of secondary and higher education in France, and the ultimate control of both educational levels by the state, were the result of a political philosophy which has lost little of its force over the past century and a half. Ultimately, there was little pedagogical basis for the centralization of the educational system in the hands of the state. Indeed, pedagogy itself came to be seen as a derivative of the political aims of the state. The state's monopoly over the educational system has had two important consequences: it has not allowed the development of institutions that might rival the state's own, and it has meant that the state has taken it upon itself to ensure that the entire responsibility for the training of its leaders would be its alone. Even at the beginning of the nineteenth century, the ultimate purpose was to regulate not only those elites destined directly for state service (military officers, engineers, teachers) but others whose functions were considered necessary for any prosperous, ambitious, and well-ordered society. . . .

It may seem a little perplexing to an Anglo-Saxon reader to be informed that even the financial and industrial elite is trained in France under the aegis of the state. This was not intended to be the case in the early part of the nineteenth century when the private sector did not loom very large and when the Napoleonic state was beginning to make inroads into all activities in the society. Today, there are no private schools that compare with the Ecole Polytechnique, the Ecole des Arts et Métiers, or the Ecole National d'Administration (ENA) and whose purpose is to train managers for the private sector. The Ecole Centrale and the Ecole des Hautes Etudes Commerciales, both of which train their students for the private sector, are no longer strictly private institutions. Indeed, the Ecole Centrale came under the control of the Ministry of Education between 1946 and 1959, after which date the school regained its "civil and autonomous personality." Nevertheless, neither of these schools, important as they are in the training of middle-level industrial managers, competes with the Ecole Polytechnique or with the ENA in the creation of the mobile elite with which this study is concerned. The state has been concerned to enhance the prestige of its own schools—the grandes écoles—to such an extent that the graduates of these schools are practically omnipresent in the key posts in the society. The administrative, financial, and industrial elites are today drawn from among the graduates of schools whose task has always been, and continues to be, the training of those destined to serve the state. . . .

The point to be stressed is that there exists in France a double-track, or parallel, sytem of higher education. Entering a university requires no more than the possession of the *baccalauréat* (the diploma granted at the termination of secondary-level studies); entering a grande école requires post-baccalauréat preparation (usually two years) for and the passing of highly competitive national examinations. Now, this parallel system of higher education that has existed for so long in France and that shows no sign of crumbling is important because it is the foundation on which rests the elite structure of French society. Consequently, no discussion of the distribution of power, of social mobility and opportunities, and even of the policy-making process can ignore the structure of higher education in France. Without this system, we would not find the elite organizations that exist in France.

The grandes écoles have a direct link to the major corporate organizations of the elites: the grands corps. These corps . . . are institutions that carry out functions on behalf of the state. At the same time, they are institutions, or clubs, that group together an elite that is united by a common educational background, common career horizons, and common corporate interests. How does one enter a grand corps? By graduating at the top of one's class in the appropriate grande école. Thus, to enter the Corps des Mines or the Corps des Ponts et Chaussées, one must graduate at or near the top of the Ecole Polytechnique. Similarly, to enter the Inspection des Finances, the Cour des Comptes, or the Conseil d'Etat, it is necessary to graduate within the top 20 percent of one's class at ENA. Hence, the educational system is tied in an unambiguous way to the society's elite structures. To be sure, the link between the grandes écoles and certain corps was not always indispensable, for some grands corps did exist in the past without having a direct link to a grande école. Nevertheless, the situation today is such that the grande écoles train the French elites and take an active part in their organizations, which in turn reciprocate by supporting the institutions that provide them with the best recruits. . . .

# 17

## Getting to the Top in West German Politics

### Lewis J. Edinger

As compared with their past and with the political realities of other countries, like France and Britain, West Germans
now enjoy more open access to government leadership roles,
although education, experience, and party affiliation are still
necessary prerequisites. Edinger outlines key criteria for leadership in contemporary West German politics and suggests
that the prevailing emphasis on social and political cooperation and stability is being challenged by younger political activists.

The processes of leadership recruitment confirm the average West
German's belief that it takes a good deal more than a sense of competence to play an influential political role. Although the Basic Law [Con-
stitution] declares for instance that "every German shall be equally eligible for any public office" it qualifies this right by stipulating that he
must also have the necessary "aptitude, qualifications, and professional achievements." When it comes to the selection of manifest as
well as latent top political leaders, such generally restrictive criteria are
translated into rather exclusive standards governing admission to the
policymaking stratum.

In the Federal Republic, as in other countries, the structured opportunities for getting to the top first of all favor university-educated males
from the highest social classes . . . [I]n the early 1970s more than 80
percent of a sample of West German leaders had a higher education,
compared to only 5 percent of the entire adult population. Except for
the labor leaders, few of them were the children of manual workers,
many had fathers who had gone to a university, and most were the off-
spring of civil servants, businessmen, and professional people. . . .

Also as in other countries, the structure of opportunities discrimi-
nates against young people. Even more than in the United States, and as

much as in England, France, and Japan, they must as a rule bide their time if they want to make it to the top. . . . West German leaders are usually in their late forties and early fifties when they get there and are then likely to stay put for a decade or more. To get ahead in government and politics today, as in other careers leading into policymaking, one must be highly motivated and have a great deal of patience and endurance. . . .

Leading participants in the West German political system usually insist that those who aspire to join or succeed them first pass through a socializing apprenticeship in various middle-range organizational positions. . . . Some followed political career lines in governmental and party hierarchies that culminated in a key position, others became leading political participants after they had made their way to the top in some nonpolitical occupation.

The accumulation of experience has become more important as room at the top has opened up more slowly. Ambitious but inexperienced young men were able to advance rather quickly in the years of socioeconomic and political disorganization and reorganization immediately preceding and following the establishment of the Federal Republic. . . .

Organizational bonds are most important in the recruitment of key public officials, particularly ties to a major party. Since the establishment of the Federal Republic, political parties have increasingly replaced other structures as routes to manifest political leadership. Party membership—rather than specific occupational skills—has become a chief criterion for ministerial posts and, frequently, for key administrative positions. Federal ministers are now almost always members of the ruling parties and their delegations in the Federal Diet. . . . Ministers in the state governments are more often recruited from outside parliament, but they, too, usually belong to the ruling parties.

Sex, education, experience, skill, and organizational affiliation are thus the principal sources of upward political mobility in contemporary West Germany. By and large, the opportunities for getting into the policymaking stratum are considerably less restricted than under earlier German regimes and in many other countries. Consider, for instance, that Willy Brandt—the illegitimate son of a salesgirl—could rise to become the chancellor of the Federal Republic in 1969. Leading participants are no longer recruited from aristocratic families and a military caste, as in the Hohenzollern Empire, nor must they fit standards of "racial" and ideological purity, as in Nazi Germany. They are neither the graduates of a few elite universities—as is still very much the case in Britain and France—nor do they belong to tight cliques based on informal social bonds and shared socialization experiences. And in West Germany wealth is not nearly as much a valuable resource for gaining entry into the policymaking stratum as it is in the United States. . . .

## THE INCOMING LEADERSHIP AND CHANGE

Some observers of contemporary West German politics believe that a conflict of generations is developing that will eventually shatter the present patterns of elite collaboration. They see a new generation of political activists coming to the fore that places less emphasis on the need for social harmony and political stability than the present leadership and is more deeply committed to divisive ideologies.

What is the basis for such prognostications? . . . [S]ome differences in the beliefs and values of West Germans who grew up before and after the establishment of the Federal Repubic [have been noted]. But also . . . [,] by and large[,] age distinctions have evidently not given rise to major political cleavages between older and younger people and have been far less pronounced than under earlier German regimes and in other countries. There seems to be little indication here of the type of generational conflict that contributed to the collapse of the Weimar Republic. Hitler's rise to power was then promoted by his ability to exploit the anticapitalist, romantic sentiments of young idealists who were alienated from what they considered the overly materialistic values of their elders and who longed for a less mundane "new order." By comparison, most young people in the Federal Republic appear to accept the prevailing order.

But what seems to hold for the youthful mass public appears to be not as valid in the case of the political public. Particularly in recent years the politically most interested and engaged young people in the universities and the major parties—the pool for the leadership of the 1980s and 1990s—have served notice on their elders that they are not prepared simply to follow in their footsteps and that they have rather different ideas about the purposes and responsibilities of political leadership. And although left-wing radicals have been most vocal on this score, young liberals and conservatives also appear unwilling to carry on as the present top leaders believe best.

The men who now rule the Federal Republic were born roughly between 1915 and 1930 and belong for the most part to what a German sociologist termed some years ago the "sceptical generation" of the post-Nazi era. The older leaders—such as Helmut Schmidt, [former] Federal Chancellor . . . —grew to adulthood under the Nazi regime, usually served in its armed forces, and launched their careers soon after its fall. Those who were once attached to the Nazi creed are now apt to consider it a youthful folly; those who were not are all the more determined to keep young West Germans from succumbing to a new perverted romanticism. The younger policymakers . . . were still children in the Nazi era. Their political views are therefore not as much the products of learning experiences under the Hitler regime as they are the consequences of resocialization in the postwar period of socioeconomic and political reconstruction.

These leaders see themselves as rational policymakers who have no use for 'woolly romanticism' and doctrinaire ideologies. They are suave, but tough and highly skilled organizational managers who prefer to focus their attention and energies on immediate rather than long-range problems. Though they may belong to different sectors of the elites, today's leading participants share what they consider a hard-nosed, pragmatic approach to public policy issues and inter-elite bargaining in domestic and foreign affairs. They place a high premium on achievement and efficient performance, on "inside information" and expert knowledge, and on the need for negotiations and compromise. Although they may not agree on what should be done and who should do it, these leaders essentially understand each other.

Partisan differences notwithstanding, most contemporary key actors basically agree that the preservation of fundamental political harmony and stability demands that government policymaking be guided by a sense of moderation and caution. The dominant policymakers hold that what has been achieved must be preserved and what does not seem feasible should not be tried. Unavoidable adjustments to changing circumstances are to be made as gradually as possible to avoid unsettling the basic patterns of West German domestic and foreign relations.

But will the elite consensus supporting the present regime outlast these leaders? The ruling elites have certainly sought to ensure its continuity by grooming as their successors men who essentially share their attachment to the prevailing political system. At the same time they have endeavored to block the ascent of young political activists who seem to them doctrinaire ideologues and radical extremists. Whether such measures will in the long run suffice to overcome frictions between members of the present and the incoming leadership generations remains to be seen.

# 18

# The British MP: Educational and Occupational Background

## Colin Mellors

In these excerpts, Colin Mellors examines the educational backgrounds of members of Parliament (MPs) over the past thirty years to shed light on the social class origins, social values, and attitudes of modern-day British politicians as well as to account for the striking differences between Britain's two major political parties. He points out that an elite education, taken in the best "public schools," actually private boarding schools, and in the preeminent universities of Oxford and Cambridge (frequently referred to as "Oxbridge"), is what distinguishes the largely homogeneous membership of the Conservative Party from the ranks of the more diverse Labour Party. Occupational backgrounds differ as well, Mellors notes, with Conservatives drawing from landed and commercial interests and Labour from workers, and with each party attracting different segments of the professions.

. . . Recruitment studies inevitably emphasize the importance of public schools, and to most foreigners it always appears ironical that the British describe those schools which are least accessible to the general public as public schools. . . . In the main these are independent boarding schools receiving no grants from public funds. . . .

### CONSERVATIVES: THE PATRICIAN TRADITION

In choosing their parliamentary candidates, the Conservative Party consistently concern themselves more with rank and achievement than party political experience. Breeding and educational attainment are customarily seen as the two most important qualifications in this party for recruitment to the political élite. The former is normally demonstrated by a public school background and the latter by graduation from one of the two ancient universities of Oxford or Cambridge. And whilst there have been some minor adjustments to this traditional picture of an exclusive patrician class, especially in view of the backgrounds of the last two Conservative leaders, it is a description which has remained largely true [since 1945]. In common with all predominantly middle class parties, Conservatives select as their candidates the younger and more educationally qualified. This applies equally to legislative recruitment and later advancement to ministerial positions. . . .

Above all else, the public school has remained the crucial channel of access into the Conservative Party. The 'old school tie' remains the most important qualification available to prospective Conservative MPs, as the success rates of public school candidates indicates. As a guarantee of electoral success, it ranks with the reliability afforded by sponsorship from the mineworkers' union in the Labour Party. . . .

[Since 1945 j]ust under half of all MPs (46.7 per cent) . . . were recruited from the public schools. By contrast, approximately four per cent of school children attend such a school. Among Conservative MPs, the proportion exceeds three quarters (77.8 per cent). It is obviously difficult to overstate the sheer numerical dominance of the public schools in the Conservative Party. Throughout, the public school/Oxbridge route has proven the most popular preparation for a Conservative career in Parliament. . . .

In terms of educational experiences in the Conservative Party there emerges a clear and relatively unchanging picture of recruitment from narrow and exclusive sources. Although there have been some adjustments at higher levels in the parliamentary party, there has been little, if any, weakening of the preference shown towards the twin attributes of rank and attainment. Those who possess these virtues have found their election easiest and earliest. Moreover, the predominance of public school recruits makes for a much more socially homogeneous party than the Labour Party.

## LABOUR: TOWARDS MERITOCRACY

Two distinct features mark the educational backgrounds of Labour MPs in this period. The first is the quite dramatic shift towards better educated Labour representatives (fashionably described as the new meritocracy) and the second, which is affected by this process, is the existence . . . of distinct educational groupings. At ministerial levels the two major parties differ less than they do at backbench level.* Whilst the Conservative Party has homogeneous educational recruitment, there are very different routes of access into Labour parliamentary politics, and over this period of thirty years, one is rapidly being displaced.

For many Labour MPs the only formal schooling which they received was in an elementary board or council school, which represented the minimum state provision before the 1944 Education Act. Some of these went on later in life to receive technical or adult training, but for most formal education did not stretch beyond an elementary school. Nearly one third of Labour MPs in this period received simply an elementary or elementary plus education. Historically, these men from the grass roots of the Labour movement have played an important part in Labour politics. In the interwar years, they comprised three-quarters of all Labour MPs. The Labour Party acted, in part, as a vehicle to secure the representation of the working classes by their own kind. Since 1945, the displacement of the elementary educated has been both thorough and rapid.

In 1945, 45 per cent of Labour MPs had an elementary education. By the time Labour assumed office in 1964 this had fallen to 29.7 per cent and by October 1974 it was 16 per cent. . . .

For some years, and especially in the sixties, there has been a concern to raise the ability of Labour recruits. Labour's leadership, which has long been middle class, has been especially vocal in pursuit of this end. The sentiments were simply expressed in the [following] words . . .: 'With all the education there is about these days Labour must show that its candidates are as well qualified as the Tories'. It is one way of establishing that Labour is 'fit to govern', a message which the Labour Party has been concerned to get across to the wider electorate since 1945. This emphasis on ability places a premium on educational qualification and fluency of speech and ideas. . . .

In one further important respect, the Labour Party does not resemble the Conservative Party. In the Labour Party, the public schools are a much less important factor in recruitment. Whilst nearly 80 per cent of Conservatives attended a public school, more than 80 per cent of Labour MPs did not, although at 18.7 per cent, the proportion of public school men in the Labour Party might be considered unduly high and, if measured in terms of ministerial positions, this figure would be even higher. Important Labour figures, of both Right and Left, have been public school products, but they remain a minority of Labour MPs. . . .

---

*Ed. note: Backbench refers to those MPs who are not members of the government in the ruling party or its equivalent in the opposition.

In educational terms, then, the pattern of Labour recruitment [since 1945] is primarily coloured by this shift from the workers to the able and articulate. It is a pattern which is repeated in occupational terms, and as with Labour occupations, there are distinct groupings. Unlike the homogeneous character of the Conservative Party, there is diversity in Labour MPs' educational origins. . . .

## CONVERGING PARTIES

In describing the patterns of political recruitment in educational terms [since 1945], it is tempting to elevate the data into some kind of thesis about the converging nature of the two main British political parties. Superficially, at least, there would appear considerable evidence to support such an interpretation. Certainly, there has been a continuing process of embourgeoisement in the Parliamentary Labour Party and the rump of the 'pure' working class representatives has suffered continuing depletion with consecutive general elections. Even the trade unions, who have customarily had the greatest affinity with the workers, have increasingly looked outside their own rank and file when selecting parliamentary candidates. In crude terms, the intellectuals have replaced the practitioners. On the Conservative side there has been additional evidence afforded to the thesis by the lesser drift away from the traditional patrician class, at the higher levels, if not at backbench level. The result is to cement the foundations of both the two major parliamentary parties firmly in the professional middle class. But to leave it at this, to settle for a semblance of overlap and convergence would be both shallow and misleading. There remain crucial differences between these two parties.

One essential difference in the educational profiles of the Conservative and Labour Parties is obscured by the crude manner in which the appropriate demographic data is assembled. The aggregate statistics tell us something about the opportunities for political recruitment from certain institutions and also about the direction of change during these thirty years, but they fail to record or examine the nature of the effort which was required in order to achieve that education. A public school education is fairly indicative of social status if only because of the financial exclusiveness of such schools, but a degree may be the natural product of a middle class education or the culmination of a protracted struggle through the state school system. Despite all the attempts to widen university entries, the proportion of working class children receiving the benefit of a university education has not changed greatly since the 1930s. Thus, whilst the actual universities or even schools attended might be the same, the effort required in order to achieve this level of education might vary considerably. It is an important distinction both in differentiating the parties and also in understanding the effect of educational training and backgrounds upon attitude formation. The notion of meritocracy is, of course, intended to meet this methodological problem and reflect effort as well as attainment.

A second, crucial, distinction is more apparent within the data itself. It is easy in looking at channels of political recruitment to concentrate upon the general and blur the particular. Thus, it might seem appropriate to deduce from the aggregate data that there is now an approximate equivalence in the recruitment of Conservative and Labour graduates. But the particular channels through which recruitment operates are, in understanding both opportunities and attitudes, probably much more important than general educational backgrounds. Actual pathways to the Commons are more important than the wider routes. The majority of Conservative graduates are Oxbridge; the majority of Labour graduates are not. Similarly, not only is there a considerable and vital disparity in the numbers from the two major parties drawn from the public schools, the actual range of public schools attended varies between parties. Some sense of this can be achieved by examining the productivity of particular educational sources of parliamentary recruits.

The public schools are, of course, the most obvious route to Westminster and nearly one half of MPs come through this channel. To probe a little deeper, however, reveals a distinct élite even within these institutions. Of those MPs drawn from the public schools, 21.7 per cent attended just one school—Eton. . . . Certain institutions not only provide access to the political élite, but plainly propagate the values and motivations necessary to seek elevation to that élite. Whilst Eton's supremacy in this field has been unrivalled, there is a clear order of rank among the public schools: 30.7 per cent of public school men attended one of three schools and over half are from what might be described as the 'Top Sixteen'. However, if we separate Conservative and Labour public school recruits, there is a notable distinction. Of the 619 public school Conservatives, 165 went to Eton and 218 to one of the top three schools—over one quarter of the party attended one of three schools. Of the equivalent 154 Labour MPs, only 8 attended Eton and 14 one of the top three schools. Therefore, not only are Labour recruits much less likely to have attended public school, but those that did were not filtered through the same narrow and particular public school channel as the public school Conservatives.

A similar pattern emerges in the range of universities attended: 909 MPs followed a university degree course and just three, admittedly the largest—Oxford, Cambridge and London—account for nearly three-quarters of these graduates. As with the public schools, there is a rank order of universities, and again if we separate the parties, there is a distinction to be made. 86 per cent of Conservative graduates hold an Oxbridge degree whilst of Labour graduates, 38 per cent come from Oxbridge, although even this figure exaggerates the proportion of the student population attending these two universities. . . .

This brief review of the particular educational paths taken by political recruits gives some indication that there remain crucial differences in the socio-economic composition of the two major parliamentary parties. Certainly, the educational backgrounds of Labour MPs have changed considerably over the past three decades, and there was a notable acceleration of this process in the sixties. But even the interpretation of this dramatic change has to be treated with some caution. A university education does not in itself necessarily imply automatic transfer to middle class status and values. A recent survey of graduates has shown how, even after obtaining a degree, a working class student's 'attitudes and aspirations are likely still to be heavily influenced by his social background'. The universities are not quite the 'melting pot' they are sometimes taken to be and, as may be seen in the choice of professions which Labour graduates select, there remain vital dissimilarities in the nature of professional groups among Conservative and Labour parties. . . .

## THE OCCUPATIONAL BACKGROUND OF MPs

The profession of politics places peculiar demands upon those who opt for public life. Robert Louis Stevenson wrote that 'Politics is perhaps the only profession for which no preparation is thought necessary'. But the reality is that a career in Parliament appeals to people of a certain type. Political life calls for fluency of mind and speech, ambition, some administrative and managerial skills and, frequently, opportunism. The profession of politics not surprisingly attracts the 'communicating' professions—lawyers, lecturers, teachers and journalists—and such professions dominate not just the British legislature but most parliamentary democracies.

The nature of employment is also important because some, more easily than others, allow for the time that is necessary in order to achieve and retain candidatures. A century ago Parliament was dominated by aristocratic and landed gentry, who had the financial resources and leisure to indulge in political life. Their places have been taken by members of the professions. . . .

. . . [A] correlation between certain professions and inclination to stand for public office is not unique to Britain as virtually the same range of occupations dominate most other legislatures. [One author] has commented that 'a glut of lawyers seems to afflict legislative bodies generally', and indeed, high as the British figure is, lawyers are even more plentiful in other legislatures. Between 1945 and 1974, the proportion of British lawyer MPs . . . [stood] at 15.6 per cent. Comparable figures for other legislatures include: United States, 55 per cent; Brazil, 50 per cent; France, 32 per cent; Italy, 27 per cent, and Germany, 19 per cent. . . .

[I]n the same way that the strong association between the Conservative Party and the public schools remains a crucial difference in the educational profiles of the two major parliamentary parties, there remain vital differences in the socio-economic composition of the parties at Westminster as expressed in their occupational profiles. Changes within the two major parties themselves should not be allowed to blur important disparities. The Conservative Party at Westminster is a much more socially and economically harmonious group. There has been a noticeable drift from the land to commerce, but it is still a party with a largely common background. Even the distinction between the professions and business is much modified by the involvement of many of the former group in commercial undertakings, if not before election, certainly subsequent to entering the Commons. The Labour Party, in contrast, has three distinct centres of occupational background—the established professions, the newer professions and the workers. The former group, who most closely resemble the Conservatives and tend to be the liberals in the party, are drawn from solid middle class backgrounds. At the other extreme are the manual group of pure working class abstraction who, as a group, have occupied a central role in the development of the Labour Party. In between these two, and displacing the latter, are the newer professions and although many of these are first generation middle class, owing their new status to recent social elevation, they are clearly not actual representatives of the working classes but neither are they identical to the established professions. . . . Without doubt, the Parliamentary Labour Party has undergone a vital social transformation in recent years, but this in itself is not sufficient to equate with converging recruitment patterns. The Conservative Party remains homogeneous; the Labour Party remains heterogeneous. What is happening in the PLP is that the men of toil are being rapidly replaced by the men of ideas.

## Conservatives: Law, Land and Business

In their occupational backgrounds Conservatives during these three decades have retained their essential cohesiveness and symmetry. . . . The description which [one analyst] has applied to the Conservatives has remained valid throughout this period: '. . . an organic union of all the groups composing the middle classes, not a juxtaposition of separate elements. It is a result which few parties of the Right have been able to achieve in other countries'.

[Since 1945] more than four-fifths of Conservative MPs have been drawn from professional and business occupations. They, together with farming and occasionally journalism, are the normal and almost exclusive access route to the Conservative Party in Parliament. . . . It was only possible to identify one worker Tory in the Commons during the whole of this period. . . .

In turning to the business group we discover the cornerstone of the Conservative Party at Westminster. Not only does the business group provide the largest number of Conservatives but the overwhelming majority of this group falls within the category of company directors. In itself, this description means little since a company encompasses a wide size range from small businesses to vast enterprises. . . .

[Between 1945 and 1974] 273 company directors were elected to Parliament; of these 245 were Conservatives. It is by far the largest single occupation represented at Westminster. They include Members with limited business connections and those with networks of business enterprises. They spread over the whole range of economic life. . . .

Before leaving the business section, a glance might be directed towards the fortunes of the small businessmen. Small businesses in the UK produce some 20 per cent of . . . industrial output, but they plainly are less successful in their output of political manpower. . . . [T]en elections [1945–74] brought the return of a mere eleven small businessmen, and of these the majority, seven, sat on the Labour side of the House. . . .

## Labour: From Men of Toil to Men of Ideas

The most distinctive feature about Labour MPs, pre-parliamentary occupational backgrounds . . . is the evidence which they furnish about the process and rate of embourgeoisement. In the simplest of terms there is a progressive, and almost perfectly correlated, displacement of workers by teachers. . . .

Taking the [post-World War II period] as a whole, the professions account for the largest segment of the Labour Party at Westminster. The overall proportions in the four groupings are: professions 40.7 per cent; business 9.6 per cent; miscellaneous 28.6 per cent; workers 21.1 per cent. Immediately this suggests a greater heterogeneity than the Conservative Party, where over 80 per cent are drawn from business and the professions. In fact, this wider spread of recruitment is not limited to more balanced groupings but also occurs in the range of particular occupations within individual groupings. This is especially well illustrated in the case of the professions. In the Conservative Party law, the armed forces and the diplomatic services form the core of professional recruits; in the Labour Party there is a much more even spread. The legal profession is again well represented (a steady 12 per cent of the PLP), but the older professions of law and medicine are balanced by the newer professions especially teaching. And this is a vital distinction, since admission to the older professions is much more likely to follow from traditional public school education and a solid middle class background. The teaching professions on the other hand are a popular choice for the lower middle classes and even the rising sons of working class families. . . .

In the Labour Party, therefore, the professions encompass two different social milieu—the established upper middle class and those who have transferred from one class to the next higher social class. The dramatic increase in the number of Labour professionals is almost wholly attributable to the rise of these Labour meritocrats. . . .

. . . [T]he increased professional group on the Labour benches is explained by the growth of one particular profession—. . . teachers . . . —who have extended their parliamentary representation by 136 per cent. . . . The other Labour professional occupations have remained reasonably stable.

The business group is the least numerically important of Labour occupations. . . . [B]usinessmen comprise between 6.7 per cent and 10.7 per cent of the parliamentary party. . . . In sharp contrast to Conservatives, Labour's business group is spread throughout the various commercial occupations and not largely limited to company directors and financiers. Middle-management is the largest single category, followed by company directors, clerical staff and business consultants. Thus, besides being much less numerous than in the Conservative Party, Labour's recruits from the commercial and business world are employed (at least prior to their election) in less prominent positions.

In the Labour Party, the miscellaneous group largely comprises three occupations—journalists, white collar workers and trade union officials. The journalists are frequently, like the teachers, examples of Labor meritocrats and tend to have lower middle class or working class origins. . . . But the key occupation here is trade union official, and 98 union officials were [elected].

However, there can be no mistaking the predominant trend in the case of manual workers. As a whole, they account for over one-fifth of Labour MPs, but at each election since 1945 they have suffered consistent and considerable depletion. In 1945 they comprised 27.6 per cent of Labour's parliamentarians, but by [1974] they had been reduced to a mere 12 per cent. If we compare these figures with the rising fortunes of the teaching profession—increasing from 12.1 per cent to 28.1 per cent—it is plain just how remarkably closely the fortunes of the teaching and working occupations are correlated. The step by step increase of teachers almost perfectly matches the step by step decrease of manual workers. . . .

# 19

## The Catholic Church in Italian Politics

P. A. Allum

In these excerpts from *Italy—Republic Without Government?*, a British analyst of Italian Politics examines the pervasive influence of the Catholic Church on government in present-day Italy, and shows how the Church's organization runs through all aspects of Italian political, social, and economic life. The author then focuses on interest-group activity in Italy, particularly on the activities of the so-called economic groups, which were formed specifically to promote and defend the interests of businessmen and industrialists, shopkeepers and farmers, artisans, and workers.

. . . The Popes have always regarded themselves as having a special interest in the Italian peninsula. This interest has increased as a result of the official recognition of the privileged position of the Roman Church and its titular head in Italian life in the Lateran Pacts of 1929. The influence of the Catholic Church in Italian politics is determined by a second series of factors, of which the most important is undoubtedly its ability to mobilize a large proportion of the Italian people. It is hardly surprising that the Church is a powerful institution in a country which is nominally 99 percent Catholic. . . .

### CHURCH-STATE RELATIONS

The present relations between the Church and the Italian State are based on the Lateran Pacts of 1929, negotiated between Cardinal Gasparri and Mussolini, which put an end to the sixty-year conflict between them. . . .

The Lateran Pacts comprised three documents—a treaty, a financial convention and a concordat—which collectively: (1) reasserted the sovereignty of the Holy Father and his complete jurisdiction over the territory of the Vatican, expressly converted into a sovereign, independent State; (2) established Roman Catholicism as the sole religion of the Italian State; (3) gave the Church sole jurisdiction in matrimonial causes; (4) stipulated Catholic religious instruction in all State schools; (5) barred former priests and those under ecclesiastical sanction from State employment (and so public office); and (6) gave the Holy See a financial settlement of some 1500 million lire (about £20 million in 1929) which is reputed to have been shrewdly invested. In return, the Catholic Church recognized the Italian State as the legal and moral embodiment of the Italian people; acknowledging Rome as the State capital; and, although asserting that ecclesiastical appointments were a responsibility of the Holy See, agreed that before appointment names should be communicated to the Italian government to ascertain their suitability, and established a secret procedure for resolving deadlock. Finally, the Pacts committed the Church to observing a strict neutrality in party politics. Article 43 of the Concordat conferred State recognition on Catholic Action organizations, on condition that they remained under the direct control of the Church hierarchy and had no party political affiliations; it also expressly forbade ecclesiastics to join political parties or be active in them. . . .

. . .[After] the fall of Fascism . . . the Lateran Pacts . . . were written into Article 7 of the Republican Constitution of 1948. . . . The Christian Democrats were . . . determined to write them into the Constitution, and they succeeded thanks to the support of the Communists, who wanted to preserve religious peace at all costs. . . .

The Church, therefore, managed to ensure the retention of an extremely favourable framework—one which is more appropriate to a confessional State than to a modern liberal democratic one. . . . Moreover, the Vatican's position in the nation's political life was strengthened by two further developments. First, the fall of the monarchy left it as the only traditional hierarchic institution at the centre of Italian political life. Second, the political triumph of Christian Democracy, which had been prepared under Fascism by the protected position secured for Catholic Action in the Concordat, brought the Papacy to the controlling centre of state power in Italy. . . .

## THE PLACE OF THE CHURCH IN ITALIAN SOCIETY

The place of the Church in Italian society derives ultimately from two factors. On the one hand, its institutional structure, and on the other, its ability to mobilize large numbers of Italians. Its institutional structure is hierarchical and has two major components. First, what one might call the state structure of the Holy See, e.g. the Curia with its various Congregations (or Departments), Offices and Tribunals, etc.; and second, its grassroots organization, e.g. the national ecclesiastical structure of dioceses and parishes, etc. . . .

In assessing the situation in Italy, we must bear in mind that it is still more favourable to the Catholic Church than elsewhere. For example, there are only 150 French bishops against 360 Italians; and 100,000 Frenchmen in holy orders compared with almost a quarter of a million Italians. . . .

The Church's ability to mobilize its supporters can be measured in a series of figures: nominally Catholic (i.e. baptized) 99 percent; practising Catholics (i.e. regular church-goers) 40 percent; Catholic voters (i.e. voting [Christian Democrat]) 35–40 percent; Active Catholics (i.e. membership of Catholic Action) 5 percent. The most important Catholic organization is Catholic Action, which is an organization of Catholic laymen associated with, and supervised by, the ecclesiastical hierarchy in its apostolic mission. It was founded after 1898 as a reaction to the triumph of liberalism and the threat to the Church's temporal power, and has acted as a kind of para-political party defending the interests of the Church in civil affairs. Hence religious and political motivations became inextricably intertwined in its action. . . .

During the postwar period, Catholic Action has counted well over three million members in some 80,000 associations, which, together with the membership of the various dependent organizations, makes 'Catholic Action effectively the largest organization numerically in the country'. . . .

Catholic Action's organization by diocese, on the basis of the existing ecclesiastical structure, provided it with a framework and an initial strength after the Liberation which other organizations founded on the fall of Fascism lacked. In this sense, it is easy to see why Christian Democracy triumphed politically in the postwar period. . . .

Thus the Church has managed to keep contact with all areas of Italian society. . . .

> Its organization in Italy runs through all levels of life: schools, parish halls (which still have an important place in Italian life), hospitals, professional associations, newspapers; and everywhere there is the presence and influence of priests. A priest is often in the best position to help in any one of the highly varied set of circumstances—or not to help. In many places for instance, particularly when unemployment was at its height, it would have been impossible for a man to find a job without the goodwill of the priest. As far as the employer was concerned, a recommendation from a priest would mean that the man was not likely to be an agitator, that he would have

voted for the governing party and taken notice of the reminders in the confession boxes about the serious consequences of voting for the extreme left or belonging to its organizations. A contractor in Rome would not expect his tender to be accepted unless accompanied by a letter from a cardinal. Such things were the common-places of Italian life. . . .

In such circumstances, it can be no surprise that the Church's place in Italian life is of the first importance.

## THE POLITICAL ACTIVITIES OF THE CHURCH

. . . [In addition] to electoral propaganda, at various times the Church has attempted to dictate policy to Christian Democrat Party leaders; and to do so, the Pope has not hesitated to take sides in internal party disputes. . . .

Another area where the Vatican has been active is in the administration. The Italian administration can help the Church in a variety of ways, from issuing regulations to authorizing grants. The Vatican has an interest, therefore, in people sympathetic to the Church occupying the important posts in the civil service. Joseph LaPalombara, in his study *Interest Groups in Italian Politics*, presents plenty of evidence of the intervention of the clergy in the administration; and of the *quid pro quo* the kinds of recommendations that civil servants seek from bishops to secure promotion. . . .

. . . [W]hatever the Catholic Church's true power, it is one which Italian governments of all political persuasions can expect to have to take account of, and ignore only at their peril. The cautious, some would say servile, attitude of the Communist Party towards the Church is proof, of a sort, of the veracity of this proposition. . . .

## INTEREST GROUPS

Interest groups apply pressure in the political system wherever they think it likely to be worthwhile. It is possible to reduce the complex activity of interest groups to a number of general propositions. Thus, for example, we can say that they are generally active in two different spheres: (1) in the decision-making centres of the state system of institutions; and (2) in the policy-forming centres of civil society. Both these spheres of activity imply different methods of pressure. Thus pressure on the decision-making centres of the state system of institutions can either be directed at the legislature, or at the executive and administration; pressure on the policy-forming centres of civil society can either take the form of trying to influence public opinion directly (for which there exist a whole range of weapons from deeds—strikes and public demonstrations—to words—control of the mass-media: press, radio, television, cinema, etc.), or of attempting to control party life (by financing parties or soliciting party office).

Interest-group activity varies from group to group and country to country. The activity of a particular group will depend on its perception of the decision-making process in the political system in which it is operating and the channels of access open to it. For example, it may well be that a particular group perceives that effective decisions are taken by the administration but lack access to it. On the other hand, it may well be represented in the legislature and hence be forced . . . to concentrate its efforts there. Nonetheless, despite these problems of individual groups, it is true to say that the predominant activity of the major groups will reflect, more or less accurately, the reality of the decision-making process in that country. Finally, it is generally believed that groups that are active in attempting to influence public opinion directly, do so because they lack access to the decision-making centres. This may well be the cause for individual groups, but, in fact, no group, however well it is served with access to and influence over decision-making centres, will neglect opportunities of creating a favourable ideological climate for itself and its claims.

## THE GROUPS AND THEIR CHARACTERISTICS

It is impossible to know how many interest groups exist and are active in Italy, because all voluntary associations as well as all organizations are, in their relations with the political system, interest groups. It is likely that their number is of a similar order to that in other Western European countries, if for no other reason than that they are similar in other respects. For example . . . [one] study of Italian interest groups . . . estimated that there were some 3000 different voluntary associations with headquarters in Rome which might intervene in the political process. . . .[The study pointed out] that most interest groups operate within the subcultures (Communist, Catholic, Socialist, etc.) of the political system, resulting in an enormous proliferation of pressure groups, because each professional/occupational category is organized in a number of parallel ideological groups. . . . Close links between parties and interest groups have been one of the characteristics of postwar Italian politics.

The most important interest groups are the so-called economic groups; those which were founded specifically to promote and defend the interests of different economic groupings, like businessmen and industrialists, shopkeepers and farmers, artisans and workers. The best known of these are those which are organized in national confedera-tions: the employers' organizations, such as *Confindustria* (General Confederation of Italian Industry), *Confragicoltura* (General Confeder-ation of Agriculture), and *Intersind* (State-Holding company em-ployers), etc., on the one hand, and the unions, *CGIL* (General Confed-eration of Italian Labour), CISL (Italian Confederation of Free Trade Unions), *UIL* (Italian Labour Union), *Coldiretti* (National Confedera-tion of Small Farmers), etc. on the other. A second series of groups are the private corporations and holdings, like Fiat, Pirelli, Montedison, Olivetti, etc., alongside which must be placed the public corporations, *IRI* (Industrial Reconstruction Institute) and *ENI* (State Hydrocarbons Corporation), as well as the insurance agencies *INAM* (National Insti-tute for Workers' Compensation), *INPS* (National Institute for Social Security) and *INAIL* (National Health Insurance Institute). Finally, there are a considerable number of associations promoting and defend-ing moral and ideological causes. The majority of these play only a sec-ondary role in the political process since the parties are, generally, bet-ter equipped for the job, and usually colonize any such associations that spring up in their ideological area. One such group which has played an important part in recent Italian politics is the Divorce League.

*Confindustria* is the central organization which claims to represent all Italian businessmen; it speaks for both trade associations and local business organizations. However . . . it accounts for only some 80,000 of Italy's estimated 680,000 firms. A further 15,000 small firms are grouped in *Confapi* (National Confederation of Small Industries), a would-be rival. If firms employing more than twenty workers are con-sidered alone, then it is generally agreed that *Confindustria* represents the overwhelming number of potential members. In this connection, it is worth recalling that the Italian business community is extremely concentrated: a relatively small number of firms (less than 200) possess most of the capital and dominate the market. In addition, *Confindus-tria* grouped all the major para-state holdings and state enterprises until the government forced them to withdraw from it in 1957, when they formed their own association *Intersind*. Thus the confederation's orien-tation towards big business is natural. In fact, it has been such that many small businessmen have complained that the big firms use the confederation to keep the small ones in line. Certainly the problem of presenting a united businessmen's front has been one of the Confedera-tion's perennial problems; in this, it has been aided by the fact that busi-nessmen are not split, like other interests, into different ideological for-mations. However the real power of Italian industry lies in the big corporations and holdings, and their leaders know it. Agnelli and Pirelli . . . do not delegate authority to subordinates or even to *Confindustria* spokesmen. They do not hesitate to intervene directly in the decision-making process when their immediate interests are at stake. . . .

The *Coldiretti* (National Confederation of Small Farmers) is the most powerful organization in the agricultural field. In the early sixties, it claimed 14,360 local sections, 1,773,618 families and 3,561,711 members, representing over 8 million persons. Its influence is based on . two institutions. First there are the *Federconsorzii* (Federation of Agricultural Syndicates) which exist in every locality to aid the farmer by bulk buying and selling of crops and equipment. They are private in conception but have been endowed with a number of quasi-public functions so that they act as field agencies for the government, and particularly the Ministry of Agriculture. At the same time they have extended their range of services of immediate economic concern to the farmer— they provide gasoline, equipment and fertilizers at cut prices (through arrangements with big business firms); can store crops to raise prices; arrange credit facilities (by arrangements with financial houses). [One study] concluded [its] survey of them in these words: 'In the course of 15 years the federation has become a powerful financial holding, controlled by Bonomi and a narrow circle of collaborators. It constitutes one of the pillars of Catholic hegemony (mediated by the *Coldiretti*) in rural Italy.' The second basis of the *Coldiretti's* influence is the *Casse Mutue* or Small Farmers' Health Insurance Agency, which was created in response to the *Coldiretti's* legislative pressure in 1955. It provides free sickness and accident benefits similar to those enjoyed by workers. The agencies administer mutual funds made available by the government and peasants' contributions on a local basis. They are managed by boards of directors elected locally for a three-year term over which the *Coldiretti*, through its massive and ruthless organization, has gained overwhelming control.

The power of the *Coldiretti* comes from its ability to mobilize a massive rural vote for the Christian Democrat Party; in consequence, it has been able to count on a following of at least a sixth of the party's parliamentarians in each postwar parliament. However, the economic miracle has done much to undermine its privileged position in party and government by promoting a massive rural exodus. Instead of being a dominant element in the Christian Democrat Party, it has become just another element in the factional struggle.

In the other fields, the groups are divided along ideological lines. Thus there are Communist, Catholic, Social Democrat, Monarchist and Neo-Fascist Veterans' Associations. Similar divisions exist in Women's movements and Family Associations, Youth and Students' movements, etc. In addition, there are groups of intellectuals, not directly attached to parties, which set themselves up as Study Centres to carry out research and provide material on subjects of their interest, since it is well-known that information is half the battle in promoting a project or interest.

# Unit VI

# Policy Formulation and ____ Implementation ____

Policymaking structures vary considerably from one Western European country to another, as do the roles that are played by executives, cabinets, and bureaucracies in the actual policymaking process. In most countries, the making of new policies is a legislative function while the implementation of already-established policies is a function of the executive and the bureaucracy. This unit contrasts policymaking procedures in three different Western European countries—Great Britain, Italy, and France—and shows how the quality of life in each is directly affected by the particular policies their governments pursue. The readings focus on the different mechanisms by which policy is formulated and then implemented in each country, as well as on the roles and functions of the heads of state, the cabinet, the legislature, the bureaucracy, local authorities, interest groups, and government commissions in bringing about desired policy changes.

In "Politics in Britain: How Power Is Used," B. Guy Peters examines the processes underlying policymaking in Great Britain and shows how the "distinctive character" of Britain's governmental institutions influences the kinds of policies that are produced. To illustrate how new policies are formulated and put into effect in the British system, Peters follows a "typical" piece of legislation through the various stages of the lawmaking process, from the point of getting the issue on the policymaking agenda through the final implementation stage, and outlines the roles different "actors" and institutions play in establishing, carrying out, and evaluating the results of these policies.

P.A. Allum, in "Italy's Executive and Legislature," examines the formal policymaking structure in Italy, where government is by coalition and where legislative initiative is largely in the hands of the executive. Since no one party has an overall majority in Italy's multiparty political system and factional conflict within the major party* is strong, the Italian government frequently comes apart when one or more of the coalition partners finds the cabinet's stance objectionable; yet when "new" cabinets are formed they often turn out to have the same party makeup as the previous cabinet and may even include the same members. Allum points to this characteristic pattern of continuous coalition as a major factor in the Italian cabinet's ineffectiveness as a collective decision-making body, and suggests that it is "political immobilism" rather than "cabinet instability" that ultimately accounts for the Italian government's inability to respond to the enormous volume of problems facing the country.

William Safran, in "Politics in France: How Power Is Used," details the roles of the executive, the legislature, and the civil service in effecting policy change in France, and shows how recent French presidents have achieved supreme decision-making power in virtually all policy areas by reducing the power of the prime minister and by actively enlisting the help of the cabinet to promote their policies as well as to shoulder the blame when these policies prove unpopular or unsuccessful. Safran goes on to discuss some of the unresolved conflicts between administration and politics that pose a potential threat to France's social and political order.

---

*The Christian Democrats have been the predominant party in Italy since the end of World War II.

# 20

# Politics in Britain: How Power Is Used

B. Guy Peters

Britain's policymaking system, which includes a number of outmoded offices and procedures, is particularly complex. Here, Peters outlines the roles that the different "actors" and institutions play in establishing, carrying out, and evaluating the results of new government policies and programs as well as in maintaining those programs already in effect.

. . . It is helpful in this discussion to think of two kinds of policy making that must go on in any government. The first is making *new* policies, as when the institutions of government decide to engage in new activities or in current activities in different ways. This is typically a legislative process, although administrative actors are certainly involved in the initiation of new policy ideas and in implementation. Also, the making of new policies tends to be more politicized, with parties and interest groups directly involved in the process.

The second major form of policy making is simply maintaining the existing policies and programs of government. This is frequently less political in a partisan sense; instead, it involves the bargaining of existing program managers with their financial overseers (in Britain, the Treasury) and overt or covert competition between existing programs. Thus the majority of this kind of policy making is not legislative but involves executive and administrative actors. We now look at the British political system as it processes both kinds of policy decisions.

## THE PARLIAMENTARY PROCESS AND NEW POLICIES

To understand how new policies are made and then put into operation, it is convenient to follow a "typical" piece of legislation through the process of lawmaking from getting the issue on the agenda for consideration through implementation. Of course, no bill is typical; some bills are passed in a matter of days the first time they are proposed, while others drag on for years before being passed. And some policy ideas never are made into law, or they have their meanings almost totally altered through implementation. Despite these differences, an underlying process is common to all.

## Agenda Setting and Policy Formulation

The first thing that must be done if a piece of legislation is to be adopted is to place it on the policy-making agenda. This is true in an informal sense in that the policy must be considered important for the government to act on, and is true in the more formal sense of being placed before Parliament for consideration and possible adoption.

In the formal sense, the easiest way for an issue to come before Parliament is to be a part of the government's legislative program. Parliament's time is limited, and the government must select those issues and bills it believes are most important. This requires difficult choices because relatively few government bills are introduced in any year. In the nine years from 1970 to 1979 governments introduced an average of forty-seven bills per session. Since several of these involved budget and finance, and a large number of others involved consolidation of existing legislation, few significant policy bills were introduced at each parliamentary session.

Bills and issues may also come before Parliament without acceptance by the government. Backbenchers can introduce legislation, although it has little chance of being passed. First, a backbencher must win a lottery to have the opportunity to introduce a bill and then there are generally only twenty Fridays—the day on which private members' bills are debated—during a session. Bills may also be introduced under the ten-minute rule, which allows for ten minutes of debate, pro and con, and is followed immediately by the vote. Both kinds of legislation allow for a consideration of issues the government may as soon forget, or issues of a moral nature on which the government does not wish to take a stance. Backbenchers cannot introduce legislation involving the expenditure of public funds.

It is easier to get issues discussed than to pass legislation. The question hour is an obvious example. Adjournment debates and motions by private members also allow individual MPs to air grievances. On average, backbenchers receive approximately 15 percent of parliamentary time, an allocation made by the government, and much of that time is spent discussing constituency grievances, thus allowing for little impact on major policy issues. The Opposition is also given a substantial amount of parliamentary time to present alternatives to the government program, the major times being the debate on the Queen's Speech (actually written for her by the government), which opens each session of Parliament, and the twenty-six supply days scattered throughout the session.

In addition to controlling the agenda and timetable, the government must be heavily involved in formulating legislation. This is generally done by Cabinet prior to the legislation's being proposed to Parliament. Much of the impetus for policy formulation comes from the party's election manifesto. Nevertheless, parties are not the only source of policy intentions and policy formulation, and many policy ideas come up from the departments themselves. And, as with many industrialized democracies, the balance of power between elective and nonelective officials may have swung in favor of the unelected. In any case, the process of formulating policy is complex, involving the interaction of ministers with their civil servants and in turn consultation with the affected interests in society. And in Cabinet, legislation is typically considered by a Cabinet committee composed of interested ministers with some Treasury representation before consideration by the entire Cabinet.

## Policy Legitimation

Once the Cabinet has agreed upon a policy it is then introduced into Parliament, with all politically controversial legislation by convention first going to the House of Commons. For a bill to become law, it must pass the House of Commons, pass the House of Lords (unless it is passed by three successive Houses of Commons), and gain royal assent.

When a bill is introduced into the House of Commons, it is given a formal first reading and then printed for distribution. After two or three weeks, there is the second reading, which is the major political debate on the principles of the legislation. For noncontroversial legislation, however, the second reading may occur in committee. After the second reading, a bill typically goes to committee for detailed consideration and possible amendment. Note that this occurs *after* Commons has agreed to the legislation in principle. The government is much more willing to accept amendments in committee than on the floor of the House where this might be seen as an admission of defeat. Finally, the bill is reported out with any amendments, a third reading is given, and the legislation is passed. The bill then goes to the House of Lords for consideration and possible amendment. Any amendments made in Lords must be considered by Commons. And although deadlocks are possible, they are infrequent. After agreement is reached, the bill is given to the Queen for royal assent, which is virtually automatic.

Of course, legislation does not necessarily move so easily through the policy-making system, and so there must be some means of regulating the flow and particularly of preventing the delay of important legislation. At the report stage, a number of amendments may be reported out of committee, and the Speaker is given the power to decide which should be debated and which would be repetitious of debates in committee. The government can also impose closure and the "guillotine" (allocation of time order). Closure is a motion to end debate made by a hundred or more MPs, but it will be accepted only if the Speaker believes all relevant positions have been heard. When there are a number of points of dissent, closure may be ineffective and then the guillotine is employed. An allocation of time order is voted by the House of Commons, and the government makes a determination of how much time will be spent on each portion of the bill. Once that time is exhausted, the Speaker must move the section to a vote. The use of the guillotine is often cited as opposed to the interests of the House as a deliberative body, especially when it is imposed on major constitutional issues, such as the devolution debates during the Callaghan government.

With party discipline, much of the activity of Parliament seems fore-ordained, but it is still important. First, legal procedures exist for the passage of legislation. Second, amendments must be accepted and legislation approved, both in the committee stage in Commons and in Lords. Finally, some legislation that seems perfectly reasonable to the majority of the Cabinet may not seem so reasonable to backbenchers in the party, and the legislation may never be passed. An average of 10 percent of all government bills introduced from 1974 to 1977 did not become law; thus, although the presence of disciplined majorities is certainly important, legislative action is not certain.

British democracy has long been representative democracy, but there were several interesting occurrences of direct democracy as a means of legitimating policies during the 1970s. In particular, there were two significant referenda on policy issues—on whether Britain should have entered the Common Market in 1975, and on the devolution proposals in Scotland and Wales in 1979. The latter proposal was voted on only in Scotland and Wales, but the principle was the same: The government and Parliament to some degree abdicated their decision-making powers to the people in an election. Although these referenda were not legally binding, they were declared binding by the major parties. Referenda represent a major departure from the traditional means of decision making in British government and have potential importance for major policy decisions.

## Policy Implementation

After a bill is passed by Parliament, perhaps the most difficult portion of the process of changing society through government action occurs: the implementation process. This is the process of taking the bare bones of parliamentary legislation and putting some meat on them. This meat consists of both substantive policy declarations and organizational structures to carry out the intent of Parliament, or at times, to thwart those intentions.

Implementation may be carried out in a number of ways. One is through the departments of the central government. Most legislation coming from Parliament is a broad mandate of power, with the ministry then having the power and the task of making the necessary regulations and activities for the intent of the legislation to come into being. A principal means of doing this is through statutory instruments developed pursuant to acts of Parliament. Statutory instruments contain more detailed regulations than the acts, and allow the executive to have a major impact on the nature of the policy implemented. Parliament exercises scrutiny over these instruments but cannot hope to fully master the volume or technical content of all such regulations. Even when the issuance of a statutory instrument is not required, the departments are heavily involved in shaping the meaning of policy and making it work. The departments may also be barriers to effective implementation, especially when the policy enacted by Parliament seems to run counter to their usual practices. In like manner, the existence of regional and local offices of the ministry is frequently associated with varying patterns of implementation and, at times, great variations from the original intentions.

Policies of the central government are also implemented through local authorities. Unlike a federal system, the local authorities in Britain are the creatures of the central government, and there is less differentiation between national and local policy than in the United States. While the major policy decisions in areas such as education, health, social services, and the police are made by the central government, these services are actually delivered by local authorities. These services are not delivered uniformly; local authorities provide different quantities and qualities of service, albeit within centrally decided parameters and subject to inspection and control by the center. This relationship between central policy making and local administration does not work without friction, especially when local and central governments are controlled by different parties. Recent examples of conflicts include Conservative local authorities delaying implementation of Labour policies for comprehensive education, and Labour local authorities refusing to implement Conservative cash limits on expenditures for health care. Thus, while it may at times be impossible to do so, the central government needs to "bring along" the local authorities when it is considering a new policy if it hopes to have that policy implemented effectively.

In return for the administration of national policies, the local authorities receive the majority of their revenue from the central government. Some of the grants to local authorities are tied to the provision of specific services (e.g., the police), while the largest single grant—the rate support grant—is a general grant. If a local authority *wishes* to do things not supported by the rate support grant or other categorical grants from central government, then it must be willing to raise funds from local revenue, generally "the rates" (property tax).

Finally, policies may be implemented by private organizations. Interest groups are usually regarded as barriers to effective implementation, but such groups may have an important positive role to play in implementation. Minimally, the interest group can serve as a watchdog on the implementation of a policy, substituting for the army of inspectors that might otherwise be required. Environmental groups have been particularly active in this monitoring role. A more important involvement of groups in implementation has the group actually implementing a policy for government. This occurs frequently in agriculture when the National Farmer's Union applies general laws to individual cases, for example, in compensation for crop or livestock damage. These activities would otherwise require huge amounts of time and public money. Further, at times government subsidizes an organization to provide a service that government supports as a matter of policy and that would have to be provided at public expense if the private organization were not willing to provide it.

### Policy Evaluation

The last stage of making a policy occurs some time after the policy has been adopted. This is the evaluation of the policy. Here we are discussing the formal evaluation of the policy, whereas informal evaluation begins almost at the time of passage. This topic is also related to policy making for continuing policy, which is our next major topic, for the annual decisions to continue policies and programs made in the budgetary process to some degree involve evaluation of policy.

Parliament is assumed to conduct ongoing scrutiny of the policies of government, and there are a number of instruments for policy evaluation housed within the government itself. . . .

A number of mechanisms for policy evaluation exist independent of the government. One of the most commonly used devices is the appointment of parliamentary or royal commissions to investigate particular policy concerns that are more fundamental than any government may want to become involved in without advice. These commissions and their reports often constitute milestones in the evolution of policy and program management. . . . The commissions have no formal powers, however, and even excellent reports often go unheeded.

Finally, there are a number of less official mechanisms for policy evaluation. The press is one, although it is severely hampered by the Official Secrets Act and the lack of access to important information. A number of policy "think tanks" also exist; some represent clearly defined ideological positions, while others strive toward greater objectivity. Finally, research units of political parties and pressure groups also produce evaluations of existing policies. A great deal of official and unofficial policy evaluation occurs, although tight control by the government over the parliamentary agenda makes consideration of many policy changes unlikely.

## POLICY CONTINUATION. . .

Most policy making is not making new policies; it is reaffirming old policies or making marginal adjustments in those policies. In many ways this form of policy making is politically more sensitive than making new policies, for existing programs have existing clients and organizations, while new policies have no inertia pushing existing commitments forward. The most important decisions for continuing policies are made in the budgetary process in which the huge number of existing policy commitments are financed each year and their relative priorities determined in pounds and pence. (Here we are speaking of the budget in an American sense, whereas in Britain the term refers to the government's revenue, not expenditure, proposals.)

The control of the public purse has been central to the powers of Parliament historically, but the existence of disciplined partisan majorities has transformed substantially the locus of effective budgetary powers. Budgeting can be best thought of as taking place in two stages. One is an administrative stage during which the spending ministries negotiate with the Treasury and with the Cabinet over expenditures. The second stage is the parliamentary stage during which these decisions are legitimated and occasionally changed. . . .

Making policy in Britain, as elsewhere, is difficult and complicated. Many good intentions are rendered ineffective by the need to gain agreement from a number of actors. British policy making is especially complicated by the many vestigial procedures and offices, although to abandon these may threaten the legitimacy of the system of government.

# 21

## Italy's Executive and Legislature

### P. A. Allum

In these excerpts from *Italy—Republic Without Government?*, the author describes how the policymaking process in Italy is impeded by a political system in which no party has an overall majority and factional conflict is strong even within the major party. Allum points to "cabinet instability," actually a succession of cabinet crises each leading to the formation of a new coalition made up of the same parties, persons, and posts, as one of the main reasons for the Italian government's ineffectiveness as a collective decision-making body, and shows how what appears to be change in the Italian political system is actually just the opposite of change, or what he and others consider to be a form of "political immobilism."

Although he is not considered a formal part of the legislative process, the President [in Italy] has been endowed with a number of powers for influencing the legislative process on his own responsibility. . . .

The Constituent Assembly expected that it would be in the appointment of the President of the Council of Ministers (or Prime Minister and, upon the latter's recommendation, of the Ministers) that the President would exercise his most important executive power. This expectation has not been disappointed, but its realization has come less from the constitutional power itself than from the parliamentary situation with which successive presidents have had to deal. The power of appointment of a prime minister is one that is always formally in the hands of Heads of State in liberal democracies. In states with strong two-party systems, the Head of State has virtually no effective choice because the leader of the majority party in Parliament effectively controls it. But in multi-party states, like Italy, where no party has an overall majority and factional conflict in the major party is strong, the Head of State's choice is more open and must be exercised more frequently.

146

Hence the opportunity for manoeuvre is real. In Italy, the limits have been, since 1948, that the Prime Minister must be a member of the dominant Christian Democrat Party. At every ministerial crisis, the President goes through a routine series of consultations with former presidents, former prime ministers, party secretaries, and the Presidents of both Houses. If the majority party leaders are agreed, they will give him a name; and he will invite that person to form a government. . . . [I]f the parties, and above all the Christian Democrats, are not agreed, the President will receive a list of names and it will be up to him to decide whom to invite. Normally he will do this on his assessment of whom he thinks is most likely to form a working majority.

There are numerous examples of the President of the Rupublic using his judgement in this way. . . .

The presidents developed two further techniques which gave them an increased control over the choice of prime minister. The first was that of laying down the type of government that should be formed, and even the contents of the proposed government's programme. . . . The second was the consultation in ministerial crises of a whole series of people extraneous to this delicate phase of the political process. . . . [O]ne of the [chief] characteristics of postwar Italian politics . . . is cabinet instability. . . . [C]abinet instability in Italy is not what it seems on the surface, because behind the façade of continuous cabinet crises, there is a significant continuity of party, persons and posts. In fact the form that cabinet instability has taken in Italy is the 'musical chairs' of continuous coalition between the same partners: frequent changes of cabinet, less frequent changes of offices and rarer changes of personnel. . . . The United Kingdom is widely believed to be an exemplar of cabinet stability, but the figures for the average length of time in the same office are not very different for the two countries. . . . Moreover, the average minister has a much longer active career in Italy than in Britain. . . . In consequence, Italy's ministers have many more years of cabinet experience than their British colleagues, for whom ten years is rare and fifteen exceptional. This is a fact of some importance when assessing the relations between executive and administration. It gives the lie to the simple proposition that in countries where cabinet instability is rife, the government is run and policy is made by higher civil servants ensconced in office because of their security of tenure.

. . .[T]here appear to be two kinds of ministerial department (what we shall call the 'command' and the 'patronage') and two types of ministerial personnel (what we shall call the 'top' and the 'middle' level politicians). Thus on the one hand there are ministries with a much more stable ministerial personnel (Interior, Defence and the Economy) . . . and others which have had a succession of them (Mercantile

Marine, Foreign Trade, Posts and Telecommunications, and Education). . . . Similarly, there are a number of key politicians . . . who over the years have alternated between the 'command' posts, often spending a prolonged period in one department. . . . On the other hand, there are Christian Democrat ministers who remain in successive cabinets but change departments. . . . Ministers from the coalition partners usually fall into the latter category, even when they receive important posts, not only because their parties are 'guests in power'. . . but because it is easier for them to reach office because of the needs of coalition arithmetic, but correspondingly more difficult to hold it for any length of time. This analysis of different types of department indicates an hierarchy of office and person which constitutes an informal mechanism for continuity and co-ordination in executive government that cabinet instability belies. . . .

## CABINET INSTABILITY AND ITS EFFECTS ON POLICY-MAKING

In spite of ministerial stability, Italy still suffers from cabinet instability and this has consequences for the quality of the country's executive government. A prime minister who is assured of a permanent parliamentary majority is able to control not only Parliament but also the cabinet. Moreover, the cabinet can be enabled to exercise the specific powers of Parliament. This happy situation has been refused to the majority of postwar Italian premiers. . . .

The two most important consequences of the cabinet's instability appear to be its ineffectiveness as a collective decision-making body, and the quality of co-ordination of executive government. This must not be exaggerated, but it forms part of the chain of political immobilism, even if it is not the cause. . . .

### The Power of Parliament

. . . The Constitution adopted a bicameral system with an absolute equality of powers between the chambers. If in federal states, like the United States or the Federal Republic of Germany, bicameral arrangements are justified on the ground of representing popular sovereignty through two channels—one the citizens the other the territorial collectivities—no such justification can be alleged in Italy's case. Indeed the only explanation of the adoption of a bicameral system with a parity of powers between each House is the centralized tradition of the state. Certainly the conservative forces in the Constituent Assembly defended such a position when they argued that a bicameral system was necessary to give balance to the legislative process, greater maturity to the legislative debate and greater stability to Parliament. . . [I]t has fulfilled none of these hopes. . . .

In common with other Western European countries, legislative initiative is largely in the hands of the executive, but private members play a more important role than elsewhere. At the same time, what is also clear is the immense legislative output of the Italian Parliament. . . . It is not surprising, therefore, that much Italian legislation is confused, fragmentary and conflicting. In any event, this productive capacity would be impossible without the recourse to legislation by committee because both Houses spend less than a fifth of their time in plenary session on legislating. The greater part of it is dedicated to ideological motions, interpellations and the draft budgets. Further, since not only is 75 per cent of all legislation passed in committee, but 90 per cent of it unanimously, it is clear that the area of agreement between all parliamentarians regardless of party is very great, however violent the ideological clashes on the floor of both Houses. . . .

. . . Italy is one of the few countries which places no limit on the initiative of back-benchers. . . . Most of the legislation is of a minor nature. In fact the system clearly encourages the presentation of Private Members' bills in favour of either a restricted number of individuals, or of occupational categories, interest groups and localities. . . .

Thus while the Italian parliamentarians can boast that they do actually participate in the 'legislative power' more than most of their European colleagues, their activity is, nonetheless, similar as far as government bills are concerned: they sometimes amend, rarely reject, and usually sanction them. . . .

## PARLIAMENT AND THE CONTROL OF THE GOVERNMENT

The Constitution has furnished Parliament with a whole armoury for controlling the government. First and foremost the cabinet must have the confidence of the two Houses of Parliament. However the use of the vote of confidence depends on the organization of the parties in Parliament. While the cabinet commands an obedient parliamentary majority, it has little to fear from Parliament. One of the paradoxes of the Italian situation is that, although all governments are coalitions, and hence by definition lack a homogeneous majority, more cabinets fall as a result of internal discord than from an adverse vote in Parliament. This is because the parties are able to impose tight parliamentary discipline on their members. Moreover, in the Italian party situation the defeat of the government in Parliament is an inefficient way of controlling the cabinet; a new coalition on virtually the same lines as its predecessor will be formed to go on from where the latter left off. Members of the government parties who are dissatisfied with government policy or legislation will endeavour to intervene in the party machinery before the Parliamentary vote. In fact, dissatisfaction with cabinet policy may well be the origin of the internal discord that causes a cabinet crisis.

A second method of control is through power of the purse. Here the same factors apply, i.e. the power of party discipline in all parliamentary votes. The situation is worsened by a number of general factors. In the first place, national budgets are very complex; few members can understand even the simplified versions prepared to help them. In addition, the budgets do not include the expenditures of many state and parastate agencies, even though they are formally accountable to Parliament. 'Their real budgets', as one observer has noted, 'are disguised.' In such a situation, it is not surprising that Parliament makes no real effort to examine them critically. In the second place, the limitation of budgeting for one year is not compatible with rational policy-making or efficient administration. Long-range planning demands that sums be committed for several years in advance; this is what, in fact, happens, but it is disguised. Moreover, Parliament only examines in any detail the provisional budgets and not the real expenditure. Hence it accepts the *fait accompli* and abdicates any real attempt to control expenditure critically. . . . In the third place, the clientele pressures put on backbenchers lead them to interesting themselves in and even contesting minor points of detail (a swimming pool or a school, or even a hospital, in their constituency and not in another locality) rather than the main lines of the budget. Interest groups of national dimensions intervene at an earlier stage with party leaders, or with the administration in the preparation of the budget. Hence the real struggle over the size and direction of the budget takes place before its presentation to Parliament, either at the planning stage, or in the Council of Ministers for the final arbitration.

A third possible method of control is through questions posed by individual parliamentarians, but it does not seem to have become a method of controlling the government in Italy. Both written and oral questions tend to get written replies; the government keeping oral replies to a minimum. Hence questions rarely lead to discussion or debate. For a debate, a motion must be presented, so there is nothing like the question time in the British House of Commons.

# 22

## Politics in France: How Power Is Used

### William Safran

In this selection from *Comparative Politics*, William Safran examines the roles of the executive, the legislature, and the civil service in the policymaking process in France, and discusses some of the unresolved conflicts between administration and politics that pose a potential threat to France's social and political order.

The mere outline of the powers of the principal institutions—the executive, the legislature, and the civil service—as defined by the constitution and the laws cannot adequately convey how policies in France are decided and implemented. The distinction between what Frenchmen have called the "legal country" and the "real country" can be seen, first, in the tendency of Fifth Republic Presidents to interpret the constitution in such a way as to increase their power at the expense of that of the Prime Minister.

This has applied not only to Cabinet appointments, in which the President has given himself an almost free hand. Most important, it has also applied to the content of policy decisions. De Gaulle (who took little interest in economics) and Pompidou gave their Prime Ministers a great deal of discretion except, of course, in the areas of foreign and defense policy; but Giscard (a professional economist) took an active lead in almost all aspects of domestic policy, and even "meddled" in the drafting of the language of government bills.

In short, the President's domain, as distinct from that of the government, has been stretched almost at will. Under de Gaulle, presidential decisions included the blackballing of Britain's bid to enter the Common Market, the raising of the minimum wage of industrial workers, and the vetoing of an appointment to the prestigious *Académie Française*; under Pompidou, the devaluation of the franc, the lowering of value-added taxes on foodstuffs, and the modification of rules on the maximum height of buildings in Paris. Under Giscard, there were hundreds of "intrusions" in matters affecting taxes, wages, social security, and interest rates.

In promoting his policies, the President is helped by the Prime Minister and the Cabinet, and he "uses" his ministers to transform his ideas into concrete legislative proposals, to defend them in parliament, and to take the blame for them when they prove unpopular or unsuccessful. The distance the President thereby establishes in the public mind between himself and his ministers is a political convenience. To provide one example: Although the austerity policies adopted between 1976 and 1980 were largely of Giscard's inspiration, public opinion surveys showed that the President was less unpopular than Raymond Barre, his Prime Minister.

The President does not rely on the Cabinet alone. He appoints, and presides over, "restricted" committees composed of selected ministers, higher civil servants, and whatever additional personalities the President may coopt. Furthermore, there is a growing staff of presidential experts who, like the White House staff in the United States, often function as an unofficial and supplementary Cabinet.

## DEPUTIES AND DECISIONS

In a formal sense, parliament has been weakened considerably by the constitution as well as by the legislature's own standing orders. Nevertheless, parliament is not *intrinsically* so weak as to be dismissed. Although in most cases—and certainly in all budget matters— the initiative belongs to the government, deputies have succeeded in significantly modifying government bills through amendments: for instance, on abortion, unemployment, farm credits, education, the structural reorganization of the public television network, and the reform of local fiscal administration.

Sometimes the government virtually abandons a legislative project to which it is ostensibly committed if it becomes apparent that there is insufficient support for the project among deputies belonging to the majority, as happened in 1976 with capital gains taxation. In still other cases, the government permits, or encourages, leaders of a parliamentary group belonging to the majority to introduce legislation. That is what occurred in 1980 with a Gaullist-sponsored bill on "participation"—the distribution of industrial shares to the workers in given firms. The government itself lacked enthusiasm for the policy but did not wish needlessly to antagonize the Gaullist party, whose support would be required for other matters.

If there are few evidences of an open conflict over policy between majority deputies and the government, that does not necessarily mean that deputies have resigned themselves to inaction from the start.

Rather, it may indicate that the deputies have made their influence felt during the bill-drafting phase through informal "backstage" negotiation with ministers or higher civil servants. Frequently, too, a government bill reflects the pressures of interest groups. The watering down of tax bills, the softening of price controls, and the government's failure to institute genuine participation of workers in industrial decisions within firms—all these have been due largely to the successful lobbying of the National Council of French Employers. It must be understood that this is not lobbying American-style by means of appearances before legislative committees; rather, lobbying is done through frequent contacts between leaders of big business and higher civil servants. In this respect trade unions continue to be at a disadvantage, since the personal links of their leaders to the upper-echelon bureaucrats are weak. In the past, unions compensated for this weakness by threatening strikes and unrest, and succeeded in pushing the government into making periodic wage adjustments in their favor, particularly during election years. (Since the capture of control of the Assembly by the Socialists, the trade unions can look forward to fruitful access to that body.)

Parliamentarians who are unhappy with government bills have a juridical weapon at their disposal: they may try to block the passage of certain bills by resorting to the Constitutional Council. That body is not a "judicial review" organ in the sense of the American Supreme Court; it is not a court of appeals to which citizens' complaints of civil rights violations may be brought; and it has not been in the habit of nullifying laws (once passed). Its major legislative function is to examine "organic" bills (which also include the budget) *before* their parliamentary passage. In recent years, the council has widened its scope somewhat; for example, in 1971 it forced the government to withdraw a bill that would have given prefects the power to forbid or cancel public meetings. Here the council acted on the ground that the bill violated freedom of association. In 1977 the council nullified a bill that would have permitted the police, without a warrant, to search parked cars, because the bill violated a constitutional provision (Article 66) on judicial safeguards of individual liberties. In 1980 the council declared unconstitutional a bill aimed at special surveillance of foreign workers on the grounds that it violated the principle of equality before the law. Yet parliamentarians have resorted to the Constitutional Council infrequently, in part because it has continued to be heavily influenced by pro-executive considerations.

If contributions of parliament to the legislative process have amounted to relatively little, this has been in large part the fault of the deputies themselves. Parliamentarians have often lacked the expertise of the administrative professionals who draft government bills. Furthermore, the deputies' absenteeism has made it difficult for them to acquire mastery over a subject or participate in parliamentary debates with consistency. That absenteeism itself must, of course, be attributed to the "accumulation of mandates" that scatters deputies' responsibilities.

Even if such obstacles were overcome, deputies would still be unable to make their wills prevail as individuals. What about deputies as members of political parties? Under Gaullist and centrist-conservative Presidents, the deputies belonging to parties of the left lacked unity and voting strength; and the Gaullist, centrist, and conservative deputies were hesitant to confront the government in open parliamentary sessions, for they, too, were divided between enthusiastic and reluctant supporters of the government. Since the elections of 1981 the tables have been turned: the right-of-center Opposition parties are too small and fragmented to fight the executive, while the Socialist deputies can be expected on most occasions to be part of an obedient machine for endorsing presidential wishes. There is, first, the factor of party discipline, and second, the fact that individual majority deputies do not wish to endanger their prospects for political advancement (i.e., appointment to ministerial posts) or "pork-barrel" favors to their constituents.

Moreover, the lack of seriousness with which deputies view their own efforts—and worth—can be attributed in part to the realization that much of the work done in parliament does not necessarily have permanent value: the decisions that count are made elsewhere.

## BUREAUCRATIC POLITICS

In theory, civil servants do not make policy, but only do the research and prepare the groundwork for it and then implement it at various levels. But administrators have been in effect co-decision makers. During the Fourth Republic, the political executive had been subject to such frequent change, and hence had been so unstable and weak, that the permanent, professional civil service was depended on for decisional continuity and even initiative. In the Fifth Republic, the distinction between the political decision-making elite and the higher bureaucracy has been obscured by the tendency of Presidents to recruit a large proportion of the Cabinet from the administrative corps. In addition, civil servants have frequently dominated interministerial committees as well as the staffs of intimate collaborators appointed by each minister (the *cabinets ministériels*).

There are also the "study commissions" whose establishment is from time to time encouraged by the President, the Prime Minister, individual ministers, or the Commissioner of Economic Planning. These commissions (which are roughly comparable to the Royal Commissions in Britain) may include academics, managers of nationalized enterprises, and even parliamentarians; but civil servants have tended to dominate them. There have been many such commissions. . . . The commissions' reports to the government, which reflect the input of interest-group leaders and miscellaneous experts, may be used by the government as a basis for legislative proposals; or, if the government does not agree with the reports' conclusions, they may be ignored.

Once the parliamentarians have passed a bill, it gains substance only when it is enforced. But governments (and higher civil servants) may demonstrate their reservations regarding a bill by failing to produce the necessary implementing regulations or ordinances. Thus the government has "denatured" acts of parliament by delaying, or omitting, follow-up regulations on bills dealing with educational reforms, birth control, and the financing of local government. Occasionally the administrative bureaucracy may, at the behest of a minister, produce regulations that contravene the intent of a law passed by parliament. For example, after parliament had passed a bill requiring equal treatment of immigrant workers, administrative regulations subjected them to special disabilities; similarly, an act of parliament forbidding discrimination on the basis of religion or race aimed at firms engaged in international trade was followed by a government regulation permitting discrimination. The Council of State may nullify such regulations after a legal challenge; however, litigation is selective and may take several years.

Parliament may intervene in the application of laws by setting up special investigation committees. But few committees have actually been established; the parliamentarians' timidity has been due less to government opposition to the appointment of such committees (which has slackened) than to an uncertainty whether they are of much use. One committee, appointed in the early 1970s to investigate the television and radio networks, proved to have little impact on government's management of the media.

## THE DELEGATION OF RESPONSIBILITY

In order to weaken the effects of long-established legislation, the executive and its administrators may resort to various forms of buck-passing. Thus, to avoid using public moneys to keep the governmentally controlled health insurance funds solvent, the funds were permitted to raise the social security contributions of the insured. Similarly, the autonomous public corporation that runs the Paris subway system contracted with private firms to obtain workers to clean the subway stations, instead of employing its own workers and having to pay them the minimum wages generally granted by legislation to public employees. Finally, although all subnational administrative activities are, theoretically, controlled or controllable by the national government, the latter has saved itself trouble and money by permitting considerable local variations in the implementation of elementary school curricula and vacation policies, public health standards, and social services for the aged.

Since the early days of the Fourth Republic, governments have been committed to a form of capitalist national planning. The four-year economic modernization plans were prepared through complex procedures involving the Cabinet (notably the Ministry of Finance), governmental statistical institutes, several hundred technocrats working in a National Planning Commission, and numerous interest-group spokesmen who were consulted regularly in the Social and Economic Council and the regional "modernization committees." This "concertation" of conflicting class interests was supposed to result in a fair plan that represented a fine balance between a "productivity" and a "social" orientation. Hence the plan was invested with a certain moral authority; it led the government and the parliament to process specific pieces of legislation that were consistent with the plan: for instance, bills on public-works investments, social welfare, wages, employment, housing, and so on. For both de Gaulle and Pompidou, the plan was an "ardent obligation"; under Giscard and his Prime Ministers, the planning institutions were retained, but planners did little more than prepare position papers and statistical forecasts, while many of their policy recommendations were ignored by the government.

There may, in fact, have been little alternative to ignoring the planners' recommendations because the projections on which they were based had increasingly acquired an air of unrealism in the face of external events (such as sudden increases in the price of oil, or the interruption of supplies of needed raw materials owing to *coups d'état*), which could not be predicted, much less controlled by the French government. Under Mitterrand national planning [is being] given new impetus. . . . [R]ecent Socialist party programs [provide for] as much attention [to] be focused on income redistribution and the provision of social goods as on growth and productivity; and [for] parliament [to] be more active in balancing the "deals" made between administrative bureaucracy and big business.

## CONFLICTS WITHIN THE SYSTEM

It should not be inferred that governmental attitudes are monolithic. Occasionally, the national administration is hampered by internal conflicts as well as conflicts with politicians. . . .

The conflict between administration and politics is seen most clearly in the relationship between the mayor and the prefect. The prefect is legally responsible only to the national government; he has the power to nullify acts of a city council, to veto the budget adopted by the General (departmental) Council and even, under certain circumstances, to depose a mayor. He takes such action only rarely, for a mayor may be more powerful than a prefect, especially if the former is, simultaneously, a member of parliament or, better, a Cabinet minister. . . . Mayors of big cities are particularly powerful because the national government cannot easily ignore their influence over a large electorate. Such mayors may bypass the prefect and have direct dealings with the finance and other ministries, and may secure funds for local industrial development projects.

Sometimes a mayor may be too political and *too* powerful to suit the taste of the national government. In 1978, Chirac, the mayor of Paris, was "punished" for his presidential ambitions and his unreliable support of the President and the Prime Minister: Chirac (probably at the President's instigation) failed to get a governmental financial supplement for the maintenance of the municipal police force—a development that forced the mayor to increase local tax assessments and threatened to reduce his popularity.

The preceding was not intended to dispel the notion that France has a hyper-presidential system. . . .

. . . While the present system is clearly presidential, the relationships between the President and the Prime Minister, and between the executive and parliament, are ambiguous enough to produce conflict. The President can exert his leadership best when there is no challenge to his decisions, the legitimacy of which derives from the fact that the President is the product of a democratic mandate (i.e., a popular election). The Assembly, which is also based on a democratic mandate, has so far not opposed the President effectively because of the lucky circumstance that the parliamentary majority, Gaullist, right-of-center, or Socialist, has more or less conformed to the political ideology of the four Presidents.

# Unit VII

## _____ Social Factors _____

It is virtually impossible to understand the differences between the various systems of government in present-day Western Europe without having at least some awareness of the diverse social milieux from which these governments emerged. Social factors invariably play an important role in shaping the political attitudes of a society, and these attitudes in turn have a direct impact on the types of political institutions that are formed as well as on the kinds of policies pursued by its government. This unit contrasts the social characteristics and political attitudes of four major Western European societies—Germany, Scandinavia, France, and Great Britain—and examines the impact of socioeconomic factors, such as level and distribution of wealth, access to education, social and occupational mobility, income, and class structure, on the way in which government is formed and carried out in each of these countries.

In "Social Structure in Contemporary West Germany," Karl W. Deutsch and D. Brent Smith describe West Germany's social structure in terms of class, occupation, income, status, and education. The authors point out that West Germans are the most affluent people in Western Europe today, adding that they are also predominantly urban-dwellers, middle class, and generally better educated than their counterparts in other Western European countries.

The Scandinavian countries are widely known for their innovations in a number of policy areas, particularly their egalitarian approach to social welfare, education, and income distribution. Francis G. Castles, in "Scandinavia's Changing Political Culture," examines the origins of Scandinavia's unusually strong organizational life, which he traces back to the second half of the nineteenth century, when the Scandinavian countries entered a period of extremely rapid industrialization that resulted in their transformation from conservative oligarchies into democratic political systems in which the working-class parties played a major role.

William Safran, in "French Politics: The Economic and Social Context," details the various economic and social factors that have influenced politics in France. He points out that until quite recently, French society was characterized by sharp class divisions, a lack of upward mobility, inequality of educational opportunity and housing, and economic policies that favored the rich. For many years, France was a country in which the gap between the white collar and the blue collar was one of the largest in Western Europe, and, as Safran explains, although that gap has narrowed in the past two decades, a long history of mutual distrust seems to have precluded the possibility of any real blurring of the lines between the different social classes.

A.H. Birch examines the political attitudes and values of the British people in "British Government: The Society and the People," and shows how these factors have contributed to the shaping of Britain's political institutions. Birch explains that the overall effect of these characteristically British attitudes, which include an unusual degree of deference toward government, is that those in positions of power within the government enjoy considerably more freedom than do their counterparts in other European democracies. Finally, in "The Social Context of British Politics," R.M. Punnett discusses politics in Great Britain by examining the various criteria that determine social class, including family background, education, occupation, and wealth. Punnett argues that social class distinctions are more significant than national, regional, religious, or ethnic variations in creating a fundamental disunity in British society, citing as evidence the results of a recent survey which showed the British to be far more class-conscious than other Anglo-Saxon societies.

# 23

# Social Structure in Contemporary West Germany

## Karl W. Deutsch and D. Brent Smith

West Germans are predominantly urban, middle class, and for the most part better educated than their counterparts in other Western European countries. They are also the most affluent people in Western Europe today. The authors of this selection describe the social structure of contemporary West Germany in terms of occupational groupings, income groups, status groups, social classes, and education levels.

Germany has long been predominantly urban and industrial, and it has become somewhat more so during the last three decades. By 1975, cities and towns contained more than nine-tenths of the population of the Federal Republic, including West Berlin. Large cities above 100,000 population accounted for 33 percent; middle-sized cities with 20,000 to 100,000 inhabitants added another 23 percent. As many as 34 percent of West Germans, however, still lived in small towns of between 2,000 and 20,000 people; and the remaining 10 percent lived in still smaller and for the most part rural communities. No political party stressing mainly rural interests could hope for a majority, but since 44 percent of the voters lived in communities of less than 20,000 people, the parties could hardly omit making an appeal to rural and small-town voters and their values. The right of center parties have been significantly more successful in attracting the vote in communities of less than 20,000 people.

World War II has left its mark on the population. At the beginning of 1974, women were still 52 percent of the population in West Germany, and in the important age group between fifty and seventy, from which many men had been killed in the war, women made up 57 percent. During World War II and the years immediately following it, fewer children were born, so that in 1974 the Federal Republic had more inhabitants aged sixty years and over than it had youngsters between six and eighteen.

The preference of the West Germans for reconstruction over reproduction between 1945 and 1955 made West Germany a country with one of the oldest populations among the large nations. Under these conditions, the appeal of youth in German politics was likely to be slightly weaker, and the appeal of age and experience slightly stronger, than in the United States. . . .

From 1968 on, however, the picture changed. Young people came to comprise a slightly higher proportion of the population; in 1971 the voting age was lowered to eighteen; the attitudes of the young began to carry over, at least to a limited extent, into the ranks of people over thirty.

The elections of 1969 and 1972 showed a markedly less conservative trend, and despite gains by conservatives in the 1976 elections, it was clear that all major political parties were placing a premium on younger leadership and a progressive image.

## THE STRENGTH OF OCCUPATIONAL GROUPINGS

About 44 percent of the people of the Federal Republic in 1974 were members of its work force of 27.2 million. The rest are their dependent children and other family members, as well as a good many pensioners, who make up a substantial 17 percent of the total population.

Only 7 percent of the work force is engaged in agriculture, and only a little less than half (47 percent) is engaged in mining or construction or in crafts. The sizable remaining group of 46 percent is occupied in commerce, transportation, and services, both private and public. There are not enough farmers to bring victory to a traditionalist party, but there are enough to press effectively for special economic and political concessions. After the blue-collar workers (47 percent), the strongest group consists of white-collar employees, who make up 38 percent of the work force. These white-collar employees are often likely to prove the decisive group in mass politics; without their support, neither labor nor middle-class appeals are likely to be successful.

Another 8 percent consists of the self-employed urban middle class and the members of their families assisting them in their enterprises. The main groups within this group of self-employed are small businessmen in commerce and the service industries, artisans, and a small group of professionals. There has been a strong tendency for blue-collar workers to vote for the SPD, and for employers, professional people, and farmers to vote for the CDU. Here again, the white-collar employees are a swing group that may well decide an election.

It is of importance to note that there are some 2.3 million foreign workers (*Gastarbeiter*, or "guest workers") and their families in the

Federal Republic. They make up some 7 percent of the work force. Most of them have been recruited from Italy, Yugoslavia, Turkey, Greece, or Spain, and are employed in unskilled or semi-skilled blue-collar work. Most originally came with the intention of returning to their home-lands, but many of these have stayed. The foreign worker may join a labor union, receive its benefits, and strengthen it by his support, but the fact that such a sizable share of West German workers are voteless foreigners cannot but weaken the potential voting strength of labor and the SPD.

## INCOME GROUPS, STATUS GROUPS, AND SOCIAL CLASSES

### The Distribution of Income

The distribution of income in the Federal Republic is somewhat more unequal than it is in Britain or in the Scandinavian countries, and the leveling effects of post-war taxation have gone somewhat less far. But by comparison with previous German regimes and with the vast majority of nations today, the average German is comparatively very well off. Indeed, on one index of the equality of income distribution, the proportion of the population with half of the income, the Federal Republic ranked with the United States (both measuring 42 percent in 1965 figures) when compared to other nations.

There remains, however, a broad range of income distribution in the Federal Republic. On the bottom end of the scale are pensioners and the unemployed, who despite inflationary trends still manage to attain a modest standard of living on government stipends, thanks to long-standing efforts to maintain an enlightened social policy. At the upper end are the relatively few (some 30,000 DM-millionaires in 1966) who command a disproportionate share of the country's wealth. The hold-ings of feudal barons, Junker landowners, and the industrial entrepre-neurs of the empire and the Weimar era have remained largely intact despite changes in regimes. Efforts to initiate widespread tax reform in the Bundestag have thus far failed. But large landowners and industrial magnates do not wield the same degree of influence they did in pre-1945 Germany.

Under the Bonn Republic, most Germans have been less interested in the just distribution of income than they have been in seeing this total income increase, and in having their own incomes rise with it. The upward shift in per capita income has been dramatic. By 1974 it was just barely below that of the United States. . . .

West Germans have become the most affluent people in Europe. Rising incomes and the increase in the number of those in the middle-income bracket, during a period in which German inflation was comparatively low, have found tangible expression in the lives of the Federal Republic's citizens. . . .The proportion of households with refrigerators, for example, rose from 10 percent in 1955 to 99 percent in 1975, while the proportion owning washing machines grew from 23 percent to 98 percent between 1958 and 1975. West German wage earners had an average of 29 vacation days in 1975. German tourists, formerly in the habit of taking their holidays in neighboring countries, have ventured in great numbers to the Mediterranean countries and beyond. An anomaly in this tale of affluence is the fact that less than half of West German households have telephones.

## Status Groups and Social Classes

Germans have long been a highly status-conscious people, and the distribution of status differs in some respects from the distribution of income. Occupations requiring more education, clerical work, and either private or public trust rank higher in status than the pay they bring indicates.

The actual distribution of social classes and status groups differed very little in the early years of the Federal Republic from the social structure of the previous several decades, but a number of factors have since contributed to greater social mobility and to a lessening of divisions among classes. A primary factor has been the rising income level and the enjoyment of material benefits on a previously unmatched scale, even among those formerly counted in the lower class. Also contributing to the lessening of class differences among Germans has been the introduction of large outside groups into the country's work force—first the refugees and expellees from the GDR [German Democratic Republic, or East Germany] and the former German territories, and now the foreign *Gastarbeiter*. Members of both groups were willing to take on the more menial tasks in society, in effect improving the lot of lower-class West German "natives." The former group has become thoroughly integrated and has become upwardly mobile in German society. In the case of the *Gastarbeiter*, strong cultural differences will likely preclude a similar assimilation.

Education has long been a major indicator of social class in Germany. Formerly accessible only to the privileged and rich, a university education served to demonstrate not only social cleavages but fundamental cultural cleavages as well. Higher education was maintained as the avenue for general elite membership. The educated few read different newspapers, engaged in different cultural activities, and even spoke a different language than did the mass of Germans.

## LEVELS OF EDUCATION

All West German children must go to school for at least eight years, but four-fifths of the students leave school at age 14 when they finish their primary education. Thus, in the early 1960s, only 18 percent of West German youth in the 15-to-19-year-old age group were full-time students, compared to 31 percent in France and 66 percent in the United States. Nearly one-quarter (22 percent) of the 16-year-olds in 1959 were getting the *Mittlere Reife*, which is the German counterpart to an American nonacademic high school education. This was a considerable improvement over the education received by their parents.

Graduation from a full-fledged German academic high school—the *Abitur*, which is comparable to two years of American college—had been achieved by only 4 percent of the general population in the mid-1950s. But by 1973, some 17 percent of German teenagers were enrolled in *Gymnasien*, or academic high schools. There was similar evidence of broader access to university education. Between 1957 and 1972, the number of university students more than quadrupled from 112,000 to 470,000, and there were an estimated 600,000 students in German universities by 1975. About 16 percent of all nineteen-year-olds in 1974 planned to attend a university.

In 1972, of the total population of all ages, almost eight out of every thousand were attending university or technical college, as against the earlier proportion of two per thousand in 1950 and in 1932 at the end of the Weimar Republic, and against only one student per thousand population under Hitler's regime in 1938. Quietly and without much rhetoric, the Bonn republic by the early 1970s opened the gates of the German universities nearly three times as wide as they had ever been opened. While the West German levels are still well below the United States figure of eighteen students per thousand population—and of perhaps twelve American students per thousand above the junior-college level, which corresponds to the German *Abitur*—and while there was no very broad college-educated group in the West German electorate, the proportion of university-educated men and women has grown significantly, and promises to continue to do so.

Before the gates were opened wider, there were probably not more than 5 to 10 percent of the sons and daughters of workers among students at West German universities, but even this proportion was larger than it had been under any previous regime.

In the late 1960s, there was a strong trend to the political left among university students and some nontenured junior faculty members, in contrast to the strong conservatism of students in the pre-1945 period. The share of students and academic personnel in the German work force had grown nearly threefold, but their political influence, social status, and economic status had not risen in proportion. At the same time that students became more numerous and more frustrated, many of them became enraged by the overload of contradictory knowledge brought to them by their studies and by the mass media, and by the normative and cognitive dissonance between their ideas and aspirations and the realities of the world in which they lived.

Such feelings of unrest and dissonance had been growing during the 1960s, and more quickly so from 1966 onward. In 1967 and 1968, they broke into the open with large student demonstrations, occupations of buildings, disruptions of academic work, and demands for university reform, more permissiveness in matters of sex and life style, and more far-reaching political changes. By the early 1970s the turbulent and variegated movement had partly succeeded in regard to the first two demands but largely failed in regard to the third. Neither the radical Marxist nor the anarchist factions among the students found much sympathy among the factory workers or among the population at large. The main thrust of the movement, however, despite much confusion, remained radically democratic and anti-authoritarian. The great majority of students and junior faculty had no interest in a bureaucratic Communist dictatorship of the sort existing in the GDR or the Soviet Union.

# 24

# Scandinavia's Changing Political Culture

## Francis G. Castles

The Scandinavian countries are widely noted for their egalitarian policies in the areas of social welfare, education, income distribution, and, most recently, even in industry. Here, Francis G. Castles examines the origins of Scandinavia's uniquely strong organizational life, which he traces back to the second half of the nineteenth century, when the Scandinavian countries experienced a late and extremely rapid period of industrialization that resulted in their transformation from conservative oligarchies into democratic political systems in which the working-class parties played a major role.

### ECONOMIC AND SOCIAL STRUCTURE

. . . In the middle of the nineteenth century, none of the Scandinavian countries had really begun industrialization. They were near-subsistence economies in which the peasantry composed the vast mass of the population. Toward the end of the nineteenth century, the comparison between Scandinavia on the one side and Britain, France, and Germany on the other was one between poverty and the beginnings of affluence based on industrial might. Sweden, today the richest country of Western Europe, was then described as "Europe's fortress poorhouse.". . .

The nature of the changes in Scandinavia is demonstrated not only by high average incomes (Gross National Product per capita), but also by a drastically altered employment structure in which agriculture has ceased to be the predominant sector. The tertiary or service economy has outstripped industrial production. . . .

. . . Within the space of a century, all the Scandinavian countries have been transformed from conservative oligarchies into democratic political systems in which working-class parties play a major role, and in which welfare state policies have in many respects been developed further than in other advanced nations. Over the last four decades, the

**TABLE 24.1 Basic Statistics, 1973**

| Country | Production | Employment | | |
| | GNP per Capita | Agriculture | Industry | Other |
| --- | --- | --- | --- | --- |
| US | $6,170 | 4.1% | 31.7 | 64.2 |
| Denmark | 5,460 | 9.5 | 33.8 | 56.7 |
| Finland | 3,720 | 17.1 | 35.7 | 47.1 |
| Iceland | 4,870 | 15.9 | 37.5 | 46.6 |
| Norway | 4,780 | 11.4 | 33.9 | 54.7 |
| Sweden | 6,140 | 7.1 | 36.8 | 56.1 |
| UK | 3,100 | 3.0 | 42.3 | 54.7 |
| West Germany | 5,610 | 7.5 | 49.5 | 43.0 |
| France | 4,900 | 12.2 | 39.3 | 48.5 |
| Greece | 1,790 | 34.1 | 25.7 | 40.2 |
| Spain | 1,750 | 26.5 | 38.0 | 35.5 |
| Portugal | 1,250 | 28.8 | 33.8 | 37.4 |

*Note:* Employment statistics for Iceland, Greece, and Portugal are estimates by OECD Secretariat.

*Source:* OECD Economic Surveys: Denmark, Norway and Sweden, 1976, statistical appendix.

strong Social Democratic parties of Sweden, Norway, and Denmark have been associated with policy innovations designed to achieve a greater level of egalitarianism in society in levels of welfare and income distribution, and more recently in terms of power in industry. . . .

Although the pace of democratic evolution in the first half of the nineteenth century varied somewhat in the Scandinavian countries, in none of them was it very rapid. This was due to the fact that the impact of industrialization was experienced later than in Britain and much of the rest of Continental Europe. But although industrialization came late, it came with extreme rapidity, and with potentially disastrous consequences for the maintenance of political stability.

Even at its most gradual, industrialization must be seen [as] a major instrument of social and political transformation. Not only does it destroy the traditional village way of life, it brings individuals into a new and unfamiliar urban setting, and subjects them to the artificial rhythms of the factory environment. Moreover, although industry increases the overall product of society, it may well, particularly in its early stages, create a small class of wealthy entrepreneurs whose ability to accumulate capital is bought at the cost of the impoverishment of the vast majority.

In discussing the process of industrialization in Scandinavia, however, we encounter a crucial paradox of political development. Extremely rapid economic development was accompanied by a wholesale democratic transformation without any dramatic change in the structure of political institutions and without any serious expression of mass violence. . . .

. . . Given the lateness and rapidity of industrialization in Scandinavia, the development of a political conflict between town and country occurred at much the same time that the lower classes were demanding access to the political system. In consequence, there was no development on British lines of an upper class party combining the interests of the urban and rural elite against the political demands of the lower classes.

Party divisions are a reflection of cleavage structures, and the Scandinavian pattern of division came to be reflected in a system of four basic blocks. The Conservatives expressed the interests of the urban elite. The Left or Liberals were in part the party of the rural counterculture and in part the party whose historical mission was the establishment of parliamentarianism and universal suffrage. The Agrarians promoted the economic interests of the farming community, and the Social Democrats expressed the demands of industrial labor. . . .

In general, the old urban-rural divide seems to have declined with the decrease in the agricultural population. The farmers' parties in Sweden and Norway have both changed their names to Center Party in the hope of attracting the white-collar groups in the towns. In Norway, issues involving national independence are capable of infusing new life into the politics of the rural counterculture, as was demonstrated in the national referendum on entry into the European Economic Community in 1972. Here it was the parties of economic modernity—the Social Democrats and the Conservatives—that proposed entry into the EEC, and the parties of the rural counterculture that opposed. The latter's victory, despite the much greater parliamentary strength of the former two groups, illustrates the power such issues still have in Norway, and the fact that in normal times they are submerged in the routine of running a social welfare society.

One of the side effects of the social welfare society may show the first signs of a new cleavage structure in Scandinavia. It is not the desirability of social welfare itself that is questioned. That has been accepted by all parties, including the Conservatives. The Swedish Conservatives even signaled their conversion by changing their name to the Moderate Unity party. The problem that has caused real trouble in recent years is that of finding the resources to pay for social welfare. Average tax rates in all three Scandinavian kingdoms are exceedingly high to finance a public expenditure in excess of 50 percent of national income, and larger and larger numbers are expressing their discontent through the ballot box. In 1973, the established Danish party system was almost completely devastated by the rise of new parties, among which by far the largest was the Progress party. Its platform was the drastic reduction of taxation and public expenditure. On a far smaller scale, something similar happened in Norway in the same year, with the party opposing taxation gaining four seats.

In Denmark and Norway, non-Socialist coalitions have held office in the last decade, and may be regarded as just as accountable for high tax levels as the Social Democrats. The consequence is that discontent has had to be channeled outside the established party system. This has not yet occurred in Sweden, but it is by no means impossible. In September 1976 the long reign of the Swedish Social Democrats came to an end in an election in which one of the major issues was the level of taxation. . . .

. . . [G]roup influence and compromise between groups have been the features of Scandinavian democracy that have most impressed observers, who have coined for them such labels as "corporativism," "corporate pluralism," and "the politics of compromise."

The origins of Scandinavia's uniquely strong organizational life lie in the development of popular movements reflecting emergent cultural cleavages in a highly literate population. The most interesting characteristic of these organizations, which makes them extraordinarily suitable agencies of compromise, is their strange combination of democratic participation and deference to leadership. Both have their origins in the period at which the popular movements developed, but each represents a wholly different side of the cultural tradition. The popular movements were organizations that represented the participatory demands of those who were on the disadvantaged side of any given cleavage. Since the way forward for all of them was the widening of the democratic sphere, all adopted democratic procedures of election, and the accountability of leaders.

At the same time, the movements developed within the context of what can only be called an "elite culture." In each country the central culture was the product of a bureaucratic elite whose claim to position and authority was less their status in the economic hierarchy than their learning and political skills. Given that educational values at this time reflected the official culture, it is not surprising that a degree of deference also became part of the organizational culture. But this type of deference is very different from the kind that in Britain produces working-class Tories. . . . [I]t is a sort of . . . deference to expertise that in no way militates against egalitarian or democratic sentiments. In fact, it prevents those in positions of leadership from assuming more commanding roles than chairmen, spokesmen, or coordinators. Moreover, deference within organizational structures tends to leave leaders that much freer to bargain, negotiate, and compromise, although always in the certain knowledge that they will be ultimately held responsible for their stewardship. . . .

# French Politics:
# The Economic and Social Context

## —————————— William Safran ——————————

Until quite recently, French society was characterized by sharp class divisions, a lack of upward mobility, inequality of educational opportunity and housing, and economic policies that favored the rich. For many years, France was a country in which the gap between the white collar and the blue collar was one of the largest of any in Western Europe, and although that gap has narrowed in the past two decades, a long history of mutual distrust, different backgrounds, and divergent concerns has precluded the possibility of any real political merger between the different social classes. William Safran, in these excerpts from *Comparative Politics*, examines these and other factors that have contributed to the shaping of contemporary French politics.

## SOCIAL CLASSES AND MOBILITY

Historically, the social system of France is much like that of any other Western European country that experienced feudalism and inherited a division of society into classes of nobles, clergy, townsmen (bourgeoisie), and peasants. . . . Today it is still possible to talk about French society as being divided into the following social groups: (1) the upper class, including the graduates of the prestigious national universities, the upper echelons of the civil service, the directors of large and successful enterprises, and bankers; (2) the bourgeoisie, including members of the liberal professions, university and *lycée* professors, engineers and *cadres* (upper-echelon technical and administrative personnel), and owners of medium-sized shops and family firms; (3) the middle and lower middle class (*classe moyenne*), including white-collar employees, petty shopkeepers, lower-echelon civil servants, elementary school teachers, and, possibly, artisans; and finally (4) the lower classes (*classes populaires*), comprising in the main industrial

171

workers and small farmers. There is in France, as elsewhere in Western Europe, a correlation between class and ideology: thus membership in the working class usually implies membership in the socialist "ideological family." There is also a correlation between social status and access to economic benefits.

But such correlations are simplistic and of uncertain reliability. Ideological and class cleavages tend to overlap in complex industrial societies. . . . There are, in addition, geographical variables. There is still a status differential between residence in Paris as against the provinces. . . . The social mobility that exists has been lateral rather than upward; recent statistics indicate that the majority of the various elites were descended from fathers who were themselves in elite positions.

. . . This lack of upward mobility (which is not decidedly different in France from that in Italy, Japan, Sweden, and even the United States), fortified by a continuing inequality of educational opportunity, housing conditions, and tax loopholes for the rich—accompanied by the existence of a pronounced lower-class life style—has sharpened the self-perception of the working classes as a deprived segment.

To some extent, class cleavages and working-class consciousness have been moderated by the gradual democratization of primary and secondary education (or at least by a public commitment to the *principle* of such democratization), and the somewhat enhanced possibilities of the recruitment of the children of working-class and lower-middle-class parents to the lower echelons of the national civil service. These class cleavages have been reduced also by the expansion of the welfare state and the introduction specifically of such features as paid vacations and the statutory medical-care system. However, the worker has had to finance social security protection by means of ever-increasing payroll deductions. . . .

After the accession of de Gaulle, co-management boards and profit-sharing schemes were introduced in order to "associate" the working class with industrial entrepreneurs and reduce proletarian resentments. In addition, interclass resentments were channeled into nationalistic (and often anti-American) sentiments, which were widespread and were counted upon to unite various socioeconomic sectors. With the partial disintegration of Gaullism that was reflected in the election of President Giscard d'Estaing in 1974, the resentments of the disprivileged had to be resolved in a more concrete fashion. . . . Giscard . . . allocated generous amounts of money for increases in unemployment and pension payments, and has even initiated measures aimed at the democratization of the tax system. . . .

For many years, the gap between the white collar . . . and the blue collar . . . in France remained one of the largest in Western Europe. . . .

During the past two decades, the salary and status gaps between blue- and white-collar employees have been narrowed. . . . Occasionally, industrial and white-collar workers discover that they have interests in common with intellectuals and students—the present and future members of the elite. . . . [b]ut such camaraderie is at best tenuous, largely because of the history of mutual distrust, the different backgrounds, and the divergent concerns of these groups. . . .

## THE EDUCATIONAL SYSTEM

. . . Since the nineteenth century, the school system in France has been public, theoretically uniform, and centralized, with the national Ministry of Education determining the educational policy and curricula at all levels, and supervising virtually all examinations. The primary schools in particular, in which attendance has been compulsory, have served as relatively efficacious agencies of republican, secular, and nationally oriented political socialization, and have prepared most pupils to find a productive place in the economy at the age of fourteen or fifteen years. The French school system was highly stratified, with the children of working class or peasant families rarely going beyond the primary school; and the bourgeois children advancing to the *lycée* in early adolescence, and thence to the university. In fact, the educational content of the *lycée*, which stressed classicism, historicism, rationalism, and formalism rather than technical or "modern" subjects, was little related to the labor market and was essentially designed for the leisure class or for those who already belonged to educated or otherwise privileged families.

In a sense, this hierarchization has extended to the structure of the French educational system. Although in theory most French *lycées* and universities are equal, certain Parisian *lycées* have been much more highly regarded than the less pretentious secondary schools in the provinces. In higher education, a distinction has been made between the ordinary universities and the specialized *grandes écoles*, such as the *Ecole Polytechnique* and the *Ecole Normale Supérieure*. These latter—most of them established in the nineteenth century—which have provided France with her intellectual and political leadership, have catered essentially to the upper-middle and the upper classes. Moreover, the clear status distinctions among the university faculty ranks . . . and between these and the student, have traditionally been rather precise and rigid, and have been a microcosm of the hierarchism of society at large.

Nevertheless, in the area of educational reforms France has been more innovative and dynamic than most other Western European countries, particularly since the advent of the Fifth Republic. In 1959, it was decided to raise the school-leaving age to sixteen by 1967 (a decision fully implemented only in 1971), and soon there was widespread agreement that secondary schooling was the right of all Frenchmen. . . . As a consequence of these reforms, an ever-increasing number of students have been acquiring some kind of academic secondary education. . . .

The pressures for university entrance created by this fact have caused serious problems for the system of higher education, which in 1974 encompassed some 800,000 students, the largest number of any Western European country. The overcrowding of lecture halls, the inadequacy of physical facilities and libraries, the impersonal relationship between the professor and the students, and above all the persistence of a university curriculum that, despite its overall excellence, has borne a constantly diminishing relationship to the labor market—all these problems demanded solution.

In the 1960s, the government began to establish additional universities, often with American-style campuses, and introduced more "technical" subjects. But these reforms were inadequate and came too late, and the clamor for a thorough overhauling of the French system of higher education figured heavily in the rebellion of May 1968. After this event, Edgar Faure, as minister of education, initiated several significant reforms, including the granting of some autonomy to universities in determining curricula; the creation of new technological colleges; the establishment of American-type academic departments (UERs); and a system of "participatory democracy" under which a university's governing personnel would in part be elected by professors, staff, and students. . . . Moreover, in the past decade, more Frenchmen have recognized that an enlarged place in the curriculum ought to be accorded to such modern subjects as economics, mathematical statistics, sociology, business management, and computer technology. . . .

It will be some time before many of the educational reforms now existing on paper are fully implemented. Despite the good intentions of politicians, the rate of expansion of university admissions has been reduced, not only because of subtle resistance by part of the traditional educational establishment, but also because of insufficient funds and the scarcity of positions for university graduates—a phenomenon observed in other industrialized countries also. In 1968, only 12 percent of the students at all universities in France were from workers' families, about one-half the proportion of such students in Britain or the United States, but higher than in West Germany, Switzerland, or the Netherlands. (Since that time, the percentage has not risen significantly in France.) In order to make access to higher education easier for a broad cross section of the population, the government had begun, in the

Fourth Republic, to grant scholarship aid . . . to students, especially from low-income families. But the stipends have often been considered insufficient. Moreover, for France as for most other advanced Western societies, there has remained the question whether hasty or piecemeal measures would provide cultural benefits on equal terms to the lower classes, or motivate them to demand such benefits, for the simple reason that workers and peasants have more pressing priorities. According to a poll conducted in 1969, 58 percent of Frenchmen do not read books, 87 percent do not go to the theater, and 78 percent have never been to a concert. Libraries are ubiquitous in France, but—as elsewhere in Western Europe—they have not been easily accessible to the working class or the peasantry. The French cultural treasure is indeed great, but the masses have been even more effectively alienated from it than from the growing economic treasure.

## THE CENTER AND THE PROVINCES

The maldistribution of the economic and cultural output of France is related to the persistent conflict between centralizing tendencies and provincialism. Since the consolidation of national power in Paris under the Bourbon kings of the seventeenth and eighteenth centuries and under Napoleon in the first decade of the nineteenth century, the provinces have declined. Yet the country is so large—by European standards—and its population, physical characteristics, and regional traditions are so diverse, that provincialism and local orientations remain significant, despite the growth of such unifying devices as radio, television, and the automobile. There are regional climatic, culinary, and linguistic differences, and there are differences with respect to the degree of economic and cultural development. . . .

Such regional differences have accounted for ideological diversities throughout France, and for the fact that the city or district . . . remains to this day the principal political base of parliamentary politicians. But the predominance of Paris is such that all provinces constitute part of a neglected backyard and a cultural and economic desert. In West Germany and Italy, several different and competing cities serve as cultural, financial, industrial, or political centers. In France there is only one significant city: Paris has the largest number of industries and controls the financial, cultural and political life of the country. . . .

The continuing dominance of Paris explains why ambitious politicians, intellectuals, and businessmen, even though they may pride themselves on their rural roots, endeavor to maintain a "presence" (i.e., an apartment or office) in the capital; and why many provincial university professors try to obtain supplementary lecture assignments in the Paris area. In order to breathe some economic and cultural life into the provinces—and incidentally to halt the excessive urban sprawl around Paris—the government has undertaken several measures. . . . But neither the economic nor the cultural decentralization attempts have been very successful. . . .

The provinces and towns of France have been hampered in their attempts at development largely because they have lacked significant powers of taxation. In recent years, the national government has allocated a greater proportion of locally collected revenues to the localities themselves, but not in sufficient amounts. There is increasing discussion of "regionalization," that is, of the devolution of more meaningful administrative powers to the regions, but it will be some time before Paris will be ready substantially to share with the provinces its political and fiscal preeminence.

## THE POSITION OF WOMEN

Nowhere is the ambiguous relationship between modernism and traditionalism illustrated better than by the role of women in France. As a Latin and predominantly Roman Catholic country, France has tended to assign to women the customary family and household roles. The Napoleonic code of 1804, under which women were legally incompetent, remained in force until 1938. Since that time, the legal and political disabilities of women have gradually been removed. In 1945, women obtained the right to vote; in 1965, married women were granted the right to open bank accounts without their husbands' express permission and to dispose of property in their own name; and subsequently, to be legal heirs. For all practical purposes, there is now legal equality of men and women.

Women have made even greater progress economically. Approximately a third of the French labor force consists of women, and the pay differential between the sexes in France, which several years ago was 9 percent, has been much lower than in Germany and Italy. . . . The entry of women into the labor market has been facilitated by the availability (especially in the Paris region) of free nursery schools for children from the age of three.

The political role of women is more difficult to assess. Traditionalism is strong enough so that women remain somewhat less than perfectly "politicized." . . . Though women account for more than half the population, they make up about two-thirds of the electoral nonparticipants. And many women who do vote are believed either to be heavily influenced by their husbands in their party preferences or to be ideologically more conservative than the latter. . . .

# 26

## British Government: The Society and the People

### A. H. Birch

In this selection, Birch examines the political attitudes and values of the British people that have played a major role in the shaping of Britain's political institutions. The overall effect of these characteristically British attitudes—which include an "almost universal acceptance of the rules of the political game," an unusual deference toward government, and a marked preference for stable governments and strong leaders—is that those in power enjoy considerably more independence and freedom from public scrutiny than do their counterparts in other European democracies.

## POLITICAL ATTITUDES AND VALUES

The British system of government is determined not only by the history and social characteristics of the country but also by the political attitudes and values of the British people. . . . However, one or two of them have played such an important part in shaping political institutions that they merit a special place in this [discussion].

The first of these is the almost universal acceptance of the rules of the political game. As was noted earlier, the British are extremely complacent about their political institutions. Most of these have a long history, and the general assumption is that they can be adapted to meet changing circumstances in the future just as they have been in the past. No important group wants to turn the country into a republic, to abolish the House of Lords, or to restrict the powers of Parliament. Minor reforms are made from time to time, such as the recent Acts enabling Life Peerages to be created and permitting hereditary peers to relinquish their titles and stand for election to the House of Commons. Other reforms are canvassed quietly in informed circles, such as the recurrent proposal . . . that the system of recruitment to the higher ranks of the civil service should be altered so as to bring in more economists and scientists. But proposals of this kind rarely become the subject of party conflict, and the central principles of the constitution are not in dispute at all.

The second point that needs to be noted is the general preference in Britain for a stable government possessing adequate powers to implement its policy. The basis of this preference is the unity and homogeneity of British society. It has been said that American society is made up of minorities, each of which wishes to preserve the power to veto government policies which it dislikes. The statement is an exaggeration, but it contains an important kernel of truth. People who feel themselves to belong to a permanent minority, whether it be ethnic or regional or economic, inevitably have reservations about the power of the majority. In Britain no sizeable group feels itself to be in this position, and people who are temporarily in a minority, in the sense that their party is out of office, are normally happy to see the government exercising a plentitude of power because they know that their turn will come next. The common attitude of the opposition is not that the government's powers should be restricted but, on the contrary, that it should be given enough rope to hang itself.

The British not only appear to like strong government (with a reservation that will be noted below), they also appear to admire strong leaders. This seems to be an enduring characteristic of the British approach to politics. In the sixteenth century the Tudor monarchs achieved popularity by resolute and often ruthless leadership. In the eighteenth century the elder Pitt was admired for his firm control of the affairs of state. In the early years of Victoria's reign Sir Robert Peel made the following comment on this topic:

> I could not admit any alteration in any of these bills. This was thought very obstinate and very presumptious; but the fact is, people like a certain degree of obstinacy and presumption in a minister. They abuse him for dictatorship and arrogance, but they like being governed.

In the twentieth century the popularity of Sir Winston Churchill suggests that attitudes have not changed.

It may be objected that these examples are all of leadership by men of the political right. However, the evidence does not suggest that there is any appreciable difference between supporters of the right and of the left in their attitudes to political leadership. Hugh Gaitskell was never so much admired by Labour supporters before 1960 as he was after he had rejected the decisions of the Labour Party's Annual Conference about defence policy and demonstrated his determination and strength by securing their reversal the following year. Harold Wilson's popularity in his first few years as party leader seems to have depended largely on the fact that he appeared to be a more powerful politician than Gaitskell had been and to have a more dominant pesonality. His success in the 1966 election, after a campaign in which his main promise was simply that he would provide strong and determined leadership, may possibly indicate the continuing relevance of Peel's remark. It is of course difficult to be confident about public attitudes on such a question, which cannot easily be measured, but certainly Wilson himself seems to share Peel's view of the matter. When John Mackintosh (a political scientist who had become a backbench Labour MP) put a list of possible cases of backbench influence on policy to his leader in mid-1967, the Prime Minister did not say—as government leaders in some other countries would have done—that he had taken account of the views of his party colleagues and the movements of public opinion they represented. On the contrary, he went through each example carefully 'to demonstrate that on no occasion was he consciously deflected from his original purpose, even over mode of presentation or timing, by any estimate of what dissident groups on his back benches might say'.

The reservation that must be made to these generalizations is that this apparent preference for a government with the power and determination to implement its decision does not mean that the British necessarily get (or would necessarily like) governments which carry through bold policies or make radical changes. In fact, many critics have observed that our governments have shown undue caution in a number of areas, notably foreign policy and economic management.

But, however one assesses the performance of British governments, the belief that they ought to have the power to provide firm leadership is of prime importance in British politics. It is one of the reasons why party discipline is accepted as desirable by politicians and public alike. It is one of the reasons, as the Liberal Party knows to its cost, why voters prefer a two-party system to a situation in which a coalition government might have to be formed. It helps to explain the general acceptance of the increase in the powers of the executive in relation to Parliament. It is not too much to say that British politics can only be understood if this public attitude towards leadership is appreciated.

A third characteristic of British attitudes towards government, which perhaps follows from the second, is that although British voters take a fairly keen interest in general elections they do not expect to exercise much control over politicians and administrators between elections. . . . It is not expected that the actions of MPs will be controlled or even closely influenced by the views of their constituents, and the rules of Parliamentary privilege are carefully designed to protect the independence of MPs from outside control. In Whitehall, civil servants are permitted to conduct their affairs in seclusion from the glare of publicity, and their anonymity is protected by press and politicians alike. Ministers are held accountable to Parliament at Question Time and in debate, but have not been expected to submit themselves either to detailed cross-examination by a specialized committee or to the ordeal of a weekly press conference. The overall effect of this general British attitude towards politics is that those responsible for governing the country enjoy a greater independence of public scrutiny and control than is enjoyed by their counterparts in the United States and a number of other Western democracies.

# 27

## The Social Context of British Politics

### R. M. Punnett

R.M. Punnett examines the various criteria that determine social class—family background, education, occupation, and wealth—in this discussion of politics in Great Britain. Arguing that social class distinctions are more significant than national, regional, religious, or ethnic variations in creating a fundamental disunity in British society, he offers the results of a recent survey that showed Britain to be far more class-conscious than most other Anglo-Saxon countries.

. . . Britain is often said to be a homogeneous nation, a united and cohesive unit in geographical, ethnic, religious, economic, and social terms. This is generally applied in a comparative sense, with the implication being that Britain is more homogeneous than most other countries. It is argued that such divisions as do exist in British society are of a minor nature, and that there is no equivalent in Britain to the racial divisions of the USA, the national or ethnic divisions of Canada and Belgium, the religious and regional divisions of France and Western Germany, or the extremes of wealth and poverty that are to be found in Italy and Spain. To place too great an emphasis on British homogeneity, however, is to over-simplify the nature of British society. . . . [N]ational, regional, religious, and ethnic variations *do* exist within the United Kingdom and are an essential part of some political questions. More important than any of these factors, however, distinctions of social class represent a fundamental disunity in British society, in many ways as significant as the regional, ethnic, or religious factors that dominate society and politics in other countries. Comparative surveys have revealed that Britain is much more class-conscious than similar Anglo-Saxon communities like the USA, Australia, and Canada. . . .

It is sometimes argued that class stratification in Britain is a national one, cutting across regional boundaries and thus helping to break down any tendencies towards regionalism. Insofar as they do this, however, class factors merely replace one form of national division for another, and thereby place an essential limitation on any notion of British homogeneity. Thus all of the factors involved in presenting a background to British politics, considerations of social class are probably the most significant of all. The various criteria that determine class groupings are essentially vague, but family background, education, occupation, and wealth are probably the main factors.

## FAMILY BACKGROUND AND EDUCATION

Despite the fact that mobility between the social classes from one generation to another has increased since the principle of free and compulsory secondary education was established, family background remains fundamentally important in determining social class. Occupation and wealth to a considerable extent are determined by education, which in its turn is determined to a large extent by family background. The earliest school leavers, in the main, become manual workers, those who stay on at school beyond the age of 15 tend to move into white collar and managerial jobs, while those with the most exclusive education generally enter the professions or the business world. As well as any general tendency there may be for middle-class parents to produce children with a higher academic ability than children of working-class parents, the educational system contains certain inequalities which help to consolidate established class distinctions. In the first place, a clear distinction emerges between the state schools, which cater for the mass of the population, and the independent public schools which provide a boarding-school education for a very small and exclusive section of the population (some 3%). This is mirrored even among the public schools themselves, and there is a clear stratification ranging from the lesser public schools to the top . . . [s]chools, with Eton, Harrow, and Winchester generally acknowledged as the top three. As well as seeking to produce an educational elite by providing excellent teaching facilities, the best public schools encourage the self-perpetuation of a social elite through their emphasis on the importance of 'character building', leadership training, and social education.

Within the state educational system a stratification does not appear at a primary level, where all children attend comprehensive infant and junior schools up to the age of 11 (or 12 in Scotland, where a separate system exists). At a secondary level, however, in many local educational authorities in England and Wales, a clear distinction still emerges between the 25% or so of the children who are allocated to grammar schools on the basis of the 'eleven plus' examination and the bulk of the children who attend secondary modern or technical schools. Over the past ten years there has been a big increase in the number of comprehensive secondary schools, which provide all types of secondary education for all levels of ability, and in 1965 the Labour Government announced plans for a rapid extension of the principle of comprehensive secondary education. With the change of Government in 1970, however, this process . . . slowed down. One of the claims advanced for comprehensive secondary schools is that they . . . remove some of the divisions within society which are partly created by the segregation of children at the age of 11 into strict educational categories. Despite the development of comprehensive schools, however, only about 15% of children stay on at school beyond the age of 15, and of these the vast majority tend to be from middle-class homes.

To some extent these educational distinctions are continued at a University level, for although there are some forty Universities in Britain, Oxford and Cambridge Universities are accorded the greatest prestige and status, both in an academic and a social sense. They are theoretically open to any student with the necessary academic qualifications, but the close link that has long existed between Oxbridge and the public schools, and which is not based entirely on academic considerations, means that the upper and middle-class section of society predominates at the two senior Universities. To some extent the upper-middle-class and public school associations of Oxford and Cambridge tends to make the children of working-class parents look to the provincial Universities for the completion of their education, thereby emphasizing further the social divisions within the education system.

In an attempt to develop a more egalitarian and more modern University system a number of new Universities were created in the nineteen-sixties, and a number of existing technological institutions were expanded and given University status. This has done something to meet the educational needs of the increased population (particularly the immediate post-war population 'bulge'), and to deal with the needs of the technological age. The problem remains, however, of the loss by Britain of many good graduates through the 'brain-drain' to the USA and other English-speaking countries. This factor, particularly in the technological sphere, represents something of a threat to Britain's future educational and industrial development.

## OCCUPATION AND WEALTH

A simple division of the community into two broad groups of middle class and working class is perhaps adequate for broad generalization, but is too vague for a detailed examination of British society. In the 1961 Census seventeen socio-economic groups were distinguished, and, excluding the armed forces, these can be simplified into three main categories to distinguish the manual groups, the non-manual groups, and the professional, managerial, and proprietorial groups. Although recent years have seen a big increase in the number of non-manual workers at the expense of the manual workers, the numerical supremacy of the manual workers is pronounced, and undoubtedly will remain for many decades.

Britain no longer exhibits the sharp inequalities of wealth and poverty that were to be found in the nineteenth century, and which are to be found today in many western countries. Industrial expansion, and the development of the welfare state and of taxation policies designed to some extent to redistribute wealth, have combined to raise general living standards and eradicate the worst poverty. The general rise in prosperity, however, has not been shared equally by all sections of the community or by all regions of the country. . . . Even this factor takes no account of accumulated wealth, and it has been estimated that as much as a quarter of the personal wealth in Britain is owned by 0.5% of the population. In social terms, many of the harsh consequences of the industrial revolution are still apparent in the slums of the major British cities. These factors are essential limitations on any broad view of Britain as a generally prosperous and egalitarian community. While in economic terms the various sections of the community may be coming closer together, this is much less the case in social terms. A well-paid car worker in Coventry, for example, may in terms of income be in much the same category as a young doctor, but he remains in a very different social category. Thus with regard to occupations and wealth the main consideration in determining social class is not so much the amount of wealth, but rather how the wealth was acquired, just as with education it is the type of school and University that is significant as well as the level of academic attainment.

Writing in 1867, Walter Bagehot presented a picture of British society as one that was essentially deferential in its attitudes towards the Monarchy, the Peerage, and the trappings of society. Indeed he argued that the secret of the constitution was that real power lay with the 'efficient' parts of the Constitution, chiefly the Prime Minister and his Cabinet colleagues, while the Monarchy and the other 'dignified' elements of the Constitution served to mesmerize the mass of the population into a respect for the system as a whole. Thus he claimed that:

In fact, the mass of the English people yield a deference rather to something else rather than to their rulers. They defer to what we may call the theatrical show of society. . .

In many respects Bagehot's interpretation of the British people as being essentially deferential remains valid today. Feelings of deference today, however, are directed not so much towards the Monarchy, the Peerage, or the dignified parts of the Constitution, as towards the vague concept of a social elite which is based on the public schools, but which in its broadest sense embraces Oxbridge, the 'officer class', and the top levels of the business and professional worlds. In the party political context this deference has extended particularly towards the Conservative Party, because the composition of the leadership of the party is based to such a great extent on this social elite. . . . [I]t may be noted here that to a considerable extent the electoral success of the Conservatives in this century can be attributed to the deferential attitude of a large section of the electorate towards the party.

Class-consciousness in social and political attitudes, a preoccupation with pageantry and with past historical greatness, and the retention of many once powerful but now largely symbolic political and social institutions, are all undoubted features of modern Britain which help to strengthen the impression of a deferential, passive, and largely politically inactive community which is content to be led by a small, select, and self-perpetuating elite. This interpretation of the relationship between a social elite and the political system thus echoes the view that Bagehot presented, and applauded, of political power in Britain lying with an elite who exercise their authority behind the shield of the 'theatrical show of society'. Unlike Bagehot, however, the modern writers who present this picture generally deplore the situation that they describe. . . .

# Unit VIII

# The Economic Scene

Between 1960 and 1973, Western Europe along with the rest of the world enjoyed a period of unprecedented prosperity. In almost every Western European country, real national product as well as output per capita increased at rates never before equaled, although some countries enjoyed a higher growth rate than others. This prosperity came to an abrupt end in 1973, however, when the quadrupling of the price of oil by the OPEC cartel triggered a reversal in Western Europe's economic climate and set off an international economic crisis whose repercussions are still being felt today.

From 1973 on, every Western European country except Norway suffered a precipitous decline in its growth rate. Indeed, in nearly all of them the annual growth of real product between 1973 and 1980 was less than half of what it was between 1960 and 1973. In addition to the decline in growth rates, the post-1973 period was also characterized by an acceleration of inflation and an increase in unemployment. In the EEC countries* as a whole, unemployment rose an average of 11.6 percent each year from 1973 to 1980, and inflation, as measured by consumer prices, rose an average of 10.7 percent during the same period.

The triple scourge of declining growth rates, high unemployment, and rising prices posed a serious threat to all the Western European governments. Their efforts to reduce unemployment had only exacerbated the inflation problem while their policies to curb inflation had invariably worsened

---

*The EEC countries (European Economic Community or "Common Market") include France, West Germany, Italy, Denmark, Belgium, Holland, Ireland, Britain, Luxembourg, and Greece.

the unemployment situation. Inevitably, it seemed to many that only a drastic change would offer any promise of reversing the downward trend. Consequently, many of Western Europe's predominantly left-of-center administrations were turned out of office in the late 1970s in order that conservative governments could assume power and be given a chance to apply their solutions. With the exception of France and a handful of other countries in which socialist governments came into power, the countries of Western Europe now saw conservative strategies as the most viable means of resolving their economic problems. There were fundamental differences between the approaches proposed by the socialists and the conservatives. Whereas the parties on the left gave highest priority to combatting unemployment and increasing the role of government in the economic sector, those on the right regarded inflation as the greater threat and tended to view government as part of the problem rather than the solution.

The table that opens this unit, "Economic Trends," provides a statistical overview of the changing economic scene in Western Europe between 1960 and 1980. The reading selections that follow focus on Margaret Thatcher's program for Great Britain and that of François Mitterrand for France—for these most clearly illustrate the contrast between the strategies adopted by the parties on the right and those adopted by the parties on the left. Through the experiences of these two countries, this unit describes the conditions and constraints typical of Western Europe as a whole and shows the opposite ends of the spectrum of political responses European governments typically employ.

In his "Speech Introducing the 1979 Budget Resolution," Geoffrey Howe, who served as Britain's chancellor of the exchequer from 1979 to 1983, outlines the economic program implemented by Margaret Thatcher's Conservative government in 1979. He describes the various budget proposals designed to provide the private sector with incentives to increase productivity and explains why these are central to Britain's overall strategy for reversing the country's economic decline. Steven Rattner presents a different perspective on the Thatcher government's policies in "Report Card on Thatcherism." Tracing changes in public attitudes toward

Thatcher's austere economic program, Rattner points out that despite the hardships Britons have been forced to endure, the majority believe that Thatcher's approach is "not only good economics but good politics." He goes on to discuss the implications of these attitudes for party politics in Britain and raises some interesting questions about their potential long-term social effects.

The authors of "France: New Government, New Strategy," describe the Socialist party's initial program for combatting inflation and unemployment in France in the early 1980s. In "Thorns Among the Roses: A Year of the Socialist Experiment in France," Janice McCormick assesses the policies pursued by the Mitterrand government during its first year in office. McCormick shows how Mitterand's early expansionary policies and tax reforms, all designed to reduce unemployment and improve the distribution of income, greatly increased the role of government in the private sector and quickly led to further deterioration in economic conditions. The following year the French government imposed a series of austerity measures in response to this situation. These are outlined in the 1983 "Ten-Point Program of Action" to restore the French balance of trade, the final reading in this unit.

# 28

# Economic Trends

## Organisation for
## Economic Co-operation and Development

**Average Annual Percentage Rates of Change for Following Periods:**
**1960–1967, 1967–1973, 1973–1980, 1960–1980**

| | Real gross Domestic product (GDP) | | | | Real GDP per capita | | | |
|---|---|---|---|---|---|---|---|---|
| | 67/60 | 73/67 | 80/73 | 80/60 | 67/60 | 73/67 | 80/73 | 80/60 |
| United States .......... | 4.6 | 3.6 | 2.3 | 3.5 | 3.2 | 2.5 | 1.3 | 2.3 |
| Japan ................ | 10.2 | 9.5 | 3.7 | 7.7 | 9.1 | 8.0 | 2.7 | 6.5 |
| Germany .............. | 3.9 | 5.3 | 2.3 | 3.7 | 2.9 | 4.5 | 2.4 | 3.2 |
| France ............... | 5.5 | 5.6 | 2.8 | 4.6 | 4.3 | 4.7 | 2.4 | 3.8 |
| United Kingdom ....... | 2.9 | 3.4 | 0.9 | 2.3 | 2.3 | 3.0 | 0.9 | 2.0 |
| Italy ................. | 5.6 | 5.0 | 2.8 | 4.4 | 4.9 | 4.2 | 2.2 | 3.7 |
| Canada .............. | 5.6 | 5.6 | 2.8 | 4.6 | 3.6 | 4.2 | 1.6 | 3.1 |
| **Total of above countries** | 5.1 | 4.9 | 2.5 | 4.1 | 3.9 | 3.9 | 1.8 | 3.2 |
| Austria ............... | 4.3 | 5.7 | 3.0 | 4.2 | 3.7 | 5.2 | 3.0 | 3.9 |
| Belgium .............. | 4.6 | 5.4 | 2.4 | 4.1 | 3.9 | 5.1 | 2.2 | 3.7 |
| Denmark ............. | 4.7 | 4.0 | 1.6 | 3.4 | 3.9 | 3.4 | 1.3 | 2.8 |
| Finland ............... | 4.1 | 6.0 | 2.7 | 4.2 | 3.5 | 5.7 | 2.4 | 3.8 |
| Greece ..... ......... | 7.4 | 8.0 | 3.4 | 6.1 | 6.7 | 7.5 | 2.3 | 5.4 |
| Iceland ............... | 5.6 | 5.2 | 3.3 | 4.7 | 3.8 | 4.1 | 2.2 | 3.3 |
| Ireland ............... | 3.6 | 5.3 | 3.7 | 4.2 | 3.3 | 4.3 | 2.1 | 3.2 |
| Luxembourg ........... | 3.0 | 6.1 | 1.3 | 3.3 | 2.0 | 5.2 | 0.8 | 2.5 |
| Netherlands ........... | 4.6 | 5.5 | 2.2 | 4.0 | 3.2 | 4.4 | 1.4 | 2.9 |
| Norway ............... | 4.7 | 3.8 | 4.7 | 4.4 | 3.9 | 3.0 | 4.2 | 3.7 |
| Portugal ............. | 6.2 | 7.6 | 3.2 | 5.6 | 6.1 | 7.9 | 1.7 | 5.1 |
| Spain ................ | 7.7 | 6.8 | 2.4 | 5.5 | 6.5 | 5.6 | 1.4 | 4.4 |
| Sweden .............. | 4.5 | 3.6 | 1.8 | 3.3 | 3.7 | 3.1 | 1.5 | 2.7 |
| Switzerland ........... | 4.5 | 4.3 | 0.3 | 3.0 | 2.7 | 3.3 | 0.4 | 2.1 |
| Turkey ............... | 5.7 | 6.1 | 4.5 | 5.4 | 3.1 | 3.5 | 2.1 | 2.9 |
| **Smaller European** | 5.1 | 5.4 | 2.4 | 4.2 | 3.9 | 4.2 | 1.3 | 3.0 |
| Australia .............. | 4.9 | 5.4 | 2.5 | 4.2 | 2.8 | 3.2 | 1.2 | 2.4 |
| New Zealand .......... | 3.9 | 4.2 | 1.3 | 3.1 | 1.9 | 2.7 | 0.6 | 1.7 |
| **Total smaller** | 5.1 | 5.3 | 2.4 | 4.2 | 3.7 | 4.1 | 1.2 | 2.9 |
| Total EEC ............. | 4.4 | 5.0 | 2.3 | 3.8 | 3.5 | 4.3 | 2.0 | 3.2 |
| Total OECD-Europe ...... | 4.6 | 5.1 | 2.3 | 3.9 | 3.5 | 4.2 | 1.7 | 3.1 |
| Total OECD *less* USA .... | 5.4 | 5.9 | 2.6 | 4.6 | 4.3 | 4.8 | 1.9 | 3.6 |
| Total OECD ........... | 5.1 | 4.9 | 2.5 | 4.1 | 3.9 | 3.9 | 1.7 | 3.1 |

*Source:* Organisation for Economic Co-operation and Development, *Historical Statistics, 1960–1980.*

| Unemployment | | | | Consumer price indices | | | | |
|---|---|---|---|---|---|---|---|---|
| $\frac{87}{60}$ | $\frac{73}{67}$ | $\frac{80}{73}$ | $\frac{80}{60}$ | $\frac{67}{60}$ | $\frac{73}{67}$ | $\frac{80}{73}$ | $\frac{80}{60}$ | |
| − 3.6 | 6.6 | 8.3 | 3.5 | 1.7 | 4.9 | 9.2 | 5.3 | United States |
| − 2.5 | 1.0 | 7.9 | 2.1 | 5.7 | 6.7 | 9.7 | 7.4 | Japan |
| 7.8 | − 8.3 | 18.4 | 6.1 | 2.7 | 4.3 | 4.8 | 3.9 | Germany |
| 6.2 | 7.9 | 14.1 | 9.4 | 3.5 | 5.9 | 11.1 | 6.8 | France |
| 6.4 | 2.3 | 16.4 | 8.5 | 3.4 | 7.0 | 16.0 | 8.8 | United Kingdom |
| − 1.3 | 2.8 | 3.8 | 1.7 | 4.4 | 5.0 | 17.0 | 8.6 | Italy |
| − 4.8 | 9.7 | 7.7 | 3.7 | 2.1 | 4.5 | 9.3 | 5.3 | Canada |
| − 1.6 | 4.6 | 9.2 | 3.9 | 2.5 | 5.3 | 9.8 | 5.8 | **Total of above countries** |
| − 4.3 | − 9.9 | 8.0 | − 2.0 | 3.7 | 4.8 | 6.3 | 4.9 | Austria |
| − 3.4 | − 0.7 | 19.8 | 5.0 | 2.8 | 4.5 | 8.1 | 5.2 | Belgium |
| − 5.0 | − 4.7 | — | — | 5.8 | 6.7 | 11.0 | 7.9 | Denmark |
| 10.7 | − 3.8 | 11.9 | 6.5 | 5.1 | 6.4 | 12.5 | 8.0 | Finland |
| − 2.4 | − 16.0 | 7.5 | − 3.5 | 2.1 | 4.7 | 17.3 | 8.0 | Greece |
| — | — | — | — | 9.8 | 14.5 | 42.8 | 21.9 | Iceland |
| − 1.7 | 2.8 | 1.6 | 0.8 | 3.9 | 8.2 | 15.4 | 9.1 | Ireland |
| — | — | — | — | 2.3 | 4.2 | 7.2 | 4.6 | Luxembourg |
| 14.5 | 6.6 | 12.3 | 11.3 | 3.6 | 6.3 | 7.1 | 5.6 | Netherlands |
| − 6.0 | — | 3.5 | — | 4.0 | 6.3 | 9.0 | 6.4 | Norway |
| — | — | — | — | 3.0 | 7.7 | 22.6 | 11.0 | Portugal |
| 4.0 | − 1.6 | 25.3 | 9.2 | 6.8 | 6.8 | 17.9 | 10.6 | Spain |
| 3.5 | 3.4 | − 1.8 | 1.6 | 4.1 | 5.3 | 10.3 | 6.6 | Sweden |
| — | — | — | — | 3.6 | 5.1 | 4.0 | 4.2 | Switzerland |
| 2.3 | 5.1 | 4.0 | 3.7 | 5.9 | 10.9 | 41.6 | 18.9 | Turkey |
| 1.9 | 2.3 | 10.1 | 4.8 | 4.3 | 6.2 | 13.4 | 8.0 | **Smaller European** |
| 7.0 | 6.2 | 16.7 | 10.1 | 2.2 | 5.1 | 11.9 | 6.4 | Australia |
| — | — | — | — | 3.2 | 6.9 | 14.3 | 8.0 | New Zealand |
| 2.0 | 2.5 | 10.5 | 5.1 | 3.5 | 6.1 | 13.2 | 7.6 | **Total smaller** |
| 1.9 | 1.2 | 11.6 | 5.0 | 3.4 | 5.5 | 10.7 | 6.5 | Total EEC |
| 2.2 | 2.1 | 10.6 | 5.0 | 3.7 | 5.7 | 11.8 | 7.1 | Total OECD-Europe |
| 1.2 | 2.5 | 10.3 | 4.7 | 3.7 | 5.8 | 11.2 | 6.9 | Total OECD *less* USA |
| − 0.6 | 4.0 | 9.6 | 4.2 | 2.7 | 5.4 | 10.4 | 6.1 | Total OECD |

# 29

## Speech Introducing the 1979 Budget Resolution

Sir Geoffrey Howe

Geoffrey Howe served as Britain's chancellor of the exchequer (secretary of the treasury) under Margaret Thatcher from 1979 to 1983 and then became foreign minister following the Conservative government's landslide victory in the 1983 general election. In these excerpts from a speech delivered to the House of Commons shortly after the Conservative party took office in 1979, Howe describes Britain's economic problems and outlines the new administration's strategies for solving them.

. . . Only a quarter of a century ago—within the memory of almost every Member of this House—the people of the United Kingdom enjoyed higher living standards than the citizens of any of the larger countries of Europe. Amongst the free nations of the world, Britain was then second only to the United States in economic strength.

It is not so today. For example, France and Germany's combined share of world trade in manufactured goods, which in 1954 was almost the same as Britain's alone, is now more than three times as large as ours. The French people now produce half as much again as we do. The Germans produce more than twice as much, and they are moving further ahead all the time. . . .

### INTERNATIONAL BACKGROUND

Of course, as inhabitants of a country that has always been deeply involved in the international economy, we pay a great deal of attention to events outside our own country. But it would be very dangerous if preoccupation with this or that world crisis—the oil crisis, the dollar crisis or whatever—led us to believe that our economic troubles could be blamed mainly on the outside world. The truth is that our troubles are very largely home-made. If we tackle them ourselves, we can pull our own economy round, even in a world of slow growth. . . .

. . . [P]rogress internationally . . . will not cure the deep-seated weaknesses of our own domestic economy. Nor will North Sea oil. Growing production will certainly put us in a better position than other countries, without oil of their own, but it must not be allowed to conceal the grim truth about what has been happening to the balance of our own trade, particularly in manufactured goods.

North Sea oil will itself do nothing to solve the problems on the supply side of our economy. Nor will it check inflation. Indeed, in some respects it may actually make matters worse, unless we correct some other aspects of policy which are at present working in the wrong direction.

## THE CAUSES OF DECLINE

. . . [W]e find ourselves, yet again, asking the question: how are we to check, and then reverse, the long decline? . . .

. . . The [previous] Government . . . consistently behaved as if it were possible for the Government to manage, indeed to plan, the economy, so as to promote efficiency and growth. . . . In five years [the Government] introduced no fewer than 15 Budgets and economic "packages", and financed a wide range of policies in the name of "the regeneration of industry".

But at the end of five years the right hon. Gentleman must ask himself, to what avail? Has th[is] industrial strategy, as he conceived it, really transformed the outlook for British industry? Are we not driven to the conclusion that the notions of demand management, expanding public spending and "fine tuning" of the economy have now been tested almost to destruction? . . .

. . . [T]he poor performance of the Bristish economy in recent years has not been due to a shortage of demand. We are suffering from a growing series of failures on the supply side of the economy.

## A NEW BEGINNING

It is our belief that many of these failures are themselves the result of actions and interventions by the Government themselves—laws that stand in the way of change and stifle enterprise; and, as important as anything, a structure of taxation that might have been designed to discourage innovation and punish success. . . .

That is why the British people are convinced—as we believe—that it is time for a new beginning. Our strategy to check Britain's long-term economic decline, which has gathered pace in the last five years, is based on four principles.

We need to strengthen incentives, by allowing people to keep more of what they earn, so that hard work, talent and ability are properly rewarded. We need to enlarge freedom of choice for the individual by reducing the role of the State. We need to reduce the burden of financing the public sector so as to leave room for commerce and industry to prosper. We need to ensure, so far as possible, that those who take part in collective bargaining understand the consequences of their actions. . . .

## INFLATION

But those changes will not themselves be enough unless we also squeeze inflation out of the system. It is crucially important to re-establish sound money. We intend to achieve this through firm monetary discipline and fiscal policies consistent with that, including strict control over public expenditure.

Financial responsibility on the part of Government must be supported by responsibility elsewhere. People must understand and accept that the only basis for real increases in wages and salaries is an increase in national production. . . .

## MONETARY POLICY

As I have already observed, my predecessor was undoubtedly right to adopt a system of monetary targets. But his other policies were seldom consistent with his own monetary objectives. Thus, although monetary growth in 1978–79 as a whole was just within the target range of 8 per cent. to 12 per cent., it was growing in the second half of the year at an annual rate of almost 13 percent. . . .

It is now clear [, moreover,] that the public expenditure policies which we inherited would have made it quite impossible to meet the right hon. Gentleman's 8 per cent. to 12 per cent. target without a further savage squeeze on the private sector, involving not just higher interest rates but also a sharp increase in the total tax burden. Not for the first time, the levels of public spending and borrowing which he permitted were far too high to be compatible with his own monetary targets. Reluctantly, I shall myself be obliged to take painful action to correct that mistake.

We are committed to the progressive reduction of the rate of growth of the money supply. . . .

Equally important, I intend to improve the way in which the monetary target is achieved. We need to rely less on curbing the private sector, and put more emphasis on fiscal restraint and economy by the public sector. That requires, as a first step, a significant reduction in the public sector borrowing requirement. . . .

. . . I intend to reduce the public sector's financial needs enough to make it possible to achieve my monetary target with less restraint on the private sector. . . .

## EXCHANGE CONTROL

I come now to. . . the question of exchange control. . . . This is . . . an appropriate time to start dismantling our apparatus of controls on outward capital flows. Our present regime is more restrictive than that of any other major industrialised country. There is an overwhelming case, in this context as in others, for giving both companies and individuals wider freedom of choice. This should reduce the distortions and costs which controls are bound to impose on economic decisions. . . .

We intend to move one step at a time. In the initial stage, the emphasis will be on direct investment overseas. . . . In response to Labour Members, I must say that this greater freedom in the financing of direct investment abroad does not, as is sometimes feared, . . . threaten jobs in the United Kingdom. The weight of evidence is that overseas investment generally strengthens our position in world export markets to the benefit of output and jobs in this country. . . .

I have also decided that there should be some immediate easement of the controls affecting individuals. I am, therefore, making significant relaxations in the rules concerning travel and emigration allowances, overseas property, and cash gifts and payments to dependants. . . .

As time goes by, I intend to take further steps in the progressive dismantling of exchange control. . . .

## PUBLIC EXPENDITURE

In order to reduce the borrowing requirement and the burden of direct taxation, we must make savings in public spending and roll back the boundaries of the public sector. We are totally committed to improving standards in the public services. But that can be achieved only if the economy is strong in the first place. So that will be our first priority. Finance must determine expenditure, not expenditure finance. Substantial reductions in expenditure can, and will, be made in the remainder of this financial year. . . .

[The Chancellor of the Exchequer proposed the following economy measures:

a. limiting pay increases for public servants to those situations where "substantial offsetting economies can be found";
b. a reduction in expenditures for industrial and employment subsidies;
c. a 3 per cent. reduction in manpower costs by all governmental departments;
d. a reduction in expenditures for environmental programs and for energy development programs;
e. an increase in prescription and dental charges for those using the National Health services;
f. a reduction in the central government's expenditures for science and education programs.

Simultaneously, the Chancellor proposed an increase in expenditures for defense, a smaller increase for pensions, and the sale of state-owned assets to the private sector. This latter proposal was the beginning of a process which was described by the Government as the "privatization" of the British economy.]

The need for substantial economies applies equally to local authority expenditure, where the Government's contribution is made through the rate support grant. . . .

### INDIRECT TAXATION

We made it clear in our manifesto that we intended to switch some of the tax burden from taxes on earnings to taxes on spending. This is the only way that we can restore incentives and make it more worth while to work and, at the same time, increase the freedom of choice of the individual. We must make a start now. . . .

. . . There are many cogent arguments at this stage in favour of value added tax. . . .

. . . I propose, therefore, that as from next Monday VAT should be charged at a new unified rate of 15 per cent. . . .

[The Chancellor proposed a 15 per cent Value Added Tax as the most efficacious way to supplement government revenues and permit a reduction in income taxes.]

I fully realise that this increase in value added tax will result in a rise in prices —in fact, a rise of about 3½ per cent in the retail price index. This is, of course, a once-for-all effect. But there never will be a time when it is easy to effect the switch from direct to indirect taxes, and the present moment is clearly no exception. That much-needed reform has been postponed too long already. . . .

## SOCIAL SECURITY PAYMENTS

Our social security system has become far too complicated and it sometimes acts to reduce the incentive to work. . . . We are therefore studying a number of aspects of the social security system to see what can be done to simplify it. My right hon. Friend the Secretary of State is also putting in hand urgent measures to tighten up on abuse and fraud. . . .

We made it clear in our manifesto that we were determined to make the taxation of capital simpler and less oppressive. The objection to capital gains tax in its present form is that most of the yield comes from paper gains arising from inflation. The tax is, therefore, a capricious and sometimes savage levy on the capital itself. The capital transfer tax, . . . is oppressive, harmful to business and a real deterrent to initiative and enterprise. It is perfectly natural that people should want to build up capital of their own and pass it on to their children, and this is particularly true of the small business proprietor. . . .

I now turn to the taxation of profits. A vigorous, profitable and expanding company sector is essential if we are to rebuild this country's prosperity. Profitability has dropped sharply in recent years and the rate of return on capital employed is now far too low, especially in manufacturing industry.

Without higher profits we shall not see the new investment and jobs which are so urgently needed. Achieving those profits is very largely the task of management and workpeople. The Government can help or hinder them, and this is no time to add to the difficulties that they face by raising taxes on profits still further. . . .

. . .[W]hile the reductions I propose are substantial, they are no more than the circumstances require. They will still in general leave people in the top income groups more highly taxed than people in corresponding positions in other industrialised countries. We have to compete with such countries, not only in the sale of goods and services but in attracting and retaining the talent required to run our industry efficiently and profitably and thereby provide the employment opportunities that our people so desperately need.

We have over the years spent far too much time and effort trying to "level down". This is no good to anybody. It is much more important to have a successful and prosperous society, and we cannot have a successful and prosperous society without successful and prosperous individuals. . . .

The . . . reductions in the burden of income tax, which are as substantial as they are unprecedented, mean that wage and salary earners will have more money in their pockets to buy the goods and services they help to produce. . . . But we have done everything we can to ensure that every family in the land will have more money coming in to pay the increased bills. What is more, the choice of the way they spend their income will rest increasingly with people, and not with the Government. . . .

I have stressed the urgent need for new policies to reverse the decline of the British economy. These policies start with our conviction that it is people and not Governments who create prosperity. This Budget seeks to reduce the role of Government. Government will spend less, Government will borrow less. This will lay the foundations for controlling inflation. . . .

That underlines the other half of the Budget strategy. It is not a give-away Budget. Indeed, it is not in the power of the Government to give anything away. However, it is an opportunity Budget. The shift from taxes on income to taxes on spending will widen choice and improve incentives. Above all, it will enlarge opportunities.

The Budget is designed to give the British people a greater opportunity than they have had for years to win a higher standard of living—for their country and for their families as well as for themselves. I dare to believe they will respond to the opportunity that I have offered them today. . . .

# 30

# Report Card on Thatcherism

Steven Rattner

In this analysis, which appeared in *The New York Times* in May 1983, just before Margaret Thatcher called for the national election which her party went on to win the following month, Rattner assesses the Thatcher government's strategies for coping with the country's economic difficulties and speculates about their long-term effects.

In the "Black Country," the tortured landscape between Birmingham and Wolverhampton that was once at the heart of Britain's industrial prowess, the sense of industrial desolation is overpowering. Abandoned factories with broken windows stare blindly down the narrow streets. Hulking buildings, where complex metalwork was proudly fabricated for a hundred years, have been reduced to warehouses. The 19th-century canal system still dissects the area, but the water is fetid. Many local craftsmen are unemployed, and some middle-aged workers may never find jobs again.

Four years after the launching of Prime Minister Margaret Thatcher's "economic revolution," this blighted region illustrates some of the consequences of her policies of austerity, naked competition and less government. Her conservative reforms have amounted to "a more drastic program than Reaganomics . . . a much bigger change than we've been offered in 20 years," in the view of Anthony Sampson, the well-known chronicler of the British system. One of the results has been a recession far worse than anything predicted when Mrs. Thatcher began her work. The Black Country has been hit particularly hard by Britain's long, dark recession, but the difficulties have reached virtually every corner of the country.

Yet any assessment of the country's economic state must take account of an astonishing paradox. Despite the shocks suffered by the economy since Mrs. Thatcher's election in 1979—unemployment up from 5 percent to 13.6 percent, manufacturing output, at its lowest point, down by more than 15 percent—the Prime Minister is widely popular in the nation at large. Although her standing has dipped from the peak it reached last summer, after the successful Falkland campaign, a recent poll found that her Conservative Government enjoys the support of 43 percent of the public, compared to 34 percent for the Labor Party and 22 percent for the Social Democratic-Liberal Alliance.

Mrs. Thatcher, in fact, may seek to exploit her popularity in an early vote. She need not call a national election for another year, but there is increasing speculation that she will call it for October or perhaps even June. And, in full awareness of the approaching political test, her Chancellor of the Exchequer, Sir Geoffrey Howe, has unveiled a budget for the new fiscal year that makes minimal concessions to those among the voters who have been hurt by the Thatcher policies. In all essential respects, the austerity program has been reaffirmed, without any adverse consequences for the Prime Minister's popularity.

For all the dislocations of the last four years, a majority of Britons today seem to believe that a dose of Mrs. Thatcher's harsh economic medicine has been necessary. As The Guardian's political columnist Peter Jenkins put it, "People who can find little to applaud in her Government's economic record may, nevertheless, be ready to concede that she is trying to go in the right direction, or, at least, that the old remedies contain little practical promise." Something like her program has to be tried, most Britons have come to believe, if the country is to survive as a leading industrial nation capable of providing its citizens with a rising standard of living.

Her political fortunes have been helped, as well, by the fact that her economic policies have yielded several significant successes. Prices rose by only 5 percent in 1982, the smallest annual increase since 1970 and far below the 12 percent average annual increases during the three-year period before her election. Interest rates have fallen dramatically; mortgage rates are down to 10.6 percent. Government spending is at last coming under control; the deficit has fallen sharply. There have been no miracles in economic growth, but the British economy has bounced back a bit from the low point of early 1981, and a recent survey found British businessmen more optimistic than at any time since 1979. Although business bankruptcies are at an all-time high, so are new business start-ups, a signal that the desired restructuring may be under way.

In the most dazzling turnabout, productivity, long the bane of the British economy, has begun to improve sharply. Efficiency in industry increased by 14.5 percent in 1981–82, better than in almost any other industrialized country. Wage settlements, particularly in troubled industries such as steel and automobiles, have moderated, and the number of strikes has decreased.

At the same time, enormous challenges lie ahead. Britain is still a stunningly inefficient country. A 1982 study by the National Institute for Economic and Social Research found that British manufacturing productivity was two-thirds that of West Germany's and still further behind the United States. At British Steel, for example, productivity doubled over the last two and a half years but remains significantly below that of the company's Japanese competitors. . . .

In the late 19th century, an American consul general stationed in Birmingham wrote that the Black Country "cannot be matched, for vast and varied production, by any other space of equal radius on the surface of the globe. . . ."

In that era, Britain dominated the world economy in a way no country had ever done before, or has done since. Britain's overseas investment was greater than those of France, Germany, the Netherlands and the United States combined. The British owned most of the world's shipping and provided more than 25 percent of the world's trade in manufactured goods. Per capita income was more than double the figure for Germany.

The reasons for Britain's decline in comparison to other large industrial countries are less clear; the causes usually cited are the complacency of prosperity, the debilitating effects of two world wars, the loss of empire, the emergence of more intense world competition, the class system and the inflexibility of the country's economic structure, with its combative labor relations. Whatever the reasons, slip Britain did, particularly in the 1970s. By the time of Mrs. Thatcher's arrival, the British economy was significantly smaller than West Germany's and France's and not much larger than Italy's.

With decline came an evident dowdiness. In their dress and their housing, even in their diets, Britons failed to keep up. A British worker today makes only two-thirds of what his American counterpart earns, and he pays higher taxes and higher prices. In a comparison of the standard of living in 15 major countries graded recently by the Organization for Economic Cooperation and Development, Britain came 10th.

It was, in large part, dissatisfaction with this economic lot that elected Mrs. Thatcher. . . .

Emboldened by certitude, Mrs. Thatcher has pursued economic policies radically different from the British norm. In her first budget, she cut income taxes by 10 percent for everyone, exempted hundreds of thousands more lower-income people from the tax and reduced the top rate from 83 percent to 60 percent. At the same time, the value-added tax, a kind of national sales tax, was nearly doubled to 15 percent. The purpose was to restore what she saw as the proper incentives—to encourage people to invest rather than consume, to work rather than play. The increase in value-added tax also raised Government revenues, helping to reduce the budget deficit.

To Mrs. Thatcher, the heart of her conservatism is a restoration of freedom of choice in economic matters. That means allowing private telephone companies to compete with British Telecom, and letting private utilities compete with the Central Electricity Generating Board. It means a massive sell-off of Government-owned companies and other properties to capitalists, who, as she sees it, are more intent than Government officials on efficiency and profits. Perhaps above all, it means curbing the power of trade unions to win inflationary wage increases and impose restrictive work practices.

Of all the startling occurrences brought on by Mrs. Thatcher's economic experiment, few have been as extraordinary as two recent votes by the traditionally militant National Union of Mineworkers to defy its leadership's call for strikes over pay and mine shutdowns. When the miners voted last fall to accept a wage increase of from 8.2 percent to 9.1 percent, it was the smallest negotiated settlement between the two sides in 10 years. At about the same time, workers at British Leyland defied their shop stewards and accepted a management proposal of an 11 percent increase over two years, the first multiyear contract reached at that company in anyone's memory. During a baggage handlers' strike at British Airways last year, other workers not only refused to strike in sympathy but crossed the picket lines and helped load and unload luggage.

Far from being aberrations, these developments reflect broad changes in public attitudes toward the country's economic problems. The central goal of Mrs. Thatcher's strategy has been to break down old relationships and rigidities within the economy and implant the consensus that creating lasting jobs depends on improving efficiency. Few Britons would acknowledge that they themselves contribute to low productivity, but most of them have been persuaded that the rest of the country needs a bit of stiffening up.

Absenteeism, which once ran at 10 to 20 percent of the work force, has dropped in many areas to 5 to 8 percent. For British industry as a whole, the number of strikes dropped in 1981 to the lowest level since the 1940's, although it rose in 1982 because of several large disputes in the public sector. The average earnings increase fell to about 7.9 percent in 1982, down from 10.1 percent in 1981 and 19.5 percent in 1980.

With Mrs. Thatcher's rhetorical and legislative assaults on the power of organized labor, antipathy toward the trade-union power structure, always high, has reached remarkable proportions. According to a survey by Market & Opinion Research International, 70 percent of the British public believe unions have too much power. The umbrella Trades Union Congress lost a million members in three years, the first such decline since the depression of 1921. Even union leaders have begun to express concern. "You cannot take out of the kitty what is not in it," said Sir John Boyd, just before his retirement as general secretary of the Amalgamated Union of Engineering Workers. "There is a realization that employers and trade unions have to create wealth before it can be shared out." . . .

Workers have not been alone in feeling the stress of change; Mrs. Thatcher's efficiency drive has been directed at management as well. British managers are becoming increasingly hard-headed, as they seek to cut costs, communicate better with workers and do a better job producing what the market wants. . . .

The controversial nature of the Thatcher revolution has helped produce the most fundamental upheaval in British politics in half a century. The Labor Party has been deeply divided by the increased militancy of its radical wing. The polarization of British politics, as the Laborites were pushed to the left and the Tories moved to the right, led to the formation of the centrist Social Democrats in troubled alliance with the Liberals. The intraparty disputes have militated against a credible alternative to the Government's austerity program.

Take, for example, the Laborites' economic spokesman, Peter Shore. Asked over a cup of coffee what his party's economic policy would be, he responded with a vigorous denunciation of Mrs. Thatcher: "Show me another country which has deflated so debilitatingly and so savagely. . . . The marginal achievements in productivity are nothing. We are now having an import boom in the middle of a recession, and exports are beginning to turn down." If Labor were returned to power, he said, it would favor higher Government spending, particularly on capital projects, an easier monetary policy to lower interest rates, a fall in the pound on foreign exchange markets, and more nationalization of industry. As for such a program's inflationary effect, "we must accept it."

Yet could Britain have gone on as before, enduring high inflation, permitting the pound to decline incessantly and imposing controls as necessary—on everything from imports to consumer prices—to insure that matters did not get out of hand? Almost assuredly not, as evidenced by the failures of the old stimulative policies elsewhere in Europe. In Ireland, which now has a higher per capita foreign debt than Poland, unemployment is at 13 percent and the inflation rate last year was 17 percent. In France, unemployment is still more than 9 percent, inflation has been running at about 9 percent, and the Government of François Mitterrand has been forced repeatedly to pull back on its expansionary program.

The political dislocations engendered by the Thatcher policies have been accompanied by social turmoil. The income-tax cuts, while intended to improve incentive for investments, have worked for still greater concentrations of wealth in a country where wealth was already shared less equitably than in the United States. The intensified competition for jobs has exacerbated racial tensions. The lack of job opportunities for young people has helped create a dispirited generation whose members, in considerable numbers, have replaced self-esteem with flamboyant life styles heavy on excessive drinking and punk-rock costumes. A country that always seemed to have a firm sense of self has become unsettled. Emigration has risen.

That there has not been even more social trouble is probably due in part to the fact that most Britons have not suffered much in their pocketbooks. For one thing, the workers who have kept their jobs have done rather well. On an average, earnings have risen by 60 percent since May 1979, while consumer prices have risen by 50 percent, and income taxes are lower.

People who have lost their jobs have been getting substantial benefits; "redundancy" payments to laid-off workers run as high as £15,000 (about $23,000). When British Airways offered its employees money to quit, more volunteered than were wanted. A Government "safety net," as it is called in Britain, provides the unemployed with benefits amounting to a large percentage of their former after-tax wage. Consumer buying is at a new high. Per capita, the British buy more videocassette players and champagne than any other people in the world.

For the future, one basic question raised by Mrs. Thatcher's adventurous economic experiment is whether the British system can be shaken up into permanent new forms or whether the improvements—like increased productivity—that have taken place will prove illusory once an economic upturn takes firmer hold.

There have been hints of some such regression. At the Ford Motor Company's Halewood assembly plant, where efficiency 18 months ago was only half that at an identical Ford plant in West Germany, productivity was brought closer to target levels. Then the improvements vanished. "The plant is still plagued by ridiculous stoppages, absenteeism and the like," said a Ford spokesman. "It's really a problem of achieving sustained improvement. There will be times when things look marvelous and then they'll fall off the edge again."

Another basic question is what the recent British experience can teach other countries. On that, there is broad agreement among British economists: Whatever the progress made in righting the economic ship, it has been the result of the old-fashioned, backbreaking recession rather than of any creative theories of "supply-side economics" or "monetarism."

Mrs. Thatcher found that monetary statistics do not always reflect the state of the economy as precisely as monetarists contend, and her efforts to implement policy through control of the money supply proved far less effective than expected. The supply-side decision to shift the burden of revenue from income taxes to a species of sales tax triggered an initial inflationary spurt, making the subsequent anti-inflation fight that much more difficult. There is little evidence that Mrs. Thatcher's income-tax incentives to work harder and invest more have had any measurable effect on the economy. Far more significant, it is agreed, has been the impact of such traditional factors as interest rates and lower budget deficits.

Perhaps the biggest question about the Thatcher program is one of degree. As in the United States, inflation has come down far more rapidly than was predicted, while the recession has been unexpectedly severe. Was austerity, however much needed, pursued too fervently? Should the Government have begun some time ago to ease up? For example, will the downward pressure on prices and the upward pressure on productivity really be any greater with unemployment at 3.17 million, as at present, than if it were half a million lower?

Despite all these questions and difficulties, the Tories continue to believe that their approach is not only good economics but good politics. A reversal at this point, they argue, would neither fix the economy nor fool the voters. At the height of the pessimism about the Thatcher program last summer, Sir Geoffrey Howe delivered a speech re-emphasizing the need for fiscal and monetary austerity and freedom of choice. That, said the Chancellor of the Exchequer in words that are still frequently quoted, requires more deregulation, more drawing in of the central Government's tentacles, more selling-off of state-owned companies, and an extension of "privatization" to areas of social policy such as health and education.

The electorate permitting, Mrs. Thatcher's revolution has only just begun.

# 31

## France: New Government, New Strategy

___ Organisation for Economic Co-operation and Development ___

This article from the *OECD Observer* outlines the Interim Plan which the new Mitterand government formulated in 1981 to fight long-term problems of inflation and, particularly, unemployment.

Between 1976 and the change in majority in 1981, the main thrust of government strategy, with certain variations in emphasis, was to control inflation. Public finance equilibrium, monetary discipline and maintaining a stable exchange rate were the instruments considered essential to keeping prices and incomes within bounds. By fighting inflation, the Government hoped to reverse the tendency for the wage share in the distribution of income to climb, a trend which began in France in the late 1960s and became more pronounced from 1973 on. The purpose was to permit modernisation of the production base and thereby restore external competitiveness, accelerate growth and reduce unemployment.

The inflation target was not met, and from 1977 to 1980 the rate at no time fell lastingly below ten per cent, even though domestic costs steadied and import prices eased from time to time. No progress was achieved in restructuring national income and demand. The public finance deficit was kept in check, unlike the situation in most of the major industrialised countries, but the weight of the public sector increased more than in many OECD countries (primarily owing to the growth of social benefits).* A relevant point here is that in 1980 France moved into first place among OECD countries for social security contributions as a share of GDP [Gross Domestic Product].

---

*Ed. note: The OECD countries include 19 European nations, the United States, Japan, Australia and New Zealand.

But it was above all in the field of employment that France's performance was poor. The rise in the number of unemployed, from which most OECD countries suffered, was extremely high in France. The Labour force projections drawn up by the French Government for the VIIIth Plan showed that, with no policy change, and assuming a growth rate similar to that recorded from 1976 on (about 2.5 per cent per year) and no change in the trend of productivity, the unemployment level would reach some 2.6 million by 1985. Of course, France is not the only country where unemployment has got worse, but it has for a long time been accustomed to full employment and the unemployment figures have certainly, for this reason, had a major influence on the change of strategy.

## A NEW COURSE

The new economic strategy, while intended to control inflation, is primarily directed towards combating unemployment. It is built around a number of objectives: faster growth, a reduction in inequalities and greater national solidarity, and building up the public sector in conjunction with the formulation of a new industrial policy. These orientations are described in the Interim Plan worked out between July and October 1981. . . . [I]t sets out the broad lines of the strategies and economic policy priorities for the coming two years. However, the Interim Plan is linked to an annual GDP growth target (in volume) of three per cent for 1982–83.

### Growth

The achievement of sustained and more rapid growth is regarded by the new government as vital if unemployment is to be reduced. The three percent target would represent a distinct improvement on 1980–81 (one percent a year on average), but would still be far short of the growth performances achieved in the 1960s and early 1970s. . . .

### Employment

In the opinion of the national experts, the growth targeted in the interim plan should make it possible to stabilize the level of unemployment, but other action must be taken if the deteriorating trend in the labour market is to be reversed. Thus the Government has worked out a national solidarity project based on the finding that wide inequalities exist in France. These inequalities are to be reduced through more progressive taxation, a tax on capital, higher unemployment and old-age benefits, etc. These are all part of the traditional armoury of social policies developed in most OECD countries over the past twenty years or so. As to that part of the national solidarity policy designed to reduce the level of unemployment, a number of measures aim to bring about a better distribution of work: progressive reduction of the working week to 35 hours in 1985; lowering of the retirement age under what are called "solidarity contracts"; encouragement of part-time working.

### Public Sector

Enlargement of the public sector's role is regarded by the French authorities as vital to the achievement of economic policy goals of growth and the reduction of external dependence. In direct contrast with the previous government's overriding strategy—and the course currently being followed by many Member countries—the new government accepts, within certain limits, an increase in the public sector deficit but is seeking to use that deficit "actively" to support demand (via the growth of social expenditure) and to finance direct job creation in the government sector. However, it is acknowledged that, as from 1983, public expenditure will have to be directed more towards research, energy conservation and productive investment whether in the private or nationalised sectors. Industrial nationalisation plans focus chiefly on basic industries, where unit investment costs are very heavy, and high-technology industries where research spending is high. The Government considers that bringing these sectors under the direct control of the State will enable them to modernise and become more competitive. In addition, nationalisation of most of the banking system is expected to enhance industry's willingness to take risks and to improve allocation of the country's resources by financial institutions in accordance with the industrial priorities set by the Plan.

### Industrial Policy

Industrial policy has changed somewhat. It is true that emphasis continues to be placed on the restructuring effort under way since the beginning of the 1970s. But two conclusions have been reached: first, specialisation has led to the decline of whole industries, many of which provided large numbers of jobs (steel, textiles); secondly, it has not prevented increasing penetration of the home market by foreign-produced industrial goods, even in those sectors where France is most competitive. The new strategy will focus on the firm instead of the sector (on the reasoning that in every sector, even one seemingly "doomed" by foreign competition, there are firms which are basically healthy and efficient though perhaps experiencing temporary difficulties) and on the product instead of the industry (since even in industries which are losing ground there are products which can successfully withstand competition). With this shift of strategy, measures may be taken to help the activities most threatened. The interim plan refers to wood and paper, textiles and clothing, steel and machine tools. The plan also puts forward the aim of "recapturing" the home market through close collaboration among producers, distributors and users and especially by building up competitive productive capacity—a process in which public enterprises would play a major role. To promote the necessary adjustment the Government may use marginal actions (financial aid to enable a firm to acquire new technology) but it may also pursue a policy of active intervention, which would be facilitated by the existence of a large nationalised sector. Emphasis is also being placed on aid to small and medium-sized businesses in the private sector, since these are considered to be a vital link in the industrial chain. . . .

## 32

# Thorns Among the Roses: A Year of the Socialist Experiment in France

Janice McCormick

With the election of François Mitterrand's Socialist government in France in May 1981 came the promise of *le changement*—a change from policies which the voters perceived as having failed to revive France's sagging economy. In these excerpts from an article published in the British journal *West European Politics*, Janice McCormick assesses the policies pursued by the Socialists during their first year in office and describes the series of events that forced them to revise their original approach.

. . . It is said that when it comes to politics the French have their hearts on the Left and their wallets on the Right. In March 1978, their wallets prevailed, seemingly endorsing the liberal economic policies of President Valéry Giscard d'Estaing and his Prime Minister Raymond Barre. Three years later either the electorate no longer trusted these centre-right politicians with their wallets or, for the first time in the history of the Fifth Republic, they voted with their hearts. Winning 51.76 per cent of the vote, Socialist Party candidate François Mitterrand defeated Giscard d'Estaing by over one million votes.

Giscard d'Estaing's defeat was due as much to a popular unease with the state of the economy as to any overwhelming French belief in the theory and goals of the Socialist candidate. . . . The electorate believed that a Mitterrand presidency would do better at easing unemployment and inflation while improving social justice.

In 1978 the French supported what one American business weekly called, 'Giscard's new French Revolution: Capitalism'; now they were ready for another revolution, a new theory, a new policy, and one more attempt at resolving the economic crisis. In the person of François Mitterrand, they were promised a 'peaceful force' with national solidarity to restore France's *grandeur*. In the seven years which had passed since the oil embargo the French were willing to try yet another economic experiment. Liberalism had been tried to heal the ills of statism; socialism would now be tried to heal those of liberalism. . . .

Although the policies proposed by the two governments to cope with the post-1974 crisis conditions of low growth, high inflation, unemployment and balance of payments problems were drastically different, they were confronted with similar problems. Both wanted to implement changes in a 'stalemated' society where social forces had historically worked against tampering with the status quo. Both governments had been elected by half of the polarised electorate—albeit different halves—yet both needed the support of both halves for their policies to show positive results. In their attempts to alter the direction of economic policy, both governments faced the dual challenges of grappling with the immediate consequences of the economic crisis *and* building a popular consensus around new policies in a nation where cooperative, consensual or corporatist arrangements for mediating interest group conflict had never been tried. In this highly polarised society there was greater concern with the highly partisan context of policy than with its methods of formulation and implementation. Balancing the needs of capital accumulation with the demands for social equity remained the elusive challenge.

## THE LIBERAL EXPERIMENT 1974–1981

In France, where protectionism and *étatisme* were the most important characteristics of policy, the campaign and election of Valéry Giscard d'Estaing symbolised the willingness of the electorate to experiment with liberalism. During his campaign for the French presidency, Giscard d'Estaing promised to rely on free market forces to adapt France to the new world economic order. The liberal experiment was slow to begin, however. Giscard d'Estaing's first Prime Minister, the Gaullist Jacques Chirac resorted to the traditional 'stop and go' policies of previous governments. His second Prime Minister, Raymond Barre, spoke a different language—that of an economic liberal.

The first choice Barre faced when he assumed power, he said, was a philosophical one—'to engage or to disengage' the state from the economy. His choice was clear. 'The State should do the least possible. When it intervenes it should only help do things and help get things done—and only in areas where market forces have proven insufficient.' He ruled out protectionism to insulate French industry from foreign competitors; France, he argued, must have an open economy competitive on international markets. The industrial infrastructure of the nation must be made more healthy: unproductive firms should be allowed to fold; layoffs should be allowed; the nationalised firms should not run deficits and their prices should be increased in line with costs. Certain high-growth industries with strong export potential were to be encouraged through state aid. The key to his strategy was an austerity programme to stabilise French costs and allow profits to rise. A strong franc and freed prices were Barre's first two instruments and wage control was the third. These, combined with monetary restraint and credit controls, he hoped, would reduce inflation to German levels. Unemployment would only improve over the long run as a result of the growth of healthy competitive firms in the new liberal environment; it would be allowed to rise in the short run.

When the Socialists assumed power in May 1981, the French economy and French firms were more competitive than they had been since the 1974 oil crisis. The recovery of French exports was general: growth had slowed but France performed better than her American and EEC trading partners; the franc held firm; the growth of the money supply had slowed; and France had the smallest budget deficit of all Western nations.

However, not all the economic results were favourable. The key to the Barre strategy was that freed prices and controlled wages would result in improved profits which would be reinvested in industry for modernisation. While the financial position of French firms was improved—debt had been reduced, and profit margins had improved—investment continued to stagnate. . . . Profits available to be reinvested had not grown. Business failed to increase productive investment for another reason: it was perceived as too risky. . . . Mergers and acquisitions abounded; and real estate purchases and bank investments were more secure. France acquired a comfortable economic position in several industries—armaments, nuclear development, aeronautics, spatial equipment and computers. These industries alone were responsible for much of France's newly gained positive balance of trade. However, fragility of these foreign sales made reliance on them for national recovery very risky: many sales were the result of government-to-government contracts; they were often to unstable Third World nations. Barre also failed to reach his second goal of bringing inflation down to German levels. In spite of credit and monetary controls and balanced budgets, inflation remained at well over 10 per cent.

The greatest failure of the liberal economic policies in the eyes of Giscard and the public was unemployment. As his third economic goal, Barre planned to reduce unemployment in the long run. He had stated that unemployment would have to rise in the short run while industry retooled with the money from increased profits. 'Improvements in employment will depend on the prior health of business, the growth of our exports, and the resurgence of investments,' Barre argued. While exports rose, investments did not grow sufficiently. Firms showed increased profits; but these did not spur the predicted massive productive investments. Barre's long-term horizon for improvements in employment became longer and longer as the number of French citizens out of work soared to a new post-war level. From 1974–80, the number of registered job seekers quadrupled, rising from 2.3 per cent of the active population in 1974 to 7.4 per cent in March 1981. Young people and women were especially hard hit.

Barre had campaigned on a liberal programme to manage the consequences of the economic crisis. Although haltingly implemented for political reasons, this programme did show some positive results. But for a complete long-run restructuring of the economy, the behaviour of business, labour and consumers had to be altered. But this cooperation for change and confidence in his policies was neither sought by the Barre Government which, uncomfortable with the workings of democracy, preferred a more authoritarian policy formulation, nor was it granted. Neither business nor labour gave him the support he needed to implement his long-run change and the population lost patience with the crisis and abandoned belief in the regime's policies.

## THE SOCIALISTS ATTACK: THE THEORY

François Mitterrand ran an astute campaign as the peaceful force (*la force tranquille*), criticising the most sensitive of Barre's policy failures—but not too vehemently. Unemployment and austerity were attacked for their effect on increasing inequality and for wounding the French humanitarian sensibilities. He distanced himself from the ideological debates and inner workings of the party he had helped create and appealed directly to the nation. . . .

As he had promised in his electoral campaign, Mitterrand's first act was to dissolve the National Assembly where the opposition had a majority. The electorate confirmed the desire for change with a landslide vote for the presidential majority in the June parliamentary elections. The new government headed by the Socialist moderate, Pierre Mauroy, proclaimed that it now had a clear mandate for sweeping social, economic and political reforms. . . .

The policies proposed by the Socialists were a reversal of those of the liberal government which they bitterly attacked, and their analysis rested on different assumptions. According to the Socialist theory, unemployment was the chief problem to be addressed, since it was sapping national energies, perpetuating inequalities, and stifling consumption.

To achieve full employment an interim plan would be enacted which included a series of measures of 'national solidarity': public-sector job creation and sharing of work. By 1983, almost 500,000 jobs were to be created in the public sector especially in the hospitals and social services. A new sharing of work (*un nouveau partage du travail*) became the theme of national solidarity to create jobs: the retirement age would be lowered to 60; early retirement possibilities would be negotiated with firms to allow early retirement after 55 years of age; and the hours of work would be reduced. . . .

In order to respond to Socialist belief in greater social justice, the consumption of the 'least favoured' French—the poor, aged, unemployed, low-wage earners—would be given special attention. The minimum wage (SMIC), family allowances, old age and disability benefits would all be raised immediately by the government, which would put pressure on industry to raise the 'scandalously low wages' paid to some workers. But to control the inflationary effect of these increases, the government would call for a special effort of national solidarity: 'If each increased wage (for these least favoured) forces increases all the way up the wage hierarchy, we will only end up with an increase in inflation. In order to give more to some of us, we must give less to others.' . . .

. . . The nationalisation of the remaining private banks and nine industrial groups was to be another tool to stimulate growth and 'break the domination of big capital in order to undertake a new economic and social policy'. Extension of the public sector, the Socialists argued, 'will give the government the determining means to conduct its economic policy'. Under their plan, the public sector would represent 32 per cent of French industrial activity and employ 24 per cent of the labour force; it would control 90 per cent of bank deposits and 85 per cent of all bank loans. . . .

An annual growth rate of 3 per cent per year was to be achieved with the help of government investment and increased public consumption. Certain industries—machine tools, wood, leather goods—were to be given specific help to restructure. Small- and medium-sized firms would be helped through a reform of fiscal and social charges. 'The central objective of our industrial policy. . . is to create the conditions for a recovery of productive investments'; loans and credit for innovation and research and development would be facilitated. . . .

Although it vehemently argued against protectionism and for the maintenance of the European Monetary System, the Socialist programme paid relatively little attention to the balance of payments issue which had been the focus of the previous government's domestic strategy. In the long run, healthy French firms would 'reconquer domestic markets' from foreign firms and a socialist energy policy would decrease dependence on foreign oil, thus balancing current accounts. A new political democracy, a 'new citizenship', the Socialists argued, would facilitate the task of the economic policy makers. Reinforced planning institutions, regular consultation with the 'social partners'— the trade unions and the employers' association—and regional decentralisation would democratise policy formulation by bringing it closer to the parties concerned. In French firms, employees were to be given new rights. Universities, radio and television were to be loosened from the control of the state: 'To build a new citizenship is first of all to return the State to the citizens . . . to assure the exercise of freedom and responsibility.'

The liberal experiment with reform had failed to gain the broad support necessary for its effective implementation and did not pass the democratic electoral test. In coping with the same economic reality, in many ways the Socialists faced an equal but opposite challenge—their traditional left-wing electorate expected change and reforms whereas the economic crisis presented immediate problems whose resolution required the cooperation of business.

Traditional left-wing constituencies—trade unions, school teachers, blue-collar workers—demanded greater political access and social equality; and higher wages, transfer payments and industrial democracy were their primary interests. The Left's victory had raised their expectations for a *grand soir* of reforms in the style of a Popular Front. Yet these reforms could fuel inflation and increase budget deficits, and weaken the currency. Although it had opposed the election of the Socialist candidate, the business community would also have to be called on for the Socialists to succeed in dealing with the economic crisis. Business confidence was necessary for the stability of the currency and for the take-off of productive investments so critical for private-sector job creation.

For their policies to stimulate growth and investment without fuelling inflation, the cooperation of a wider constituency than the traditional Socialist electorate was necessary. . . .

Yet if the Socialists' proposals were to have any chance of success, the government would have to be daring and creative in building confidence in and support for its policies. It was this lesson, rather than one of *revanche*, that they could have drawn from the failure of the liberal Barre government.

**THE ROSE IN POWER**

In spite of a solid parliamentary majority and a surprising trade union quiescence—the new government has found the task of building a socialist island in a capitalist world more difficult than it had anticipated. . . .

The policies of the Mauroy government were revised over the course of its first year in power. Confronted with the economic realities, the government's forecasts grew more pessimistic and its policies more austere. The policies formulated and the results obtained fell into three distinct phases. From June 1981 to March 1982, the new administration benefited from a grace period of support and tolerance for its inconsistencies and social innovation and reform; there were signs that the economy was picking up and the policies were succeeding. But in March 1982 serious economic reversals were experienced amidst calls both for a pause in reforms from business interests and many Ministers, and also demands for an acceleration of change from the people and trade unions. Entering its second year in power after a serious monetary crisis, which forced it to question the viability of its economic strategy, the Socialist government implemented wage and price controls and austerity measures.

## 1. The Period of Grace: June 1981–March 1982

The new government faced difficult challenges in its first months in power, even though they were rewarded with some positive results. The monetary and fiscal policies were the first to be enacted in the form of action to defend the currency. Within 24 hours of the Left's victory in May the franc was collapsing. Despite the immediate support of the Banque de France, it fell to a ten-year low against the dollar, and hit its agreed floor against the other European currencies in the European Monetary System. The Paris Bourse was flooded with sell orders, and the Napoléon gold coin, the traditional index of political tension, rose nearly 10 per cent. After his first Cabinet meeting, Mauroy imposed strict exchange control restrictions to block the flight of capital and speculation on the franc. But instead of devaluing the franc immediately. . . the new government took a series of popular but costly initiatives before the June legislative elections. The minimum wage was increased by 10 per cent; family and housing allowances were raised 25 per cent; 54,000 public sector jobs were created and 4 billion francs were made immediately available to firms for job-creating and export-stimulating activities.

After a landslide victory in the legislative elections of June, the Socialists began to implement their programme. The consumption of the least advantaged was once again stimulated by increases in social transfer payments to the aged, handicapped and poor. . . . Consistent with its policy of solidarity with the most disadvantaged citizens, the social transfers and minimum wage increases exceeded the inflation rate.

An agreement on hours of work was negotiated between the CNPF and FO and was later signed by all other unions except the CGT.* This agreement suggested the negotiation at the industry and company levels of a gradual reduction of the working week to 39 and then 35 hours and an additional week's paid vacation. However, under pressure from the CGT and the Communist Party, who claimed that the employers were deliberately prolonging the negotiations, in February the government granted by law a fifth week's paid holiday and a 39-hour week with no reduction in salary. . . .

The debate over the proposed nationalisation of the banks and nine private industrial groups was the most heated of the first year of the new government. . . . In the autumn of 1981 the Cabinet proposed a law for the complete and immediate takeover of five industrial groups . . . the conversion of the debt of the two leading steel companies . . . into state holdings; and a fifty-one per cent state holding in [two other large corporations]. . . .

. . . The two leading investment-bank holding companies . . . were also to be taken over. . . . A majority of French citizens now supported this 'attack on big capital' through the nationalisation plan. After legal snags and a ruling by the Constitutional Council that certain clauses of the bill were unconstitutional, the nationalisation bill became law. The estimated cost of the takeovers was over 44 billion francs.

For the remaining private industries, the government's policies were at best ambiguous. Credits for research and development in promising high-technology industries were increased. But control over this money resided with the controversial Minister of Research, Jean-Pierre Chevènement, and he gave little indication as to how these industries would be identified. 'Recapturing the home market' would be accomplished by a close cooperation among producers, distributors and users and especially by building up competitive productive capacity.

Through the Minister of Industry money would be channelled into shrinking industries by giving them ambitious five-year plans. These were not to be bail-outs, but funds for making them competitive. Aid to small- and medium-sized business was expanded. Sceptics called the 34.4 billion franc industrial policy a combination of the old Gaullist bail-outs for lame ducks and rewards for national champions. Its purposes were highly political and often inconsistent. Once again, it seemed the government wanted to please everyone, counting on

---

*Ed. note: The CNPF, or Conseil National du Patronat Français, is an important French employers' association. The FO (Force Ovriers) and the CGT (Confédération Générale de Travail) are two of France's leading trade unions.

growth to expand the economy fast enough both to satisfy simultaneously all groups and to modernize French industry. . . .

. . . In early October at the request of France, the value of the franc within the European Monetary System had to be readjusted to block the continued erosion of France's foreign exchange reserves. The franc's value against the mark was reduced by 8 per cent and the government restricted some prices. It was hoped that these measures would ease the balance of payments deficit—the oil bill had to be paid in dollars—making French exports more competitive abroad, and foreign imports more expensive in France.

To pay for immediate deficits in the unemployment compensation system, an income tax surcharge was placed on high incomes. . . . In spite of the Socialists' aversion to indirect taxation, sales taxes were increased on petrol, tobacco and alcohol. . . . With a 27.6 per cent increase in public expenditure and an 18 per cent increase in revenue, the first projected deficit of 76 billion francs for 1982, (compared to 30 billion francs of 1980), by December 1981 was revised upward to about 95.4 billion francs or 2.6 per cent of the gross domestic product. The government counted on the effects of its expansionary measures to stimulate consumption and investments and thus increase its tax receipts.

## 2. The Transition: Signs of a Setback

By February–March 1982, the situation had soured. There were signs that the recovery of late 1981 had been ephemeral; the franc was falling again and the government's political and trade union support was being eroded. . . . Although the success of Socialists' economic policy depended on the behaviour of French firms, only 4 per cent of those interviewed said their companies were planning to increase employment in 1982, 6 per cent their capacity utilisation and 8 per cent their investments. . . .

The remaining economic news looked as gloomy in the first few months of 1982: French inflation was running at an annual rate of 17 per cent. High inflation further reinforced the strength of the dollar on already nervous international money markets; and there were no signs that a decrease in the American prime rate was imminent, making credit more expensive for financing either productive investment or the French deficit which was revised upwards every month. In spite of lower world oil prices, the French balance of trade had also worsened—for two reasons. First, the French stimulation of consumption had also stimulated the sale of foreign consumer goods in France; unable to meet the rapid increase in demand, French businesses saw their foreign competitors move in. But French exports had also failed to meet their goals due to the deflationary policies of its trading partners; within the other EEC nations the recession was far more severe. Each of these economic problems snowballed to further complicate the task of the government, and make the success of the policies of a socialist France in a competitive capitalist international environment less likely.

There were also signs that any social and political truce was over as well. An outbreak of strikes, often led by the CGT, seemed to be aimed as much at the Mauroy government—in which there were four very loyal Communists—as at their employers. . . . In February, they hit their peak: there were three times more days lost in strikes than in January 1982 and four times more than in February 1981. . . .

### 3. The Thorns on the Roses: 'The Second Phase of Change'

As the economic forecasts grew gloomier in early spring, the tone of government statements changed. . . . 'Discipline', 'economic rigour' and 'national effort for the economy' were the new slogans and stimulating investment the new priority. . . . The government was forced to suffer the consequences of not having worked out a compromise between its electorate which anxiously awaited reforms and the owners of capital whose cooperation was necessary for the success of those reforms. If French industry was to create jobs and export competitively it would have to expand, investing in the latest technologies. Responding to the business community's complaints about being overtaxed to pay for the first year of social reforms, the Mauroy government granted business a series of concessions that did not create tax incentives for investment but were aimed at improving the climate for business: any further reduction in working time would not be enforced until 1983; a freeze was placed on the level of employers' social security contributions until July 1983; and the company tax (*taxe professionnelle*) was cut by 10 percent. To pay for these tax cuts to business, the value-added taxes were revised upwards on many consumer items and downwards on many food products. Three billion francs were given to the newly nationalised firms to finance their losses which were estimated as high as ten billion francs. The nationalised banks were to be 'encouraged' to help cover the remaining seven billion francs. It was hoped that this public-sector investment would also help stimulate other private investment. Although aimed at increasing profits, these measures could not guarantee those profits to private investment.

These measures could not show immediate results but instead exacerbated the basic 'stagflationary' condition of high inflation and high unemployment; March and April registered the most serious rise in the wage-price spiral. Increases in hourly wages for the first third of 1982 were 5 per cent after a 4.1 per cent increase in the fourth quarter of 1981 making an annual rate of over 18 per cent. Price increases for March and April were over 1.2 per cent per month, and economists predicted that the inflation rate would rise above 15 per cent for 1982. Finance Minister Delors stated that he refused to consider a price or wage freeze because, 'One doesn't freeze an economy one is trying to stimulate. We have opted instead for a gentle disinflation.'

Unemployment had not fallen in spite of massive public-sector job creation, in fact it seemed to be worsening. In March 1982 it was 8.7 per cent whereas it had been 7.4 per cent in March 1981. The average length of unemployment had risen from 253 days to 271, and the unemployment of adult males had grown more rapidly than the national unemployment rate. At the same time, projected budget deficits for 1982 increased to over 125 billion francs and 200 billion francs for 1983. The government searched for new ways to finance the deficits of the social security and unemployment compensation systems without penalising business or braking public consumption. Speculation continued to weaken the franc. In May the franc once again hit its floor in the European Monetary System, as the dollar reached another all time high. The Banque de France had to intervene massively to defend the parity of the franc as France's reserves fell from 37 billion francs in early March to 16 billion francs in June.

These remedial measures were not sufficient. In June the Mauroy government reverted to more classical deflationary and austerity policies. After devaluing the franc 10 per cent vis-à-vis the dollar—the second devaluation in nine months—the government pledged to hold the budget deficit to 3 per cent of the GDP. The whole nation was asked to participate in the effort as the government recognized its vulnerability to foreign economic conditions: 'We are changing speed in order to reduce the gulf that separates us from some of our partners and that affects our currency and the balance of trade.' In order to reduce inflation to below 10 per cent, all wages except the minimum wage and all prices except milk, fruit and vegetables were to be frozen at 11 June levels until 31 October. To control an inflationary surge after the lifting of controls, the government pledged to reinforce the collective bargaining mechanisms to force unions and management to moderate the increases in both wages and prices.

The official language changed rapidly from optimism to pessimism. The new goal was to 'combine social justice with economic efficiency'. But the government was unable to get labour and management to agree to negotiate a form and a method of controls; instead it pushed a law through Parliament effectively suspending the 1950 law on collective bargaining and imposing state-monitored price controls. . . .

# 33

## Ten-Point Program of Action

_____ **French Government Communiqué** _____

In early 1983, faced with a massive balance of payments problem, the French government moved to impose further austerity measures. This excerpt from a press release issued following a cabinet meeting held in late March of that year outlines a new program of action designed to restore the French balance of trade.

The government has decided on national action to restore French external equilibrium in two years. To attain this central objective, it has adopted a ten-point program of action that continues the policy of austerity defined in June 1982.

### REDUCTION OF PUBLIC DEFICIT: FOUR SERIES OF MEASURES

1.   The state budget deficit will be held to 3% of the gross domestic product in 1984 as in 1983.
For 1983:

- seven billion francs of credit currently held in reserve will be cancelled;
- an additional eight billion francs will be saved;
- a special tax will be levied, starting in April, to offset reductions in the price of crude oil.

In all, the budget deficit will be reduced 20 billion francs.
2.   Equilibrium will be the goal for the social security system in 1983 and 1984. An additional 13 billion francs will be raised by:

- a proportional levy of 1% imposed before July 1 on all taxable income and allocated to an equalization fund for the social security system;

- a supplementary savings program of four billion francs in 1983;
- a new tax on liquor to take effect April 1, 1983;
- a new tax on tobacco to take effect July 1, 1983;
- a mandatory payment for hospital stays (20 francs a day towards the cost of meals) to take effect April 1, 1983;
- the current negotiations on the future of UNEDIC (unemployment compensation fund) will be speeded up. They should, in accordance with the law, ensure the strict equilibrium of the unemployment insurance fund for 1983;
- the nation's social budget will be discussed at the spring session of Parliament. Parliament will decide on the guidelines and directions of the social budget and on appropriate methods of financing it.

The government will see to it that all the social partners are involved in the discussions on these points and that the renewal of the contractual policy is consistent with the main goals of equilibrium.

3. The deficits of the major state-owned companies will be systematically reduced; seven billion francs in new savings will be made in 1983.

In addition, the earnings of these companies will be increased by rate increases of approximately 8% for gas, electricity, telephone and passenger train service starting April 1.

4. A savings of two billion francs will be made on loans to local townships in 1983.

## ENCOURAGEMENT OF SAVINGS AND CONTROL OF THE MONEY SUPPLY: SIX MEASURES

The law on the protection of savings and the development of investments has provided incentives to increase long-term savings and money invested in stocks.

To complement this action the volume of savings will be increased by 20 billion francs in 1983 by the following provisions:

5. A mandatory loan equal to 10% of the tax payable on income and on large fortunes. Taxpayers paying less than 5,000 francs' income tax a year will be exempt. The loan will be collected in May and the money held for three years. It may be reimbursed before the due date when the equilibrium of France's external accounts has been restored on a durable basis. The loan will amount to 14 billion francs. It will enable the government to maintain the necessary effort to restructure French industry and promote exports despite budget restrictions.

6. A vigorous incentive for savings in special home-ownership accounts (*épargne-logement*). This will include among other things higher interest rates and a higher ceiling on the amounts allowed in these accounts. These measures will take into account the size of the family.

7. The ceiling on savings bank and post office type-A accounts (tax exempt) is raised to 58,000 francs.

8. In the framework of contract negotiations special funds to promote industrial development and generate jobs might be set up.

9. The target for the growth of the money supply is reduced to 9% from 10%.

10. Spending by French tourists traveling abroad will be limited to 2,000 francs per adult and 1,000 francs per child per year. The tourist exchange card will be revived for this purpose.

A delegation for external trade has been set up at the Ministry of External Trade and Tourism. Its task, an interministerial one, will be to promote and coordinate actions to correct France's foreign trade balance.

In preparing this program the government has sought a fair distribution of the efforts asked of the French people.

It has also taken care that the measures adopted do not entail higher costs for companies.

Parliament will be closely involved in implementing this program, which will be presented to it by the Prime Minister on April 6. The necessary legislative provisions will be submitted shortly thereafter.

In accordance with the appeal made by the President of the Republic on March 23, the French people must mobilize both as consumers and as producers in order to succeed in correcting France's external trade balance within the next two years.

# Unit IX

# Industrial Policy and Economic ——————— Nationalism ———————

In the past, Western European governments have placed more or less reliance on the market to determine the allocation of resources. In recent years, however, there has been a growing tendency among almost all the advanced industrialized nations of Western Europe to move away from reliance on market forces. This tendency has been exacerbated by the serious economic problems—most notably unemployment and inflation—that have plagued Western Europe since the oil-price explosion of 1973. Along with these problems, many of Western Europe's traditional industries—particularly steel, textiles, and automobiles—have suffered severe declines in their ability to compete on world markets, and this has prompted many governments to develop "industrial policies" designed to protect national industries from foreign competition and, where possible, to foster their modernization. Moreover, a number of governments have taken an active interest in promoting new technologies and are diverting resources into industries which they consider to have the strongest growth potential—primarily aerospace, computers, biogenetics, and other high technology industries. This trend has been accompanied by a widespread resurgence of economic nationalism, most clearly evidenced by the fact that in many Western European countries, government is now making the kinds of decisions that were previously made by the market. Today, government plays a leading role in determining resource allocation in Western Europe, as well as in deciding which industries shall be protected against competition and which shall be left to fend for themselves.

Industrial policy, then, embraces not only attempts by government to choose the industries that are to be favored, it also embraces the various policies designed to protect industries that are threatened by competition from abroad, particularly from the newly industrialized countries (NICs) of the Third World and from Japan. This unit focuses on a number of important issues within the rubric of industrial policy and examines the nature and impact of these policies on Western Europe's economies.

"The New Interventionism," an excerpt from a report published by the Organisation for Economic Co-operation and Development (OECD) in 1983, explains the emergence in many OECD countries of policies aimed at sheltering industries from severe international competition. Wyn Grant, in "A Typology of Policy Alternatives," defines four basic approaches to industrial policy in terms of their general application to the British economy since 1972. In "Industrial Policy: The British Case," Grant takes a closer look at the policies pursued by the British government in recent years. He shows how industrial policy is translated into specific acts in Great Britain and provides examples of the kinds of legislation typically involved in the implementation of a broad policy.

In "France: New Strategies in Industrial Policy," the OECD discusses the policy changes instituted by the French Socialist government since 1982 and considers the implications of these new strategies for both the private and nationalized sectors in France. Juergen B. Donges, in "Industrial Policies in West Germany's Not So Market-Oriented Economy," describes how, in the 1970s, the West German government shifted its approach to industrial policy from one that was primarily complementary to the market mechanism to one that has increasingly favored government intervention in the economic sector. Analyzing the factors that led up to this transition, Donges examines its effect on West German industries in recent years.

In "The European Community and Industrial Policy," Wyn Grant details the difficulties the European Economic Community has encountered in attempting to meet the demands of its member nations for a Community industrial policy aimed at improving the Common Market countries' competitive position in international trade. Finally, "The New Protectionism," another selection from the OECD, details the weapons of economic nationalism the various kinds of import restrictions and export subsidies that have grown up in the place of tariffs, allowing Western European nations, like many world traders, to profess a continued commitment to "free trade" while at the same time sheltering or subsidizing home industries.

---
# *34*

# The New Interventionism

## __ Organisation for Economic Co-operation and Development __

The OECD was organized in 1960 to promote constructive world economic policies. Its members now include nine-
teen European countries, the United States, Canada, Japan,
Australia, and New Zealand. This excerpt from *Positive Adjustment Policies*, a 1983 OECD publication, explains the
emergence in many OECD countries of government policies
aimed at sheltering industries from severe international competition.

---

. . . A relatively new phenomenon in many OECD countries is that
governments try to influence directly the structural composition of
production. They do this by discriminating between economic activities, not primarily with the aim of achieving certain non-economic
goals, but to influence industrial or regional structures in order to promote overall economic objectives, e.g. economic growth or the maintenance of high employment. This "new interventionism" has been directed specifically at the structure of manufacturing industry, in some
instances to protect industries against market forces that are bringing
about a decline, in other instances to promote industries with a promising growth potential. . . .

The spread of the new interventionism is primarily a response to
the slow economic growth and high unemployment experienced since
the mid-1970s which make continued structural adjustment in the industrial countries difficult. Also, the social environment and increased
interdependence among national economies generate more adjustment
pressures than economic growth alone has done in the past. Moreover,
the advantages accruing from an intensified international division of
labour or from innovative competitors—i.e. gains in overall economic
growth and productivity, the creation of new jobs in new sectors and
new regions and a contribution to combatting inflation—are widely dis-

persed and often difficult to identify. By contrast, the burdens associated with international competition often occur in concentrated form and visibly, so that they generate interest-group pressure for defensive government intervention. Finally, as a result of the experiences of the 1970s and early 1980s, governments may sometimes have doubts about the long-term cohesion of the world economic system and may therefore be prepared to sacrifice economic efficiency for the sake of maintaining a certain degree of self-sufficiency in essential products and materials.

Much of the new interventionism has been focussed on industry, partly because some other sectors have always been more subject to regulation than industry and partly because industry was particularly hard hit by the unforeseen trend breaks of the 1970s. Shifts in macroeconomic income distribution pushed up wage and tax costs in many industries, especially in labour-intensive activities. This affected the profitability of the manufacture of internationally traded goods more than purely domestic activities (like most services), because international competition constrained the passing on of higher costs in the form of higher sales prices.

In particular, many labour-intensive, mass-produced manufactures with rather low income elasticities, such as standard textiles, garments, shoes and simple electronics, were supplied competitively to world markets by newly industrialising countries. This trend will—if anything—accelerate in the 1980s, as the newly industrialising countries of the 1960s–70s gain experience in industrial production, improve product quality and marketing and widen their product range, and as large new industrial suppliers—including the industrialised parts of China—may join them.

Although overall demand growth has slowed down, it is not clear that there has been any reduction in the supply of new knowledge and new technologies. This frequently posed pronounced problems in industries where the new technologies required large and risky capital investments at a time of reduced cash flow and inflated interest rates. . . .

Industry was less sheltered than many other sectors against the risks of an increasing international interdependence and changes in the international economic environment. These changes have become less predictable. For example, the oil-price increases, the political developments in the post-Vietnam era, the Iranian revolution, and heightened East-West tensions have shown the risks to industries which depend on international economic integration. . . .

The problems which industry, labour and sometimes the general public had to face under these changed circumstances arose basically from the fact that industrial supply structures could not always adjust as rapidly as needed. . . . It was therefore not surprising that governments of industrial countries were confronted with increasing pressures by individual industries to intervene in rapidly changing markets, either to stem the decline of activities (such as textiles, steel or shipbuilding) or to assist with accelerated moves into promising activities (such as electronics or energy-saving transport equipment). . . .

# 35

## A Typology of Policy Alternatives

### Wyn Grant

In these excerpts from his 1982 study, *The Political Economy of Industrial Policy,* Wyn Grant defines four basic approaches to industrial policy in terms of their application to the British economy during the 1970s.

. . . Four strategic approaches to industrial policy are set out in a typology of policy alternatives. The four categories used in this typology are:

1. Pure market
2. Social market
3. Selective intervention
4. Socialist approaches

### THE PURE MARKET APPROACH

Strictly speaking, there is no such thing as an economy in which all allocations of resources are made through the market. Even the most extreme exponents of the efficacy of markets as distributive mechanisms have to make some exceptions. As Hirsch points out, 'Even under the most favourable conditions for market society, certain things have to be kept off the market.'

Nevertheless, the pure market approach is important as a theoretical model which exerts an intellectual pull on social marketeers, shifting them in the direction of a version of the social market approach which is more market than social. The absence of anything that would be recognized as an industrial policy within the framework of the pure market approach means that the case against it cannot be made in terms of the industrial policy it produces. Two general arguments may be advanced against the pure market approach. First, it has a corroding effect on social relations, e.g. by strengthening the selfish aspects of the individual character at the expense of values which stress obligation to others, so that even if it results in a more efficient economy, a high price is paid in terms of a less tolerable society. Second, the attempts by proponents of the pure market approach to justify those small areas of state intervention and regulation which are to be permitted produce principles which could be applied in such a way as to justify intervention on a far wider scale than the advocates of the approach would ever envisage.

In his discussions of the role of government in a free society, Milton Friedman accepts that there cannot be exclusive reliance on the market mechanism. He accepts that once paternalistic justifications for government activity are allowed, for example in relation to the mentally ill or to children, 'doing so introduces a fundamental ambiguity into our ultimate objective of freedom'. The particular cases of children and the mentally ill discussed by Friedman illustrate the difficulty of erecting watertight barriers against further government intervention, once one has allowed even a little intervention. After all, if one can help the mentally deficient on paternalistic grounds, why not the unemployed? To use Friedman's own words, 'There is no formula that can tell us where to stop.' The boundaries to government intervention then become no longer a question of the general superiority of market over political mechanisms, but rather the subject of a practical political judgement about the relative effectiveness of different kinds of policies.

## SOCIAL MARKET APPROACH

Advocates of a social market approach to industrial policy recognize the inevitability of some intervention by government in industrial affairs, but they regard such intervention as inherently undesirable and consider that it should as far as possible be infrequent, temporary and limited in scope. Perhaps the major difference between the social market and selective intervention approaches is that advocates of the former believe in a policy *for* industry rather than the comprehensive industrial policy advocated by selective interventionists. . . .

The stress placed on the general economic framework rather than on a specific industrial policy in the social market approach leads to an emphasis on economic and fiscal controls and legal regulation, and to policies that are neutral between firms and industries. In particular, there is an emphasis on competition policy as a means of curbing monopoly and other hindrances to the effective operation of the market mechanism. . . .

Nationalization in the social market model is largely confined to what are viewed as public utilities with the boundaries of their operations being strictly defined. Although the desirability of natural monopolies being in public ownership is acknowledged, the length of time that a public monopoly in a particular field has been in existence is not automatically taken as a guarantee that it is natural rather than artificial. Wherever the justification for industries remaining in public ownership is insufficiently strong, they should be returned to the private sector or converted into 'mixed enterprises' involving the participation of both private and public capital. Industrial innovation policy under the social market approach relies on integrating public research and development capacity with industry and disseminating and transferring technology. . . .

A major problem for the proponent of the social market approach is that of deciding where intervention should stop, given that it is regarded as a distasteful necessity. The same problem arises for the advocate of the pure market, but it is more acute for the proponent of the social market as he is prepared to tolerate more departures from the market principle. . . .

## SELECTIVE INTERVENTION

. . . Selective interventionists believe that macro-economic measures are by themselves insufficient as a means of attaining such objectives as fuller employment and the avoidance of a chronic balance of payments deficit and that resorting to micro-economic measures by government is inevitable. Pursuing the right general economic policies, although important, will not be enough to prevent continuing economic decline. In particular, selective interventionists believe in the need for, and efficacy of, financial inducements that discriminate between firms and industries. In order to seek advice on the operation of such a policy, and to try and ensure the co-operation of the affected interests, one sees the proliferation of tripartite bodies of various kinds concerned with industrial policy. In addition, the selective interventionists, although not favouring the wholesale nationalization of major areas of industry in private ownership which is advocated by socialists, see a significant role for nationalization and various kinds of mixed enterprise as a means of both rescuing declining industries and stimulating emerging industries.

In general, however, the selective intervention approach is based on voluntary co-operation between government and industry, rather than compulsion. Although the use of compulsion is not ruled out, the emphasis is on persuasion. Industrialists must be induced by means of subsidy, exhortation and tripartite working party to take those decisions which government considers to be in the national interest. . . .

## SOCIALIST APPROACHES TO INDUSTRIAL POLICY

Industrial policy in Britain in the 1970s was dominated alternately by the social market (1970–72, 1979–) and selective intervention (1972–79) approaches. What both approaches have in common is an assumption that, given the right conditions and/or incentives, a form of capitalism can be made to work in Britain. It is true that the two approaches take a different view of the efficacy of market mechanisms as a means of achieving industrial policy objectives. Proponents of the social market approach regard the market as a generally efficient allocator of resources, with government intervention being permitted only where it can clearly be shown that the necessity of such intervention offsets the inevitable distortion of the market which will result. Thus, government intervention is tolerated to *facilitate* the operation of the market (e.g., by sponsoring or licensing appropriate regulatory mechanisms to avoid malpractice); to *correct* unavoidable market malfunctions (e.g., to inhibit monopoly through a competition policy and to regulate inherently unstable markets such as those for agricultural commodities); and to *offset* some of the grosser social inequalities produced by the operation of the market mechanism (e.g., those who have personally to accept the burden of industrial change through redundancy should be compensated).

Selective interventionists take a more sceptical (even agnostic) view of the efficacy of the market economy. They believe that quite extensive areas of economic activity have to be insulated from market forces either because the market is failing to work properly or because the social costs which would be imposed by market operation are perceived as being too great. The areas of market failure are not, in their view, confined to special types of market which are inherently unstable and cannot always be offset by a vigorous competition policy or by the use of taxation so that the price mechanism takes some account of social costs. Thus, one *replaces* the market where it is believed to have failed; in other areas, where there is some hope of resuscitation, there is a resort to financial inducements to *modify* the behaviour of market actors.

What unites both approaches is that they strive to avoid as far as possible the element of compulsion inherent in socialist approaches to industrial policy. Although selective interventionists are more willing to accept that capitalism has certain inherent flaws than are the supporters of the social market approach, they appear to believe that these can be overcome with the right mix of paragovernmental agencies, funding packages, networks of tripartite committees and the like. Socialists would argue that neither approach will work because capitalism is beset by internal contradictions which are now manifesting themselves in a terminal global crisis, the effects of which are especially apparent in Britain's weakened economy. However, it should be recognized that going beyond either of these models in the direction of a socialist solution (or, for that matter, a pure market solution) would involve creating a society fundamentally different from that in which British people have been used to living. Ultimate limits to the range of industrial policy options are set by a polity which accepts, on the one hand, certain responsibilities to care for its citizens and, on the other, limits to compulsion arising from a recognition of property rights and of certain basic individual liberties. . . .

# 36

# Industrial Policy: The British Case

## Wyn Grant

Here Grant provides a closer look at the changing approaches to industrial policy followed by the different British governments in the 1970s and early 1980s. This selection, which describes in detail how industrial policy is translated into specific acts, sheds light on the kinds of legislation that are typically involved in the implementation of a broad policy.

### THE FORMS OF SELECTIVE AID

The period 1972–1979 in [British] industrial policy was characterized by a complex series of selective assistance schemes, largely operated under the terms of the 1972 Act. The most important parts of the Act as far as selective assistance is concerned are Sections 7 and 8. Section 7 of the Act provides for discretionary government assistance to projects that create or safeguard employment in the assisted areas or regions. Such assistance has usually been provided in the form of interest relief grants to 'top up' the major form of regional assistance, the 'automatic' Regional Development Grant which has been given since 1972 to all qualifying assets in the assisted regions without any job creation or retention test being applied.

Assistance under Section 8 of the 1972 Act is not restricted to the assisted areas and is supposed to benefit the economy and serve the national interest. Section 8 has been used to assist capital-intensive projects in the regions, but its main use has been to support projects in the non-assisted areas. The Section 8 powers were used by the Labour Government in three main ways.

First, a number of schemes of aid were devised for individual industrial sectors. Lippitt described the purpose of these schemes as being 'to take a particular industry and over a reasonable period of time to jack it up into a modern, efficient competitive situation.' The first two schemes were introduced by the Conservatives in 1973 covering wool textiles and offshore supplies to oil installations. The Labour Government introduced a further fourteen schemes covering such diverse industries as machine tools, paper and board, footwear and red meat slaughterhouses. Up to March 1980 £272 million of assistance had been offered under the sectoral schemes, with another £52 million of payments under the offshore supplies scheme.

Second, there were general schemes to encourage new industrial investment. The first of these, Labour's Accelerated Projects Scheme (APS), was open for applications from April 1975 to June 1976 and was designed to have a counter-cyclical effect in the recession and to encourage companies to bring forward investment projects that might otherwise have been deferred. A total of 111 projects were assisted involving £72 million of assistance and £568 million in project costs. The Selective Investment Scheme (SIS) which succeeded APS was intended to encourage companies to go ahead with projects costing more than £500,000, particularly in the engineering industry, which might otherwise have been abandoned, built abroad, or executed on a smaller scale. By the closing date in June 1979 742 applications had been received and by March 1980, grants totalling £106.5 million had been offered to 166 projects involving capital outlays of over £1000 million. The assistance offered varied between three per cent and twenty-one per cent of project costs, averaging at 10.5 per cent. The scheme was very successful in attracting inward investment projects to the UK, with thirty-five such projects being offered assistance up to March 1980 with eighty per cent of the resultant investment being located in the assisted areas.

Finally, Section 8 was also used for one-off rescues such as those of British Leyland and Chrysler. At one stage, rescues accounted for about one-half of Section 8 payments, but they declined in relative importance in the latter part of Labour's term of office. Section 8 powers were also used by the Labour Government in 1978 to introduce a scheme designed to facilitate energy conservation by industry. Apart from small scale assistance towards consultancies, £12.2 million of assistance to capital projects had been offered by March 1980.

The Product and Process Development Scheme (PPDS) launched in 1977 consolidated a number of earlier aid schemes supporting research and/or development operated under the 1965 Science and Technology Act such as the Pre-Production Order Scheme. PPDS was designed to assist firms in bearing the cost of product and/or process development from the design stage up to the point of commercial production, special attention being given to new products and processes.

The Microprocessor Application Project (MAP) was launched as a crash programme in 1978 under the 1965 Act against a background of concern at the UK's slow rate of takeup of this key technology compared with major competitors. The objectives of MAP were to raise significantly national awareness of the potential of micro-electronics at all levels in UK industry; to increase substantially the supply of people retrained in micro-electronics skills; to help firms to establish the relevance of micro-electronics to their business; and to improve the rate of application of micro-electronics in firms' products and processes, particularly by first-time users. The Government also launched in 1978 the Micro-electronics Industry Support Programme (MISP), funded through the 1965 Act and Section 8. The scheme particularly emphasized assistance for the design and manufacture of silicon integrated circuits and the infrastructure companies supplying goods and services to the industry. . . .

## THE POLITICS OF REGIONAL POLICY

Regional policy, as the oldest form of industrial policy, has attracted more academic attention than any other aspect of the subject. . . .

### The Political Preference for Regional Policy

In the seven-year period from 1971/2 to 1977/8 inclusive, total direct expenditure on regional policy was just under £5,000 million pounds at 1978/79 prices. The principal form of regional aid throughout this period was the non-discretionary Regional Development Grant introduced in 1972 and given to all qualifying assets in the assisted areas. Even allowing for expensive rescue cases like British Leyland, the amount spent on regional aid over the 1972–79 period exceeded the amount spent on aid to individual industrial sectors, particularly in the earlier part of the period.

It might seem that governments favour regional policies simply because they are necessary and efficacious. Certainly, there is a great deal of evidence and argument that can be adduced to support such a view. Governments throughout the world support regional policies because gross imbalances between regions are regarded as socially undesirable, politically intolerable, and injurious to national economic efficiency. . . .

Regional imbalances manifest themselves in a number of ways: net outward migration, an ageing population, run-down public amenities, derelict land, out-of-date factories and industrial plants, incomes below the national average, and a vicious cycle of collective despondency and low economic growth. However, despite the importance of all these indicators, 'unemployment discrepancies have always been the basic, almost exclusive, dynamic of regional policy.' As long as a person has a significantly higher chance of being unemployed because he or she has the misfortune to live in, say, Strabane, Greenock or Penzance rather than Croydon, Reading or Chelmsford, there will be political pressure, and a social need, for a regional policy. Even if one is not prepared to accept arguments based on a notion of approximate equity of treatment of persons living in different locations in terms of their chances of obtaining employment, it must be accepted that it is not in the interests of those living in the more prosperous regions to be subject to a continual influx of seekers after work, leaving the rest of the country as the haunt of the unskilled, the disabled, the retired-on-state-pensions and other socially-disadvantaged groups.

However, the necessity of having some kind of regional policy does not resolve questions about the relative shares of public funds that should be devoted to location-specific policies and general aid schemes. . . . [A] study by Political and Economic Planning of new factories in Special Development Areas found that financial incentives were not an overriding reason for the choice of location; among main reasons, the availability of incentives ranked third after the availability of a factory or site and the availability of suitable labour.

General aid schemes may, of course, themselves provide aid to regions in difficulty. Almost ninety per cent of the aid provided under the Wool Textile Scheme went to plants in assisted areas, and most of the applications under the Clothing Scheme emanated from assisted area plants. Forty-nine per cent of the funds provided under APS and seventy-one per cent of SIS offers went to projects in assisted areas up to March 1980. However, an industrial policy that emphasizes schemes designed to promote the development of high technology is likely to lead to the more prosperous regions receiving a disproportionate share of the available aid. Of 271 applications for grant approved under the microprocessor application scheme to June 1980, 164 were located in the South East of England. The next highest numbers of applications were also from relatively prosperous regions: the South West (23), the West Midlands (16) and the East Midlands (17). These figures do not reflect a lack of willingness on the part of government to give such aid to the regions, but rather the concentration of workers with the relevant skills in the more prosperous regions. Recent research suggests that 'the South East possesses an environment external to the enterprise and establishment which is conducive amongst other things to invention and innovation,' a finding which has disturbing implications for the efficacy of conventional forms of regional policy.

## The Efficacy of Regional Policy

The assessment of the efficacy of British regional policy is not an easy task, given the range of variables involved, the lack of reliable regional statistics in relation to many relevant indicators, and the discontinuities in government policy. Nevertheless, official figures do suggest that 'differences in regional economies have narrowed over the past decade but there are signs that the trend may have been reversed in the last couple of years'. This reversal at the end of the 1970s coincides, of course, with the rundown in regional policy, although undoubtedly other factors have played their part. The general picture over the decade is one of incomes becoming more equal, unemployment differences reducing, and spending patterns becoming more alike. In part, however, this is because formerly prosperous regions have become less prosperous; where formerly less prosperous regions have started to catch up, this has often been the result of fortuitous factors such as North Sea oil rather than government assistance. The harsh fact remains that 'the areas with highest unemployment are those which had highest unemployment at the inception of regional policy some fifty years ago'.

Nevertheless, regional policy does seem to have had some beneficial impacts. Manufacturing output in Scotland, Wales and Northern Ireland appears to have been significantly higher in 1976 compared with 1958 'than would have been expected in the absence of regional policy . . . by far the major part of the increase appears to have occurred in the period of strong regional policy since 1965'. However, the case for regional policy often seems to rest on an argument that, although things are bad, they would have been far worse without it. Minimizing one's losses is sometimes the best available strategy, but what is particularly worrying is that the outlook for the future, at least in terms of the efficacy of conventional policy measures, looks bleak. Fewer firms are moving and 'whilst regional incentives may still have some influence on the location of expansions and new openings, the influence appears to be much weaker than formerly.'

Although economists disagree about the precise impact of regional policy, it is clear that it has ameliorated the basic problem of regional imbalance rather than gone very far towards solving it, despite the quite considerable share of industrial policy funds which has been devoted to regional policy. The continuing attachment of politicians of all parties to regional policy, until recently in preference to other forms of industrial policy, cannot simply be explained in terms of socio-economic necessity and efficacy. Moreover, the problem could have been tackled in other ways than the relatively indiscriminate provision of location-specific aid for industrial development. . . .

## ASSISTING HIGH TECHNOLOGY UNDER THE THATCHER GOVERNMENT

In 1980 the phrase 'constructive intervention' started to be used by [the] ministers [of Britain's new conservative government] to describe their industrial policies. In so far as the phrase meant anything, it appeared to represent a growing commitment to assisting high technology industries and to stimulating the application of new technologies to the production processes of older industries. Expenditure on general industrial research and development increased from £66 million (at 1980 survey prices) in 1978–79, the last year of the Labour Government, to £82 million in 1979–80 and £108 million in 1980–81. It was projected to increase to £124 million (at 1980 prices) in 1981–82, representing an increase of eighty-nine per cent since the Labour Government's last full year in office. In particular, expenditure on micro-electronics and its applications was more than doubled between 1978–79 and 1979–80, as was expenditure on the development of new products and processes. Of a £50 million additional allocation of funds for industrial aid announced by the Chancellor in November 1980, £16 million was set aside for the PPDS and two micro-electronic aid schemes. . . .

### Product and Process Development Scheme

The survival and further development of Labour's Product and Process Development Scheme under the Conservatives represents an interesting aspect of the Thatcher Government's industrial policies. Clearly, PPDS was seen as less politically controversial than the sector aid schemes sponsored by Labour under Section 8 of the 1972 Industry Act. [This] scheme was introduced in 1977 with the aim of encouraging UK companies to invest more of their resources in development work to launch new or significantly improved products and processes more quickly and more effectively.

Assistance under the scheme usually takes the form of a twenty five per cent grant towards development costs, though in exceptional cases a fifty-fifty shared-cost contract, with the Department contribution recoverable through a levy on sales, may be offered. . . .

After a slow start, PPDS applications increased, and by the end of December 1980, 1073 applications had been received. . . .

Applications are judged against four criteria. The Department must be satisfied that the company has the financial and technical resources to carry through the project to commercial exploitation. . . . Second, the project must offer good prospects of success and must be likely to lead to a significant improvement in the company's performance, for example by widening its product range. . . . Third, there is the additionality criterion which requires that the project or programme would not be undertaken in the form proposed or within a reasonable time scale without government aid. . . . Finally, the total qualifying cost must normally not be less than £25,000 or more than £2 million, although consideration is given to projects of less than £25,000 from small firms.

Britain has suffered not so much from a lack of research into basic technology, but rather a neglect of commercial product development and market considerations. PPDS goes a long way to fill that gap. . . .

**TABLE 36.1  Britain's Industrial Policy Expenditures (£m, current prices)**

| | 1976–1977 | 1977–1978 | 1978–1979 | 1979–1980 | 1980–1981 | 1981–1982 | 1982–1983 | 1983–1984 | 1984–1985 |
|---|---|---|---|---|---|---|---|---|---|
| Department of Industry | | | | | | | | | |
| Regional and general industrial support | 519 | 502 | 629 | 509 | 644 | 807 | 534 | 680 | 590 |
| Scientific and technological assistance | 98 | 100 | 106 | 142 | 344 | 212 | 249 | 280 | 300 |
| Support for aerospace, shipbuilding, steel and vehicle manufacture | 351 | 349 | 326 | 376 | 599 | 1,043 | 606 | 60 | — |
| Other central and miscellaneous services | 25 | 29 | 32 | 35 | 42 | 48 | 51 | 50 | 50 |
| | 993 | 980 | 1,094 | 1,062 | 1,628 | 2,109 | 1,440 | 1,070 | 940 |
| Department of Energy | | | | | | | | | |
| Regional and general industrial support | 9 | 20 | 16 | 22 | 29 | 27 | 32 | 30 | 20 |
| Scientific and technological assistance | 148 | 127 | 143 | 174 | 218 | 264 | 265 | 270 | 280 |
| Support for nationalised industries | 82 | 100 | 193 | 266 | 265 | 398 | 778 | 200 | 230 |
| Other central and miscellaneous services | 15 | 32 | 31 | –16 | 14 | 25 | 26 | 30 | 30 |
| | 253 | 279 | 385 | 445 | 526 | 715 | 1,101 | 530 | 560 |
| Department of Trade | | | | | | | | | |
| Regional and general industrial support | 15 | 15 | 18 | 23 | 26 | 29 | 33 | 30 | 30 |
| Export Credit Guarantee Department | 725 | –146 | 359 | –50 | –155 | 85 | 367 | 190 | 310 |
| Total outlays | 1,986 | 1,128 | 1,856 | 1,480 | 2,025 | 2,938 | 2,941 | 1,830 | 1,850 |

*Source: The Government's Expenditure Plans 1982–1983 to 1984–1985*, Vol. 2, HMSO, Cmnd. 8494-11, 1982. Reprinted by permission from *OECD Economic Surveys: United Kingdom* (OECD, February 1983), p. 49. (Originally titled "Industrial and Regional Support Expenditures.")

# 37

# France: New Strategies in Industrial Policy

## Organisation for Economic Co-operation and Development

This selection from a larger OECD economic survey describes the changes in industrial policy instituted by the French Socialist government since 1982. Intended to foster the modernization of France's production system in the "spearhead" as well as the "traditional" industries, these new strategies have implications for both the private and nationalized sectors.

. . . There is a long tradition of government economic intervention in French industrial policy. The French reaction to the first oil shock of 1974 was in the form of a deliberate industrial and energy "redeployment" policy designed to bring about large-scale structural changes in the country's production system. In the case of energy, this policy has, by and large, continued up to the present time and because of it a significant degree of adjustment has been made to the new world situation. In the case of industry, high priority was given to the production of capital goods and other high value-added products, and to exports.

As time went by, it became clear that the policy was swallowing up considerable amounts of public money, in the support of exports or firms in difficulty, without achieving the hoped-for results. Budgetary restraint became a more important concern and, with the resumption of economic growth after the 1975 recession, greater selectivity was pursued and less ambitious objectives set. Firms and activities that appeared to be doomed had to be run down smoothly. Firms and sectors with a chance of becoming competitive had to be given limited help. Others that were fully competitive internationally did not need any special measures. A number of bodies were set up during this period, some to help small and medium firms adapt (e.g. CIASI*), and some to

---

*Ed. note: Comité interministériel pour l'aménagement des structures industrielles.

244

strengthen the competitiveness of the high-technology sectors "of the future"(e.g. CODIS\*\*). The deepening of the recession after the second oil crisis and rising unemployment have shown that this policy did not suffice to halt a process coming to be called "disindustrialisation", whose symptoms (in France, as in many industrial countries, incidentally) have been the continuous decrease in industrial jobs since 1974 and the decline in industrial investment.

With the change in government in 1981, industrial policy was reframed and the first and most important measure introduced by the new government was the nationalisation of certain large industrial groups early in 1982. Relations between the new competitive public sector and the government will be defined under the terms of "plan contracts" negotiated for periods of three to five years and, since the beginning of 1983, are in the process of being signed with 12 industrial groups in the sectors of steel, chemicals, motor vehicles, aerospace, and electronics. These plan contracts set strategic objectives which are defined by the government as a shareholder, the aim being to ensure consistency of enterprises' action with the government's industrial policy options and to establish the framework within which enterprises exercise autonomy of management.

It is extremely difficult to attempt a first analysis of the role that the nationalised enterprises have so far played in industrial policy. In the 1981–82 period they were more the physical expression of an objective than a real instrument of intervention. One thing is already quite clear, however. The weight of the nationalised sector in industry is now very considerable: the public groups control 29.4 per cent of sales, 22.2 per cent of the workforce and 51.9 per cent of total industrial investment, energy included. If only the large firms (over 2,000 payroll) are considered, these figures obviously become much higher. It seems certain now that the government intends to use the new nationalised enterprises to reactivate productive investment in 1983. The financial resources put at their disposal have been significantly increased: the equity contribution to the competitive public sector has been raised from Frs. 15 billion in 1982 (of which Frs. 10 billion in capital endowments from the budget and Frs. 5 billion in contributions from the banking and financial sector) to Frs. 20 billion in 1983.

The general objectives of industrial policy (for both the nationalised and private sectors) will be set out in the industrial development act for 1984–1988 due to be put to the vote at the bill stage at the end of 1983. Already, however, the first schemes introduced and the programmes now under study reveal the broad policy thrusts. The French

---

\*\*Ed. note: Comité d'orientation pour le développement des industries stratégiques.

government's major stated objective is to accelerate modernisation of the productive system in order to establish increased growth potential in the spearhead industries, but also in the "traditional" sectors (machine tools, wood, textiles, etc.). As regards the spearhead industries, just as much emphasis as previously, if not more, has been placed on support for new technologies. The legislation on "orientation and programming of research and technological development" enacted in 1982 specifies that the share of GDP allocated to research and development expenditure will be increased to 2.5 per cent by 1985 (compared with 1.8 per cent in 1981); the 1983 finance act provides for a 17.8 per cent volume increase in the civilian research budget (compared with 14.1 per cent in 1982). In the context of the preparatory work on the Ninth Plan, the priority given to the electronics "cycle" is likely to be reflected in a block appropriation of Frs. 140 billion over 5 years; already, certain sectoral plans are in operation (electronic components, automated office systems) or being drawn up (cable networks, bio-medical applications).

Policy in regard to the traditional sectors takes a rather different line in that the intention not to abandon these industries, many of which are labour-intensive, reflects the priority given to employment. The five sector plans already introduced (leather, furniture, toys, machine tools, textiles, clothing) include employment-support aids pending the effects of measures designed to restore the capacity for response to international competition: modernisation of plant, but also development of domestic producer linkages between upstream and downstream activities in the same industry cycle and also with distribution channels, so that the assisted industries may be better integrated in the French market.

All in all, industrial policy seems to be still in a phase of transition. The general shift in economic policy since mid-1982, particularly in the direction of tighter budgetary control, will tend to accelerate restructuring measures in the nationalised sector—with their inevitable effects on employment. The concentration and modernisation of the basic industries could certainly have positive effects in the medium term. On another level, the policy of maintaining a diversified industrial fabric takes the concrete form of sector assistance. The policy in favour of new technologies and the "industries of the future" has not yet been defined. The degree of interdependence now binding France to its industrialised partners, the maintenance of which is not at issue, will make a choice of priorities necessary if industry is to be capable, at one and the same time, of standing up to the most advanced competition, meeting the requirements of the home market, preserving sectoral coherence, ensuring at least a stable level of employment and keeping up with the structural and technological change whose pace seems to be dictated to it. If all these ambitious objectives are to be achieved, then a considerable volume of savings will have to be channelled to industry. The problem therefore arises of what national resources are available for total investment and how those resources are to be allocated among the various sectors of the economy.

# 38

## Industrial Policies in West Germany's Not So Market-Oriented Economy

### Juergen B. Donges

In the 1970s, West Germany shifted its approach to industrial policy from one that was primarily complementary to the market mechanism to one that increasingly favors interventionism. In these excerpts from an article in *The World Economy,* a British journal on international economic affairs, Donges analyzes the factors leading up to this change in policy and the effect it has had on West German industries.

The Federal Republic of Germany is often thought to resemble the textbook model of a market economy. This is a misconception. The Federal Government as well as the governments of the *Länder* [States] interfere in the market mechanism in a number of ways. In some cases, the interventions take place with a remedial intention, when the market clearly fails (or is supposed to fail) in allocating resources in an optimum way and in promoting growth. In other cases, the intervention goes further, aiming deliberately at obtaining sectoral and regional structures of industrial production, employment and foreign trade different from those which the market would presumably generate.

The purpose of this article is to discuss the concepts which have governed industrial policy in the Federal Republic since its inception. . . .

### INDUSTRIAL POLICIES IN A MARKET-ORIENTED ECONOMY

The objective of industrial policies in the Federal Republic of Germany has never beeen sharply defined by the Federal Government. There is a consensus, however, that it is determined by the basic goals of overall economic policy, which consist of the simultaneous attainment of price stability, full employment and steady as well as adequate growth of output, in addition to balance-of-payments equilibrium and an equitable personal and regional distribution of incomes and wealth. The industrial sector, which contributes about 50 per cent to GDP and employs roughly 45 per cent of the labour force (for manufacturing alone, the shares are approximately 10 percentage points lower), bears significantly on the degree to which these national economic goals are accomplished. Industrial policy then embraces all government actions which affect industry: its domestic and foreign investment, foreign trade, regional location, innovation activities, labour absorption, access to capital markets, environmental use and any other aspects.

The shaping of industrial policies started out from the principle that the market mechanism in combination with effective price competition would ensure dynamic efficiency in industry. Decentralised decision-taking and *ex post* coordination of individual plans was regarded not only as a precondition for individual freedom (as guaranteed by the Constitution of 1949) but also as the arrangement most likely to stimulate private initiatives, speed up technological progress and rapidly improve the living standards of the population.

This principle of decentralised decision-taking has two important implications. On the one hand, it charges entrepreneurs (and the owners of firms capable of controlling their managers) with the task of being responsive to structural changes. They have to take the risk on their investments. Consumer acceptance or refusal of goods offered on competitive markets is the ultimate test of whether the investment is a success (yielding a profit) or a failure (leaving a loss). On the other hand, the Government has to refrain from policies that impede structural change or introduce unnecessary entrepreneurial risks; and it should pursue policies that properly support the functioning of the price mechanism, including the provision of an adequate infrastructure for industrial growth. Industrial promotion policies should be considered only if external economies to the benefit of society are generated; and promotion should concentrate on particular industries only if externalities are generated by that particular industry and cannot otherwise be realised. Whatever government support is given, it should be restricted to a finite period stipulated in advance. Otherwise, industries may do little to adjust to shifts in comparative advantage or to venture into new long-run investments which have high social benefits. So much for the principles.

In reality, it has always proven difficult to get such principles fulfilled in a pure form. The Federal Republic is no exception to this rule. Yet during the 1950s and 1960s industrial policies were rather complementary to the market mechanism. It is only since the early 1970s that they have become more interventionistic and distorting. . . .

Quite consistent with the market-oriented philosophy, which has dominated thinking about economic policy in the Federal Republic of Germany, the Federal Government has attached much weight to competition policy. On the external side, the West German market has been opened for foreign suppliers of manufactured goods. Although a number of industry-specific protectionist devices prevail, there is no doubt that liberalisation of international trade has constituted an important channel for strengthening competition. In periods of cyclical booms and increasing inflationary pressure during the 1950s tariff reductions were used to enlarge the supply of goods on the domestic market.

The internal pillar on which the competitive system was built was the 'law against limitations on competition' of 1957. This law had two main provisions. One established as a general principle the prohibition of cartels and other competition-limiting agreements (with certain exceptions). The other provision authorised the cartel authorities to prohibit the abuse of firms, market power. This second provision has not been very effective in practice because it is difficult to prove a misuse of market power in a concrete situation. The first provision, on the other hand, has worked reasonably well, although it could not prevent an increase in horizontal and vertical concentration in West German industry. While competition is not necessarily more intense when there are more suppliers on the market—in fact oligopolistic competition can be socially more efficient—the trend towards concentration may well reflect attempts by individual entrepreneurs to escape the pressures of competition. The control of market power will therefore remain a major task for any Federal Government, although, presumably, no clearcut solutions will be reached. This task applies also to consciously parallel behaviour among individual firms, which is forbidden by the anti-trust law but so far has not intimidated firms in the automobile industry and petroleum refining from increasing the selling prices of their products in a more or less similar way on various occasions. . . .

## TOWARDS SELECTIVE GOVERNMENT INTERVENTIONISM

Although officially the Federal Ministry of Economics still assigns to the market mechanism the task of steering structural changes in industry, unofficially it also recognises that the Government has become increasingly involved in this process. The deeper the structural changes become and the weaker the economic outlook, the more are both entrepreneurial associations and labour unions tempted to demand government assistance and the harder it is for a government to resist such demands, particularly when electoral considerations are taken into account. Up to now, interventions can be classified into two groups:

a. protection of domestic industries against imports from low-wage countries, and
b. direct financial assistance to domestic firms.

What they all have in common is that they are not neutral among industries, but deliberately discriminate among activities and, in some cases, even among firms in the same sector of activity.

The *import protection issue* reveals quite well the significant change which has occurred in the West German policy framework with regard to industry. Although the country fared well from the liberalisation of trade in the 1950s and 1960s and owed part of its rapid industrial growth to the advantages of increasing international specialisation, manufactured imports from low-wage countries (including Japan) are now regarded by many as a source of serious market disruption. It is true that responsibility for trade policy has lain since the early 1970s with the European Community. And it is known that the Federal Government has tried on various occasions to stem the tide of protectionism. Protectionist sentiments, however, have gained ground in the Federal Republic, and the Federal Government may sometimes be in the comfortable position of keeping the 'free trade' flag flying while at the same time obtaining relief from import competition through protectionist measures implemented at the Community level.

The system of import protection in the Federal Republic (and the European Community) has always favoured the production of labour-intensive and raw material-intensive manufactures at the expense of engineering industries which were the ones with the highest growth potential. . . .

Nowadays, however, non-tariff protection is much more important than tariff protection. Moreover, selective non-tariff protectionism has been proliferating, thereby undermining the principles of non-discrimination and multilateralism, which have been the keystone of the General Agreement on Tariffs and Trade (GATT). Instances are the implementation of new import quotas and so-called anti-dumping duties, the Multi-fibre Arrangement of 1974 (renewed in 1978 and due for a second renegotiation in 1981) and bilaterally negotiated 'voluntary' export restraints on a wide range of products. In addition, the Commission of the European Community has encouraged international cartelisation of industries with a view to defending market shares against foreign competition (the Davignon Plan for the steel industry implemented in 1977).

The Tokyo Round agreements did not make much progress towards removing this type of import restriction. In addition, the European Community seems to be determined to retain the possibility of discrimination against any country whose imports are regarded as growing too fast (and, one should add, which has little scope for effective retaliation). . . .

Government interference with the operation of the market mechanism has been increased by *aid to domestic industries*, particularly in the form of direct subsidies, tax relief, special depreciation allowances and credits at preferential terms. It appears that these measures have come into increasing use as a substitute for the loss of autonomy by the Federal Government in trade policy matters and to allow both Federal and *Länder* authorities to pursue regional-policy objectives more effectively. In addition, research-and-development undertakings have increasingly been promoted by financial aid. . . .

The concentration of government industrial aid in a few sectors partly reflects regional policy concerns, as some of the industries which have benefited most are located in backward regions (coal mining, steel, shipbuilding, electrical industry). It also reflects the distribution of assistance to research-and-development undertakings which the Federal Government considers of paramount importance for future industrial growth. The Kiel study shows that five industries (computer equipment, energy, chemical industry, machinery and electrical engineering) received 77 per cent of government research-and-development aid in 1974 (mainly in the form of project financing). Since 1975, the aircraft industry has also become a major beneficiary of such aid. Within these industries, the Federal Government has revealed a distinct preference for a few large companies, such as Siemens, VEBA, AEG-Telefunken, Bosch, Brown Boveri, Ruhrkohle, Metallgesellschaft and Messerschmitt-Bölkow-Blohm. Small-size and medium-size firms have found it more difficult to get access to government support. Precisely because of their small size, they cannot afford to lobby for funds as effectively as big companies and are less able to comply with the many bureaucratic requirements for applications. . . .

Direct government aid to industry has been justified officially in various ways. One argument stresses the need to eliminate a technological backlog *vis-à-vis* the United States. Cases in point are the aircraft industry and computer technologies. Sometimes the 'infant industry' argument is used as a justification for government aid in fields considered vital to the economy as a whole. The nuclear-energy industry and other technologically-advanced activities have qualified here. A third type of argument revolves around international trade and regards government aid as a necessary tool to correct distortions of competition in both West German and foreign markets which result from production or export subsidies available to foreign suppliers. The steel industry and shipbuilding have requested and received assistance on these grounds.

The merit of these arguments, however, is open to question. The technological-gap argument may disguise the political desire to develop prestige industries. On economic grounds there is no reason why West German industries should be competitive in all fields and, in any case, it is logically impossible that they (as with industries in any country) can acquire a comparative advantage in every single activity. One may argue that the assisted activities involve positive externalities for society as a whole. In that case, though, one would expect a decrease in the amount of aid received over time, whereas in fact the amount has increased relatively to the value added. The infant-industry argument would be more convincing if it rested upon solid analyses of social benefits and costs, which is not the case; and such analyses are difficult to undertake due to the lack of adequate data and information about the future. It might make more sense to aid all research-and-development activities equally in terms of value added rather than to adhere to the principle of project-oriented assistance as practised in the Federal Republic. Finally, the argument about correcting for trade distortions would be more appealing from an economic point of view if subsidies and other public aids were less subject to considerations of policy competition among governments (thereby frequently transforming production subsidies into export subsidies) and were more oriented towards restructuring the industries affected.

In sum, even when governments seek in good faith to promote industrial developments considered socially desirable, selective public assistance to industry may in practice be applied with a strong protectionist or nationalistic bias. Furthermore, it is likely that the more the state intervenes in the operations of the market, the more distortions will be created (since help for one branch or firm will be a charge on the rest) and the more one measure may conflict with another. Forces which work for repeal of such detailed interventions in the market are usually weak in representative democracies; they may also prove to be weak in the Federal Republic, if micro-policies proliferate further. . . .

# 39

# The European Community and Industrial Policy

## Wyn Grant

Since its organization by treaty in 1957, the European Economic Community has remained committed to a free-market philosophy. In recent years, however, a Community-wide industrial policy has developed in response to member demand. Here, Grant assesses the success of that policy and describes some of the conflicts that exist between Community policy objectives and the national policies of the individual member states.

### THE LIMITATIONS OF COMMUNITY INDUSTRIAL POLICY

The development of an effective European Community industrial policy is inhibited by the Community's ideology, its organization, the national interests of its member states, and the conflicting interests of different industries within and between member states. The Community was formed at a time when it was assumed that a continually expanding West European economy would absorb any labour displaced from declining industries; hence, an interventionist industrial policy, even one designed to promote adjustment, was not seen as necessary. . . .

However, it became apparent that the creation of a customs union, the removal of technical barriers to trade and the pursuit of competition policy would not lead, in particular, to the creation of European firms operating on a scale that enabled them to compete effectively with American firms. This concern led to the Colonna Report on Industrial Policy of 1970; a commitment to the establishment of a single industrial base for the Community at the Paris Summit in 1972; and an action programme by December 1973. However, despite all this activity in 1972–73, 'little was really achieved beyond the acceptance of the idea that the EEC should have an industrial policy'. . . .

. . . The central problem is that each member state defines Community industrial policy largely in terms of its own self-interest, and pressure for a Community policy only arises when things have got so bad that an industry is beyond salvation on a national basis. The Commission finds itself faced with a situation in which 'On the one hand the Governments of our Member States take differing positions on most issues; on the other hand a substantial part of the private sector in Europe in practice values its autonomy higher than the possible contribution the Community could make to its future. Given the absence of any positive political support for a Community industrial policy, it is the worst industrial problems that are most readily sent to Brussels. It is not entirely the fault of the Community if it cannot find solutions to problems which have defeated the national governments.

## SECTORAL POLICIES

The steel sector is the one area where Community policies have had a significant impact. In relation to the steel industry, the Community has been able to achieve more than in other sectors because of the wider powers given to it by the Treaty of Paris which set up the Coal and Steel Community, the longer tradition of European co-operation in steel policy, the parlous state of the industry in recent years, and the energetic leadership of the responsible Commissioner, Viscount Davignon. A series of measures combining minimum prices and import controls, backed up by fines imposed on offending Community producers and a series of Voluntary Restraint Agreements negotiated with major steel-supplying third countries, culminated in the declaration in October 1980 of a state of manifest crisis in the Community's steel industry. After some concessions to the Germans, production quotas were agreed at the end of October. . . .

The difficulties that the Community faces in developing an adequate policy even for industries that are in crisis are illustrated by the case of shipbuilding. The Community would prefer assistance to the shipbuilding industries of member states to be lower, but recognizes that, given the price gap between European and Asian yards, most Community yards would go out of business without such aid. However, the Commission is also worried that 'such aids will drive back market forces and that the economic selection of the most competitive yard will become a matter of only secondary importance'.

The 1978 Fourth Directive on Aid to Shipbuilding did go some way to providing a framework for a Community shipbuilding policy. The directive required that aid and intervention should be progressively reduced, and must be linked to the reduction of capacity. The draft Fifth Directive attempted to tackle the more contentious question of aid to state owned nationalized industries, the question of the controversial Polish Order negotiated for British Shipbuilders by the Callaghan Government being at the back of the Commission's mind. However, ambitious plans by Viscount Davignon to parallel the Community's steel policy with a similar shipbuilding policy led to very litte in the way of policy innovation.

The Community's impact in other industrial sectors has been even more limited, although it has influenced sectors such as textiles through its responsibility for commercial policy and the handling of negotiations for the Multi Fibre Arrangement which provides for the restraint of the rate of growth of imports of textiles into the EEC from low-cost countries. The Commission is taking an interest in the Community's troubled motor industry, and there has even been speculation about the possibility of assistance for compensatory payments to redundant automobile workers. As far as regional policy is concerned, ninety-five per cent of the Regional Development Fund is carved up on a quota basis between member states. . . .

All too often Community industrial policy looks like a belated response to changes in the industrial structure that have already taken place, rather than an attempt to anticipate the problems of the future. The important area of information technology offers a good illustration of this tendency. The Community admits that 'The Nine have become concerned about this only recently,' and it was not until June 1979 that the heads of state and government meeting in Strasbourg asked the Commission to look into the matter, a request which led to the submission of proposals by the Commission to the Council of Ministers in September 1980. The proposals centred on a traditional reliance on competition policy, combined with an attempt to concert public procurement policies and the promotion of cross-frontier projects by undertakings. Member states are inclined jealously to defend their procurement policies because they offer a means of promoting 'national champions', and cross-frontier projects have hardly been a sparkling success in the past.

The general absence of effective sectoral policies is in large part a reflection of the social market orientation of the Community's approach to industrial policy. Those who would not want to see the integration process taken too far might argue that the ambiguities and ineffectualness of Community industrial policy is really a good thing, because it leaves member governments a freer rein to pursue their own national policies. . . .

## THE COMMUNITY AND NATIONAL INDUSTRIAL POLICIES

Article 92(1) of the Treaty of Rome provides that 'Save as otherwise provided in this Treaty, any aid granted by a Member State or through State resources in any form whatsoever which distorts or threatens to distort competition by favouring certain undertakings or the production of certain goods shall, in so far as it affects trade between Member States, be incompatible with the common market.' However, Articles 92(2) and (3) list a series of exemptions, one of which is so worded as to provide a means of allowing regional aid, and another which contains a clause which permits aid 'to remedy a serious disturbance in the economy of a Member State'. Much, then, depends on the way in which the treaty is interpreted.

In 1979, the Commission prohibited the Dutch Government from giving aid to Philip Morris International to enlarge a cigarette factory. The firm subsequently appealed to the European Court of Justice, the first time that a recipient of proposed aid has lodged such an appeal, and the decision of the Court in favour of the Commission is an interesting clarification of the Commission's power to prohibit state aids.

In its judgement dismissing the appeal, the Court pointed out that Article 92(3) gives the Commission power of discretion by stating that the types of aid listed 'may' be considered as compatible with the common market. The Court ruled that the Commission had rightly considered the standard of living and serious under-employment in the area in question not by reference to the national average in the Netherlands but in relation to the level throughout the Community. The compatibility of the aid in question with the treaty must be considered within a Community context and not simply in relation to one Member State.

Aid to the tobacco industry is controversial even at a national level and the Commission is on relatively safe ground in mounting a challenge to it. The Commission has kept out of politically more sensitive areas like state aid to the motor industry and has only gone through the motions of vetting the state aid, although this may change. There were hints from Brussels in 1981 that clearance for the latest Government aid package for British Leyland would not automatically be granted.

Another potential area of conflict concerns the nationalized industries. Article 90 of the Treaty of Rome provides that the relevant provisions of the treaty extend to public undertakings and gives the Commission the power to address appropriate directives or decisions to Member States. In June 1980, the Commission adopted what proved to be a controversial directive based on Article 90 which required each member state to place at the Commission's disposal data relating to the financial relationship between the state and public undertakings in each country. The Commission's stated objective in collecting this information was to 'be able to assess whether the public resources thus placed at the disposal of a public undertaking constitute, for example, an aid and must therefore be treated as such, or whether, on the contrary, the resources are being made available simply in accordance with normal practice in a market economy'. Despite reassurances by the Commission that it did not intend to discriminate against the public sector, this directive concerned a number of member states and Britain, France and Italy launched a challenge against the Commission on the way it had used its powers in the European Court. The United Kingdom sympathized with the Commission's broad objective, but challenged the Commission on the technical grounds that the Commission could issue a directive on its own initiative under Article 90(3) only when it has been established that a member state is breaching the competition regulations, whereas the Italians based their case on the procedure and the principle. The underlying issue, which is likely to emerge again, is the Commission's belief that nationalized industries should follow market principles as well as private industries.

## THE IMPACT OF COMMUNITY INDUSTRIAL POLICY

Even where conditions for a Community industrial policy are most favourable, i.e., where member states have a common interest in the problems resulting from the collapse of an industry, this common interest in the problem is often outweighed by conflicts of interest over possible counter-measures. Other Community policies often have more impact on industry than the attempts to develop an industrial policy. Thus, it has been argued that 'the trade agreement with the People's Republic of China will have a much greater effect on the textile industry than the Community's attempts to restructure the industry'. All too often, the Commission tends to retreat into the pursuit of technicalities where it knows it will not encounter much opposition from the member states, even if the results it achieves have a minor impact on the industrial structure of the Community. Thus, it has achieved the passage of a whole series of directives on tractors, with work underway on the harmonization of the location and attachment of statutory plates and inscriptions to tractors. A directive on spa waters has been another area of activity. In many ways, the OECD has made a more positive contribution to the international debate on industrial policy, with its attempts to evolve an agreed framework for industrial policy which will shift the emphasis away from the short-term defence of weak sectors to a longterm strategy of adjustment. . . .

Despite its hesitant steps towards an industrial policy, the Community remains attached to the free market philosophy embedded in the Rome Treaty and it is unlikely in the foreseeable future that the member states, individual firms or the rather weak European industrial pressure groups will provide sufficient political impetus to shift the Community from that position. It is difficult to argue with the European Democratic Group's recommendation that 'Industry needs to be given equally important status and attention as Agriculture in the Community.' However, that is unlikely to happen, given the institutional momentum behind, and cluster of interests associated with, the CAP [(Common Agricultural Policy)].

# 40

# The New Protectionism

## Organisation for Economic Co-operation and Development

Tariffs, or taxes on imports, are not the only means by which countries can "protect" their home industries from foreign competition. This excerpted report describes the several kinds of trade barriers that now impede the course of nominally "free" trade.

The liberalisation of international trade since the Second World War has led to a level of tariffs on trade in manufactures that is now lower than it has ever been in modern times. Only very few OECD countries now rely to any marked extent on tariffs to promote industrial production. . . .

### THE INCREASED RELATIVE IMPORTANCE OF NTBs*

The very success of the abolition of quantitative restrictions as a first step and of subsequent tariff cutting has led to a new game plan in international trade policy: countries often intervened in the 1970s on behalf of their immediate national interests by imposing new non-conventional barriers to trade which are not proscribed by international agreements and cannot be easily controlled. In some instances, long existing restrictions—like textile quotas and health regulations—were reaffirmed or narrowed; in other instances, new restraints were introduced in the world trade of manufactures that had been relatively free of controls—like automobiles. In the 1970s, some OECD countries also strengthened protectionist coal policies for the sake of greater self-sufficiency in energy supplies. Other important areas of trade—such as tex-

---

* Ed. note: Non-tariff barriers

tiles, East-West trade, agricultural products and important areas of the service sector—have in any case remained virtually exempt from the rules of free trade. . . .

. . . [T]hese other forms of protectionism often have a relatively large distorting effect, negating many of the benefits of past trade liberalisation. The lesson of the 1950s and 1960s, that international co-operation and competition can normally overcome limits to economic growth better than many other means, often seems to be forgotten in the face of the economic concerns of the 1970s and 1980s. It is frequently overlooked that interventions in free international exchange merely remedy the symptoms or, at best, create solutions that are viable in the short run but weaken the underlying competitive constitution of markets and the long-term growth potential.

Among the non-conventional instruments of trade policy that have become more widespread since the late 1960s have been import quotas which set limits to imports. . . . Thus, Australia limits the number of cars that can be imported to 20 per cent of expected domestic car sales, France restricts imports of Japanese cars to 3 per cent of domestic sales, and Italy to 2,200 vehicles per annum. Because quotas shield national economies fully from international cost and price movements, they tend to induce domestic producers and privileged quota holders to collect monopoly rents from their buyers. This creates resistance to structurally adjust to a condition in which the beneficiaries of quota protection would have to compete.

In response to the rapid structural changes of the 1970s and the pressure on many industries in OECD countries to reduce capacities, governments often guarantee a minimum price for certain products by imposing a supplementary duty on imports which are supplied at a lower price. Such a "trigger price" system was first practised by European countries to maintain the price of agricultural products above world-market levels and has since spread to such markets as steel.

Apart from the immediate effect on inflation, such policies tend to retard structural adjustment (but, of course, such retardation may be the intended objective). . . . Like all interventions that impede price flexibility, they weaken the underlying adaptability of the market system and pave the way for subsequent government induced "market failure". . . .

Voluntary export restraints have increasingly been imposed by importing nations on successful exporting countries. Agreements to limit exports to new markets have usually occurred where there have been rapid shifts in international comparative advantage in the production of labour intensive manufactures from high wage countries to producers in newly industrialised countries, who have combined relatively low wages with rapid improvements in productivity and product quality. . . .

These developments have led to adjustment pressures which are part of normal growth processes but are sometimes concentrated in certain regions and felt to be too abrupt. Instead of resorting to GATT [(General Agreement on Trade and Tariffs)] procedures, many OECD governments have tried to solve the resulting dilemma by seeking cooperation of new exporters to obtain so-called voluntary export restraints. . . .

Although such voluntary restraints may be less durable than tariffs or quotas, they have reduced incentives to declining industries for structural adjustment. They also create considerable uncertainties for efficient suppliers to world markets and limit growth opportunities in newly industrialised countries. . . .

The spreading of voluntary export restraints has often led to increased pressure on OECD countries that did not resort to this practice, leading to chain reactions. . . .

Resistance to prompt structural adjustment has played a particularly marked role in the conflict which led to the prolongation until 1986 of the Multifibre Agreement, which exempts a large share of international trade in textiles and related products from the principal rules of GATT. It appears that this Agreement has almost lost its originally intended temporary nature. Prolongation of agreements such as these conflict directly with the objectives of positive adjustment, since major sectors under particular adjustment pressures become exempted from those pressures. This then often shifts adjustment burdens onto non-exempted areas.

The Multifibre Agreement is an example of "orderly market arrangements" which increasingly weaken the stimulus of international competition. In such market arrangements, industry organisations, governments or supranational organisations control international trade in sensitive products, normally in markets in which substantial excess capacities exist (like steel) or in which recent innovations have shifted competitive positions (like motor cars or consumer electronics). Such arrangements tend to be supported by large-scale producers who prefer safe, government-protected profits to the larger, riskier profits of the market place. But less efficient and innovative producers are maintained as a result, which is in direct conflict with the long-run objectives of positive adjustment. Among the costs are likely to be losses in dynamism and a shift from entrepreneurial to administrative attitudes in business.

International competition has for a long time also been distorted by government procurement policies that favour national suppliers in many innovation intensive industries in which government agencies are important buyers. This is, for example, the case in defence industries where there has been a tendency to buy nationally, either by granting local producers a preferential price margin or refusing outright to buy internationally. Similar policies have been used by governments to secure markets for their national aircraft, communications and data-processing industries. . . .

## EXPORT SUBSIDIES DISTORT ALLOCATION

In reaction to post-war trade liberalisation, which concentrated on imports, the "new protectionism" of the 1970s has frequently also affected the export side. Exports may be subsidised by preferential export credits (as is the case for many sales of large-scale investment goods and plants abroad), or by reimbursement or reductions of the taxes that usually apply to domestic business activities. Exports may also be subsidised by governments guaranteeing prices against the effects of general price change or exchange rate fluctuations (export insurance).

There has also been a proliferation of other forms of export subsidisation in trade with relatively new participants in the world trade system who are often not fully committed to the principles of free international competition. This is both true of relations with developing countries, where public development aid and trade are often intertwined, and with East-bloc countries whose governments' procedures often induce market economies to assume traits of state trading.

Export subsidies, including subsidised export credit, are frequently used to help national producers to reap scale economies and to push them faster along the learning curve in innovative activities. This tends to be particularly the case in industries which governments promote by R & D subsidies, or where they are major customers. Once an industry has been identified as promising and once public funds have been committed to it, there is a natural tendency to ensure that previous expectations are not proven wrong. Governments tend to have the resources of the budget or of market intervention to pursue the support of loss making activities. By contrast, one of the socially most valuable functions of the market is to act as a mechanism for cutting losses and eliminating non-viable ventures.

Whereas governments generally acknowledge the welfare costs of cartels in domestic markets, they tend to be more lenient with respect to anti-competitive co-operation between firms in export markets. The expressed rationale behind this attitude is that competition in world markets is keener than in domestic markets and requires larger units of suppliers. The tacit rationale, however, is that frequently export cartels help countries to postpone adjustment problems, often without the affected foreign countries noticing the full consequences for their economies. It is of course true that export cartels may sometimes facilitate innovation and rationalisation and thus promote technical efficiency, but they also weaken competitiveness and hence may damage overall economic efficiency.

Although different interests are affected by subsidies rather than by trade protection, and although a subsidy normally has a more positive image than a trade barrier, the new export trade interventionism has in principle many of the same drawbacks for national economic welfare and international co-operation as traditional tariffs. Both distort spontaneous market signals and raise doubts as to whether decision makers in the government are better informed about the complex, long-term structural changes and emerging technical solutions than the many, self-interested market participants. They create administrative difficulties similar to those of selective interventions, and they tend to shift the interest of market participants from cost cutting and product improvement to lobbying the government and the bureaucracy.

As most structural problems of the 1970s are shared by the majority of industrial countries, artifical export supports run a serious danger of aggravating the problems of excess capacity in other countries. Whilst one country can always solve its own problem of excess capacities by subsidising exports, all nations taken together cannot. Export subsidies can thus amount to structural beggar-thy-neighbour policies which lead to international repercussions in the form of countervailing interventions. The final effect would be an overall deterioration of the world trade system. In the face of the real dangers of trade confrontation, it seems necessary to set up faster and more positive mechanisms of structural adjustment in the industrial economies and to find ways to speed up the orderly solution of international trade conflicts.

# Unit X

## _____ Social Welfare _____

Since the end of World War II, all Western European nations have implemented vast expansions in their systems of social welfare. During the decades of rapid economic growth that followed the war, increased resources enabled governments to meet continually greater political demands for "cradle to grave" protection against economic adversity. In addition to providing often generous benefits for the unemployed, governments adopted general welfare programs that covered a wide spectrum of social needs—health care and hospitalization, pension plans, public housing, child care, and income allowances to families with children. In many cases, these benefits evolved into legal "entitlements," which the public has since come to consider basic rights. Although the particulars vary from country to country, these comprehensive "safety nets" have constituted a growing percentage of both gross national product and total government expenditures. Consequently, with the slowdown in economic growth and the continuing recession that followed the oil crisis of 1973, these social welfare programs began to pose serious problems of governance. Demands for increases in public services despite falling tax revenues have prompted different political responses, involving social and ethical questions as well as economic policy choices.

This unit traces the development of Western Europe's social welfare systems, describes governance problems related to social welfare, and examines the entitlement programs which were in place in the early 1980s, when their expansion appeared to have come to a halt. The first reading in this unit, "Social Welfare and Politics," presents statistics showing the expansion of social welfare expenditures in Western Europe during the past two decades and suggests some of the social and ethical dimensions involved in the political debate surrounding the social welfare issue. In "The Development of Welfare States in Europe," Peter Flora and Jens Alber set the historical context for the unit with a brief survey of the origins of the social welfare state and a detailed analysis of the growth of social insurance legislation since the turn of the century. "Trends and Problems in Postwar Public Expenditure Development" by Jürgen Kohl examines recent patterns of growth in public expenditures, the roles that different political parties have played in that expansion, and alternative fiscal policies. Kohl also discusses significant differences among Western European countries in regard to social policy.

Reports from two countries present political "case studies" of responses to changing social welfare realities. David Brand, in "Generosity's Price: Social Welfare Costs in the Netherlands," details one example of the high comfort level of European welfare programs and the impact on government when rising welfare expectations can't easily be met. We see what happens when increasing costs and abuses of the system require government to propose social welfare retrenchment while recipients are asking for more benefits. In "Sweden's Welfare State Under Stress," Barnaby J. Feder focuses on popular resistance to a new tax to highlight the political problems the Swedish government faces in trying to bridge the gap between the costs of social services and the government's capacity to pay for them.

# 41

## Social Welfare and Politics

### Elliot Zupnick

This introduction to the growth and scope of welfare services in Western Europe since 1960 points out the economic, social, and moral aspects of political decision making concerning welfare. The accompanying tables and figure are based on statistics compiled by the Organisation for Economic Co-operation and Development; the figure was formulated by *The New York Times*.

---

In a period of fiscal stringency resulting from low growth rates and economic recession, a question that looms large among many Europeans is whether their societies can afford to maintain the extensive social welfare programs that have been set into place over the past century. To many others, however, the more pressing question is whether these societies can afford not to maintain these programs. For while it is almost universally acknowledged that these programs impose enormous strains on the available economic and financial resources of almost all Western European countries, there is a widespread feeling that attempts to reduce them, or even to freeze them at their present level, would be unacceptable to societies that have come to expect ever increasing benefits.

The magnitude of the problem posed by Western Europe's extensive social programs is suggested by an examination of Tables 41.1 and 41.2. Table 41.1 shows government consumption as a percentage of gross domestic product. The large increase in the share of total output absorbed by most Western European governments between 1960 and 1980 is manifest. For the EEC countries alone, this share increased from 14 percent in 1960 to almost 19 percent in 1980. The data in Table 41.2 refer to total outlays of governments. These include, in addition to payments for goods and services—shown in Table 41.1—government transfers. It is through these transfers that governments redistribute income from the taxpayers to the recipients of the transfers. Expressed as a percent-

**TABLE 41.1  Government Final Consumption as a Percentage of GDP**

| | 1960 | 1967 | 1968 | 1969 | 1970 | 1971 | 1972 | 1973 | 1974 | 1975 | 1976 | 1977 | 1978 | 1979 | 1980 | Average | | | |
|---|---|---|---|---|---|---|---|---|---|---|---|---|---|---|---|---|---|---|---|
| | | | | | | | | | | | | | | | | 60–66 | 67–73 | 74–80 | 60–80 |
| United States | 16.9 | 19.3 | 19.2 | 18.8 | 19.2 | 18.4 | 18.4 | 17.7 | 18.3 | 18.9 | 18.5 | 18.0 | 17.4 | 17.4 | 18.1 | 17.6 | 18.7 | 18.1 | 18.1 |
| Japan | 8.0 | 7.7 | 7.4 | 7.3 | 7.4 | 8.0 | 8.2 | 8.3 | 9.1 | 10.1 | 9.9 | 9.9 | 9.7 | 9.8 | 10.0 | 7.9 | 7.8 | 9.8 | 8.5 |
| Germany | 13.5 | 16.3 | 15.6 | 15.8 | 15.9 | 17.1 | 17.4 | 18.1 | 19.7 | 20.8 | 20.2 | 19.9 | 20.0 | 20.0 | 20.4 | 14.8 | 16.6 | 20.1 | 17.2 |
| France | 13.0 | 13.0 | 13.5 | 13.3 | 13.4 | 13.4 | 13.2 | 13.2 | 13.6 | 14.4 | 14.6 | 14.7 | 15.0 | 14.9 | 15.3 | 13.2 | 13.3 | 14.6 | 13.7 |
| United Kingdom | 16.6 | 18.0 | 17.7 | 17.2 | 17.7 | 18.0 | 18.5 | 18.4 | 20.1 | 22.0 | 21.6 | 20.4 | 20.1 | 20.0 | 21.5 | 16.9 | 17.9 | 20.8 | 18.5 |
| Italy | 12.8 | 14.4 | 14.5 | 14.2 | 13.8 | 15.5 | 16.1 | 15.5 | 15.1 | 15.4 | 14.8 | 15.3 | 15.9 | 16.1 | 16.1 | 13.8 | 14.8 | 15.5 | 14.7 |
| Canada | 13.6 | 16.5 | 17.3 | 17.6 | 19.2 | 19.2 | 19.1 | 18.5 | 18.6 | 20.0 | 19.8 | 20.4 | 20.3 | 19.4 | 19.5 | 14.9 | 18.2 | 19.7 | 17.6 |
| **Total of above countries** | 15.5 | 17.0 | 16.8 | 16.5 | 16.7 | 16.6 | 16.4 | 15.9 | 16.6 | 17.5 | 17.1 | 16.7 | 16.2 | 16.3 | 17.0 | 15.9 | 16.6 | 16.8 | 16.4 |
| Austria | 12.8 | 14.6 | 14.8 | 15.1 | 14.7 | 14.8 | 14.6 | 15.1 | 15.8 | 17.2 | 17.6 | 17.4 | 18.3 | 18.0 | 17.8 | 13.1 | 14.8 | 17.4 | 15.1 |
| Belgium | 12.4 | 13.5 | 13.6 | 13.6 | 13.4 | 14.1 | 14.5 | 14.5 | 14.7 | 16.4 | 16.5 | 16.9 | 17.5 | 17.7 | 18.1 | 12.6 | 13.9 | 16.8 | 14.4 |
| Denmark | 13.3 | 17.8 | 18.6 | 18.9 | 20.0 | 21.3 | 21.3 | 21.3 | 23.4 | 24.6 | 24.1 | 24.1 | 24.5 | 25.2 | 26.8 | 15.3 | 19.9 | 24.7 | 20.0 |
| Finland | 11.9 | 15.1 | 15.5 | 14.7 | 14.7 | 15.5 | 15.6 | 15.3 | 15.5 | 17.5 | 18.5 | 18.9 | 18.8 | 18.4 | 18.6 | 13.1 | 15.2 | 18.0 | 15.4 |
| Greece | 11.7 | 13.0 | 12.9 | 12.7 | 12.6 | 12.5 | 12.2 | 11.5 | 13.8 | 15.2 | 15.1 | 16.0 | 15.9 | 16.3 | 16.1 | 11.6 | 12.5 | 15.5 | 13.2 |
| Iceland | 8.5 | 9.6 | 10.0 | 9.5 | 9.7 | 10.0 | 10.4 | 10.1 | 11.0 | 11.1 | 11.0 | 11.0 | 11.5 | 11.7 | 11.6 | 8.6 | 9.9 | 11.3 | 9.9 |
| Ireland | 12.5 | 13.4 | 13.4 | 13.5 | 14.6 | 15.2 | 15.3 | 15.7 | 17.2 | 19.1 | 18.4 | 18.0 | 18.2 | 19.3 | 21.2 | 12.9 | 14.5 | 18.8 | 15.4 |

| | | | | | | | | | | | | | | | | | | | |
|---|---|---|---|---|---|---|---|---|---|---|---|---|---|---|---|---|---|---|---|
| Luxembourg | 9.8 | 11.9 | 11.8 | 10.9 | 10.7 | 11.7 | 11.9 | 11.3 | 11.5 | 14.9 | 14.8 | 16.0 | 15.7 | 15.9 | 16.6 | 10.8 | 11.5 | 15.0 | 12.4 |
| Netherlands | 12.8 | 15.5 | 15.2 | 15.3 | 15.6 | 16.0 | 15.9 | 15.6 | 16.3 | 17.4 | 17.2 | 17.4 | 17.7 | 18.1 | 18.1 | 14.2 | 15.6 | 17.5 | 15.8 |
| Norway | 12.9 | 16.1 | 16.6 | 16.8 | 16.9 | 17.9 | 18.2 | 18.2 | 18.3 | 19.3 | 20.0 | 20.2 | 20.4 | 19.7 | 18.9 | 14.1 | 17.2 | 19.6 | 17.0 |
| Portugal | 10.9 | 13.5 | 13.5 | 13.3 | 14.2 | 13.9 | 13.8 | 13.2 | 14.5 | 15.4 | 14.1 | 14.4 | 14.7 | 14.8 | 15.4 | 12.4 | 13.6 | 14.8 | 13.6 |
| Spain | 7.4 | 8.4 | 8.2 | 8.3 | 8.5 | 8.6 | 8.6 | 8.6 | 8.8 | 9.2 | 9.8 | 10.0 | 10.4 | 10.8 | 11.3 | 7.4 | 8.5 | 10.1 | 8.6 |
| Sweden | 15.8 | 19.6 | 20.6 | 20.8 | 21.6 | 22.5 | 22.8 | 22.7 | 23.2 | 23.8 | 25.0 | 27.6 | 28.0 | 28.4 | 29.2 | 17.1 | 21.5 | 26.5 | 21.7 |
| Switzerland | 8.8 | 10.3 | 10.4 | 10.5 | 10.5 | 10.9 | 10.9 | 11.2 | 11.6 | 12.6 | 13.2 | 13.0 | 12.9 | 12.9 | 12.8 | 10.1 | 10.7 | 12.7 | 11.1 |
| Turkey | 10.5 | 12.3 | 12.6 | 12.4 | 12.9 | 13.4 | 13.8 | 14.4 | 11.3 | 12.2 | 12.8 | 13.9 | 13.5 | 13.7 | 13.0 | 11.6 | 13.1 | 12.9 | 12.6 |
| Small European countries | 11.9 | 13.9 | 14.2 | 14.2 | 14.5 | 15.0 | 15.0 | 14.9 | 15.2 | 16.3 | 16.7 | 17.2 | 17.3 | 17.4 | 17.8 | 12.7 | 14.5 | 16.8 | 14.7 |
| Australia | 9.4 | 12.3 | 12.5 | 12.1 | 12.2 | 12.5 | 12.6 | 13.0 | 13.9 | 15.5 | 16.0 | 16.4 | 16.9 | 16.2 | 16.6 | 10.3 | 12.5 | 15.9 | 12.9 |
| New Zealand | 10.6 | 11.8 | 12.1 | 12.1 | 12.6 | 13.1 | 12.9 | 12.9 | 14.5 | 15.1 | 14.2 | 15.6 | 16.6 | 16.0 | 17.5 | 10.8 | 12.5 | 15.6 | 13.0 |
| Total of the small countries | 11.5 | 13.7 | 13.9 | 13.9 | 14.2 | 14.6 | 14.6 | 14.6 | 15.0 | 16.2 | 16.6 | 17.1 | 17.3 | 17.2 | 17.7 | 12.3 | 14.2 | 16.7 | 14.4 |
| Total CEE | 14.0 | 15.4 | 15.3 | 15.1 | 15.3 | 16.1 | 16.3 | 16.3 | 17.3 | 18.3 | 18.0 | 17.9 | 18.1 | 18.1 | 18.7 | 14.6 | 15.7 | 18.1 | 16.1 |
| Total OCDE-Europe | 13.5 | 15.0 | 15.0 | 14.9 | 15.1 | 15.8 | 15.9 | 15.9 | 16.6 | 17.7 | 17.5 | 17.6 | 17.7 | 17.7 | 18.3 | 14.2 | 15.4 | 17.6 | 15.7 |
| Total OCDE less U.S. | 12.8 | 13.9 | 13.8 | 13.7 | 13.9 | 14.5 | 14.5 | 14.4 | 15.1 | 16.2 | 16.1 | 16.0 | 15.8 | 16.0 | 16.6 | 13.3 | 14.1 | 16.0 | 14.5 |
| Total OCDE | 15.0 | 16.6 | 16.5 | 16.2 | 16.3 | 16.3 | 16.2 | 15.7 | 16.4 | 17.2 | 17.0 | 16.8 | 16.4 | 16.5 | 17.1 | 15.5 | 16.2 | 16.8 | 16.2 |

*Source: OECD Economic Outlook: Historical Statistics 1960–1980* (Paris: OECD, 1982), p. 58.

TABLE 41.2  Total Outlays of Government as a Percentage of GDP

| | 1960 | 1967 | 1968 | 1969 | 1970 | 1971 | 1972 | 1973 | 1974 | 1975 | 1976 | 1977 | 1978 | 1979 | 1980 | Average | | | |
|---|---|---|---|---|---|---|---|---|---|---|---|---|---|---|---|---|---|---|---|
| | | | | | | | | | | | | | | | | 60–66 | 67–73 | 74–80 | 60–80 |
| United States | 27.8 | 31.2 | 31.3 | 30.8 | 32.2 | 32.2 | 31.9 | 31.2 | 32.9 | 35.4 | 34.4 | 33.5 | 33.1 | 32.8 | 33.2 | 28.7 | 31.5 | 33.6 | 31.3 |
| Japan | 20.7 | 22.7 | 22.6 | 21.5 | 19.3 | 20.8 | 21.8 | 22.1 | 24.5 | 27.3 | 27.9 | 29.0 | 31.1 | 31.6 | 32.7 | 22.4 | 21.5 | 29.1 | 24.4 |
| Germany | 32.0 | 38.2 | 37.6 | 37.6 | 37.6 | 38.9 | 39.7 | 40.5 | 43.4 | 47.1 | 46.4 | 46.5 | 46.5 | 46.4 | 46.9 | 35.0 | 38.6 | 46.2 | 39.9 |
| France | 34.6 | 39.0 | 40.3 | 39.6 | 38.9 | 38.3 | 38.3 | 38.5 | 39.7 | 43.5 | 44.0 | 44.2 | 45.2 | 45.4 | 46.2 | 37.1 | 39.0 | 44.0 | 40.0 |
| United Kingdom | 32.6 | 38.5 | 39.6 | 41.5 | 39.3 | 38.4 | 40.0 | 41.1 | 45.2 | 46.9 | 46.1 | 44.1 | 43.7 | 43.5 | 44.6 | 34.5 | 39.8 | 44.9 | 39.7 |
| Italy | 30.1 | 33.7 | 34.7 | 34.2 | 34.2 | 36.6 | 38.6 | 37.8 | 37.9 | 43.2 | 42.2 | 42.5 | 46.1 | 45.5 | 45.6 | 31.6 | 35.7 | 43.3 | 36.9 |
| Canada | 28.9 | 32.1 | 33.0 | 33.5 | 35.7 | 36.6 | 37.2 | 36.0 | 37.4 | 40.8 | 39.6 | 40.6 | 41.0 | 39.3 | 40.7 | 29.5 | 34.9 | 39.9 | 34.8 |
| Total of above countries | 28.9 | 32.4 | 32.6 | 32.2 | 32.6 | 33.0 | 33.1 | 32.9 | 34.8 | 38.0 | 37.2 | 36.8 | 37.3 | 37.5 | 38.3 | 30.2 | 32.7 | 37.1 | 33.3 |
| Austria | 32.1 | 40.5 | 40.6 | 40.3 | 39.2 | 39.7 | 39.8 | 41.3 | 41.9 | 46.1 | 46.9 | 46.8 | 49.7 | 48.8 | 48.5 | 35.3 | 40.2 | 47.0 | 40.8 |
| Belgium | 30.3 | 34.5 | 36.3 | 36.1 | 36.5 | 38.0 | 38.8 | 39.1 | 39.4 | 44.5 | 45.1 | 46.6 | 47.9 | 49.5 | 51.7 | 31.2 | 37.1 | 46.4 | 38.2 |
| Denmark | 24.8 | 34.3 | 36.3 | 36.3 | 40.2 | 42.4 | 41.9 | 40.2 | 44.3 | 47.5 | 47.6 | — | — | — | — | 28.4 | 38.8 | 46.5 | 35.9 |
| Finland | 26.7 | 33.4 | 33.4 | 31.8 | 31.3 | 32.8 | 33.2 | 31.9 | 32.9 | 37.1 | 38.3 | 39.5 | 39.1 | 38.5 | 38.2 | 29.1 | 32.5 | 37.7 | 33.1 |
| Greece[1] | 17.4 | 23.6 | 23.5 | 22.5 | 22.4 | 22.8 | 22.0 | 21.1 | 25.0 | 26.7 | 27.4 | 29.0 | 29.9 | 29.7 | 30.3 | 19.1 | 22.6 | 28.3 | 23.3 |
| Iceland | 28.2 | 32.2 | 33.8 | 30.2 | 29.6 | 32.6 | 33.6 | 35.5 | 36.6 | 38.7 | 33.9 | 34.0 | — | — | — | 26.7 | 32.5 | 35.7 | 30.8 |
| Ireland | 28.0 | 34.8 | 35.2 | 36.6 | 39.6 | 40.5 | 38.8 | 38.9 | 43.1 | 47.2 | 46.8 | 45.5 | 45.7 | — | — | 30.9 | 37.8 | 45.7 | 37.3 |
| Luxembourg | 30.5 | 37.5 | 37.3 | 34.1 | 33.1 | 36.3 | 37.0 | 35.7 | 35.3 | 47.9 | 48.6 | 52.6 | — | — | — | 32.2 | 35.8 | 44.0 | 35.8 |

| | | | | | | | | | | | | | | | | | | | |
|---|---|---|---|---|---|---|---|---|---|---|---|---|---|---|---|---|---|---|---|
| The Netherlands . . . . . . | 33.7 | 42.5 | 43.5 | 43.9 | 45.5 | 47.5 | 48.1 | 48.7 | 50.8 | 55.9 | 55.9 | 56.0 | 57.5 | 59.5 | 62.5 | 37.1 | 45.7 | 56.9 | 46.5 |
| Norway . . . . . . . . | 29.9 | 36.4 | 37.9 | 39.9 | 41.0 | 43.0 | 44.6 | 44.6 | 44.6 | 46.6 | 48.5 | 50.2 | 52.3 | 51.4 | 49.4 | 32.3 | 41.1 | 49.0 | 40.8 |
| Portugal . . . . . . . | 17.0 | 20.9 | 20.9 | 20.9 | 21.6 | 21.3 | 22.7 | 21.3 | 24.6 | 30.2 | 35.1 | 27.5 | 29.3 | — | — | 19.4 | 21.4 | 30.0 | 22.1 |
| Spain . . . . . . . | 13.7 | 21.1 | 21.3 | 21.7 | 22.2 | 23.6 | 23.2 | 23.0 | 23.1 | 24.7 | 26.0 | 27.5 | 29.3 | 30.5 | 32.4 | 15.8 | 22.3 | 27.6 | 21.9 |
| Sweden . . . . . . | 31.1 | 40.0 | 42.6 | 42.8 | 43.7 | 45.5 | 46.4 | 44.9 | 48.1 | 49.0 | 51.9 | 57.9 | 59.6 | 65.1 | 65.7 | 34.0 | 43.7 | 56.8 | 44.8 |
| Switzerland[1] . . . . . | 17.2 | 20.4 | 20.7 | 21.8 | 21.3 | 21.9 | 21.9 | 24.2 | 25.5 | 28.7 | 30.3 | 30.4 | 30.1 | 30.2 | 29.7 | 18.8 | 21.7 | 29.3 | 23.3 |
| Turkey . . . . . | — | 21.0 | 21.9 | 23.1 | 21.9 | 22.1 | 22.5 | — | — | — | — | — | — | — | — | 19.8 | 21.9 | — | 21.0 |
| **Small European countries** . . . . . . . . | 26.1 | 31.6 | 32.7 | 33.0 | 33.7 | 35.1 | 35.3 | 35.8 | 37.2 | 40.5 | 41.9 | 43.4 | 44.4 | 45.3 | 46.6 | 27.7 | 33.9 | 42.8 | 34.8 |
| Australia . . . . . . | 22.1 | 26.3 | 25.1 | 25.1 | 25.5 | 26.2 | 26.3 | 26.8 | 30.4 | 32.4 | 32.9 | 34.3 | 33.7 | 33.2 | 34.1 | 23.9 | 25.9 | 33.0 | 27.6 |
| New Zealand . . | — | — | — | — | — | — | — | — | — | — | — | — | — | — | — | — | — | — | — |
| **Total of the small countries** . . . . . . . | 25.5 | 30.9 | 31.7 | 31.9 | 32.6 | 33.9 | 34.1 | 34.4 | 36.1 | 39.3 | 40.6 | 42.1 | 42.9 | 43.7 | 44.9 | 27.2 | 32.8 | 41.4 | 33.8 |
| **Total CEE** . . . . . . . | 32.1 | 37.5 | 38.2 | 38.3 | 37.9 | 38.6 | 39.5 | 39.8 | 42.1 | 45.8 | 45.5 | 45.4 | 46.2 | 46.2 | 47.0 | 34.4 | 38.5 | 45.5 | 39.5 |
| **Total OCDE-Europe** . . . . | 30.9 | 35.9 | 36.6 | 36.8 | 36.5 | 37.3 | 38.0 | 38.5 | 40.4 | 43.9 | 44.0 | 44.4 | 45.2 | 45.4 | 46.2 | 32.9 | 37.1 | 44.2 | 38.1 |
| **Total OCDE** *less U.S.* . . . | 29.3 | 33.3 | 33.6 | 33.4 | 32.9 | 33.8 | 34.3 | 34.4 | 36.4 | 39.9 | 39.8 | 40.2 | 40.9 | 41.5 | 42.6 | 31.1 | 33.7 | 40.2 | 35.0 |
| **Total OCDE** . . . . . | 28.5 | 32.2 | 32.5 | 32.1 | 32.6 | 33.1 | 33.3 | 33.1 | 35.0 | 38.2 | 37.7 | 37.6 | 38.1 | 38.4 | 39.3 | 29.8 | 32.7 | 37.8 | 33.4 |

[1]Only current disbursements.

*Source: OECD Economic Outlook: Historical Statistics 1960–1980* (Paris: OECD, 1982), p. 59.

Figure 41.1

The New York Times/April 25, 1983

age of gross domestic output, total outlays by EEC governments increased from 32 percent in 1960 to 47 percent in 1980.

Quite aside from the ever increasing difficulty of financing these outlays through increased taxes (see Figure 41.1), the growing importance of governments in the economic sector, as evidenced by the data in Tables 41.1 and 41.2 has had, according to many observers, an adverse impact on productivity by reducing the level of private capital formation and affecting incentives. The need to increase productivity and improve incentives is thus a major argument used by those who advocate a reduction in the social welfare programs. On the other side are, of course, those who argue that a serious reduction in the level of social welfare expenditures would not only generate a high level of social unrest but would also be tantamount to depriving those who remain poor in an affluent society any semblance of hope for the future. Thus economic, social and ethical questions are intricately interwoven in the current debate regarding the future of Europe's social welfare programs. The choice governments make in this sector will have a profound effect not ony on the nature of European societies in the future but also on their ability to govern in the short and medium runs.

# 42

# The Development of Welfare States in Europe

———————— Peter Flora and Jens Alber ————————

Part of a larger study, this selection examines the origins of social expenditures in different Western European countries and traces their patterns of growth, particularly in the area of social insurance.

## THE BEGINNINGS OF THE MODERN WELFARE STATE

While the modern welfare state is a product of the last ninety years, it has an important early history. Gaston Rimlinger has convincingly demonstrated the need to distinguish between two phases of this "prehistory": the "Poor Law" period from the sixteenth to the eighteenth and nineteenth centuries and the "Liberal Break" of the nineteenth century. Poor relief became a matter of national concern in the sixteenth century with the emergence of national states and economies. It was a "relief of the poor within a framework of repression." However, the poor laws contained an element of reciprocal social responsibilities, but they were much more reliant on punishments than on relief. The reciprocal social responsibilities mainly referred to the relationship between individuals and their local communities, since the execution of the national poor laws was left to local authorities.

Whereas the old European welfare states developed very similarly during the poor law period, the liberal break produced many divergences. The core ideas of liberalism—individualistic freedom, equality, and self-help—were antithetical to the former concepts of dependence and protection. The importance of this second phase lies primarily in the coincidence of new social problems created by industrialization and urbanization with an emerging philosophy that facilitated the destruction of old protective institutions.

### The Take-Off Period

The take-off of the modern welfare state occurred in the last two decades of the nineteenth century. We use two measurements to delimit this breakthrough: the increase and structural change of public expenditures with respect to social welfare (social expenditure ratio), and institutional innovations (above all, the institutionalization of social insurance systems). Here, the long-term development of public social expenditures can only be illustrated for three countries for which longitudinal studies are already available: Germany, the United Kingdom, and Sweden. However, they reflect the average level and variation in Europe at the turn of the century, since Germany then had a comparatively high ratio of public social expenditures to GNP and the United Kingdom one of the lowest.

Between the turn of the century and the end of World War II, the ratio of public expenditures to GNP roughly tripled in the three countries. As Figure 42.1 illustrates, social expenditures disproportionally shared in this tremendous increase: in Germany the proportion of social expenditures in the budget rose from about 30 percent to 62 per-

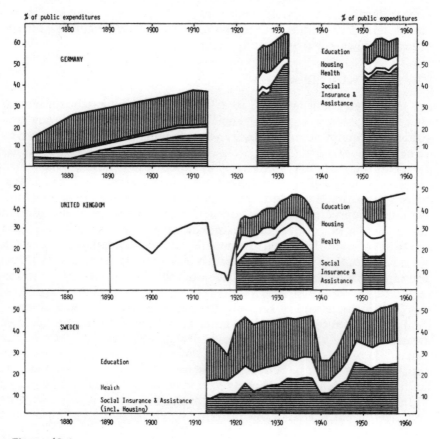

Figure 42.1.

cent, in the United Kingdom from about 20 percent to 47 percent, and in Sweden from about 30 percent to 53 percent from the beginning of the century to 1960. This steady increase was curbed only in times of war, and accelerated during economic depressions.

The trend and time pattern of social expenditures has been predominantly shaped by social security outlays in the sense of transfer payments for social insurance and public assistance. Although the structure of expenditures cannot be given for a common base-year at the start of the century for all three countries, Figure 42.1 illustrates that these payments have absorbed an ever increasing share of the budget. The widening scope of income redistribution through social transfer payments thus seems to be the most significant structural change in the development of social expenditures and of public expenditures in general.

This may justify our concentration on social insurance legislation as the basic institutional breakthrough of the modern welfare state. Four main social insurance (or security) systems developed in relation to different risks: industrial accidents; sickness (and invalidity); old age (and invalidity, survivors); and unemployment.

## The Break with Liberalism

Although there is no uniform sequence in the establishment of these four systems, in general, social insurance for industrial accidents came first, unemployment insurance last, with the other two systems in between. . . .

This sequence may tentatively be explained by the degree to which the introduction of each system represented a break with the liberal ideas concerning the assignment of guilt and responsibility among individuals, groups, and the state. The break with liberalism lay above all in the principle of compulsory insurance as well as in the recognized amount of state (financial) responsibility. In comparison, the break with patrimonial traditions was much less vivid, lying primarily in the principle of individual legal entitlements that is from the liberal tradition.

The introduction of accident insurance or workmen's compensation constituted the least radical break with liberalism since it could be rationalized by redefining the old idea of liability for individually caused damages. Two aspects of employers' liability, however, represented a clear break rather than a mere redefinition. The first was that industrial accidents were increasingly viewed as an inevitable element of industrial production, thus weakening the notion of guilt (with its reliance on court trials) and introducing the principle of automatic compensation for the loss of earnings through work injuries. The other aspect was that the individual liability of employers usually was replaced by a pooling of risks among all employers of an industrial branch. Of our twelve countries, five introduced workmen's compensation schemes first (Belgium, Denmark, France, Sweden, the United Kingdom) mandating employers to provide relief, while the other seven started with compulsory insurance schemes (Austria, Finland, Germany, Italy, the Netherlands, Norway, Switzerland) that, today, all countries possess.

Providing security against risks of nonoccupational origin (sickness and old age) that could not be viewed as individually caused damages constituted a much deeper break with the liberal tradition. Both of these risks at that time were the main causes of poverty and destitution, and their mitigation required the commitment of much greater financial resources than were needed for the compensation of industrial accidents. The primary object of sickness insurance, whether compulsory or only subsidized, was to provide cash benefits in the event of lost earnings due to nonoccupational sickness. The degree of substitution between private (subsidized) and public (compulsory) schemes seems to have been somewhat higher for sickness insurance than for old age insurance. This is suggested by the fact that six countries introduced subsidized voluntary sickness insurance schemes that usually were retained for long periods and reached comparatively high coverage (high coverage: Denmark 1892–1933, Sweden 1891–1947, Switzerland 1911 ff; low coverage: Belgium 1894–1944, France provisional 1852–1930, Italy 1886–1928), whereas only three countries introduced subsidized voluntary old-age insurance (Belgium 1900–1924, France provisional 1856–1910, Italy 1898–1919) with only Belgium reaching a higher level of coverage. Pension insurance schemes usually group together three different risks of long-term character: invalidity, old age, and the death of the family breadwinner (survivors). Of these, old age has generally been the first (together with invalidity) and by far the most important. Besides controlling and subsidizing voluntary schemes, the state intervened primarily in establishing either compulsory public insurance schemes or demogrant (noncontributory) universal pension schemes financed by general revenues.

Unemployment insurance was usually introduced last because the notion of state support for the "undeserving poor" required the most radical break with liberal and patrimonial principles. Due to the special difficulties of solving unemployment through insurance techniques, public assistance programs persisted with subsidized voluntary and compulsory insurance schemes. Three countries still have only subsidized voluntary schemes (Denmark, Finland, Sweden), whereas five others have retained such schemes for a long period (Belgium 1907–1944, the Netherlands 1906–1949, Norway 1906–1938, France 1905–1967, Switzerland 1924–1976). Only four countries introduced compulsory insurance systems from the outset (Austria, Germany, Italy, the United Kingdom).

## THE DEVELOPMENT OF SOCIAL INSURANCE SYSTEMS

### Steps in the Extension of the Social Insurance Schemes

The expansion of social security systems may be described qualitatively by the risks and social categories successively covered, as well as in quantitative terms by the number of insured persons. In general, the sequential steps of extension within each system have followed a similar pattern in including new groups of persons and new types of benefits. Initial provisions for industrial accidents were frequently limited to workers in a few especially dangerous industries. By 1911, when Switzerland introduced its program, all twelve countries had workmen's compensation schemes of some kind, and by the outbreak of World War I all had extended them to the majority of industrial workers. In a second step, the schemes were extended to additional groups, primarily agricultural workers and later to the majority of all employed persons. This step usually was completed between the wars, although Norway and Switzerland did not extend their schemes to agricultural workers until the 1950s. The third step was marked by widening the concept of industrial accidents to include new risks such as occupational diseases. With the exception of the United Kingdom and Switzerland that had broad definitions of industrial accidents from the very beginning, this step was made after World War I. A last step of extension, which largely did not begin before the 1950s and which is not yet complete, consists in the extension of coverage to self-employed persons.

Sickness insurance, at the time of its introduction, was usually limited to industrial workers and a few categories of employees below an income limit. By 1913, when the Netherlands passed a law on compulsory insurance, all countries had taken legislative action to provide some kind of insurance scheme. In the next step coverage was extended to groups such as agricultural workers or higher paid employees. In the countries with compulsory schemes, this step usually occurred in the 1920s. The consolidation of the schemes through the provision of medical benefits, either introduced for the first time (the Netherlands 1941) or improved and extended to new groups, represents a third step. With the exception of the pioneer Norway (1909), medical benefits were generally extended to family members between 1930 and 1945, while their extension to pensioners usually came about a decade later, between 1941 (Germany) and 1955 (Italy). As in the case of industrial accidents, the extension to self-employed persons marks the last and fourth step, mainly in the years after 1950.

In the introductory phase of pension insurance, coverage was usually limited to workers and certain groups of employees, with benefits limited to old age and/or invalidity payments. A first major modification occurred when survivors' benefits were included: Germany was first in 1911 with most countries following by 1930. However, introduction in Switzerland and Sweden did not occur until 1946, with other Scandinavian countries following as late as the 1950s and even 1960s. Another consolidating step consisted in the inclusion of self-employed persons. Here, the old age insurance schemes in Scandinavia covered the entire population from the very beginning, while the other countries moved toward this goal only after World War II. The introduction of periodic adjustments of pensions to price or wage levels, and the combination of fixed (national minimum) benefits with earnings-related pensions may be understood as a fourth and last significant step. Most countries introduced pension adjustments only after World War II and between 1955 and 1965. While countries with earnings-related pension programs moved towards supplementary flat-rate pensions, such as the Netherlands (1956), Italy (1965), and, in a sense, also Germany (1972), countries providing flat-rate pensions, such as the Scandinavian countries and the United Kingdom, introduced supplementary earnings-related pensions in the period of 1959 to 1966.

Unemployment insurance initially was typically limited to industrial workers or specified industries. After the differentiation between insurance benefits of limited duration and unlimited assistance benefits independent of contributions, the major consolidating steps of the insurance systems consisted in the extension of the schemes to wider groups, including agricultural workers, and the introduction of dependants' benefits.

## Stages in Social Insurance Legislation

Considering the general chronological development of all these schemes, it is possible to distinguish four phases or stages of social insurance legislation:

1. A classical introductory phase from the early German legislation until 1914. By the outbreak of World War I, all twelve countries had

some kind of workmen's compensation schemes, ten had introduced either compulsory or subsidized voluntary sickness insurance programs, eight countries provided for old age, while only five had established some kind of unemployment insurance.

2. A phase of extension between the two World Wars. Social insurance was adopted in additional countries and was extended to cover new risks (especially unemployment and occupational diseases) as well as new groups (particularly nonemployed persons such as family members and pensioners), thus adding the idea of a national minimum to the older concept of just wage substitution. At the start of the second World War, the majority of the twelve countries had made accident and sickness insurance compulsory, all countries had introduced some kind of unemployment insurance, and, with the exception of Switzerland, they all provided for old age.

3. A phase of completion immediately after World War II. In this phase, extensive reforms in several countries (Belgium, France, Sweden, Switzerland, the United Kingdom) made the catalogue of covered risks complete, so that by 1950 all nations had rather comprehensive programs for all the four main risks. All countries had a compulsory pension insurance or demogrant scheme; eleven possessed compulsory accident insurance, nine had compulsory sickness insurance, while seven had adopted compulsory unemployment insurance.

4. A phase of consolidation and reorganization after 1950. Two major changes occurred in this phase. The first consisted in extending social insurance to self-employed persons, often accomplished through the establishment of universal insurance systems. This step was to some degree related to Lord Beveridge's idea of national solidarity as the core principle of social security. The second change was constituted by a coordination, and even unification, of existing schemes based on a more comprehensive conception of social security. By 1965, all countries except Germany had extended their pension and sickness insurance schemes to some categories of self-employed, and, beginning in the 1960s, several countries tried to reorganize and unify their social security systems (particularly Italy from 1965, the Netherlands from 1966, Norway from 1970, Belgium from 1970 and Germany from 1972).

## Measuring the Scope of Social Insurance Systems

Quantitative data on the extension of social insurance coverage partly reflect these broad legislative phases. In order to facilitate a comparison of national scheme extensions, an index of social insurance coverage has been developed that consists of a weighted average of the percent of the labor force covered by the four systems. The weights given to the four systems, tentatively derived from their varying financial as well as sociological significance, are: 1.5 for old age insurance coverage, 1.0 for sickness and unemployment insurance coverage, and 0.5 for accident insurance coverage. The percent covered by subsidized voluntary systems only is divided by 2.

The mean index value demonstrates a steady rise in social insurance coverage over this period. After a gradual and modest increase up to 1910, coverage expands quickly in the interwar period and after World War II up to 1960 and then levels off. Judging from the mean and median quinquennial percentage growth of coverage in the twelve countries, the period from 1945 to 1960 stands out as the phase of major extension. The years from 1925 to 1930 and from 1935 to 1940 also witnessed rapid growth, but only the decade from 1950 to 1960 has seen a major and general extension of social insurance coverage. In single countries, the growth of coverage in general has been relatively steady, with only a few periods of very rapid extension (Germany 1885–1891, the United Kingdom 1906–1911, Sweden 1913, Italy 1919, Denmark 1933, Norway 1936–1940, Finland 1939, Belgium 1944–1946, Switzerland 1947–1948, the Netherlands 1951–1957, Sweden 1955, Norway 1956, Italy 1955–1960, and Finland 1963–1964).

Looking at the differences among the European countries . . . we can see that the classical introductory phase before World War I was relatively homogeneous. Most countries kept the initial scopes of the systems limited, and only Germany and Denmark stood out as pioneers. The second phase of extension between the two world wars witnessed the greatest divergence with the Scandinavian countries of Sweden, Denmark, and Norway, as well as the United Kingdom, extending the scope of their systems, while Finland, Switzerland, France, Belgium, and Italy lagged far behind. The greatest divergence occurs in 1935. The phases of completion and consolidation after World War II demonstrate a slow convergence still characterized by the lead of the Scandinavian countries and the United Kingdom that all have national insurance schemes in at least one of the four systems. This group is followed by five countries with index values close to the mean with compulsory insurance systems of a more limited coverage (Italy, France, Austria, Belgium, Germany). Switzerland, which still mainly relies on subsidized voluntary insurance, is last with an extraordinary low index value. The international differences began to diminish especially in the 1960s, when several countries approached complete coverage of the resident adult population. . . .

# Trends and Problems in Postwar Public Expenditure Development

—————————— Jürgen Kohl ——————————

This selection provides further historical perspectives on the political problems of governance that stem from expanded entitlement programs. Kohl analyzes patterns in the growth of social expenditures by different Western European countries since 1950, including the impact of the ideological stance of the party in power on the spending behavior of governments.

## INTRODUCTION

A widely shared concern of both political scientists and politicians is that Western democracies are confronting a fundamental crisis. In recent years, they appear to be more and more ungovernable because their governments are suffering under the burden of overload. There is consensus that this crisis is most clearly manifested in certain dilemmas of public choice, specifically the structural problems of budgeting public resources to meet public needs. Some neo-Marxist critics refer to "the fiscal crisis of the (capitalist) state" that will eventually be transformed into a decisive "legitimation crisis" of (bourgeois) parliamentary democracy. Conservative and liberal critics, on the other hand, blame exaggerated and unrestricted welfare state development for eliciting "the revolution of rising expectations" which is now exceeding the fiscal capacities of the state.

The origins of the present problems, according to both perspectives, lie in the policy-making structure of capitalist mass democracies. The rapid economic growth of the recovery period after World War II enabled Western democracies to increase public spending in almost all fields because of greater fiscal resources. Now, as the prospects for sustained economic growth diminish, political pressure is exerted on governments and parliaments to maintain and even expand the present level of public expenditures. Both former obligations and increased needs during economic crisis suggest that relative expenditure growth (public spending as a percentage of GNP) is disproportionately expanded when economic development slackens. Thus, public expenditure development is less a function of economic growth and is instead primarily determined by political and ideological factors.

Certainly, the general growth of public expenditures has been accompanied by structural shifts within them. For a better understanding of the prime determinants of these growth tendencies, one must differentiate between expenditure items to determine which are growing most rapidly and thereby shaping the general trend. Most authors, whether conservative or radical, agree that social expenditures have been the outstanding component in the secular rise of public expenditures, accounting for the larger share of general growth during past decades. Furthermore, it is significant to note the internal shifts within social expenditures between transfer payments (for purposes of income redistribution) and the provision of social services (such as health and education).

The sociopolitical mechanism underlying the disproportionate growth of social expenditures is often explained by the growing political power of the working class, represented by trade unions and (socialist) labor parties, which have first demanded social security and later income redistribution. After the institutionalization of social security systems, coverage has been extended and the relative levels of benefits raised repeatedly. Similarly, when private consumption reached a certain level of saturation, demands for superior public goods, especially in education and health care, have been advanced. Minimum standards for the provision of social services have been typically established as social rights and have maintained that identity even as basic standards have vastly increased. Moreover, since such demands are usually tied to the social goals of equality of opportunity and social justice, social spending is not easily reduced when economic resources decline. The fiscal problem is further compounded when increasing demands for public expenditures are not met by a corresponding willingness of the electorate to accept the necessary financial burden, such as higher taxes or social security contributions. While this tension exists in the provision of public goods in general, it is even more problematic in the case of social expenditures when claims are advanced for the sake of social justice or redistribution.

The logic of competitive politics holds that governments faced with the alternative of losing public support will tend to meet new demands without imposing new burdens. Various possibilities exist, which can be used in combination: increasing budget deficits to be financed by loans; cutting other expenditure items in favor of social transfer and social service expenditures; and, because no immediate pressure is exerted on behalf of them, reducing public investments. In all cases, the prospects for future economic development will be adversely affected.

These demands and expectations do not arise in all countries with equal intensity, nor do different political systems respond to the problems they pose in the same way. There are great differences between countries concerning, for instance, the organizational strength of the working class, ideological traditions, and existing program structures. Moreover, the political structure of interest articulation, aggregation, and representation varies greatly, so that even similar problems will probably lead to different political solutions regarding revenue and expenditure decisions. Last but not least, one must consider the role of political leadership in managing and responding to popular demands since this will lead to varying degrees of popular satisfaction.

For an appreciation of both present problems and future prospects of welfare state development, it may be helpful to compare and examine in greater detail the relevant empirical evidence. The above considerations have been formulated into the following questions for our analyses: First, what is the relationship between economic growth and public expenditure growth? Second, what is the significance of social expenditures as the driving force in public expenditure growth? Third, has the party composition of government influenced expenditure growth (and how)? Finally, what are some alternative political answers, as represented by fiscal policies, to the problems of expenditure growth?

The following analyses are based mainly on the series of OECD Statistics of National Accounts for 1950 to 1975. Within this framework, the public sector is broadly defined as all levels of government and the institutions of social insurance. This is a rather comprehensive definition of the consolidated public sector compared to a more narrow conception of the state excluding social security which typically prevails in budgetary statistics. Because the framework of national accounting does not always provide adequate functional classifications of expenditures, especially for social expenditures, we have established an additional data set based on the Social Accounts series of the European Community covering the original member countries from 1962 to 1975.

## PUBLIC EXPENDITURES AND THE CONSTRAINTS OF ECONOMIC GROWTH

### Trends in the Development of Total Public Expenditures

Total public expenditures are defined as the sum of central and local government expenditures plus social security outlays. On this basis, the size of the public sector varies considerably among the Western European (and North American) nations, although all have experienced substantial expansion of the public sector in the postwar period.

At the beginning of the period, public expenditure/GNP ratios ranged from about 20 percent to 30 percent, the latter mark reached only by the European big powers of the United Kingdom, France, and Germany. As a consequence of the general rise of expenditures, the 1975 levels ranged from an exceptionally low 30 percent in Switzerland to more than 50 percent in Sweden and the Netherlands.

The differing paces of development have led to significant changes in the rank order of countries. Those departing from high initial levels have expanded at comparatively moderate rates, while in Sweden, Denmark, Norway, and the Netherlands, countries with low 1950 levels, the rise has been extremely rapid. From an initial level of 20 to 25 percent, the public expenditure/GNP ratio has increased at a rate of about 1 percent per year, thus doubling within a quarter of a century. A rising public expenditure/GNP ratio means that public expenditures have grown faster than total economic output; this is even the case using constant prices, that is, when the usually higher inflation rates in the public sector are accounted for. This is even more striking since almost all of the countries have experienced rapid economic growth of more than 4 percent per year in the postwar period. . . .

## Expenditure Trade-offs: Public Consumption vs. Social Transfers

Public consumption expenditures (for the provision of public services including defense) and transfer expenditures (for the redistribution of cash income) form the two largest budget shares in the public sector and are of roughly equal size. . . . [T]wo different patterns can be discerned. These are the Scandinavian pattern (Denmark, Sweden, Norway, and Finland), largely followed by the United Kingdom and Ireland, where public consumption expenditures prevail, and the Continental pattern (France, Italy, Belgium, the Netherlands, and Luxembourg), where more resources are devoted to transfer expenditures. Germany and Austria are somewhat between, but are moving closer to the Scandinavian pattern in recent years. These patterns proved sufficiently stable when tested at successive points in time.

It is suggested that these patterns reflect two different approaches to public policy, and to social policy in particular. The Continental pattern emphasizes the redistribution of cash income relegating final consumption decisions to individual preferences. While this may be an effective way to achieve income maintenance or greater income equality, cash transfers encourage reliance on the market provision of social services and thereby reinforce private modes of producing and delivering such services. Governments preferring this approach sometimes explicitly rely on the principle of the superiority of market production, even for social services such as health care.

The Scandinavian pattern, on the other hand, favors the public provision of services whereby collective choice more directly shapes the structure of supply and the mode of control. This approach seems especially suitable to effect changes in the quality or kind of services and to counterbalance disadvantages of private market provision. . . .

## THE ROLE OF SOCIAL EXPENDITURES IN EXPENDITURE GROWTH

### Social Transfers

Disaggregating budget components is once again appropriate for explaining the general growth pattern of public expenditures. Social expenditures are of crucial importance because a great part of present political and economic problems is often attributed to accelerated welfare state development and its financial burdens.

Efforts to quantitatively assess the significance of social expenditures must resort to approximations. The category of social transfers is a good example of this, since social security benefits that have traditionally formed the core of social expenditures . . . comprised from 80 to 90 percent of transfer payments. . . .

By 1975, social transfers have risen to levels of more than 10 percent of the GNP in all countries (except Finland) whereas in 1950, only Germany and France had surpassed this level. In 1975, the most advanced level was attained by the Netherlands (26 percent) followed by France, Italy, and Belgium. But relative growth, as indicated by the income elasticities, has also been considerable in the United States and the Scandinavian countries. They started at very low levels (about 5 percent) and have almost tripled their transfers/GNP ratio. From the mid-sixties on, an acceleration of these growth tendencies can be observed in almost all countries. . . .

. . . Regarding transfers . . . as "publicly supported private consumption" and comparing them to private final consumption reveals a rapid increase at even higher rates than the social transfers/GNP ratio increase. The share of private consumption in the final use of the GNP is on the decline everywhere by an average of more than 10 percentage points since 1950. This means that in most countries, one-fifth to one-fourth of private consumption is financed by public budgets through social transfer payments. The share of "pure" private consumption (total private consumption minus social transfers) has fallen below the level of 50 percent of the GNP.

Despite the current variations in the level of resources devoted to social transfer expenditures, their growth rates have been consistently higher than those for total public expenditures. . . . As a result, they have gained additional importance in the consolidated budgets of all countries (except Germany). In those countries that followed the Continental pattern (France, Italy, the Netherlands), transfers accounted for more than 70 percent of the total expenditure growth. . . . This is partly explained by the fact that defense expenditure shares (which are included in public consumption) have gradually, but considerably declined from the mid-fifties to levels of less than 10 percent in 1975. This decrease has to some extent compensated for the increase in *civil* public consumption (which can be considered as the production costs of public goods and services), so that only small differences appear between civil public consumption and transfer expenditure growth when compared at current prices. But differences are again pronounced when compared at constant prices because the former are usually subject to higher rates of cost inflation than cash transfers which are usually deflated by the consumer price index.

## Total Social Outlays

But if inter-country comparisons of social expenditures are restricted to transfer expenditures only, the picture is likely to be distorted. The total outlays for health, for instance, also include employee wages and investment expenditures, in addition to subsidies and transfers. The comparison may be extremely misleading unless differences in institutional arrangements of services are taken into consideration. . . . It is essential to note that social expenditures are defined here as all expenditures for social risks or needs irrespective of their economic nature (i.e., whether they are spent as cash transfers, as reimbursements for private outlays, or as employee wages for the provision of certain services in kind).

Because of this more comprehensive definition, compared to the narrow concept of social transfers, the GNP shares are in general substantially larger and inter-country differences are less pronounced. But the basic trend is confirmed again: while in 1962 the social expenditures ratio did not exceed 20 percent of the GNP in any of the original member countries, it had crossed this benchmark by 1975 in practically all of them. The rate of increase, however, has been very different for the individual countries: extremely rapid in the Netherlands which started from the lowest level in 1962 and now holds the top position with a ratio twice as high as the former one, but very slow in France which only climbed from 16 percent to 20 percent over a 12-year period.

The differential rates of change reveal another interesting feature: In the 1960s, a trend toward convergence and greater harmonization, and a leveling of inter-country differences seemed to emerge in accordance with the hopes and political objectives associated with the formation of the European Economic Community. In the seventies, this trend is somewhat reversed, widening the gap between the leading countries (the Netherlands and Germany) and the laggards (France, Belgium, and Luxembourg). . . .

The differences are even more pronounced when expressed in absolute terms. For instance, social expenditures per capita in Germany, Denmark, and the Netherlands are twice the level of those in the United Kingdom and Italy. This strongly suggests that attainment of large per capita increases in social expenditures has been facilitated by fairly effective economic performance. Those countries suffering most from economic difficulties have remained at low absolute levels, despite their efforts to raise relative expenditure levels.

### Determinants of Social Expenditure Growth

In order to achieve a more precise understanding of the prime determinants of social expenditure growth, expenditures are subdivided here into the functional categories health, old age, invalidity and occupational injuries, unemployment, and family. . . . Such functional classifications should be approached cautiously because national social security institutions do not cover a similar range of problems nor can the benefits they provide be attributed to just one single function. Therefore, the task of converting national statistical series and assigning identical functions cannot be solved unambiguously.

Despite these reservations, some conclusions concerning the average structure and the direction of change may be drawn: Expenditures for health services and old age (including survivors') pensions are the most important items in all countries. Taken together, they account for two-thirds of all social expenditures in most cases. Expenditures for old age, still the largest single item, range from 30 percent to almost 50 percent, while health expenditures cluster around 30 percent. Expenditures for invalidity and occupational injuries seem to vary greatly between countries, but this is probably due to differing institutional arrangements and statistical difficulties rather than political priorities.

Despite their political salience, expenditures for unemployment represent only a small portion of social expenditures. They show a distinctly upward trend in all countries in recent years, undoubtedly due to the increasing inability of Western economies to absorb potential members of the labor force. But interestingly enough there is only a low association between unemployment rates and unemployment expenditures when tested cross-nationally. This probably suggests differing priorities for governmental action and/or highly different standards and requirements for benefits.

Family allowances and related measures are on the decline in most countries, particularly in those following the "Romantic" pattern that traditionally gave high priority to family policy. In France they declined from almost 30 percent to 20 percent and in Italy from more than 20 percent to about 10 percent within a decade. Family-related expenditures are stabilizing now at a lower limit of about 10 percent, while somewhat higher levels are still maintained by some predominantly Roman Catholic countries (France, Ireland, Belgium).

The trend in expenditures for old age pensions and survivors' benefits is closely linked to demographic factors such as changes in the age structure, longevity, and mortality rates. While these conditions vary somewhat from country to country, on the average this expenditure item requires a fairly constant share in social expenditures, but of course a larger share in the GNP.

Health expenditures have exhibited the most rapid increases during the last decade and gained additional importance in all countries. In contrast to the outlays for pension, invalidity, or occupational injuries' insurance, which are almost exclusively cash transfers to private households, an increasing part of health expenditures is not for income maintenance during sickness, but for the provision of medical services. Because of the comparatively high rate of cost inflation that affects the direct public provision of services, an important part of rising health expenditures must be attributed to this factor.

In short, we can conclude that the development of social expenditures is conditioned mainly by three sets of factors:

*Demographic shifts*, particularly changes in the age structure of the population creating greater demand for social services. It is plausible to assume that, given certain standards for individual benefits, health expenditures will develop at the rate of growth of the total population, old age expenditures at the growth rate of the population group aged 65 years or more, and family allowances and related grants at the rate of change of the younger population group under twenty. All these expenditures must be financed mainly by taxes and contributions of the gainfully employed labor force. Since in almost all Western European countries the labor force is growing at a much lower rate than the other population groups, total outlays will *ceteris paribus* exceed the receipts. This eventually results in the necessity to raise the relative burden on the active labor force, or to cut certain services or transfer payments.

*Cost inflation*, resulting from differential productivity gains on the supply side. Because the production of public goods and services is subject to low productivity gains (compared to the industrial production sector) and at the same time lacks the supply-demand equilibrium provided by market production, rising nominal expenditures are required just to maintain the same level of performance. This applies primarily to health and educational services that are extremely labor-intensive and must be controlled for when attempting to infer real improvements in services from an increase in social expenditures.

*"Real" improvements*, in standards and quality of services. Such improvements have been numerous in practically all fields of social policy. The coverage of established social security schemes has been extended, for instance, to include additional population groups. In addition, the level of benefits compared to previous earnings has been raised, or the eligibility requirements have been reduced. The quality of health services is improved, for instance, when new risks are covered by health insurance or when medical care is intensified and made more effective.

Obviously, this last set of factors is largely dependent on political decision making and subject to political controversy. Therefore, it is expected that governments with different political and ideological commitments will influence social expenditure growth in particular and public expenditure growth in general. Although demographic and cost inflation factors unfortunately cannot be controlled for in the following analyses, it is assumed that they probably affect expenditure development in different countries in a similar way. Thus, we shall turn to an analysis of governmental influence on public expenditures in order to explain further the differences in growth rates.

## PARTY IN POWER AND PUBLIC SECTOR DEVELOPMENT

It has been clearly demonstrated in the preceding discussion that there are impressive differences between Western European countries with regard to the development of public expenditures, despite the similarity of general growth tendencies. They started at different levels after the war, experienced differing paces of development during the last decades and have now arrived at considerably different expenditure levels. These variations must now be examined against sociopolitical factors that might have encouraged or impeded public expenditure growth.

The sociopolitical mechanisms leading to increased state activity and expenditures have been briefly sketched in the introduction. Taking regard to national variations in political conditions, we can now venture some more specific hypotheses. Different expenditure levels after the Second World War, for instance, may be due, among other factors, to the degree of war involvement that required (and made possible) extraordinary efforts to raise resources. Once the machinery for extracting resources [the tax system] was built up, revenues could easily be directed to other expenditure purposes. The social security institutions developed earlier are probably of major importance in explaining social transfer expenditure levels. Similarly, the older ideological traditions of liberal and authoritarian rule and the corresponding conceptions of the responsibilities of the state have probably exerted lasting influences on the size of state bureaucracies and public budgets. Likewise, the different approaches to social service provision outlined above have had an impact on the emphasis placed upon transfer as opposed to public consumption expenditures. However, the following considerations may serve as a background for our analysis of welfare state development in the postwar decades and our understanding of the impact of political and ideological structures.

Increased welfare spending is most favored by the lower strata of the population both because of their urgent need for income maintenance measures and their potential gains from income redistribution while the middle and upper classes typically resist such attempts. The political articulation and aggregation of these interests and demands are, of course, structured by the opportunities for political organization and by the existing party system. While other social cleavages may be important, these economic interests will take precedent in the programs and the political rhetoric of the socialist or labor parties on the one hand and conservative and liberal ones on the other. Religion-based parties, common in Western Europe, are more difficult to assess, depending on whether traditional or social reformist tendencies prevail.

Because socialist parties traditionally stood for progressive taxation, both to advance social justice and to mobilize the fiscal resources needed to carry out social reforms, it is assumed that they also favor increasing the levels of total expenditures. Conversely, conservative and liberal parties are expected to oppose not only welfare state development, but increased activity beyond the classic functions of the state in general and interventions in the capitalist economy in particular. Therefore, they are expected to keep expenditure levels and increases as low as possible.

We can hypothesize then that countries with a large, strongly organized working class will lead in welfare spending and eventually in public expenditure increases in general. But party strength expressed as the number of electoral votes is not directly translated into political power since electoral systems and parliamentary rules of representation intervene. Moreover, participation in government is the decisive threshold since ultimately executive power and the command of a parliamentary majority will most effectively determine budget decisions. . . .

. . . A few generalizations are suggested. . . . With respect to total expenditures, "pure" socialist or socialist-dominated governments seem to increase their expenditures more rapidly than "pure" conservative governments. However, the strongest propensity toward disproportionate increases is found with Center governments (mostly conservative-socialist coalitions). The difference between Center-Right and Center-Left/Left governments is only small.

The growth pattern of social transfer expenditures is somewhat different. Social transfers most rapidly increased under Center-Right and Center coalitions. While conservative majority governments again show the smallest increases, leftist governments also remain below the average. . . .

------------------------------ *44* ------------------------------

# Generosity's Price: Social Welfare Costs in the Netherlands

-------------------- **David Brand** --------------------

This *Wall Street Journal* report summarizes the Netherlands' response to the political dilemma which faced Western
European governments in 1982, when unemployment, already high, was rising as economic growth was declining in a
period of extended recession. The question was how to pay for
existing entitlement programs without impairing recovery
and how to deal with demands for expanded benefits.

Frits van Gompel is the well-nurtured product of Holland's benefi-
cent society. A comfortable home, take-home pay of $186 a week, de-
cent schools for his children and no worries about medical bills would
seem to frame a portrait of a satisfied man.

Satisfied, that is, except for one problem: Frits van Gompel, car-
penter and family man, has been unemployed for the past two years and
sees little hope of finding a job soon.

This is unemployment, Netherlands style. Two decades of an increasingly generous social-welfare system have resulted in the world's
most-comfortably-off jobless workers. Unemployment benefits that
last for 2½ years, state-subsidized housing, child allowances and free
medical care are shielding Holland's fast-growing ranks of the unemployed against the worst financial hardships of the recession.

Western Europe generally is a comfortable place to be today even if
you're unemployed with a family and a mortgage to worry about. Belgium's unemployment benefits never run out; Denmark pays its jobless
workers a handsome 90% of their previous wage; several countries pay
child allowances for full-time students well into their twenties, and
Holland gives its unemployed workers vacation pay.

Although many of the 11.3 million unemployed workers in the
U.S. might look enviously at such benefits, Europe has come to regret
its excess of generosity and is starting to cut back. As the recession
deepens and more workers are thrown onto the unemployment rolls,
the rate of public spending is outpacing economic growth, resulting in

widening budget deficits. "The expansionary era for Europe's social-se-curity systems is over," says a Common Market official in Brussels. "The programs have to be adapted to economic reality."

In recent days the Common Market has warned its 10 member countries that they must give priority to cutting back on public spend-ing. The reason for the community's alarm is clear. It estimates that member countries last year spent 26% of their combined gross national product on social programs. That compares with 1981 estimated U.S. spending of just 10% of GNP. . . .

The fast-rising growth of unemployment over the past two years is the major villain. The Common Market countries now have 10.1% of their work force, or about 11 million people, out of work. And within a year the community expects a further one million workers to go on re-lief.

## PEAKING IS FORECAST

A labor official at the Organization for Economic Cooperation and Development, in Paris, says that government spending on unemploy-ment benefits in Western industrialized nations will reach peak levels this year. In Western Europe the problem is particularly acute, he says, because far fewer jobless workers than in the U.S. are finding new em-ployment quickly. About 70% of unemployed workers in the U.S. find work within three months, compared with only about 41% in France and less than 37% in Britain.

Because the rising unemployment means that there are fewer workers in private industry to provide the financing for social-security programs, European payroll taxes are rising alarmingly. Last year Dutch companies and their employees contributed nearly 58% of payroll to fund everything from unemployment benefits to health care. This year their contribution has risen to over 59%. Both West Germany and Swe-den last year contributed over 35% of payroll in social-security taxes—but the U.S. contribution was a mere 18%.

As a result, the ax has started to fall on social spending. Britain has tightened the rules for receiving unemployment benefits, and Denmark has stopped adding inflation adjustments to all social-security benefits. West Germany probably will delay increases in pensions next year, Bel-gium is reducing family allowances and France appears to be on the verge of raising social-security payroll taxes.

## MORE WAYS HUNTED

Most Western European states—Sweden being the one exception—are looking for more radical ways to stop the steep rise in social spending. Some countries, such as Holland, are talking about entirely re-vamping their systems. There is much interest in a forthcoming OECD conference on social security that will discuss such possibilities as sharply limiting unemployment benefits and channeling more money into retraining programs. The European Trade Union Confederation in Brussels is attracting attention with a suggestion that unemployment schemes should be funded on the basis of a company's profits rather than on the size of its work force.

But the cuts in the systems are likely to be limited, and there clearly is little sentiment for dismantling welfare states. There was a public outcry in Britain recently when a government think-tank report suggested replacing the National Health Service with private insur-ance—a suggestion quickly disavowed by Prime Minister Margaret Thatcher.

The U.S. is often singled out as having the type of social-security system that many European countries don't want to emulate, both be-cause of the relatively low benefits in the U.S. and the mixture of pri-vate and publicly financed social welfare schemes. Victor Halberstadt, professor of finance at Leiden University in Holland, reacts in horror to the suggestion that "we should ever go to the extreme of the situation in the U.S." and Martin Hutsebaut, a labor specialist at the European Trade Union Confederation, declares that "you certainly won't find any European workers supporting the U.S. unemployment-benefits scheme."

Europe's unemployed, with their access to elaborate systems of long-lasting jobless benefits, free medical care and subsidized housing, are "very well off" when compared with their U.S. counterparts, ob-serves an OECD labor expert. Unemployed Americans are receiving an average jobless benefit of $112 a week. Once this is exhausted, the main recourse is welfare and food stamps.

Most U.S. states provide a basic 26 weeks of benefits, and 38 states are providing a further 10 weeks under a new six-month federal program (three other states are allowing eight weeks and the rest six weeks). Workers in 15 states with high unemployment rates are receiving an extra 13 weeks of benefits under a federal-state program.

For many Americans, mainly those who haven't worked long enough to build up qualification credits, there are no benefits at all. The U.S. Bureau of Labor Statistics estimates that only 52% of jobless workers now are able to qualify for unemployment benefits. Holland, where nearly all jobless workers qualify for benefits, would appear to be the land of milk and money by comparison.

Holland's social-security system has grown like topsy since the in-troduction of its retirement-pension scheme in 1957. In the 1960s, as profits from the country's rich natural-gas fields began to flow, the sys-tem increased in generosity. Even during the 1970s, when other Western economies began to slump, the Dutch increased their social spending. "We assumed that economic growth would be with us for decades—we made a drastic mistake," says Mr. Halberstadt of Leiden University.

This year the social-security program will soak up about 35% of all government spending. Unemployment benefits, the fastest-growing part of this outlay, will cost $3.1 billion this year, and the estimate for next year is $4.8 billion. But the financing base for the system is crumbling as the dole lines grow. Unemployment is 10.8% of the labor force, and a 14% rate is forecast for next year.

Mr. Halberstadt, who is also an adviser to the government on social-security policy, says the system is getting out of hand because the number of people receiving benefits of some kind almost equals the number of workers in the private sector. "We are simply overcaring," he says. "For too long we've lived with the illusion that you can carry a welfare state at this level in a recession." But how can the social-security system continue to be financed, he says, when the budget deficit has doubled over the past four years? The only answer, he says, is to introduce a less expensive system.

Dutch workers are loath to see any cutbacks in the system. Garage mechanic Klaas de Jong, 35, has been out of work for nearly two years and complains that he "just can't get by" on his take-home benefits of $147 a week. For the first six months of unemployment he was paid 80% of his salary under the state unemployment-insurance plan. Then he began drawing benefits at the rate of 75% of his salary under the two-year plan run by the municipalities.

Mr. de Jong pays only $161 a month in rent for his house in Vianen, a pleasant town about 20 miles from Amsterdam. The rent is low because the local building society that owns the house gets financial support from the government. Mr. de Jong's rent is lowered even further by the $100 a month he receives in direct rent subsidy from the government. He also receives $278 every three months in family allowance for his two children.

If he is still out of a job at the end of 2½ years, he will begin drawing welfare payments, which are tied to the minimum wage of $171 a week. But Mr. de Jong won't be applying for welfare. "It won't be enough to pay my bills, and anyway they put you through a means test," he complains. Instead, he plans to open his own garage.

One thing that increasingly worries Dutch officials in their efforts to pare social-security costs is the abuses that have grown along with the unemployment rolls. A major problem is moonlighting workers who are also collecting unemployment benefits. "Like everyone else, I work on the side to get by," confesses an Amsterdam man who is collecting jobless benefits. "It's very dangerous," says another Amsterdam man. "With so much unemployment about, you risk being denounced by your neighbors. A friend of mine went to jail for three months for moonlighting."

Another widespread abuse that is only now being checked involves Holland's disability-insurance program, which allows incapacitated workers to spend the rest of their working lives on 80% of their previous pay, adjusted each year for inflation. There now are 750,000 workers on this program, a fact that Mr. Halberstadt calls "incredible." He says, "You cannot tell me that 15% of the Dutch working-age population is disabled."

Typically, he claims, the program is used by employers who want to avoid the red tape of getting the regional employment office's approval to lay off workers. Workers agree to the collusion, he says, because of the high lifetime benefits they will receive. First, he says, a worker will remain at home for up to a year on 80% of his pay under the state sick-pay program, with the usual complaint being low-back pain. (By paying a low insurance premium to the government, a worker can draw 100% of his salary for the year.)

At the end of the year, says Mr. Halberstadt, it has been increasingly common for the disability plan's medical service to declare a worker permanently disabled so that he can draw 80% of his pay until he qualifies for state retirement benefits at 65.

As an example of the benefits awarded by the program—although certainly not as an example of fraud—Anton van den Ham, 43, of Vianen has been living on disability benefits since 1971. His weekly check is $135, supplemented by his wife's earnings as a packer in a book club. He pays a mere $116 a month for his spacious, subsidized house and gets an educational supplement to send one of his three children to a special school.

Sitting in his airy living room, which is filled with plants and caged parrots, Mr. van den Ham explains that he suffers from asthma and that "I'm sick so often it's impossible to hold down a job." Once he was a crane operator at a local plant, now he spends his time providing free counseling for local residents on how to apply for social-security benefits.

Mr. Halberstadt exclaims that "this is a country of free riders that is about to spend itself into poverty unless changes are made." The changes now being discussed aim at trimming $5.4 billion from the Dutch budget, mostly in social-security cuts, by next year.

It is proposed that all benefits and family allowances be frozen at present levels and that health-care services be reduced. In the past the social-security system acted as a "good stabilizer" for Holland's economy, says Social Affairs Minister Louw de Graf. "But because we went too far in social-security expenditures," he says, "we're on a downward spiral. We've got to stop the decline now."

# 45

## Sweden's Welfare State Under Stress

### Barnaby J. Feder

Returned to power in late 1982, Sweden's socialist government attempted to raise revenues to pay for welfare entitlements without discouraging economic expansion. This report from *The New York Times* outlines the political quandary the government faced when strong public opposition developed to some of those revenue measures.

The more that Swedes think about their Government's latest efforts to prop up their welfare state by raising taxes, the less they like it.

They went along with December's increase of two percentage points in the value added tax, making a total charge of 23.46 percent on most of the things consumers buy. They also grudgingly accepted large increases in inheritance taxes, a rise in payroll taxes paid by employers, special taxes on video equipment and a proposed cut in tax concessions for stockholders.

But their irritation boiled over with a new law intended to help the Social Democratic administration collect income taxes from a vast army of part-time workers. These are Swedes who do repair and service work on a barter basis or for cash. This "gray" area of the economy has provided savings for consumers and extra income—none of it reported—for the moonlighting workers.

The new law, requiring all Swedes to report the names and social security numbers of people doing work for them, is widely known as the "informers' law." Even Swedes who lack sympathy for those earning money outside the tax system are troubled by the implication that individuals must become, in effect, Government tax agents.

"It's a typical example of Sweden at its worst—a drive toward perfection, even perfection of stupidity," said Carl Bildt, a Moderate Party member of Parliament. The Moderates, Sweden's major conservative party, have argued that the ruling Social Democrats should reduce both social services and taxes.

In early April the Government tried to calm the uproar by softening the new law. It said that Swedes who had not had any work done for them would not have to file forms, that the minimum amount to be reported would be doubled (to 1,000 kronor, about $133) and that the workers' social security numbers would not be required. This final concession could make the law hard to enforce.

In many ways, the surge of protest against the new law sums up the problems Sweden has faced in dealing with the yawning chasm between the cost of the social services its citizens expect the Government to provide and the capacity of the Swedish economy to finance them. The budget deficit this year is expected to be about $12.5 billion, or 12½ percent of the gross national product.

"We are a very slow people," said Hans Werthen, chairman of the Confederation of Swedish Industries and one of the nation's most influential businessmen. "It takes a long time to change peoples' minds."

"By the time the problems are unmistakable," Mr. Bildt said, "they might also be unmanageable."

Conservatives insist that Sweden cannot afford huge budget deficits, record trade imbalances and a public sector that spends about two-thirds of the gross national product. They argue that public spending must be slashed to meet the problems without fueling inflation, which is expected to be at least 11½ percent this year.

The Social Democrats agree that these problems exist, but they fear unemployment even more. They regard economic expansion as the proper cure. A lively debate within the party on what policies are needed to encourage such expansion—and how much can be spent to keep unemployment from rising above 3.5 percent—has been called the "War of the Roses," an allusion to the party's symbol.

So far, the Social Democrats have supported the position of union leaders on employment. Harry Fjallstrom, head negotiator for the Swedish Confederation of Trade Unions, sums up labor's attitude this way: "A job in the private sector may be better than a job in the public sector, but a job in the public sector is better than no job at all."

The Social Democrats, however, have promised to cut subsidies to some of Sweden's troubled nationalized sectors, including the shipyards and textile groups.

Last October the Social Democrats were returned to power after six years on the outside. During that period, Sweden's economy deteriorated steadily and the public sector grew dramatically. In the election campaign, the Social Democrats promised recovery and restoration of social services that the non-Socialist incumbents had begun to pare.

The new Government's first step, taken Oct. 9, was a 16 percent devaluation of the krona that shocked Sweden's neighbors but enhanced prospects for the country's exporters. Prime Minister Olof Palme and Finance Minister Kjell-Olof Feldt then introduced other measures, including temporary domestic price controls.

One gain came when the labor unions supported the Government by proposing what amounted to a 5 percent cut in real wages. But the Social Democrats, clearly in tight straits, are moving gingerly. The outcry against the "informers' law" is not the only sign that Sweden's willingness to make sacrifices to preserve social solidarity may be fraying.

The most dramatic development was the decision of the engineering companies and Metall, the union representing their workers, to negotiate their own labor agreement. This ended 30 years of centralized negotiations in Swedish industry.

But no one here wants to read too much into the split. Most of Swedish society remains committed to a wide redistribution of wealth to make a broad range of social services and medical care available to everybody at virtually no cost. Many Swedes resist the idea that the welfare state is facing a financial crisis.

"What's wrong with Sweden is that it's been a long time since we have had something to really make us feel united," observed Leif Erik Staalberg, a chauffeur for a Swedish pharmaceutical company.

# Unit XI

# Energy

In the years following World War II, there was a sharp increase in the demand for energy in almost all the countries of Western Europe. Because energy requirements that had previously been met by coal and other solid fuels could now be met far more efficiently and at a much lower cost by energy supplies from abroad, increasing quantities of oil began to move into Western Europe from foreign refineries, and by the mid-1960s imported oil had replaced domestic coal as Western Europe's primary source of energy. Falling oil prices eventually led to cutbacks in domestic coal production as well as a slowing down of the development of nuclear energy, making the countries of Western Europe almost totally dependent on imported oil to meet their rapidly expanding energy needs. By 1973, imported oil, derived almost exclusively from the Middle East, accounted for over 64 percent of Western Europe's total energy consumption, and coal consumption in those countries has remained virtually unchanged since that year.

Against this background, it is not difficult to understand why the quadrupling of the price of oil by the OPEC countries in 1973 dealt such a serious blow to the Western European economies, particularly those of the heavily oil-dependent industrialized countries in the northern section of Western Europe. Since that year, the governments of all the Western European countries have made major efforts to reduce their dependence on foreign oil and to regain a degree of self-sufficiency in the area of energy supply. Different countries have employed different strategies in attempting to cope with problems stemming from the energy crisis. Some, like France, are driving hard toward nuclear power. Others, particularly Sweden, are taking serious measures to reduce reliance on nuclear power and are attempting to cultivate renewable energy sources from within their own borders. Still others, notably Great Britain, are looking very questioningly at their reliance on nuclear power while at the same time increasing their dependence on it. All have moved in the direction of energy conservation, more intensive use of indigenous resources, and the development of alternative energy supplies.

This unit focuses on the different energy policies pursued by the various Western European countries following the energy crises of the 1970s, and details recent efforts on the part of these countries to meet their immediate as well as their long-term energy needs. "The European Community and the Energy Problem," a report prepared by the Commission of the European Communities, examines the energy problems facing the European Community as a whole and sets out the need for a common energy policy. Tracing the changes in economic conditions after World War II that led to the shift from coal to oil during the 1950s and 1960s, the report explains why the energy crises of the 1970s had such a devastating effect on Western Europe's economies. It goes on to describe the various steps that have been taken to formulate a common energy policy and the measures that have been proposed to ensure the future energy independence of the Community's member nations through planning and the diversification of energy sources.

The Swedish Institute, in "Energy and Energy Policy in Sweden," describes recent efforts on the part of the Swedish government to reduce dependence on nuclear energy and imported oil and to provide for the country's future energy needs by utilizing renewable energy sources from within its own borders. Since the country has long been dependent on external energy supplies, achieving this goal will require careful planning, conservation, and diversification. At the present time, major efforts are being made to cultivate new forms of indigenous energy and to expand currently under-utilized energy sources.

The Commission of the European Communities' "Review of Member States' Energy Policy Programs" details the progress of four of its member nations—Germany, France, Italy, and the United Kingdom—toward achieving their 1990 energy policy objectives. The report examines the major issues and problems currently facing each of these countries and shows how each one proposes to meet its future energy needs.

---

# 46

## The European Community
## and the Energy Problem

_____ Commission of the European Communities _____

This report from the Commission of the European Communities reviews the energy problems of the European Community as a whole and sets out the need for a common energy
policy. Beginning with the reindustrialization period that followed World War II, it traces changes in economic conditions
that led to the shift from coal power to oil power during the
1950s and 1960s, and explains why the energy crises of the
1970s had such a disruptive effect on Western Europe's economies. Although preliminary steps have been taken to formulate a common energy policy, no comprehensive policy has
been implemented to date. However, as reported here, a number of measures have been proposed, most of them aimed at
ensuring the future energy independence of the Community's
member nations through long-range planning and the diversification of energy sources.

---

**INTRODUCTION**

Belgium, Denmark, the Federal Republic of Germany, France,
Greece, Ireland, Italy, Luxembourg, the Netherlands and the United
Kingdom as members of the European Community share a common
economic and social destiny.

The Community's 272 million citizens already enjoy an average
standard of living among the highest in the world and if they are to
maintain and improve living and working conditions they will require a
regular, stable and adequate supply of energy at reasonable prices.

Energy is a determining factor in the operation and development of
a modern economy.

Most of the Community used to be relatively self-sufficient in energy, but over the last 30 years has gradually come to depend, as a whole, on imports—especially of oil—to cover much of its needs; total imports exceeded 64% in 1973 and are still over 47% in 1982.

To begin with, this heavy dependence on imported energy promoted economic development and social progress within the Community countries, because of the low prices and regular deliveries.

But in the final quarter of 1973 and, once again in 1979–80, there were serious disruptions whose effects are still being felt. However, this 'energy crisis' was only apparently precipitated by the political and military events which marked its beginning. Instead, its roots are to be found in the market patterns throughout the previous decades.

As early as 1962 the European institutions became aware of the need to control developments more effectively and outlined an energy policy for the Community.

The 'energy crisis' could only make the need for such a policy more imperative for it demonstrated clearly the vulnerability of the economy of Western Europe to interruptions or restrictions of supply and also to sharp increases in energy prices. Furthermore, it emphasized the ineffectiveness of isolated or uncoordinated national reactions, as well as the dangers of an absence of solidarity among the oil-consuming countries. Lastly, it showed the need for changing the pattern of supply so as to reduce dependence on imports: greater energy conservation, more intensive use of indigenous resources and the development of sources other than oil.

It must, however, be clearly realized that no discovery or technical innovation—whether it be energy from nuclear fission, North Sea oil or gas, the possible underground gasification of coal, or even controlled thermonuclear fusion—can by itself solve the problem. Moreover, even a very intensive effort to increase self-sufficiency in the Community's energy supplies will in no way remove the need for considerable imports in the foreseeable future.

The key to the future as regards energy, for the European Community as for any other developed geopolitical entity, lies in diversification: diversified requirements must be met by technically and geographically diversified sources of supply. It is, moreover, absolutely essential to normalize trade relations with the producing countries.

The mere spontaneous action of economic forces on the energy market quite clearly cannot guarantee the attainment of these objectives. It is necessary to have policy measures concentrated on energy but encompassing various facets: market organization, research and development, international relations, finance, etc.

The number and diversity of the economic and social factors which determine or have repercussions on the energy situation mean that, in order to respect the unity of the common market and achieve economic and monetary union, national energy policies shall converge towards an energy policy which, by collective discipline aimed at attaining common objectives, shall ensure equivalent efforts and results throughout the territory of the European Community.

Unity on policy is essential if that policy is to be effective, since it alone allows the Member States to cope with problems beyond their individual capabilities and reduces the risk of duplication in research and investment. It enables the Member States to enjoy the advantages of a large market and share the cost of certain major projects. Such a policy makes it possible, finally, to take advantage of the economic and political strength of an entity of more than 270 million inhabitants in relations with the multinational oil companies, with other importing countries and even in the dialogue with the oil-producing countries.

But a European energy policy is not a prefabricated system which can be imposed as a whole and at one stroke. Member States' energy situations differ widely and flexibility is therefore required in adjusting to developments which will undoubtedly contain uncertainties and surprises.

Community policy is gradually being formulated through a series of decisions by the institutions of the Community, arrived at successively in the spheres in which a common attitude is considered feasible and advantageous, or urgent.

This implementation process may seem slow and unspectacular, but it is also realistic and practical. It is rule-of-thumb in appearance only, since it is consistently based on a body of clearly recognized principles and objectives and, from now on, will apply an overall energy strategy which, in accordance with well-defined priorities, will direct the Community as it progresses.

## THE MARKET BEFORE THE CRISIS (1950–73)

With particular regard to Western Europe and more specifically the countries of the European Community, market trends exhibited the following features:

### Volumes

In the course of the period—something under a quarter of a century—running from the early 1950s to the last years before the crisis, demand for energy—already high compared with the world average—increased very sharply.

In the industrialized countries, primary energy consumption increased generally by more than 100% and, by 1973, the nine Member States then forming the Community had a combined energy consumption of almost 1,000 million tonnes of oil equivalent (mtoe). At that time, there were no signs of demand saturation in Europe or of a decline in growth. The European Commission was still forecasting a doubling of energy requirements in 15 years and estimated total requirements for 1985 at some 1,800 mtoe.

## Supply Structure

This boom in primary energy consumption was accompanied by radical changes in the patterns of supply.

Immediately after the Second World War more than 80% of the total energy requirements of the countries which now form the European Community were met by solid fuels (coal and lignite), while oil accounted for only about one tenth of the total. By 1973, however, solid fuels covered scarcely more than one fifth of total requirement (23%), whereas oil accounted for nearly three fifths (59%), and natural gas—a source recently established in Europe—accounted for over 12%, and hydroelectric, geothermal and nuclear energy accounted for the balance (just over 4%).

It was, therefore, hydrocarbon fuels (oil and natural gas) that made the rapid growth in consumption possible. In addition, the uses to which petroleum products are put have been extended considerably.

Whereas in the past they were used mainly as motor fuels, they have been increasingly used to produce thermal heat (heating, furnaces, electricity, etc.) and as raw materials for the petro-chemical industry.

The changing pattern of Community energy consumption has been accompanied by a change in the ratio between energy produced in the Community and imported energy. The Community has long been poor in oil resources. Even today, despite the recent North Sea discoveries, these are enough only to meet part of the demand and will be able to do so only for a limited period. The increase in consumption was covered chiefly by imported oil; consequently, whereas energy imports accounted for scarcely 10% of Community supplies around 1950, they have now come to constitute over 60% of the total energy supplies of the Member States in 1973.

Furthermore, according to the forecasts made before the crisis of 1973, it did not appear that this degree of dependence on external supplies was likely to decrease. The expected contribution from the North

**TABLE 46.1 Share of the Various Sources of Primary Energy in Gross Consumption (mtoe*)**

| | | Hard Coal and equivalent | | Brown coal and equivalent | | Oil and equivalent | | Natural gas | | Other fuels | | Electrical energy | | Total | |
|---|---|---|---|---|---|---|---|---|---|---|---|---|---|---|---|
| | | 1973 | 1981 | 1973 | 1981 | 1973 | 1981 | 1973 | 1981 | 1973 | 1981 | 1973 | 1981 | 1973 | 1981 |
| West Germany | mtoe | 59.6 | 55.5 | 23.6 | 30.1 | 145.9 | 114.1 | 27.4 | 41.8 | 0.7 | 1.0 | 8.3 | 15.7 | 265.6 | 258.2 |
| | % | 22.4 | 21.5 | 8.9 | 11.7 | 55.0 | 44.2 | 10.3 | 16.2 | 0.3 | 0.4 | 3.1 | 6.0 | 100 | 100 |
| France | mtoe | 27.8 | 28.0 | 0.9 | 1.0 | 123.6 | 95.8 | 13.7 | 21.6 | 0.1 | 0.1 | 13.2 | 32.8 | 179.5 | 179.3 |
| | % | 15.5 | 15.6 | 0.5 | 0.5 | 68.8 | 53.4 | 7.7 | 12.1 | 0.1 | 0.1 | 7.4 | 18.3 | 100 | 100 |
| Italy | mtoe | 7.7 | 11.5 | 0.4 | 0.3 | 95.3 | 91.0 | 14.5 | 22.2 | 0.3 | 0.2 | 9.7 | 5.6 | 127.7 | 130.8 |
| | % | 6.0 | 8.8 | 0.3 | 0.2 | 74.6 | 69.6 | 11.3 | 17.0 | 0.2 | 0.1 | 7.6 | 4.3 | 100 | 100 |
| Netherlands | mtoe | 3.2 | 4.1 | 0.0 | — | 29.3 | 27.0 | 29.0 | 28.9 | 0.0 | 0.3 | -0.1 | 0.9 | 61.4 | 61.2 |
| | % | 5.1 | 6.7 | 0.1 | — | 47.7 | 44.1 | 47.2 | 47.2 | 0.0 | 0.5 | -0.1 | 1.5 | 100 | 100 |
| Belgium | mtoe | 11.7 | 11.1 | 0.0 | — | 27.5 | 20.8 | 7.3 | 8.3 | 0.0 | — | -0.1 | 3.3 | 46.4 | 43.5 |
| | % | 25.1 | 25.5 | 0.0 | — | 59.3 | 47.8 | 15.8 | 19.1 | 0.1 | — | -0.3 | 7.6 | 100 | 100 |
| Luxembourg | mtoe | 2.5 | 1.5 | 0.0 | — | 1.8 | 1.1 | 0.2 | 0.3 | 1.1 | — | 0.6 | 0.3 | 5.1 | 3.2 |
| | % | 48.7 | 46.9 | 0.4 | — | 32.9 | 34.3 | 4.4 | 9.4 | 0.1 | — | 13.5 | 0.4 | 100 | 100 |
| United Kingdom | mtoe | 80.7 | 67.2 | — | — | 108.2 | 72.5 | 25.6 | 40.5 | — | — | 8.2 | 11.1 | 222.6 | 191.3 |
| | % | 36.2 | 35.1 | — | — | 48.6 | 37.9 | 11.5 | 21.2 | — | — | 3.7 | 5.8 | 100 | 100 |
| Ireland | mtoe | 0.6 | 0.9 | 0.8 | 0.9 | 5.5 | 5.1 | — | 1.1 | — | — | 0.2 | 0.1 | 7.1 | 8.1 |
| | % | 8.2 | 11.1 | 11.4 | 11.1 | 77.8 | 63.0 | — | 13.6 | — | — | 2.6 | 1.2 | 100 | 100 |
| Denmark | mtoe | 2.3 | 5.1 | 0.0 | — | 17.3 | 11.5 | — | — | — | — | -0.0 | 0.6 | 19.6 | 17.2 |
| | % | 11.5 | 29.6 | 0.1 | — | 88.6 | 66.9 | — | — | — | — | -0.2 | 3.5 | 100 | 100 |
| Greece | mtoe | — | 0.2 | — | 3.1 | — | 10.9 | — | — | — | — | — | 0.3 | — | 14.5 |
| | % | — | 1.4 | — | 21.4 | — | 75.2 | — | — | — | — | — | 2.1 | — | 100 |
| EUR 10** | mtoe | 195.9 | 185.0 | 25.8 | 35.6 | 554.4 | 449.6 | 117.8 | 164.8 | 1.1 | 1.7 | 40.0 | 70.6 | 935.0 | 907.3 |
| | % | 21.0 | 20.4 | 2.8 | 3.9 | 59.2 | 49.5 | 12.6 | 18.2 | 0.1 | 0.2 | 4.3 | 7.8 | 100 | 100 |

*Source:* Eurostat
*mtoe: million tons of oil equivalent.
**The European Community as a whole.

Sea, in the form of oil and gas, would have been partly offset by an increase in imports of coal, natural gas and nuclear fuel.

## Prices

During the first half of the period between the end of the Second World War and the onset of the energy crisis, Community energy prices were governed largely by the price of coal—at that time still the largest source of energy. Independently of the systems of aid to the coal industry, which moreover varied widely from one country to another, the general policy was that coal should not be priced out of the energy market and so high price levels for other sources of energy and, in particular, those of imported energy—especially oil—were maintained so as to protect indigenous coal and allow it to compete favourably.

During the 1960s, however, after coal had declined in importance, there was a change of policy, and it became more advantageous to allow imported energy to compete more freely on the energy market—even if this meant increasing aid to coal, accompanied by a planned cutback on production.

From that time onwards and to an increasing extent, the energy market, particularly within the Community, came to be dominated by the price of oil products.

From 1960 to 1970, however, the world oil market was characterized by an abundance of supplies and, consequently, low and stable prices; indeed, in real terms, prices, if anything, tended to fall. Moreover, because it was available at low prices, oil was able to capture the lion's share of the increase in demand.

During this period, the Community benefited from the active competition which prevailed on the oil market and, consequently, on the energy market as a whole; it was indeed possible for the Community to secure its energy supplies at very advantageous prices, as oil was able to cover the increase in demand at low prices and thus influence the price of other energy sources.

But the relative fall in prices also had the effect of speeding up the cutback in coal and of slowing down the development of nuclear energy.

## Effects Within the Community

The Community's energy supply pattern has therefore undergone a change, the major features of which have been a drop in the relative importance of solid fuels, greater use of liquid and gaseous fuels and increased dependence on imported fuel, principally oil.

This change has had important results within the Community.

First, it has brought closer together national situations which had previously differed fairly widely. Among the countries now belonging to the European Community, a distinction used to exist a short time ago between, on the one hand, the energy-producing countries (i.e., mainly those producing oil) such as the Federal Republic of Germany, France, the United Kingdom and (to a lesser extent) Belgium and the Netherlands, and, on the other, the mainly energy-consuming countries: Denmark, Greece, Ireland, Italy and Luxembourg. This distinction was somewhat blurred, as the producing countries were already importing energy—particularly oil—while some consumer countries could rely on a certain amount of national production (hydroelectric power, peat and so on). Nevertheless, a real distinction did exist some 25 years ago, and influenced consumer behaviour.

As a result of the cutback in coal production, which affected all the producing countries, albeit to differing extents, and the constant increase in demand which reduced the relative share of internal energy sources, all the Community countries had become net importers of energy by the 1970s—the amount varying in 1973 between half their supplies and almost their entire requirements.

Furthermore, the shift from coal to oil has had an impact on the regional distribution of industry within the Community. Originally based in the coalfields, industry was still, immediately after the Second World War, concentrated mainly in the coal-producing central areas of north-western Europe. Oil, which was imported mainly by sea, reached Europe and the Community via the seaports. Related activities (e.g. refining) and those attracted by the difference in transport costs (petrochemicals and various other industries) have therefore provided opportunities for industrial development in coastal regions. At the same time, the cutback in coal production has given rise to problems in regions where coal-mining was an important activity or which were the traditional centres of industries consuming large quantities of coal.

Finally, the oil-refining industry has developed its operating installations in step with a sustained growth in demand for petroleum products. The early action required in respect of investment projects with lead-times running into several years was to result in an aggregate capacity which was very large even before the crisis; once the crisis had arrived, this capacity proved very much in excess of needs, thus threatening the viability of the refining industry. . . .

**Harbingers of Crisis**

The situation . . . began to change towards the end of 1969. At that time the world demand for energy, especially oil, was increasing at a constant rate and rather more rapidly than the producing companies had foreseen. A poor level of investment in some areas—particularly transport—together with difficulties and delays in the development of new resources, especially for environmental reasons (e.g. Alaska), combined with a high level of demand from Europe and Japan and expanding purchases by the United States, turned the world market from a buyer's into a seller's market.

The exporting countries, grouped together under the banner of OPEC [Organization of Petroleum Exporting Countries], realizing the advantage to be gained from this new situation, tried to pursue a concerted policy for obtaining an increase in their oil revenues. . . .

**Impact of the Crisis**

Two successive oil-price shocks, in 1973–74 and 1979–80, took the price of a barrel of crude oil from less than USD 3 to nearly USD 36. [These price increases] obviously had considerable economic consequences. However, although these two price rises were of similar magnitude in real terms, their economic results were not strictly comparable since they took place in different circumstances. In 1973, when production-capacity utilization rates were high, the very large increases in the price of non-energy raw materials and the rise in the dollar *vis-à-vis* European currencies reinforced the inflationary effects of the oil-price shock. The rise in prices within the Community went up from an average of less than 4% in the 1960s to about 12% for 1973, 1974 and 1975, with a wide range of increase from country to country: rates of 15% to 20% were recorded in Italy, Ireland and Greece, whereas Germany managed to limit the rate to about 7%. The different reactions of the oil-importing countries, expressed notably in the economic policies implemented and the different behaviour of economic operators, lent powerful support to the deflationary effect of the oil-price shock, and the world economy went into its first recession since the war. Community GDP fell in volume terms by more than 1% in 1975.

The quadrupling of the price of oil in 1973–74 also resulted in a spectacular reversal of the industrialized countries' balance of payments, but still more so in the case of the non-oil-producing countries, which finally bore the brunt of the OPEC surplus. As well as causing considerable monetary disruption such changes had a restrictive effect through the lasting contraction of world trade which resulted.

The second oil-price shock came when the world economy, without having adapted sufficiently to the constraints arising from the new energy situation, was again growing, albeit at a slower rate than in the 1970s. Thus the average growth rate for the Community in the period 1976–79 was 3.5% compared with 5% for the period 1960–70. As the economic situation was different—under-utilization of production capacity, stagnation or a fall in the prices of several raw materials, better coordination of economic policies—the effects of the second oil-price shock were more successfully controlled in the short term, and it was possible to avoid a recession in 1979 and 1980. However, in contrast to what happened after 1975, the crisis is lasting longer in most economies: the average rate of growth for the three years 1980, 1981 and 1982 is slightly less than 1% for the OECD countries, nearly 0.8% for the Ten, 0% for the United States and about 3% for Japan. In addition, the employment situation, which got seriously worse in 1975 as a result of the recession, has only deteriorated further; the number out of work in the Community went up from 3.5 million in 1974 to 5 million in 1975 and passed the 10 million mark by the end of 1981. Naturally, the successive rises in the price of oil are not the sole cause of the deterioration in the general economic situation, and efforts to adjust to the energy constraints have been kept up. Thus energy consumption per unit of GDP at 1970 prices and exchange rates fell from an index of 99.9 in 1979 to 88.7 in 1982, and the consumption of oil per unit in GDP also fell from an index of 96.1 to 75.8 over the same period. Such modifications clearly entail much structural, and hence lasting, change, which makes it possible to hope that in the medium term the return to economic growth will not be hampered by another energy crisis. Nevertheless, the deterioration in the economic situation of the weakest countries, in particular of the non-oil-producing countries, is becoming more and more dramatic: their external debt has reached an exceptionally high level, which may create anxiety lest a financial crisis result from the energy crisis. The resulting freeze on the process of development is already prolonging, by its effects on world trade, the economic crisis situation and aggravating the problems of competition and the tendency towards protectionism appearing around the world.

### The Community and the New Factors Governing the Energy Market

The economic recession and the changes in energy prices have not been without repercussions on energy consumption.

Within the Community, gross consumption of primary energy has shown the following trend (mtoe):

| | | | | |
|---|---|---|---|---|
| 1973: | 969 | 1978: | 969 | |
| 1974: | 941 | 1979: | 1,012 | |
| 1975: | 890 | 1980: | 970 | |
| 1976: | 947 | 1981: | 934 | (provisional) |
| 1977: | 942 | 1982: | 930 | (estimate) |

This has been an exceptional phenomenon, and one which previous experience since the Second World War made it absolutely impossible to predict. Whereas, from 1950 to 1973, energy consumption grew continuously every year, it has since fallen twice, in two consecutive years each time—with a slight upturn between each decline. An average and relatively constant increase of 4.5% per annum broke off abruptly and was followed by eight years of stagnation, bringing energy consumption in 1981, and probably in 1982 as well, to some 3.5% below the 1973 level.

This trend is explained partly by the decline in economic activity—particularly industrial activity. It was noted that the latter fell at certain times and that even now recovery is only half-hearted. The trend is also explained by the features of the oil crisis itself. In 1974 it was, above all, physical factors which played a part: the interruption of supplies to some countries and the measures taken by certain governments to impose a reduction in consumption. Thereafter, the additional factors to be taken into consideration are the effect of the price increase, which caused consumers to moderate their consumption somewhat, and of measures to encourage more rational use, which are also beginning to have an impact, as structures and consumption habits gradually adjust to the new market situation.

The trend of recent years has led to a downward revision of energy consumption forecasts for the coming years.

Whereas, as early as 1974, the gross domestic consumption of primary energy forecast for the Community for 1985 was reduced from some 1,800 mtoe—a figure often cited before the crisis—to around 1,450 mtoe, it now appears that it will not exceed 1,100 mtoe, and will be below 1,200 mtoe in 1990.

The hoped-for economic revival should mean an increase in energy consumption, which will prove modest (as expected) only if a greater effort is made to save energy and use it more rationally.

## AN ENERGY POLICY FOR THE COMMUNITY

Even before the energy crisis the Community had attempted to formulate and implement a common energy policy. However, the measures forced upon the governments of the Member States by the threatening situation of late 1973 and early 1974 were conceived and adopted haphazardly and without much coordination or solidarity, which reduced their effectiveness and endangered the process of building Europe.

On the other hand, it is now more apparent than ever that the convergence of national policies and the creation of a common energy policy are fundamental factors in the creation of European unity, and that the measures to be taken inside the Community and also the positions to be adopted on the international scene will carry far more weight and be far more effective if they are taken jointly on behalf of a group of industrialized countries with 270 million inhabitants than if they are the outcome of separate and discordant policies.

The Community has been working towards an energy policy for a long time.

Even though there is no mention of such a policy in the European Treaties, a working party on energy adopted, in June 1962, a memorandum on energy policy which was designed to achieve the free circulation of energy within the common market, and which included detailed provisions regarding the diversification of external supplies, aid to Community production (principally that of coal), the rapid development of nuclear energy, storage, taxation and import regulations. This memorandum constituted, in fact, the first outline of a real energy policy for the Community.

Thereafter, further efforts were made by the European Commission. . . .

Given the gravity of the situation in early 1980, the Commission drew up a communication . . . entitled 'Energy—A Community initiative'; this noted a disquieting gap between what had been done and what remained to be done to work out and implement an effective energy policy. So as to reduce the gap and render the Community able to meet the serious threats to its present and future energy supplies more effectively, the Commission sent the Council on 30 September 1981 a communication on the development of an energy strategy for the Community. . . .

The guidelines adopted for 1990 are as follows:

- to reduce to 0.7 or less the average ratio for the whole Community of the rate of growth in gross primary energy consumption to the rate of growth of the gross domestic product;
- to reduce oil consumption in the Community to a level of about 40% of gross primary energy consumption;
- to cover 70 to 75% of primary energy requirements for the production of electricity by means of solid fuels and nuclear energy;
- to encourage the use of renewable energy sources so as to increase their contribution to the Community's energy supplies;
- to pursue an energy-pricing policy aimed at achieving Community energy objectives.

These various recommendations are in keeping with the Community's three basic concerns, which are:

(i)   to dissociate economic growth and growth in energy consumption;

(ii)  to place a ceiling on oil imports;

(iii) to prepare a more satisfactory energy supply for the more distant future.

The elements of the energy balance have developed more or less in accordance with these broad outlines.

From 1973 to 1981 energy consumption did not increase; it even fell slightly, whereas the gross domestic product increased in volume by about 16%. Although this trend is explained largely by the persistence of a relatively low level of economic activity, it is nevertheless certain that rational energy-utilization policies and reactions in the economy to price rises have also had an influence. . . .

## The Development of Alternative Resources

### Coal

After long being the major, and almost the sole, source of energy supply for the Community, coal rapidly declined in importance after 1960. Until the crisis, European coal policy was based principally on a progressive cutback in production, within the limits imposed by regional requirements and the problems of employment.

The upheaval that occurred in 1973 led to reappraisal of this policy, with a view to halting the decline in output.

Among the objectives adopted in 1974 was the maintenance, in 1985, of the pre-1973 production level. It is now clear, in the light of the subsequent fall in production and the lower-than-expected growth in total consumption that it will probably not be possible to reach this objective.

However, Community production, together with an increase of coal imports, would still enable solid fuel to play a major role in 1990: about one fifth of energy supplies. With nuclear energy, coal is one of the main substitutes for oil in the centralized generation of heat.

The coal industry was faced with a difficult situation in 1975 owing to the low level of demand and, despite the increase in energy prices, its financial position deteriorated between 1976 and 1979, since cost increases outpaced earnings. It is, therefore, more necessary than ever to aid the Community's coalfields financially; consequently, at the beginning of 1976 the Commission formulated a new set of Community arrangements coordinating at Community level national policies for, and intervention on behalf of, the coal industry. . . .

As regards the potential substitution of coal for oil in the industrial heat sector, the Commission takes the view . . . that market forces and technical development will result in greater use being made of coal in this area. The rate of conversion, however, may be slower for economic and ecological reasons than is desirable from an energy-policy point of view. Measures must therefore be found to accelerate this development and change the consumption patterns of Community industry with a view to freeing the latter from the oil constraint.

The Commission is also trying to promote the marketing of solid-fuel liquefaction and gasification techniques.

Monitoring of coal imports has also been introduced, in order to ascertain market trends more accurately and rapidly. In addition, the research into coal technology pursued in recent years will be maintained in the future.

As a follow-up to these endeavours and achievements, the Commission, in its communication of 10 February 1982, redefined the role for coal in the Community's energy strategy, the aim being to increase its use, even if that were to mean importing more. Coal reserves are vast, and their geographical distribution is such that, unlike petroleum, there is an alternative to dependence.

However, the consumption of coal has not gone up since 1973. There are many reasons for this: the nature of coal as a fuel, the uncertainty surrounding price movements and the security of supplies, and the role of coal in the energy policy of the Member States. Measures should be taken to remove these obstacles as far as possible and overcome the environmental problems.

To improve the prospects for consumption, the Commission proposes that:

(i)    prices should be made more transparent;
(ii)   investment in coal-fired plant should be encouraged throughout industry, in public buildings and district heating schemes;
(iii)  research, development and demonstration activities should be stepped up, so as to create more scope for the utilization of coal.

In addition, the coal industry's situation should be improved. At present, of the Community's total production some 50 to 60 million tonnes (20 to 25%) are profitable, some 140 to 150 million tonnes (60 to 65%) are not profitable under present market conditions and about 40 million tonnes (15%) cannot be produced competitively at all. A healthy Community industry is in the interests both of consumers and workers. The coal industry's situation can be improved by continued modernization and rationalization, the progressive closure of mines which are no longer economic and the opening-up of new, economic, production capacity. The Commission accordingly intends to continue to support modernization and rationalization. It will also continue to carry out its responsibilities regarding the retraining of miners and any other social problem which may arise. The long-term situation of the industry would be improved by concentrating national aid measures on the promotion of structural change and improving productivity.

Finally, the expected increase in coal imports is bound to have certain consequences. In the coming years much of the extra demand for coal will be met by imports, which may increase by a factor of three or four over the next 20 years. In this respect, the major producers of the industrialized world will remain the Community's principle source of imported coal.

Regular talks should be held between the Community and those producers so as to improve the general understanding of market trends and reduce the danger of unnecessary tension in a period of real or threatened shortage.

It is also to be desired that European companies engaged in supplying coal should take action (e.g. by setting up a trade association) to ensure that information about short-term market trends and longer-term prospects, potential problems and their possible solutions should be exchanged on a regular basis.

Finally, the Community's increasing dependence on external sources of supply requires that the current policy with regard to stocks must be modified to provide means of dealing with any serious shortage of coal.

## Natural Gas and Community Oil

Today, coal is no longer the Community's only resource, and efforts on a wide scale must be made to develop the Community's considerable resources of oil and gas—under the North Sea in particular. Community oil production reached 101 million tonnes in 1981, and that of natural gas 125 mtoe. Their respective situations are somewhat different however: oil production still has a little room to expand, whereas natural gas production is tending to fall. Consequently, everything must be done to maximize the exploitation of the fields discovered and ensure that dwindling reserves are replaced by fresh discoveries, the objective being to achieve and permanently maintain the highest possible level of production. It is therefore hoped to achieve 125 million tonnes of oil a year in 1990 and almost the same volume of natural gas.

In order to maintain this effort, the Community grants financial assistance to Community research and development projects using new techniques for prospecting for and exploiting hydrocarbons in particularly difficult areas such as the North Sea. . . .

As part of its programme on the rational use of energy, the Community is restricting the use of natural gas and petroleum products in power stations, in order to reserve available hydrocarbon fuels for those uses in which they offer a specific advantage or for those in which, as in the case of vehicle fuels, there is currently no substitute.

Recent developments concerning natural gas prompted the Commission in February 1982 to propose various measures designed to make supplies more secure within the context of the energy strategy for the Community. The new contracts recently concluded by Member States for deliveries of gas from Algeria and the USSR indicate that the volume of imports will be going up, from 28% of the present total supply to possibly as much as 36% by 1985 and more than 45% by 1990. This increased dependence on external supplies means that better guarantees must be sought for the stability of the Community's overall supply. The Commission is therefore advocating amongst other things, and aside from the expansion of Community exploration and production mentioned above, that sources of imports be diversified, additional storage and reserve production capacity be set up, encouragement be given to research into the production of natural gas substitutes and, finally, that the capacity of the Community's transport grid be expanded.

*Nuclear Energy*

The importance of the atom for Europe's energy supplies was acknowledged back in 1957 in the report by the 'Three wise men' which as its title indicated made the development of this new energy source 'an objective for Euratom' and hence a major objective of European energy policy. According to that report, nuclear energy after an interval of about 10 years, that is from 1967 onwards, would begin to relieve the Community of the burden of oil imports thus improving its supply structure and its overall position.

The subsequent favourable conditions obtaining in the energy market—abundance of oil supplies and favourable prices—sharply reduced the Community's effort in this and curbed the development of nuclear energy utilization. It took the 1973 oil crisis to bring nuclear energy once again into the foreground among the sources which can be used to replace imported oil. . . .

But as the impact of the oil crisis wore off, nuclear programmes lost their momentum. . . . Current figures and estimates for nuclear capacity and production are less than half the target set in 1974: this shortfall is equivalent to around 100 million tonnes of oil a year, but the effect of this delay is cushioned by the fact that the increase in electricity consumption is lower than forecast.

Thus, the objective of achieving in 1985 a nuclear contribution of more than one third of electricity production should now be reached before 1990, when it is expected that nuclear-generated electricity will account for about 38% of the total. This evolution, nevertheless, is too slow when set against the possibilities inherent in nuclear energy for reaching a balanced energy supply. The delay is due partly to the fact that the effort, firmly intended when supply difficulties began to be felt, is beginning to seem less urgent and even less warranted now that the tensions in the market are becoming slightly less acute.

Although nuclear power stations produce electricity at a lower cost than conventional thermal power stations, they are extremely expensive to build, and large-scale programmes require very considerable quantities of capital, which in the present economic situation gives rise to serious problems. The Community is now able to use its credit, as a borrower on the world capital market, to facilitate through loans the acquisition of the sums needed for investment in nuclear projects: since 1977 it has earmarked more than 800 million ECU in appropriations, and the Commission has managed to get the financial resources available for this purpose doubled.

A further difficulty lies in the supply of nuclear fuels. It is generally thought that although these fuels would have to be largely imported, their supply does not entail risks comparable to those which affect oil deliveries. . . . [T]he Commission has considered it necessary to formulate a policy for the supply of nuclear fuel; the aims of such a policy would be to ensure the availability of sufficient quantities of natural uranium at reasonable prices, and also of capacity for enrichment and for reprocessing of spent fuels, while at the same time strengthening European industry in these sectors. . . .

However, the supply of fuel to nuclear power situations will . . . be largely dependent in future on external supplies of natural uranium. Moreover, concern about the problem of nuclear proliferation means that exports are subject to political considerations inspired *inter alia* by concern over non-proliferation of nuclear weapons. . . .

However, for some time past the chief obstacle has been public reluctance to accept expansion of the nuclear industry, because of the possible hazards to workers in such installations, to the population in their vicinity and to the environment. . . .

This distrust has been deepened by the accident which occurred in March 1979 at the nuclear power station at Three Mile Island, near Harrisburg, in the United States. . . . The Community has been engaged since 1958 in a programme of action in the sphere of public health protection against radiation. In both the field of research and that of regulations continuous efforts are being made to improve the design of nuclear installations and their methods of operation from the point of view of safety and protection of the environment. . . .

But nuclear safety is not restricted to the operation of power-station reactors: it must also cover all the industrial stages of the fuel cycle. The problems raised by radioactive waste must be dealt with. A plan drawn up by the Commission aims to step up research into conditions in which radioactive waste can be disposed of in the safest possible manner for, in some cases, almost unlimited periods, and also the identification, at Community level, of the sites offering the best guarantees in this respect.

There is also a Community research project designed to ensure that the dismantling of nuclear installations at the end of their economic life is fully compatible with safety and environmental protection requirements. . . .

. . . Community research is also seeking to extend the applications of nuclear energy and encourage the development of new types of reactor[s] which will be more economical and make more efficient use of nuclear fuel. These are fast-breeder reactors (FBRs)—a new type of nuclear reactor which makes it possible to extract much more energy from fissile fuels than do current reactors.

With the prospect of a persistent and increasingly rapid deterioration in the Community's hydrocarbon supply position after the year 2000, it is important to maintain and, if possible, increase the proportionate share of nuclear fission in the energy balance of the Community during the first half of the next century. Fast-breeder reactors should therefore be available for electricity generation on a commercial basis during the 1990s. A considerable effort will be required, however, to develop the technology and, above all, to ensure safe working methods and the protection of the environment. . . .

All the activity and achievements on these many fronts will be continued and expanded in future. The 'energy strategy' guiding the Commission's action from now on was supplemented on 10 February 1982 by a 'nuclear section' which reiterates nuclear energy's contribution to the present, and especially the future, security of the Community's energy supplies. The main advantages of nuclear energy are stressed: low cost per kWh, creation of added value and of jobs, easy storage for large volumes of fuel, alleviation of the balance of payments, etc. The task therefore is to encourage the optimum development of nuclear energy. . . .

*New and Renewable Sources of Energy*

However important and indispensable they may be, the solutions which a policy based on voluntary cooperation can bring to energy supply problems are subject to limitations which can be overcome only by technological progress and its industrial application. The implementation of an overall strategy in the energy sector therefore makes the continuation of Community research programmes particularly necessary.

In addition to the projects already under way, in respect of coal, hydrocarbons and nuclear fission and fusion, since 1975 the Commission has been running research projects in the fields of energy saving and new and renewable energy sources. . . .

. . . Alongside the aid granted to demonstration projects in the field of energy saving, financial support is given to projects to exploit alternative energy sources.

The following have received support so far:

(i) some 40 projects relating to the exploitation of geothermal energy: 28 million ECU in financial support as against about 300 million invested;

(ii) about 70 projects relating to solar energy: 23 million ECU in financial support as against some 80 million invested;

(iii) a dozen projects on the liquefaction and gasification of coal, 75 million ECU in financial support as against more than 225 million invested already in the initial stages.

The current contribution of renewable energy sources to the Community's energy balance is low: 1.5% in 1980, attributable primarily to hydroelectric power and geothermal energy. The efforts undertaken to increase this contribution should bear fruit by 1990, providing they are actively pursued and the new sources are not made less competitive by a fall in the price of conventional energy. With these reservations, renewable energy's share by volume could double to 2.3% of supply, the increase resulting from solar energy and biomass, while hydroelectric power and geothermal energy remain more or less at their current levels.

One research and development project of particular importance is that relating to controlled thermonuclear fusion. This project, which has been under consideration for a long time, was finally decided upon in October 1977 when, after two years of discussion, the Council of Ministers agreed to entrust its realization to the Culham Nuclear Research Establishment in the United Kingdom. This project, which has been named JET (Joint European Torus) will be jointly conducted and financed. If all the technical problems can be resolved, JET, which is a most promising project, may represent a decisive step towards the production of energy from deuterium and lithium, raw materials which are available in almost unlimited quantities. At present, it appears that the fusion of light atoms may, along with solar energy, make a major contribution to the energy supply in the third millenium if it can be mastered industrially.

### Security of Supply

Most of the measures described above are designed to increase the security of supplies, directly or indirectly. However, they do not protect the market from all fluctuations. It is therefore necessary to organize storage arrangements which constitute a buffer against the effect of accidental or deliberate interruptions in supplies, providing, in the case of deliberate interruptions, a certain capability for resistance to economic or political pressures applied by the suppliers.

The Community has for a long time had a regulation providing for the obligatory storage of oil and oil products; the level of this is fixed, at present, at 90 days' consumption, based on the figures for the previous year. In February 1982, however, as a temporary precaution, the Commission proposed to keep 1980 as the reference year, lest the recent fall in oil consumption should reduce the volume of emergency stocks by too much.

Moreover, since the beginning of 1978 the Member States have ensured that electricity producers maintain in thermal power stations sufficient stocks to ensure a supply of power for at least 30 days. The Community has also given itself the means to ensure that the trade flows between the Member States are maintained if there is an accidental interruption in certain oil supplies and that the burden resulting from the shortage is evenly shared. A decision of February 1977 regulates trade in crude oil and petroleum products between the Member States in the event of supply difficulties. A decision of November 1977 permits a harmonized reduction of energy consumption throughout the Community in the same circumstances. A directive of July 1973 calls for the coordination of the measures to be taken by the Member States to make withdrawals from stocks, restrict consumption and regulate prices in order to avoid any abnormal increases. The Commission is also trying to improve the organization of mutual assistance between Member States in a period of tension on the oil market.

In October 1981, the Council stressed the advisability of taking, in conjunction with the other industrialized countries, the measures needed to ensure that limited shortages in the supply of oil do not have undesirable effects for the world economy on the market and on prices.

It is scarcely possible to predict what form exactly any shortages might take, in future, and in each case appropriate solutions can only be devised in the actual circumstances.

Nevertheless, the Council decided in October 1981, and confirmed in March 1982, that it would implement a procedure making rapid action by the Community possible if circumstances so required. It also produced a list of measures from among which it reserved the right to select those which the Member States should apply, under the Commission's supervision. . . .

# 47

## Energy and Energy Policy in Sweden

### The Swedish Institute

The example of Sweden presented in this article illustrates how a nation that is highly industrialized, subjected to a harsh climate, and largely dependent on external energy sources faces up to its energy future. Through planning, conservation, and diversification, the Swedish government is attempting to provide for its country's future energy needs utilizing renewable energy sources from within its own borders while at the same time reducing its dependence on nuclear energy and imported oil. To accomplish this, Sweden must develop new forms of energy, optimize and expand currently under-utilized forms of energy, and develop dynamic cooperation between government, industry, and the private and public sectors.

---

Sweden's energy situation is characterized by a high level of consumption, negligible supplies of indigenous oil, natural gas and coal, and considerable dependence on imported energy. The main policy objective is to develop an energy system based primarily on long-lasting sources of energy—preferably renewable and indigenous ones—with the least possible impact on the environment. To this end, measures aimed at reducing Sweden's dependence on imported oil are of central importance.

Total final energy consumption in 1982 was about 33 milllion tons of oil equivalent(mtoe). The industrial sector accounts for about 40% of the total, the transport sector for 20%, and the remaining 40% is consumed by the housing, commercial and service sectors. Total energy demand amounted to about 50 mtoe. This meant that annual consumption per capita was equivalent to six tons of oil.

During the first post-war decades, total energy demand rose quickly. It has more than tripled since 1945. The annual increase in the 1960's was around 5%. However, the trend was broken during the

| TABLE 47.1   Key Data, 1982, in mtoe | |
|---|---|
| Total energy demand | 46.7 |
| Indigenous energy produc- | 24.4 |
| tion of which solid fuels | 3.0 |
| nuclear power | 8.8 |
| hydroelectric power | 12.5 |
| Net imports of oil | 20.4 |
| Total final energy consump- | |
| tion | 30.5 |

| TABLE 47.2   Electricity Supply, 1982, in TWh | |
|---|---|
| Electricity production | 96.5 |
| of which | |
| hydroelectric power | 54.0 |
| nuclear power | 37.5 |
| oil | 5.0 |
| Imports | 6.0 |
| Exports | 2.6 |
| Electricity consumption | 99.9 |

1970's and by the beginning of the 1980's the annual rate of final energy consumption was lower than in 1973. Oil consumption fell by 2.8% a year between 1973 and 1981 and over the same period the proportion of oil in the total energy supply dropped from 60% to 45%. Total energy demand in mtoe grew by 0.6% a year during this period while annual economic growth was 1.5%. Energy has been used more and more efficiently during the 1970's.

Three factors explain Sweden's relatively high level of energy consumption: heating requirements in a severe climate, an energy intensive industrial sector and the need for long-distance transportation. Heating accounts for about 40% of final energy consumption. Of net heating requirements in the housing, commercial and service sectors in 1982, individual boilers accounted for 60%, piped-in district heating for 25% and electrical heating for 15%. Forestry, iron, and steel absorb a significant share of the total energy used in industry.

## INDIGENOUS ENERGY RESOURCES

Sweden's own reserves of conventional energy are very limited. There is almost no oil, natural gas or coal. A little oil has been found on the island of Gotland. There are sizable reserves of *uranium* but the ore is mainly low-grade and is not being mined at present. The question of uranium mining in Sweden has been widely debated, among other reasons because of its impact on the environment.

Sweden's reserves of *peat* are very large. It is estimated that peat bogs make up 12% of Sweden's land area, covering 5.4 million hectares (13.3 million acres). The estimated fuel content of the peat reserves is 3,000 mtoe. Peat is still used only to a limited extent for energy purposes but steps have been taken to stimulate exploitation.

The *forests* are Sweden's most important natural resource. They also play a vital role as a source of energy, not least in the paper and pulp industries, where residual products provide a valuable energy supplement. *Woodchips* have been increasingly utilized in recent years, for instance in district heating plants.

Indigenous solid fuels, chiefly peat and forest residues, accounted for 8% of total energy demand in 1981, or 4 mtoe. Their contribution can be raised to 7 mtoe in 1990 and 9 mtoe in the year 2000.

*Hydroelectric power* is the most important indigenous source of energy. Early expansion of hydroelectric capacity was a significant factor in the transformation of Sweden into an industrial State. In 1981, the hydroelectric power stations produced 60 TWh [(thermal watt hours)], amounting to 13.5 mtoe or 28% of total energy demand. Present production capacity is 62 TWh, which is to be expanded to 65 TWh by 1990.

It has been estimated that another 30 TWh of hydroelectric power per annum could be economically harnessed. Four unexploited rivers in northern Sweden account for half of this potential. The limited expansion of hydroelectric capacity is due to environmental considerations. In 1982, hydroelectric power accounted for 56% of total electricity production.

In the same year, nine *nuclear power* reactors accounted for 39% of Sweden's electricity production. A tenth reactor was ready for use but not operational. After certain structural alterations this reactor is expected to be brought into operation by stages over the coming year. It is estimated that the final two reactors in Sweden's nuclear power programme will go on line towards the end of 1985. Total capacity of this 12-reactor programme will be 9,400 MW. The uranium for the nuclear fuel used in the Swedish reactors is imported. Sweden's ASEA-ATOM is supplying nine of the 12 reactors. Great importance—and interest—has been attached to various aspects of the nuclear fuel cycle. A central plant for the interim storage of used nuclear fuel will be completed in Oskarshamn in 1985. Situated alongside the nuclear power station there, the storage centre is designed to accommodate 3,000 tons of spent fuel pending final disposal.

*Electricity* is produced by state, municipally or privately owned power companies. The State Power Board provides about 45% of total electricity production. The Swedish electric power grid has several cross-connections with Denmark, Finland, and Norway.

The proportion of *electricity* in total final energy consumption has grown steadily and in 1982 amounted to 23%. So Sweden can well be described as an electrified country, per capita consumption being about 12,000 kWh a year. In 1982 hydroelectric power and nuclear power together accounted for 95% of total electricity production.

## OTHER ENERGY RESOURCES

*Natural gas* is not at present used in Sweden. Agreement has been reached with Denmark on the introduction of limited supplies of natural gas in southern Sweden from 1985.

In recent decades, *coal* has been little used in the Swedish energy supply. Its share of total energy consumption in 1982 was less than 3% (or about two million tons of coal). The use of coal is expected to increase to between four and six million tons a year by the end of the 1980s, most of it going to district heating plants. All of the coal will be imported. In 1982, it came primarily from the United States.

*Oil* remains the single most important source of energy, even if its overall share in the Swedish energy system has dropped from 60% in 1973 to 45% in 1981.

Oil consumption in 1982 was about 21 million tons, compared with almost 30 million tons at the beginning of the 1970's. The drop in consumption has been particularly rapid since the oil price rises of 1978/79. Most of the decline has been in the consumption of heavy fuel oils.

In 1982, net imports of crude oil and oil products were about 19.5 million tons at a cost of almost SEK 32,000 million (SEK 1 (Swedish krona) = USD 0.13 or GBP 0.08 (approx.)), which represents around 18% of total Swedish imports. Sweden exported a significant amount of refined oil products.

Of the 12.8 million tons of crude oil delivered to Sweden in 1982, the United Kingdom supplied 3.5 million and Norway 2.7 million. During the year the supply picture changed radically—OPEC's share of Sweden's crude oil imports fell from 68% in 1981 to 47% in 1982.

Refined oil products are imported mainly from Western Europe and the Soviet Union.

Annual capacity in Swedish refineries is approximately 22 million tons. The largest of the refineries—Scanraff in the Brofjord—is jointly owned by the Swedish cooperative oil company OK, Texaco, and the state-owned Svenska Petroleum AB. OK is building a catalytic cracker at Scanraff which will be ready in 1985. BP and Shell also have refineries in Sweden.

The international oil companies play an important part in keeping Sweden supplied with oil. Their market share in 1981 was 56%.

## DEVELOPMENT OF ENERGY POLICY

In 1975, the Swedish Parliament approved a large number of measures in the field of energy policy on the basis of a comprehensive Government bill. The chief objective of these measures was to limit the growth of energy consumption and reduce dependence on imported oil. Among important features of the policy were new or reinforced programmes in the fields of energy conservation and energy R&D. It was followed up in 1979 by a Government bill establishing the general direction of Sweden's long-term energy policy.

The current policy is founded on the 1981 Energy Bill setting out policy guidelines for the period up to 1990.

The main policy objective is to move towards an energy system based on lasting sources of energy, preferably renewable and indigenous ones, with a minimum of impact on the environment. Two important factors influencing energy policy decisions were the result of the national referendum on nuclear power held in 1980 (see below), and the need for further measures to reduce dependence on imported oil.

Measures to promote *energy conservation* are of central importance in Swedish energy policy. In this field, the goal is to bring down energy use to the lowest possible level, with due regard to social and economic conditions. Special attention is given to reducing oil consumption. Measures taken include price and tax regulation, the supplying of information and advice on energy-saving techniques, the Oil Substitution Fund (see below), a stricter building code, government grants for energy-saving measures in housing, a long-term plan for energy conservation in existing buildings, measures to do with communal energy planning, and a variety of measures in the transport sector.

*District heating* already plays an important part in Sweden's heating supply. Steps have been taken to stimulate further expansion.

*Oil-substitution* efforts are also of crucial importance. The 1981 Energy Bill provides for a special oil-substitution programme during the 1980's. An important instrument in the search for other sources of energy to replace oil is the Oil Substitution Fund. It can provide financial aid in the form of loans (and, in certain cases, grants) to stimulate investment and other measures in the oil-substitution field. The Fund primarily supports efforts to replace oil with peat, woodchips, biomass, coal, synthetic fuels, etc. It is financed by a special tax on oil and oil products (except petrol). The Fund is expected to accrue SEK 1,700 million during the 1981–83 period.

Even if reduced dependence on oil is the main objective, there is still a need for an active *oil policy* to ensure security of supply both in the short and long term. The state-owned oil company Svenska Petroleum AB was established in 1975. Government aid is available for prospecting activities and special credit guarantees are offered for oil extraction projects. There are also special programmes for the military storage of oil in case of war and blockade, or of "peacetime crises".

An important feature of the oil-substitution programme is greater use of *coal* in district heating and hot-water plants. It also plays an important part in efforts to increase investment in the energy field. Special emphasis is placed on finding ways to come to grips with the pollutive effects of coal, in particular the acidification of soil and water.

The 1981 Energy Bill called for an expanded programme in the field of *energy R&D*. New technology and know-how are vital if the long-term energy policy goals are to be achieved. Priority is given to more energy-efficient processes in certain industrial branches, and to solar heating, heat pumps and heat storage, peat, forest-based fuels, fuel-processing and windpower. This programme of energy research, development and demonstration is financed by a special tax on the consumption of oil and petroleum products.

As a result of the 1980 referendum on *nuclear power*, it was decided to complete the present 12-reactor programme but to phase out nuclear power in due course, closing down the last reactor in the year 2010.

In the autumn of 1981, the Government gave a parliamentary committee the task of planning the phase-out of nuclear power and further reduction of Sweden's dependence on oil. The committee is to propose long-term measures for a secure Swedish energy supply. A report is expected towards the end of 1984. This report will constitute an important part of the material on which the Government will base a bill on long-term energy policy scheduled for early 1985.

# 48

# Review of Member States' Energy Policy Programs

—————— Commission of the European Communities ——————

In this report published in mid-1982, the Commission of the European Communities details the progress made by four of its member nations toward achieving their 1990 energy policy objectives. The program objectives of Germany, France, Italy, and the United Kingdom are outlined, as are the trends, issues, and problems facing each of these nations. These excerpts contrast the differing energy requirements of these four western European countries and show how each one proposes to meet its energy needs in the future.

## GERMANY

### Programme Objectives

The Third Revision of the German Energy Policy Programme was adopted by the Federal Government in November 1981. . . . The programme restates the Government's intention to rely primarily on the market and on the price mechanism to bring about the necessary changes in supply and demand. But it also recognises a role for continuing regulatory, fiscal and financial incentives to facilitate the process of adjustment in certain sectors (notably, conservation in buildings and in industry, district heating) and the need for financial support for coal gasification plants. The programme emphasises the desirability of continuing diversification in energy supply, including a growing role for nuclear power.

### Forecast Trends

The German government does not make energy forecasts of its own. But the programme includes the forecasts prepared by three independent research institutes (Berlin, Cologne, Essen) using basic assumptions developed after discussion with the government. The figures used in the Commission's review are those drawn from the forecast of DIW [(Deutsches Institut fur Wirtschaftsforschung)]. Berlin which was the most recently prepared.

According to the DIW forecast:

- oil would fall from 48% of total primary energy demand in 1980 to 40% in 1990;
- coal (53%) and nuclear (33%) would together supply 86% of total primary fuel inputs to power stations, compared with 72% in 1980;
- the energy coefficient would fall from 0.69 (1980/75) to 0.52 (1990/85).

## Key Issues

Given the importance of the nuclear power programme in the forecast energy balances particular attention must continue to be paid to possible constraints. The Federal Government reached an agreement with the Länder in October 1981 to streamline the licensing procedures for pressurized water reactors. But decisions have still to be taken to begin construction of upward of 3 GW [(Gigawatt)] of the nuclear capacity projected to be needed by 1990.

The energy projections were prepared by the three institutes before the signature by German companies on 20 November 1981 of a long-term contract for additional supplies of Soviet gas starting in 1984. If supplies became available in the amounts and on the time-scale planned some 9.2 mtoe or 15% more gas will be available to German consumers in 1990 than is currently shown in the projections. This could have implications both for other gas supplies and for the substitution of natural gas for other energy sources, including district heating.

## FRANCE

### Programme Objectives

In October 1981 the French Parliament approved a new French energy plan which envisages a boost to energy conservation (particularly in the residential, transport and tertiary sectors) and an accelerated development of domestic energy sources, including new and renewable energies, to replace imported oil. Solid fuels produced domestically are expected to provide nearly 50% of requirements in 1990, compared with 20–25% assumed earlier. The expansion of consumption of natural gas ( + 40% 1980–1990) will, however, continue to require a substantial increase in imports (up to 12% of total primary energy demand by 1990). The largest single element in reducing dependence on imported oil will remain the nuclear programme: nuclear could meet over 30% of total primary energy demand in 1990 and provide 80% of electricity.

### Forecast Trends

- the share of oil in total primary energy demand is expected to fall from 60% in 1980 to 35% in 1990;
- coal (over 9%) and nuclear (nearly 80%) could together supply some 89% of the total primary fuel inputs to electricity-generation compared with 61% in 1980;
- the energy coefficient, however, is expected to rise over the decade to 0.68%. This appears to be due in part to the shift from oil use to nuclear energy.

### Key Issues

The Plan assumes high rates of economic growth (5% a year). Its sensitivity to lower growth deserves especially careful consideration, given the inter-relationships between lower GDP growth, the rate of introduction of new energy-efficient technology and the pace of electrification.

The target for renewables is ambitious. It will be affected by the pace of commercialisation of new technologies, the rate of economic growth and by the availability of and trends in the prices of competing fuels. The impact of oil price developments and of the likely availability of increased amounts of imported natural gas could be important factors in influencing its realisation.

### ITALY

### Programme Objectives

Italy's new National Energy Plan was approved by the Italian Parliament in December 1981. . . . It involves a substantial expansion of installed nuclear capacity, requiring the construction of 4 GW new capacity between now and 1990 over and above the 2 GW already under construction; the construction of new coal-fired stations with a total capacity of 17 GW as well as the conversion of a further 3.7 GW from oil to coal; the construction of 3 major coal handling ports to receive the large increase in coal imports; and substantial penetration of natural gas, both in industry and in the domestic and commercial sectors.

The total plan is estimated to involve investment of over 83,000 bn 1980 lire, of which nearly one-quarter will be required for the construction of new power plants. This also includes 8,000 bn lire needed for energy saving incentives (3,000 bn in transport alone), reflecting the provisions of the Bill approved by the Italian senate in February 1981.

## Forecast Trends

According to the Plan:

- oil is expected to fall to 53% of total primary energy demand by 1990;
- solid fuels (35%) and nuclear (13%) should provide together 48% of total primary energy inputs to electricity generation by 1990. But oil use in power stations is expected to rise by 40% during the first half of the decade as power stations ordered in the 1970s come into operation; and even in 1990 oil will continue to supply 38% of power station inputs;
- the energy coefficient is expected to rise during the first half of the decade and then to fall to 0.66 in 1990/85.

## Key Issues

The current plan provides for greater diversification of energy supply in 1990 than envisaged previously, with a somewhat more limited role for nuclear and an enhanced role for solid fuels and natural gas. It has been widely welcomed not only by the Italian Parliament (where it was passed unanimously) but also by regional governments.

But the ambitious new power station programme in particular will require vigorous resolution in its implementation and attention to a number of continuing difficulties, notably:

- over the selection of sites for new nuclear stations;
- in the availability of the necessary finance

The latter will depend heavily on the financial position of ENEL, the Italian state electricity corporation, which has been adversely affected both by the recession and by the pricing of electricity below cost to certain categories of consumer. Particular attention must be paid to measures to enable ENEL to finance the new construction, including a more rigorous approach to electricity pricing.

If the forecasts are achieved, imported gas will provide some 80% of total natural gas supplies in 1990 and Italy could have the highest level of dependence of any Community country on Soviet gas supplies (35% of total requirements). The implications of these developments will require careful consideration, particularly if there is any slowdown in the other aspects of the programme to diversify away from oil.

## UNITED KINGDOM

### Programme Objectives

. . . [Energy] policy [in the United Kingdom] continues to be based on the economic development of the four main domestic supply sources (coal, oil, natural gas and nuclear), with economic pricing of energy remaining the essential instrument in encouraging more rational energy use, fuel-switching and the development of indigenous resources.

The energy balance projections used in the Commission's report were prepared by the British Government in mid-1980. They are understood to be currently under revision to reflect developments since that date. The main assumptions are that:

- the United Kingdom can expect to remain energy self-sufficient and a net exporter of oil for most of the 1980s, with oil production probably reaching its peak in the middle of the decade (figures here, as elsewhere, are based on the mid-point of the ranges submitted by the British Government);
- the production of natural gas will grow but this will be outpaced by a growth in domestic consumption. There is therefore likely to be an increase in natural gas imports;
- there will be a modest increase in domestic coal production which should provide a small exportable surplus;
- there will be a substantial increase in the contribution from nuclear power. Three new advanced gas cooled reactors (AGRs) are expected to come on stream this year. A public enquiry into the planned pressurized water reactor (PWR) is due to begin in January 1983.

A major policy development in 1981 was the introduction into Parliament of the Oil and Gas (Enterprise) Bill to enable the disposal of the exploration, development and production assets of the British National Oil Corporation (BNOC) and to reduce the powers of the British Gas Corporation (BGC) as sole producer and distributor of gas supplies.

## Forecast Trends

In terms of the three quantitative guidelines agreed for the Community as a whole the forecasts present the following picture:

- oil use is expected to grow in volume terms during the decade. But by 1990 it could be down to 39% of total primary energy demand;
- coal (63%) and nuclear (24%) are expected to provide 87% of total primary energy inputs to electricity generation. This will involve something of a shift from coal to nuclear. Oil use in power stations is expected to grow in the mid-1980s as oil-fired plant ordered in the 1970s comes into operation. By 1990 oil use in power stations could be 17% above its 1980 level;
- the energy coefficient is expected to fall to 0.52 during the second half of the decade.

## Key Issues

Existing forecasts are based on an increase of some 17% in total primary energy demand over this decade. If this estimate is now believed to be too high, the anticipated growth in electricity demand is also likely to be revised downwards. A continuing low level of growth in electricity demand is now thought likely by the electricity generating industry. The implications of such a development will require close attention, particularly if it is combined with any substantial weakening of oil prices. It could influence (positively or negatively) the pace of closures of older plant and the planned nuclear programme.

A second major uncertainty relates to the prospects for the UK coal industry in the light of the possible delay in the development of the Belvoir field; the pace of closures of uneconomic pits; and the financial position of the NCB [(National Coal Board)] (with its very substantial burden of debt interest). The longer-term prospects for the industry will clearly be affected by developments in the Electricity markets which represent the major outlet for NCB coal.

The likely pace of exploration and development of North Sea oil and gas is difficult to predict. Factors will include the effects on the attitudes of market operators of applying the provisions of the Oil and Gas (Enterprise) Bill; their reaction to recent changes in taxation and royalty arrangements; trends in crude oil prices; and possible Government intervention to smooth out the depletion curve so as to optimise production on a long-term basis. A further element of uncertainty in the gas sector has been introduced by the collapse in September 1981 of the efforts to put together agreed arrangements for the construction of a gas-gathering system in the North Sea. It is not clear whether attempts will be made to resuscitate this idea or similar arrangements.

# Unit XII

# Immigration

Beginning in the 1950s successive waves of immigrants from the countries bordering the Mediterranean, from West Africa, from the Caribbean, and from parts of Asia flooded the nations of Western Europe in search of work. And for the most part, work was available—particularly in the heavily industrialized countries in the northern section of Western Europe, which were enjoying a period of sustained economic expansion. The influx of immigrants into Western Europe reached its peak during the 1960s and early 1970s, when the importation of "guest workers" from abroad was a standard response by many nations to labor shortages resulting from rapid economic growth. But, as we saw in Unit VIII, the mid-1970s brought a major reversal of this upward trend, and many Western European countries entered a period of sustained economic decline which caused a corresponding decline in the demand for immigrant labor.

Today, Europeans are facing a number of problems stemming from the fact that the vast majority of these immigrants, whose total number was recently estimated at over 15 million, have not returned to their home countries, despite the lack of job opportunities, but have remained in Western Europe, along with their families and children who were born in Western European countries. In addition to placing heavy strains on Western Europe's already overburdened social welfare systems, the presence of two generations of immigrants in these countries has generated a whole host of social concerns, and racial tensions have become so severe that, most recently, rioting has erupted in several countries.

Not only are most immigrants racially and culturally different from the natives of Western Europe, the majority do not even speak the language of their host country. Moreover, immigrants generally hold the least desirable, lowest-paying jobs, and, for the most part, they are not accepted by the local populations and have not assimilated into the societies in which they live. If immigrants' efforts to find their place in an alien society have been thwarted by barriers of language and culture, Europeans' problems in attempting to deal with these racially and culturally diverse minorities have been repeatedly exacerbated by their own economic problems. No easy solutions exist, but some progress has been made.

This unit traces the history and evolution of immigration policy in Western Europe over the past three decades and examines the transition from what was previously a largely homogeneous society to one in which minorities now constitute a significant percentage of the total population. It focuses specifically on the types of problems that exist both for the immigrants and their host countries and on the various responses that the different European governments have made to these problems.

Jonathan Power, in "The Migrants: Who Are They?" describes the typical immigrant in Western Europe today, traces both recent and historical patterns of migration and settlement, and suggests some of the problems posed by the large concentrations of foreigners now making their homes in Western European countries. "Mediterranean Migration" examines patterns of labor flow into Western Europe from the Mediterranean Basin between 1950 and 1975, and shows that while the impact of immigration has been favorable from the economic standpoint, the political and social costs have been extremely high.

Clearly, as Ray C. Rist points out in "Paying the Price: The Social Costs of Immigration," the large-scale importation of foreign workers into Western Europe, so widely practiced during the economic boom of the 1960s and early 1970s, has resulted in a host of unexpected and unwanted problems for Europeans. Arguing that effective approaches have not yet been found, Rist urges policymakers to step up their efforts to resolve the problems that are impinging not only on Europeans' freedoms but also on the freedoms of the immigrants, whose decision to come to Western Europe was founded on the same dreams that inspired Europeans to invite them in the first place.

Racial tensions are widely felt throughout Western Europe today. In "British Race Riots Not Wholly Racial," Godfrey Hodgson analyzes the underlying causes of the so-called race riots that swept urban Britain in the summer of 1981, and suggests that these events were more likely the result of economic despair, widespread unemployment, and pervasive feelings of malaise stemming from frustrations over an economic climate that seemed to show little promise of improvement. If Jonathan Power's "An Algerian in Paris," an interview with a 35-year-old skilled laborer whose past 20 years have been spent as a migrant worker in France, is typical of what life is like for the migrant worker, then the situation can be no better for the immigrant, who must similarly endure a life of loneliness, alienation, estrangement from family, and limited personal freedom.

In a deliberate attempt to solve one of the immediate problems of immigration, the Swedish government made an unusual policy decision in the late 1960s to extend free education to its second generation immigrant children in their own language. Swedish writer Britta Kellgren, in "Sweden Goes Multilingual," explains the rationale behind this unusual policy and describes how Sweden is rapidly evolving into a multicultural society, many of whose "educated" immigrants are now experiencing renewed pride in their ethnic origins and deciding to return to their home countries while others are choosing to remain in Sweden as active, productive members of Swedish society.

# 49

## The Migrants: Who Are They?

### Jonathan Power

In these excerpts from *Migrant Workers in Western Europe and the United States*, Jonathan Power describes both recent and historical patterns of labor migration in Western Europe and suggests some of the social, political, and economic problems posed by the large numbers of immigrants now living in European countries.

Upward of 15 million migrants are now living in Western Europe, . . . workers and their families who have come to meet the growing demand for labour from industry, agri-business and the expanding service sector over the past 20 years. Many were actively recruited: Southern Europeans mainly from the Mediterranean countries—Greece, Turkey, Spain, Portugal, Italy and Yugoslavia—travelling northward to Holland, Belgium, France and Germany to build roads and houses, work in hotels and restaurants and supply the factory conveyor belts. They came to France from North Africa and the former French colonies of West Africa; to Federal Germany from Turkey, Greece and Yugoslavia; to the United Kingdom from former British possessions further afield—India, Pakistan and the West Indies; they came to The Netherlands from Indonesia and from Surinam—both former Dutch colonies. . . .

The figure of 15 million migrants in Western Europe is a very rough estimate. It does not show the full number of people affected by the migration there since the late 1950s: millions more came there for periods of a few months or years and then went home. Some returned because they had saved enough, and seen enough, or because they could not find any more work, or because the personal pressures of working and living away from their families for 11 or 11½ months a year were too painful to be borne any longer. . . .

There is a definite pattern of migration in the European experience. One person arrives first and finds work and a home. Then the family comes later. In most families the first to come was a father or husband or a single man. But single women and wives also came alone, even from countries like Turkey where traditionally women rarely work in

**340**

urban jobs and more rarely leave home alone. They came to earn money for their families, or sometimes for a dowry. Or they came hoping to save enough to go back and buy land or a small business. But many stayed on and brought their families to join them and no longer plan on a voluntary return in the short run. Indeed, the longer they stay and the closer their involvement in the amenities and expectations of the host country, the greater their commitment to their newly acquired living standards and raised expectations. If they are sending remittances home to other family members, these expectations may, in a sense, be exported, as the home-based community invests in higher education for family members, or major projects, such as building a house. In short, family immigration and settlement tend to encourage closer assimilation to patterns and expectations of life in the affluent West. . . .

The migrant workers usually have a high birth rate, compared to the population of the countries they are living in. In West Berlin, for example, the numbers of babies born to Turkish and Yugoslav and Greek migrant workers are much higher than those born to the German Berliners. The migrants are young, and in the age group most likely to have children. They come from countries where birth rates are high (though the migrants have lower fertility rates than comparable age groups in their home countries). Meanwhile the German population of Berlin is ageing, and the younger people have a very low fertility rate.

Perhaps the most intractable problem posed by new migrant settlement patterns in . . . Europe is the arrival on the labour market (and in the unemployment queues) of the second generation of immigrant children, who were either born in the host country, or arrived at an early age. In 1975/76, under-15s accounted for 25% of the foreign population in France, 23% in West Germany; under-16s represented 30% of the Swiss foreign total, and under-17s 34% of Sweden's. Youngsters seeking work tend to get a raw deal both from their inexperience and from their foreignness (even those born in the country). Yet at the same time, they tend to assimilate the rising expectations—thanks to their liberation from menial jobs, amongst other things—of the country's own youth, and refuse to do the type of work which first attracted their parents' generation. This conflict between rising expectations and diminishing opportunities is generally recognized, in every country with a sizeable "foreign" population, as one of the most acute social, political and economic significance for the future.

## A BRIEF HISTORICAL PERSPECTIVE

The migration of some fifteen millions to Western Europe . . . in the past twenty years or so is just the most recent of the migrations which have been taking place since before the beginning of recorded history. . . . The scale of this latest migration can be compared with the largest migrations in modern history. . . .

. . . Even before the First World War, several Western European countries were importing labour to do jobs they could not find local workers for. On 12 July 1907, for instance, a census showed nearly 800,000 foreign workers in Germany—126,000 of these workers were from Italy, 52,000 from Holland and 542,000 from South and Eastern Europe. Of the 800,000, 280,000 worked in agriculture, the rest in industry, construction and mining. By 1914 the number of foreign workers in Germany had risen to 1.2 millions.

France had a similar history. In 1886, there were already more than 1.1 million foreigners working and living in France. 482,000 were Belgians, 246,000 Italians, and the rest were mainly German, Spanish and Swiss. About 25% of these foreign workers were seasonal agricultural workers; the rest were in industry and mining. By 1888 and 1893 the French government was adopting measures obliging foreigners to register with the locality where they were living. Numbers of foreign workers continued to rise in both France and Germany until the start of the war in 1914. After the First World War, France again found it necessary to recruit foreign workers to meet the needs of her industry. To make up the losses of manpower from the war and the ageing of the native French population, the state and employers negotiated contracts with several countries for labour recruitment. Countries which sent workers to France under contract included Poland, Czechoslovakia and Italy. The number of foreign migrants in France rose from 1.4 million in 1919 to 2.5 million in 1926 and 3 millions (7% of the total population) in 1930. After the start of the depression, in 1930, the recruited workers were shipped home again by train, as they had come.

Germany had employed very few foreigners in the period after the First World War. In 1932, for example, there were only about 100,000 foreign workers in industry and 42,000 in agriculture. But during the Nazi period, Hitler forcibly brought millions of civilians and prisoners of war to work in her war industries. By 1943, there were 5.2 million foreign "Zwangsarbeiter" (compulsory workers) in Germany. After the Second World War, German industry found for ten years that it could meet its rapidly growing manpower needs from the twelve million refugees from East Germany who came to the West. After 1955 this source was drying up, and the West German government signed recruitment agreements with a series of countries for organized recruitment of unskilled workers for her industry. The first agreement was in 1955 with Italy, followed by Spain and Greece in 1960, Turkey (1961), Morocco (1963), Portugal (1964), Tunisia (1965) and Yugoslavia (1968). As a result of the official recruitment, and additional direct recruitment by private employers, the number of foreign workers in West Germany rose from 10,000 in 1954 to over 650,000 in 1962 and to over 2.3 millions in 1972. In France recruitment of foreign workers for industry started immediately after the war when between 1946 and 1949, Italian workers were imported. But in France, as in Germany, massive labour immigration started after 1956. The first, Italian migrants, were followed by Spanish workers (after 1957), then Portuguese (after 1962); other migrants came from Algeria, Morocco, Tunisia, and later from Senegal and the other former black African colonies.

The history of labour migration in Belgium is similar. Imports of labour started before the Second World War with Italians and Poles working in the coalmines of Eastern Belgium. After the war, official bureaux recruited foreign labour, first for the coalmines, which were made a priority sector in 1946, later for other sectors such as transportation and construction. As Italian workers emigrated less in the mid-fifties, new sources were tapped in Greece and Spain, in the 1960s by agreements with Algeria, Yugoslavia, Portugal and Tunisia. Many of the workers coming to Belgium came spontaneously or were recruited by private employers until conditions were made more stringent after 1967. This was the result of public pressures as the numbers of foreign workers increased. But since employers still wanted cheap foreign workers and were willing to hire them, a flow of illegal migrants developed early in Belgium. After the boom years of the sixties came the ending of all new recruitment in 1974, with a final act of regularization, conceded with ill grace by the government after a hunger strike of undocumented workers. But, in Belgium as elsewhere, family immigration has continued to push up the immigrant figures. One in ten of the Belgian population is now a foreigner—more than the entire population of Brussels, though without a vote.

In Switzerland there has always been a large foreign population. In 1910, 14.7% of the population were foreigners. Until the beginning of the 1960s, immigration was not controlled; it was determined by "the demands of the economy" and the availability of migrants. As a result, the proportion of foreign residents and workers in Switzerland came to be one of the highest in Europe. The number of foreigners living in Switzerland rose from 224,000 in 1941 to 506,000 in 1960 and over 1 million in 1970 (in a total population in 1970 of 6.2 millions). This rapid growth of the foreign worker population brought strong opposition, first from labour unions who pointed out that it was keeping wages down; later from other groups who objected to the "over-alienization" of Switzerland.

Like the other Western European countries discussed here, the UK long considered itself not an immigration country. From 1871 to 1931, for instance, Britain lost a net outflow through migration of well over 3 million people. But at the same time, Britain was already receiving immigrants. The first and largest stream was from Ireland. In 1851 there were over 700,000 Irish immigrants in Britain. They were followed by Italians and by about 120,000 Jews who came to Britain between 1875 and 1914 from Eastern Europe. This, like the earlier Irish immigration, aroused anti-alien propaganda. To deal with it a "Royal Commission on the Aliens Question" was set up, which reported in 1903 that the number of aliens in Britain was very small: 0.69% of the British population were aliens, compared with 1.38% in Germany, 2.68% in France and 9.58% in Switzerland. They found that "alien labour is chiefly employed in doing work for which the native workman is unsuited or which he is unable to perform." The number of aliens settling in the UK fell sharply during and after the First World War. The annual average increase in the number of aliens was under 1,000 between 1921 and 1930 compared with 21,000 from 1906 to 1914. After 1930 the number rose to 5,000 a year on average between 1930 and 1935 and to 18,000 a year between 1935 and 1940. These were mostly refugees and others coming for non-economic reasons. Foreign workers were again needed to meet labour shortages after the Second World War. The first were 120,000 Poles who had come to Britain during the war and who were employed in areas of labour shortages (such as the mines) in the UK.

Others were recruited among displaced workers in Europe under what were called the "European Voluntary Worker" Schemes. Stringent conditions designed to discourage or prevent these workers from settling were imposed by the government when it admitted them. The Aliens Acts, dating back to the late nineteenth century restricted the import of other labour from Europe. But recruitment of labour from the colonies and ex-colonies was possible. From 1948 on, a growing stream of immigrants came to Britain from the West Indies—in substantial numbers from 1954 on. Others came from India (from 1955) and from Pakistan (in large numbers from 1957) to fill jobs in labour-short British industries.

The case of Holland has parallels both with the UK and with other Western European countries. Holland experienced large inflows of population from former colonies, first from Indonesia and later from the Antilles and Surinam. But Holland has also recruited workers for its industries from "recruitment countries" with which it has official agreements in Southern Europe and North Africa. The migrants from the recruitment countries are from Spain, Turkey, Greece, Morocco, Algeria, Portugal and Tunisia. In all, there are about 200,000 migrants from these recruitment countries, another 99,000 from EEC countries (mainly Italy), 135,000 from Surinam and 75,000 from other countries. A total of about 509,000 out of a total population of 13½ millions. . . .

# 50

## Mediterranean Migration

### Glenda G. Rosenthal

This selection presents data showing patterns of labor flow between the countries of the Mediterranean Basin and Western Europe from 1950 to 1975, when the influx of migrant workers in the European North reached its peak. It goes on to examine the costs and benefits of labor migration to both the sending and receiving countries, and details recent efforts on the part of many Western European governments to curtail the inflow of migrant workers and to limit the length of time these foreigners can legally remain in their country.

By the time emigration from the Mediterranean developing countries to the industrial regions of Western Europe peaked in 1970, more than 800,000 workers were emigrating annually. Although emigration started to taper off gradually from 1970, there was no marked reduction until the 1973–74 oil crisis and the ensuing international recession brought the process of recruitment of foreign workers to a near standstill. Thus, by 1974, . . . northern and Western Europe were hosting approximately 7.5 million immigrant workers, of whom approximately 5 million were from the countries of the Mediterranean Basin.

By the mid-1970s also, migrant workers represented a considerable proportion of the total labor force of their countries of origin. Algeria topped the list, followed closely by Portugal. Yugoslavia, Greece and Tunisia were also significantly linked to Western Europe through migration. Similarly, the dependence of all Western European countries, with the exception of Italy, on migrant labor rose steadily until the early 1970s. For example, Luxemburg's proportion of foreign workers in its employed force rose from about one-fifth to one-third and Germany's went up from 1.4% to about 10%. Indeed, in some years, migrant labor exceeded by far the increase in domestic demand for labor, as in Germany in 1965 and 1970. In 1968, 65% of Germany's immigrant labor, 79% of that of the Netherlands and 62% of that of France came from

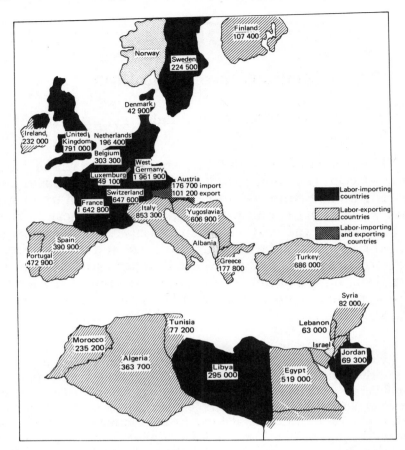

**Figure 50.1.** *Labor migration in the Mediterranean Basin, 1978. Source:* "International labor migration," *The Conference Board*, New York, Economic Road Maps, Nos 1890–1891, November 1980.

non-European Community Mediterranean countries. As late as 1970, migratory flows from the Mediterranean were extremely heavy, with 74% of new migrants in the EC coming from non-member Mediterranean countries (Yugoslavia: 25%, Turkey: 16%, Portugal: 13%, and Greece and Spain together: 15%).

In addition to these very large numbers of migrants, the direction of their movement is of some significance since it was heavily influenced not only by geography but also by historical ties. For example, by the end of the 1960s Algeria and Portugal were by far the biggest suppliers of migrant labor to France, whereas Germany relied mostly on Turkey and

**TABLE 50.1  Migrant Workers in Western Europe, 1974**

|                    | Immigrant countries | | | | | | | | | |
| Emigrant countries | Germany | Switzer-land | France | Belgium | Netherlands | Luxembourg | Austria | Sweden | United Kingdom | Total |
|---|---|---|---|---|---|---|---|---|---|---|
| Portugal   | 81,000     | 3,000    | 475,000    | 4,000   | 4,000   | 9,000[c] | —       | 1,000    | 10,000    | 588,000   |
| Spain      | 160,000    | 75,000   | 265,000    | 34,000  | 19,000  | 2,000    | —       | 2,000    | 17,000    | 574,000   |
| Italy      | 405,000    | 305,000  | 230,000    | 70,000  | 10,000  | 11,000   | 2,000   | 3,000    | —         | 1,037,000 |
| Yugoslavia | 495,000    | 23,000   | 50,000     | 3,000   | 9,000   | 1,000    | 166,000 | 23,000   | —         | 770,000   |
| Greece     | 223,000    | 5,000    | 5,000      | 6,000   | 2,000   | —        | —       | 8,000    | —         | 249,000   |
| Turkey     | 585,000    | 14,000   | 25,000     | 10,000  | 33,000  | —        | 29,000  | 2,000    | —         | 698,000   |
| Finland    | 5,000      | 1,000    | 1,000      | —       | —       | —        | —       | 105,000[f] | 1,000   | 113,000[g] |
| Morocco    | 14,800     | —        | 130,000    | 30,000  | 23,000  | —        | —       | —        | —         | 197,800   |
| Algeria    | —          | —        | 440,000    | 3,000   | —       | —        | —       | —        | —         | 443,000   |
| Tunisia    | 10,600     | —        | 70,000     | —       | 1,000   | —        | —       | —        | —         | 81,600    |
| Others     | 415,600[a] | 158,000  | 209,000[c] | 70,000  | 57,500[d] | 18,000 | 32,000  | 53,000   | 1,772,000 | 2,784,000 |
| **Total**  | 2,395,000  | 585,000[b] | 1,900,000 | 230,000 | 158,500 | 41,000   | 229,000 | 197,000  | 1,800,000 | 7,535,500 |

[a] Of which 10,000 Austrians
[b] Settled and annual; excludes 152,000 seasonal and 98,000 temporary workers
[c] Particularly Africans and citizens of EC countries except for Italy; excludes 130,000 seasonal workers
[d] Excludes 25,500 West Indians and Surinamese
[e] 15,000 according to Portuguese figures
[f] 100,000 according to Swedish figures; 110,000 according to Finnish figures
[g] Excludes 1,000 Finns in Denmark and 2,000 in Norway
Source: OECD Observer, July/August 1975.

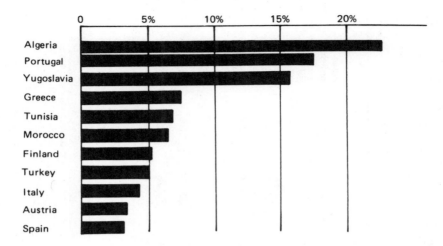

**Figure 50.2.** *Workers abroad as percentage of total employment in country of origin, 1977. Source:* "International labor migration," *The Conference Board*, New York, Economic Road Maps, Nos 1890–1891, November 1980.

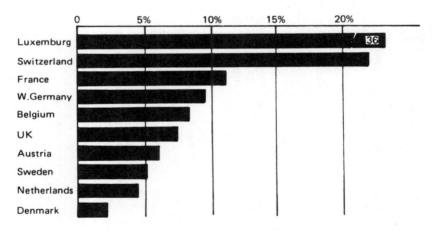

**Figure 50.3.** *Foreign workers as percentage of total employment in host country, 1977. Source:* "International labor migration," *The Conference Board*, New York, Economic Road Maps, Nos 1890–1891, November 1980.

Yugoslavia for its immigrant workers. There were, however, some secular changes in the trends during the 20 years of peak migration. In France, for instance, Spanish predominated over Portuguese immigration in the early 1960s, while West Germany relied heavily on Greek and Spanish workers until 1965.

Most important of all, however, is the fact that even though the oil crisis signaled a halt in recruitment of labor from the Mediterranean countries, since then there has not been any important drop in the *total* number of immigrants in Western Europe. In the first place, the number of dependents of foreign workers has hardly decreased at all owing to the continued immigration of family members and the ever-increasing numbers of foreign children born to immigrants in the receiving countries. Migrant workers usually have a high birth rate compared to the populations of the countries they are living in since they are young, are in the age group most likely to have children, and come from countries where the birth rates are traditionally high. As one study has indicated, one in six of all children now born in West Germany is the child of immigrant parents and in West Berlin the number of children born to Turkish, Yugoslav and Greek workers is much higher than the number born to native Berliners.

There has not been any massive return either of foreign workers from Western Europe to the Mediterranean countries. The majority of foreign workers have tried to survive the difficulties by remaining on the labor markets of the more industrialized countries, particularly since in many cases access to unemployment insurance benefits eased the situation and undoubtedly allowed for better conditions than if the migrants returned home to almost certain unemployment. The result has been that, even where a total ban on new immigration was instituted, there has been a consolidation rather than a reduction in the existing migrant workforce.

## THE COSTS AND BENEFITS OF LABOR MIGRATION

Initially, both sender and recipient countries were committed to the idea that the northward and westward movement of Mediterranean workers was *mutually* beneficial. Only later were the costs perceived to outweigh the benefits but, by then, both were firmly locked—economically, socially and politically—into the relationship. It would be useful, therefore, to examine briefly here the various arguments that have been advanced from both the sending and receiving ends with respect to the costs and benefits of these migratory flows.

There has been little dispute over the assertion that immigrant labor has permitted job vacancies to be filled with reduced upward pressure on wages and prices. This is particularly the case in the more onerous and badly paid jobs that are no longer compatible with the social and economic expectations of indigenous workers; labor shortages in these sectors worsen even in times of rising overall unemployment.

**TABLE 50.2  Short-Term Costs and Benefits of Migration**

| | Benefits | | Costs | |
|---|---|---|---|---|
| | Individual | Social | Individual | Social |
| Emigrant countries | 1. Increased earnings and employment opportunities<br>2. *Training (human capital)<br><br>3. *Exposure to new culture, etc. | 1. *Increased human capital with return migrants<br>2. Foreign exchange for investment via migrant remittances<br>3. Increased output per head due to outflow of unemployed and underemployed labour<br>4. Reduced pressure on public capital stock | 1. Transport costs<br>2. Adjustment costs abroad<br><br>3. Separation from relatives and friends | 1. Loss of social investment in education<br>2. Loss of 'cream' of domestic labour force<br>3. *Uncertainty of continued inflows of remittances may hinder development plans<br>4. *Social tensions due to raised expectations of return migrants<br>5. *Demonstration effects on consumption patterns worsen the balance of payments<br>6. *Remittances generate inflation by easing pressure on financing public sector deficits |
| Immigrant countries | 1. *Cultural exposure, etc. | 1. Permits growth with lower inflation<br>2. Increased labour force mobility and lower unit labour costs<br>3. Rise in output per head for indigenous workers | 1. Greater labour market competition in certain sectors | 1. *Dependence on foreign labour in particular occupations<br>2. Increased demands on the public capital stock (e.g. provision of more social services)<br>3. *Social tension with concentration of migrants in urban areas |

*Indicates uncertain effects.
*Source: OECD Observer*, July 1978.

The influx of immigrant workers prepared to accept lower wages and poorer working conditions, and excluded (initially at least) from the benefits extended to organized labor, permitted the industrialized countries to increase their output and protect their competitive positions in world trade.

It is hardly surprising that unemployed, marginally employed or unsatisfactorily employed young men in rapidly growing cities in the developing countries of the Mediterranean Basin, or working the land and eager to move away, were quick to seize the opportunities offered by the growing industry of Western Europe in the 1950s and 1960s. Indeed, it is estimated that it would have cost the rich countries $60 billion in aid to create the number of jobs in the developing world equivalent to the number of immigrant workers in Europe. . . .

Although the impact of immigration on the receiving countries has for the most part been a useful one from the economic standpoint, the political and, above all, the social costs have been quite high. These have ranged from greatly increased public spending to provide decent living conditions and social benefits for immigrant workers and their families, to the blatant racism displayed with ever-increasing frequency as rising unemployment creates growing resentment toward all alien elements. Even further along the line, Western Europe's industrial countries are having to face the many problems associated with alienated, unemployed and increasingly militant second-generation immigrants.

The presence of large concentrations of poorly paid foreign workers has been a source of tension in Western Europe going back to the earliest days of immigration. When Western European workers started feeling the pinch of inflation and unemployment, xenophobia and hostility mounted and reached the point of open racism and even violence in a number of countries. Although foreign workers frequently perform menial jobs that Europeans disdain, like garbage collection and construction work, the notion that immigrants take jobs from local citizens is deeply ingrained.

Much of the social tension has been compounded by a cluster of other problems. In the first place, workers often migrate without their families. In West Germany in the early 1970s, for example, although 82% of all Turkish workers were married, 54% were there without their wives. There is no doubt about the hardships encountered by immigrant workers who may see their wives and children only once a year over a period of many years. In West Germany, for example, dependents of foreign workers can enter the country only if they agree in advance not to take jobs, yet workers who seek permission for their families to join them often find that their applications are delayed by local administrations. Moreover, while approvals are pending, immigrant workers must pay Germany's high tax rate for bachelors. According to one Turkish official quoted in the American press: 'On the one hand, they forbid a man to bring his family in, and on the other they penalize him financially for not doing so'. Although the situation of migrants' families tends to vary according to the terms of the different bilateral treaties on labor recruitment, as well as to the interpretation that the authorities give to the conditions for family transfers, there is no question that much greater public spending is required if a worker's family is admitted. A German study estimated that the cost of infrastructural investment for a single immigrant worker was DM30,000 as compared with DM150,000–200,000 for a family. A Dutch study came to a similar conclusion with a figure of eight times the public expenditure on a family than on a single worker. In both cases, it was assumed that the kinds of services provided would be the same for foreign workers as for the indigenous population.

However, the conditions under which immigrant workers live are often very far from being the same as those of the native work force. French estimates suggest that at least one-quarter of immigrant workers live in poorly serviced shanty towns. Indeed, the poor living conditions in the 'bidonvilles' surrounding Paris have attracted considerable international publicity. Even though the conditions may not be so bad in other Western European countries, in many cases poor housing and social services give rise to severe social problems.

Finally, the receiving countries must face the problem of the arrival on the labor market of the second generation of immigrant children who were either born in the host country or arrived there at an early age. In both France and West Germany, approximately one-quarter of the foreign population is made up of under-15s. The problem here is that these young people suffer under a double hardship: they are labeled as foreign, even though they may have been born in the country, and they have also assimilated the rising expectations of the country's own youth so they refuse to do the type of work that first attracted their parents' generation. Thus, whether immigrants arrive with or without their families or whether they settle and send for their dependants, host governments have to face the realities of vastly increased social costs and mounting labor tension just at a time when inflationary pressures and other economic constraints are pushing them in the direction of greater restrictiveness.

The social costs could probably have been borne as a necessary burden had the migratory flows in reality been temporary as was originally believed in the late 1950s when immigration first became significant. As one commentator points out, the conviction that the 'need for migrant labour would vanish once the unusual conditions of the prolonged boom that followed the post-war reconstruction in Europe no longer prevailed' turned out to be an illusion. In fact, far greater numbers of immigrant workers remained in the host countries than was originally predicted. Moreover, use of foreign manpower has taken on a structural character that affects both the deployment of national manpower and the functioning of essential sectors, including the public services. The host countries are thus caught in a dilemma: they can neither afford to send the immigrants home, nor can they bear the heavy cost of keeping them where they are.

Nevertheless, Western European governments have taken a variety of steps to extricate themselves from the dilemma, mostly directed at severely limiting the inflow of immigrants and then making sure that they do not stay too long. In France, for example, the government has adopted various schemes involving payments of $2,000 and up to induce immigrants to leave. Even so, the government's strategy has not come anywhere near dealing with the 8-9% of foreigners who are unemployed. In West Germany, there has always been fairly strict supervision of the labor force and strong resistance to the idea that it is a country of permanent immigration and yet, despite restrictive measures and a complete halt on new work permits, the percentage of foreigners in the population has stabilized at 6.5, or approximately double that in the late 1960s. Overall, therefore, the receiving countries are now having to face many more problems associated with the presence of large immigrant populations in their midst than they enjoy benefits.

## Sending Countries

There has been discussion for some time now about the relative costs and benefits of migration to the sending countries. Benefits claimed have centered on the relief of unemployment and underemployment. In addition, it has been suggested that migrant workers acquire skills that can be put to good use when they return home. Finally, the remittances sent home by emigrants have turned out to be the main source of foreign exchange for many of the sending countries and thus provide a base for financing imports of the capital equipment required for development.

Many of these benefits turned out to be costly in the long run. For example, had emigration claimed only unskilled and unemployed labor, it would have been economically beneficial to the sending countries. What in fact happened, as numerous studies have illustrated, is that the authorities in the receiving countries selected only the most dynamic and productive applicants for emigration who usually were also the best educated and most qualified. Furthermore, through what has been described as a 'skimming off' process, importers often renew the contracts only of those who demonstrate the most capacity for social and occupational adjustment as well as the lowest levels of labor union and political activism. The repetition of this skimming off process over a number of years means that the sending countries are disadvantaged over and over again. Clearly they run the risk of losing just those workers who are most needed, who are in short supply, and in whom they have placed a certain educational investment. It is also likely that in those countries where the shortage of skilled workers is greatest, the jobs vacated by migrant workers will be filled by less skilled workers. Finally, it has been suggested by some observers that the skimming off frequently means that those workers who return home tend to be less skilled than those who stay abroad for longer periods of time or even settle abroad and send for their families. This has been called the 'return of failure'.

Similar kinds of conclusions have also been drawn recently with respect to the training benefits initially assumed to accrue to the sending countries. The severest critics roundly condemn this assumption, but even the usually reticent OECD and International Labour Organization (ILO) conclude that migration has done little to further the development of the sending countries. The *OECD Observer* asserts:

> The hope that migrants would have opportunities for training which on their return would enable them to make a contribution to the development of their own countries has not been realised. For in the receiving countries immigrants have generally been confined to subordinate positions where they could assure the local labour market of a flexibility which it would otherwise have lost. The fragmentation of the work generally assigned to the foreign worker tends to make him a performer of repetitive tasks, his only 'training' a familiarisation with industrial discipline. . . .

The final link in the labor chain that joins the countries of the Mediterranean Basin to those of Northern and Western Europe is financial. This takes the form of workers' remittances, transferred savings and investment. Almost all observers acknowledge that the volume of remittances from foreign workers in Western Europe represents an immense economic potential. . . .

Remittances have been an important source of foreign exchange for most of the countries of the Mediterranean Basin in recent years and, in a number of cases, have played a crucial role in their balance of payments' situations. Remittances by Turkish and Yugoslav nationals working in Germany, for example, have on occasion been more than twice as large as the total value of Turkish and Yugoslav exports to Germany for the same year. In 1973, remittances covered 79% of Yugoslavia's negative trade balance, 26% of that of Spain and over 100% of those of Portugal and Turkey. In addition to their global effects, remittances also tend to serve as aids to development at the individual and family levels. An estimated two thirds of repatriated savings are spent on housing. As a result, they have improved the living standards of significant sections of the home populations. This in turn has tended to increase the size of farms, which has somewhat relieved agricultural underemployment.

By the opposite token, remittances also perpetuate inflationary tendencies. It has been noted, for instance, that there is frequently a close correlation between the growth in imports of capital goods and emigrants' remittances and an increase in the share of imported capital goods in total investment—the so-called boomerang effect. Labor migration has not facilitated the task of the sending countries in expanding their share of foreign markets. In fact, some observers have suggested that there is no hard evidence of any observable general economic relationship between flows of migrant workers and trade flows and that there was not any dramatic evolution of trade between the two groups of countries during the period when mass migration movements took place. Quite the contrary: trade relations between the manpower-receiving countries and other countries have developed better than those between the manpower-sending and manpower-receiving countries. Thus, the possibility of replacing manpower flows by trade flows has not materialized.

# 51

## Paying the Price: The Social Costs of Immigration

### Ray C. Rist

The practice of importing labor from abroad, which was widespread in Western Europe during the economic boom of the 1960s and early 1970s, has backfired in recent years and left Europeans to wrestle with a number of unanticipated and unwanted problems. In these excerpts from an article published in the *Journal of International Affairs*, Ray Rist analyzes the roots of these problems and shows how current provisions for education, housing, employment, residential mobility, and other policies governing the lives of immigrants reflect both ambiguity and ambivalence toward the foreign workers.

. . . With the movement of the EEC in particular and the European North in general outside its own boundaries in the pursuit of manpower, the repercussions of the large-scale importation of labor began to be manifest. While the boom years of the 1960s and early 1970s hid much of the social debt that was accumulating, it could not be ignored for long. The belief was naive that labor could be imported and then exported on a rotational basis. The assumption was that the workers would come to take up the tasks gladly left behind by the national workers and then leave with a minimum of impact upon the fabric of the host countries. There have been social costs and they have been considerable.

At one level, one can survey the broad consequences of the migration of tens of thousands of Turks, Yugoslavs, Spaniards, or North Africans to the industrial countries. What one finds are the clashes of cultures, the growing ghettos, the evidence of racism, and discrimination. Second generation immigrant youth wander in a cultural limbo, and thousands of children enter school systems that are neither prepared nor anxious to undertake the efforts necessary to create a milieu in which all can flourish. The result, as in Germany, is that more than 60 percent of all second generation youth leave school with no diploma of any kind. At another level, that of the solitary worker, the tragedy is of a more personal sort. The workers of the South were brought North as if they were an abstraction or an image. Behind terms like "guestworker" or "migrant worker" was a belief that such workers were like replaceable parts. Like cogs in a machine, for every part that broke down there was a seemingly endless supply of replacements.

Beneath the abstraction, however, lay a human being who was more than simply the sum total of his/her working hours per week. Beyond the role of worker were other roles that each migrant filled, and each role had its own implications for the host society. The worker was father/mother, husband/wife, friend, countryman, neighbor, consumer, believer, and carrier of language, to name but a few. Amidst all this has lingered the unresolved ambiguity of whether the worker was in fact a "guest" or, more likely, an unwanted but tolerated intruder.

The policies governing the lives of the immigrant laborers in the countries of the European North are a patchwork of confusion and contradiction. This is particularly evident when one examines the slippage between pronouncements of concern for the integration and well-being of the workers and the realities that tend to produce opposite outcomes. The fact that, until very recently, each country was essentially addressing the needs and concerns of the workers on an *ad hoc*, country-by-country basis has meant discrepancies in the provisions for education, housing, residential mobility, access to the labor market for children and other dependents, reunification of families, and legal protections. While many of these issues have been addressed by the EEC with regard to its own workers, it should be reiterated that these workers constitute but one quarter of all workers in the Community.

The cumulative result of the approaches taken by the individual countries is a reflection of the deeper ambiguity and ambivalence toward the foreign workers. That one finds economic integration coinciding with social marginality is entirely predictable if one accepts the rationale that the workers and their families are not immigrants, but rather migrants. The evidence is that many if not a majority of those who have come in the waves of manpower migrations from the European South consider themselves to be immigrants. Their children are growing up with characteristics of second generation immigrants. For these youth in particular, rural Turkey or the coast of Yugoslavia are abstractions. Their lives are being lived in Berlin, Paris, Brussels, and Amsterdam, not in Ankara or Belgrave. . . .

# 52

# British Race Riots Not Wholly Racial

Godfrey Hodgson

The summer of 1981 witnessed unusual violence in Great Britain, as riots broke out in almost every major British city. In this wire service release which appeared in late August of that year, television commentator Godfrey Hodgson points out that economic decline and record unemployment levels were far more significant than racial tensions in contributing to the country's widespread social unrest.

Looking back, this summer's unusual violence in Britain's cities had two immediate causes—racial tensions and the insensitive conduct of the police. But it would be wrong to see the eruptions as simply race riots, though racial hostility was surely an ingredient in the explosive brew. Young whites in many areas pelted cops and looted stores along with blacks. In Liverpool, rioting broke out in a district where whites and blacks get along, and both dislike the police. Nor would it be fair to lay the blame entirely on the police. They have been summoned to deal with mounting street crime and other urban problems without either training or resources. Except in special cases, they are not armed. Deep down, therefore, the causes of the unrest reflect British society itself today—a land of record unemployment and economic decline, its decayed inner cities a sign of the malaise.

A large non-white minority entered this society relatively recently, and the country has not been able to adapt. A generation ago, there were only a handful of Asians, Africans and West Indians in Britain, most of them seamen living in port cities. Now the immigrants number 2.5 million, or about 5 percent of the population, disproportionately crowded into the poor neighborhoods of London, Liverpool and Manchester. The British generally treat them politely but patronizingly. Discrimination exists in the job market, for example, but it is concealed.

In their poor urban neighborhoods, however, the immigrants come up against whites as deprived as themselves. But there, too, racism is usually covert. Yet a mood of conflict exists—and it can surface, as it did in the riots. The impoverished whites and blacks share a common problem. Both are suffering from the worst unemployment since the depression of the 1930s. Teenagers have been the hardest hit. In some places, like the area of Liverpool where rioting broke out, the jobless rate for young whites last year was 43 percent, for blacks 47 percent. This disaster mirrors the drop in industry and the rise in the service professions, which put a premium on education. The cities have been overtaken by office buildings, with here and there some renovated older houses. The middle classes have moved to the leafy suburbs.

The latest census, just published shows the shift of population, and it tells the story statistically. Remote regions like Cornwall and Norfolk have experienced the fastest growth. The London population, once 9 million, was down to 7.5 million in 1971 and now stands at 6.7 million. The inner city has lost 20 percent of its residents in the past decade. The same is true in other large cities. Liverpool's inner core, for example, has lost nearly one-third of its population over the past 20 years.

Economic change has been the culprit. Offices and factories have moved out to the country, often to new towns conceived by modern planners. The old industries—shipbuilding, textiles, steel, cars—are dying.

Not only are the jobless white and black kids frustrated. So are the police and the politicians who issue them orders—and so are the voters who elect the politicians.

Thus the riots this summer were more than a narrow urban phenomenon. They were symptomatic of present-day Britain, and they could happen again.

# 53

## An Algerian in Paris

### Jonathan Power

This interview with Said, a 35-year-old Algerian laborer who has lived and worked in France since the age of 17 and sees his wife and children only once a year, makes it painfully clear that the life of a migrant worker is typically one of loneliness, estrangement from family, and highly limited personal freedom.

Q: Hello, Saîd. Do you have a minute to spare?

A: I've all the time in the world. No one waiting for me, no wife or children. Or rather, I have, but they're back home in my village, Tibchari, not far from Tizi-Ouzou.

Q: How long have you been in France?

A: I came to Marseilles in 1960, when I was 17. We arrived at precisely 6:15 in the evening on 3rd September, 1960. It's stamped on my memory for ever: France, on a rather dull Monday evening. You see my grey hairs? That's what comes of living alone.

Q: Why France?

A: Well, I left my village first of all to go to the town. I looked for work, but didn't find any. . . .

Q: How much do you earn?

A: I'm a skilled labourer. I had to fight for it. I take home about 3,000 Fr. a month. I pay 200 Fr. rent for the room I share with a colleague (he pays the same amount), and I send 1,000 Fr. a month to Algeria.

Q: Are you able to save at all?

A: A little. During 18 years' service in France—it's funny, but it's just like the Army: when I go back to Algeria in the summer, I feel as if I'm on leave. . . . I've been able to build a small house in my village. Not very big, only 4 rooms. One for my parents, one for my two sisters, one for my wife and our two children, and another where we eat. . . .

Q: How old are your children?

A: There's my daughter, Houria (the word means "liberty" in Arabic)—she's eight. And then my son, Mokhtar ("the chosen one") is 6½.

Q: Were you in France when they were born?

A: Yes. I received a cable once, but I couldn't go back. I didn't see Houria or Mokhtar when they were born. The first time I saw them, they were already big—well, no longer babies. It was my father who gave them their names.

Q: Do they recognize you?

A: They know my father as their Dad. At first, when I go home, for about a fortnight I'm a stranger to them. They get used to me, little by little. But as soon as that happens, it's time for me to go. That's why I always go at night, while they're asleep. I always leave in the night, on purpose. It's not so hard that way. To see them cry. . . . You know, a fortnight before I have to leave, I begin to get this sick feeling in my stomach. It hurts. I buy the ticket without telling anyone, not even my wife. I only tell her two days beforehand, because she feels bad, too, when I have to go. That's not living.

Q: Have you ever thought of bringing your family to France?

A: Yes, when I was first married. But it meant finding a place to live, then paying rent for six months and filling in lots of forms. . . . No thank you. No lodgings for Algerians here, except this room: 12 square metres in a run-down building, with no sun and no hygiene. We're treated like animals here. In the evening when I come home from work, it's like entering a tomb. So at first I thought of bringing my wife, since it's no way to live, her over there and me here. Then, after I saw what racism was like and how awful the living conditions were, I said to my-self: it's already bad enough like this, why ask anyone to share it? And, besides, it shows a lack of respect to ask my father. It's shameful how I have to live.

Q: So you see your wife only once a year?

A: In eleven years of marriage, I must have seen her altogether 12 or 13 months. For some years now, I've been taking a month's paid holiday, and another month without pay. Two months a year: it's not much. Do you know any French people who would be prepared to live apart from their wives and children like that? . . . It's easy to make laws prohibiting things. But they don't know how we live, what we have to go through. No, they just don't know. . . .

Q: Do you ever think you'll go back for good?

A: Of course I do. [My friend] Habib here has decided to go back at the end of the year. He's sure to find work. In any case, the returned migrants have priority for jobs in Algeria. You know, each time I get back to my village, for me it's like the day I was born. It's a new beginning.

Q: Have you personally suffered from racism?

A: When I go to Marseilles, I don't speak to anyone for 2 or 3 hours. On the bus, in the street. Talk to whom? Nobody. We're always home early, by 9 or 10 o'clock at night, because of the spot-checks. You have to be careful. Everyone's afraid. If one of us did something silly, well. . . . But there are good ones and bad ones. Not everyone in this country is a racist. But I take a responsible attitude myself. That's to say, I take care not to go into areas where there is racism. I don't go out much at all. What's hardest, is to be a man in the factory and a woman at home in the evenings—doing the shopping, getting the meal ready, washing up afterwards. . . . We don't have time to go out, so we don't meet racists. . . .

Q: How do you see [the] future?

A: Look—me, I didn't go to school. I've told you why not. But my kids will go through school, all the way, until they have a skilled trade. My children won't have to live as I do. No, definitely not. By the year 2000, it will all have changed. It's already beginning to. . . .

Q: Your son won't emigrate?

A: No fear! I was the 1960 generation, he is 1978! Quite a different matter. Now there's work to be had at home. He doesn't go around with his eyes closed like I did. And anyway, if I'm here, it's so that he won't have to emigrate. . . .

Q: And your future, what do you see in store?

A: Work, you get used to it. It never occurs to me to drop everything and go off to sleep. If I had a trade, I would have a future. I'd like to be in mechanics, an engineer would be grand. The future? I'll go on until I retire, maybe sooner, because my friend Habib isn't going to wait till then—he's going. . . .

Q: Do you belong to a union?

A: Sure. The workers have to stand up for themselves. It's important. I'm taking a risk in not being nice to the boss all the time. If he sacks me, I'll just go home. It's degrading to be unemployed. I'm here to work, not to be unemployed. I once was, for 50 days. I went around looking for work. I didn't want to wait for the unemployment people to find me work. I looked for it, and I found it.

Q: You might say you were the last generation to emigrate?

A: The last one, yes. My son won't emigrate, never. We are the last, I can swear to that. . . .

---

# *54*

---

# Sweden Goes Multilingual

---------------- **Britta Kellgren** ----------------

Since 1968, Sweden has assumed full responsibility for educating its second generation immigrant children in their own language. In this wire service release issued in June 1983, Swedish writer Britta Kellgren explains the rationale behind this unusual policy and describes how Sweden is rapidly becoming a multicultural society.

---

If the United States, Britain, France and other big countries are bedeviled by the problem of foreign immigrants, consider the challenge to a little land like Sweden, where aliens represent 10 percent of the population. The problem here has not been easy to tackle, especially since the Swedes are a relatively homogeneous people. But an effort is being made to absorb the immigrants without compelling them to erase their ethnic identities.

Following a deliberate policy decision made by the government a few years ago, Sweden is becoming a multicultural society, with the authorities assuming the burden for educating the children of immigrants in their own language. The decision was predicated on the notion that it was essential for kids to become proficient in the tongues they spoke at home before they could become fluent in Swedish. In short, they had to learn one language well before learning another. Otherwise, educators warned, Sweden would spawn a generation of youngsters who were "semilingual" rather than bilingual—and, as a consequence, might be misfits both in Swedish society and in the presence of their parents. Legislation passed in 1968 therefore extended to all children of non-Swedish families the right to free schooling in their mother tongue—euphemistically known here as the "home" language. The expectation was that the children would adapt more easily to life here if they were aware of their national origin. In addition, fluency in their own language would give them pride in their heritage. And perhaps, it was believed, they might return to their countries of origin.

The educational system now handles pupils starting from two-year olds in day care centers up to teenagers in high school, and it works in different ways. Foreign children attending regular schools are excused from their classes for a few hours a week for special language training. In some instances, classes are conducted in a foreign language, as if the school existed outside Sweden. There are also bilingual classes, in which two teachers teach in two different languages. For newly arriving children, preparatory classes have been set up to introduce them to Swedish while continuing their training in their own tongue.

Of the more than 400,000 foreigners resident in Sweden, roughly half are Finnish, with the rest from Greece, Turkey, West Germany, Poland, Latin America and other areas. An equal number are naturalized, bringing the total with alien backgrounds to nearly a million. The alien influx began during World War II as refugees fled to Sweden. The immigration swelled during the 1960s, when the economic boom caused a labor shortage that required the importation of workers from abroad. What makes the problem relatively manageable is that the numbers involved are small and the immigration has been orderly. There is nothing here comparable to the invasion of Mexicans or Cubans into the United States.

Here in Stockholm, for example, about 75 percent of the 8,000 students entitled to special language training are enrolled in such classes. By the seventh grade, teachers estimate, most who started their schooling in their mother tongue can cope with Swedish. The public educational system is unusually flexible, and it is rare that a child cannot be matched to a language. Some 50 tongues are taught, among them Nepalese, Thai, Singalese, several Chinese dialects and Tagalog, the Philippine idiom. The government furnishes books in these languages. An obstacle, of course, is to find teachers capable of teaching some of the more esoteric tongues. An instructor has yet to be found, for instance, for the one family here that speaks Waloff, an African dialect. On the other hand, the system managed to locate a teacher to train a little girl from Iraq who spoke a local variation of Kurdish. The teacher, by chance, happened to be living in the city of Uppsala.

None of this is going to transform Sweden into the Tower of Babel. On the contrary, the hope is that most of the children will eventually become proficient in Swedish without forgetting their native tongues.

# Unit XIII

## —————— Security ——————

Communist gains in Eastern Europe made the Soviet Union and its satellites the primary focus of Western European security concerns after World War II. In 1949, the United States formally tied its own security interests to those of Western Europe by joining in the signing of the North Atlantic Treaty. Since that time, the North Atlantic Treaty Organization has served as the institutional vehicle for the defense of Western Europe as a whole, although each member country maintains its own national security forces. In the early years of NATO, the United States reigned as the unchallenged leader, but declines in U.S. economic and political power along with shifts in the transatlantic balance of power have led to a gradual weakening of U.S. influence over the NATO allies and have called its leadership into question. Shifts in economic and political power have not, however, produced corresponding changes in security arrangements. Instead, Western Europe continues to be dependent on U.S. nuclear forces while at the same time questioning U.S. commitment to its defense. In the late 1970s, the United States responded to Western Europe's growing concern over security by agreeing to increase the number of its nuclear weapons in Western Europe. Although this move has allayed the fears of Western European governments as to the strength of the United States' commitment to their defense, it has also spawned considerable opposition from growing numbers of Western Europe's citizenry.

This unit examines NATO and its security policies, the varying perspectives of and relationships among its members, and the recent controversies which have called NATO's future into question. Excerpts from the *NATO Handbook* summarize the purposes and operational structure of this complex organization. Through NATO, sovereign member nations pursue mutual deterrence and defense goals while working cooperatively toward better East-West relations and arms control agreements. "Squaring Off Without the Bomb" charts the changing military strengths of NATO and the Warsaw Pact in both personnel and conventional forces in recent years. Another table, "NATO and Warsaw Pact Military Expenditures: 1975-1981," shows military expenditures by members of the two alliances. The authors of "Western Security: What Has Changed? What Should Be Done?" trace shifts in the U.S.-Soviet balance of power and in the balance of economic and political power between the United States and the European members of NATO which have increased transatlantic tensions. They argue that a growing disparity in world views is the key to recent NATO divisions, but they are convinced that neither the U.S. nor Western Europe can face the challenges of the 1980s alone and they recommend that the Europeans assume a more equal role within the organization.

Although all member governments generally continue to support the Alliance, popular concern regarding the proper response to the East bloc's large military build-up, particularly the Soviet Union's deployment of nuclear missiles with greatly improved precision, mobility, speed, and range, has severely challenged NATO's viability. In "The Theater Nuclear Weapons Debate," two figures chart NATO's response to the nuclear threat and outline other proposals and counterproposals which were offered at the end of 1982. In "NATO and Nuclear Weapons: Reasons and Unreason," political scientist Stanley Hoffman examines the formidable new anti-nuclear movement, showing how it differs from past protest movements. He also shows how the nuclear missile debate, which he considers to be one of NATO's "most dangerous tests," is symptomatic of a fundamental divergence of views between Alliance members on both sides of the Atlantic, and he argues that these differences must be resolved if NATO is to survive as the key security structure in Western Europe.

# 55

# The North Atlantic Treaty Organization (NATO)

————— North Atlantic Treaty Organization —————

In the following excerpts from the 1982 *NATO Handbook*, the NATO Information Service summarizes the treaty which established the organization in 1949 and the major features of the Alliance's operating structure. For closer study, we also include the first six of the treaty's fourteen articles.

## EXCERPTS FROM THE NORTH ATLANTIC TREATY

The Parties to this Treaty reaffirm their faith in the purposes and principles of the Charter of the United Nations and their desire to live in peace with all peoples and All Governments.

They are determined to safeguard the freedom, common heritage and civilization of their peoples, founded on the principles of democracy, individual liberty and the rule of law.

They seek to promote stability and well-being in the North Atlantic area.

They are resolved to unite their efforts for collective defense and for the preservation of peace and security.

They therefore agree to this North Atlantic Treaty:

### ARTICLE 1

The Parties undertake, as set forth in the Charter of the United Nations, to settle any international disputes in which they may be involved by peaceful means in such a manner that international peace and security, and justice, are not endangered, and to refrain in their international relations from the threat or use of force in any manner inconsistent with the purposes of the United Nations.

### ARTICLE 2

The Parties will contribute toward the further development of peaceful and friendly international relations by strengthening their free institutions, by bringing about a better understanding of the principles upon which these institutions are founded, and by promoting conditions of stability and well-being. They will seek to eliminate conflict in their international economic policies and will encourage economic collaboration between any or all of them.

## ARTICLE 3

In order more effectively to achieve the objectives of this Treaty, the Parties, separately and jointly, by means of continuous and effective self-help and mutual aid, will maintain and develop their individual and collective capacity to resist armed attack.

## ARTICLE 4

The Parties will consult together whenever, in the opinion of any of them, the territorial integrity, political independence or security of any of the Parties is threatened.

## ARTICLE 5

The Parties agree that an armed attack against one or more of them in Europe or North America shall be considered an attack against them all, and consequently they agree that, if such an armed attack occurs, each of them, in exercise of the right of individual or collective self-defense recognized by Article 51 of the Charter of the Untied Nations, will assist the Party or Parties so attacked by taking forthwith, individually and in concert with the other Parties, such action as it deems necessary, including the use of armed force, to restore and maintain the security of the North Atlantic area.

Any such armed attack and all measures taken as a result thereof shall immediately be reported to the Security Council. Such measures shall be terminated when the Security Council has taken the measures necessary to restore and maintain international peace and security.

## ARTICLE 6

For the purpose of Article 5, an armed attack on one or more of the Parties is deemed to include an armed attack

• on the territory of any of the Parties in Europe or North America, on the Algerian Departments of France,* on the territory of Turkey or on the islands under the jurisdiction of any of the Parties in the North Atlantic area north of the Tropic of Cancer.

---

*Ed. note: Inapplicable since July 3, 1962, when Algeria became independent of France.

- on the forces, vessels, or aircraft of any of the Parties, when in or over these territories or any area in Europe in which occupation forces of any of the Parties were stationed on the date when the Treaty entered into force or the Mediterranean Sea or the North Atlantic area north of the Tropic of Cancer. . .

## ANALYSIS OF THE TREATY

The North Atlantic Treaty is the framework for a military alliance designed to prevent aggression or to repel it, should it occur. It also provides for continuous co-operation and consultation in political, economic and other non-military fields. It is of indefinite duration.

The signatory countries state their desire to live in peace with all peoples and all governments. Reaffirming their faith in the principles of the United Nations, they undertake in particular to preserve peace and international security and to promote stability and well-being in the North Atlantic area.

To achieve these goals, they sign their names to a number of undertakings in different fields. They agree, for example, to settle international disputes by peaceful means, in order to avoid endangering international peace, security and justice. They also agree to refrain from the threat or use of force in any way which would not be consistent with the purposes of the United Nations. They undertake to eliminate conflict in their international economic policies and to encourage economic collaboration between their countries.

Under this Treaty, the member countries therefore adopt a policy of security based on the inherent right to individual and collective self-defence accorded by Article 51 of the United Nations Charter, while, at the same time, affirming the importance of co-operation between them in other spheres.

The Treaty consists of fourteen Articles and is preceded by a Preamble which emphasizes that the Alliance has been created within the framework of the United Nations Charter and outlines its main purposes.

Article 1 defines the basic principles to be followed by member countries in conducting their international relations, in order to avoid endangering peace and world security.

Article 2 defines the aims which the member countries will pursue in their international relationships, and their resulting obligations.

In Article 3 signatories state that they will maintain and develop their ability, both individually and collectively, to resist attack.

Article 4 envisages a threat to the territorial integrity, political independence or security of one of the member countries of the Alliance and provides for joint consultation whenever one of them believes that such a threat exists. In practice, this consultation takes place in the North Atlantic Council and its subordinate committees.

Article 5 is the core of the Treaty whereby member countries agree to treat an armed attack on any one of them, on either side of the Atlantic, as an attack against all of them. It commits them to taking the necessary steps to help each other in the event of an armed attack.

Although it leaves each signatory free to take whatever action it considers appropriate, the Article states that individually and collectively the member nations must take steps to restore and maintain security. Joint action is justified by the inherent, individual and collective right of self-defence embodied in Article 51 of the United Nations Charter; but it is agreed that measures taken under the terms of the Article shall be terminated when the Security Council has acted as necessary to restore and maintain international peace and security.

Article 6 defines the area in which the provisions of Article 5 apply. However, it does not imply that events occurring outside that area cannot be the subject of consultation within the Alliance. The overall international situation is liable to affect the preservation of peace and security in the Treaty area and the North Atlantic Council must therefore devote its attention to consideration of this situation as a matter of course.

In Articles 7 and 8 member nations stipulate that none of their existing international commitments conflict with the terms of the Treaty and that they will not enter into any commitments in the future which do so. In particular they state that rights and obligations pertaining to membership of the United Nations are unaffected by the Treaty, as is the primary role of the United Nations Security Council in the sphere of international peace and security.

Under Article 9, the parties to the Treaty establish a Council, on which each of them shall be represented, which shall be able to meet promptly at any time. The Council in turn is charged with the creation of such subsidiary bodies as may be necessary to implement the provisions of the Treaty. This is the basis on which the North Atlantic Treaty Organization has been gradually built up.

Article 10 provides for the possibility of accession to the Treaty by any other European State in a position to further the principles of the Treaty. In 1952 Greece and Turkey, in 1955 the Federal Republic of Germany, and in 1982 Spain acceded to the Treaty under the terms of this Article.

Article 11 describes the process of ratification of the Treaty in accordance with the constitutional processes of the signatories, and the manner in which the Treaty is to enter into force.

Articles 12 and 13 deal with the possibility of revision of the Treaty after a period of ten years and denunciation of the Treaty by any party to it, after twenty years. They have never been invoked.

Article 14 gives equal authority to the English and French texts of the Treaty and arranges for their safe deposit in Washington, D.C.

## HOW THE ALLIANCE WORKS

The North Atlantic Treaty Organization serves a defensive Alliance which maintains military preparedness in order to prevent war. It is an inter-governmental, not a supranational organization, in which member states retain their full sovereignty and independence. The political task of NATO is to provide for consultation on all political problems of relevance to its members or to the Alliance as a whole and to give direction to the military side of the Organization. The military task of NATO in peacetime is to draw up joint defence plans, to set up the necessary infrastructure and to arrange for joint training and exercises. In peacetime national forces receive orders only from national authorities. Apart from the integrated staffs at the different NATO military headquarters, the only exceptions to this rule are certain air defence units on constant alert and the Standing Naval Forces mentioned [later].

The aim of all member countries is to achieve a just and lasting peaceful order, accompanied by proper security guarantees, and to defend the North Atlantic Treaty area. The Alliance seeks to achieve these purposes through a policy based on the twin principles of defense and detente. To this end the Allies have been active in promoting political initiatives and armaments control measures designed to ease East/West tensions.

### Defence Policy

The primary role of the Alliance is to safeguard the security of member nations by deterring aggression. This means that a potential aggressor should have no doubt that if he initiates an attack he will be taking a risk out of all proportion to any advantage he may hope to gain. In the event of aggression, the role of the Alliance is to re-establish the territorial integrity of the North Atlantic area. NATO must therefore maintain sufficient forces to preserve the military balance with the Warsaw Pact and to provide a credible deterrent.

NATO forces are made up of three interlocking elements known as the NATO Triad. They are:

- conventional forces strong enough to resist and repel a conventional attack on a limited scale, and to sustain a conventional defense in the forward areas against large-scale conventional aggression;
- intermediate- and short-range nuclear forces to enhance the deterrent and defensive effect of NATO conventional forces against large-scale conventional attack, with the aim of convincing the aggressor that any form of attack on NATO could result in very serious damage to his own forces, and of emphasizing the dangers implicit in continuing a conflict;
- United States and United Kingdom strategic nuclear forces which provide the ultimate deterrent.

Together, the conventional and nuclear forces must provide a whole spectrum of military capabilities which will enable NATO to meet aggression at any level with an appropriate response. It must be made impossible for the aggressor to calculate in advance the cost to him of aggression, by presenting him with the risk that the situation could escalate beyond his control. The Soviet Union and its allies have continued to build up and improve both their conventional and nuclear forces, their offensive capabilities and their operational readiness in every field, including a large-scale expansion of the Soviet Navy, which is now active all over the world. Strong conventional and adequate nuclear forces are therefore vital elements of the overall NATO deterrent. An agreement between East and West on the balance of forces at the conventional level has not yet been achieved, although this is still the objective of the Western powers in the Vienna negotiations on Mutual and Balanced Force Reductions in Central Europe. Negotiations are also underway in Geneva on possible reductions in intermediate-range nuclear forces.

The policy of maintaining deterrence goes hand in hand with efforts to improve East-West relations. NATO must continue to maintain its defensive strength in order to provide a firm basis for negotiations and to guarantee its security until the time comes when security can be achieved by firm agreements to reduce military strengths on both sides. . . .

## THE CIVIL AND MILITARY STRUCTURE OF THE ALLIANCE

### The North Atlantic Council, the Defence Planning Committee and the Nuclear Planning Group

NATO is an organisation of sovereign nations equal in status. Decisions taken must therefore be expressions of the collective will of member governments arrived at by common consent.

The highest decision-making body and forum for consultations within the Alliance is the North Atlantic Council, composed of representatives of the fifteen member countries.

At Ministerial Meetings of the Council, member nations are represented by Ministers of Foreign Affairs. These meetings are held twice a year. The Council also meets on occasion at the level of Heads of State and Government. In permanent session, at the level of Ambassadors (Permanent Representatives), the Council meets at least once a week.

The Defence Planning Committee is composed of representatives of the member countries participating in NATO's integrated military structure. It deals with matters specifically related to defence. Like the Council, it meets both in permanent session at the level of Ambassadors and twice a year at Ministerial level. At Ministerial Meetings, member nations are represented by Defence Ministers.

The Council and Defence Planning Committee are chaired by the Secretary General of NATO at whatever level they meet. Opening Sessions of Ministerial Meetings of the Council are presided over by the President, an honorary position held annually by the Foreign Minister of one of the member nations.

Nuclear matters are discussed by the Nuclear Planning Group in which thirteen countries now participate. It meets regularly at the level of Permanent Representatives and twice a year at the level of Ministers of Defence.

## The Permanent Representatives and National Delegations

The Permanent Representatives of member countries are supported by national delegations located at NATO Headquarters. The delegations are composed of advisers and officials qualified to represent their countries on the various committees created by the Council.

## The Secretary General and the International Staff

To assist it in its task, the Council has established a number of committees whose main areas of responsibility are indicated in the diagram. These committees are supported by an International Staff, made up of personnel drawn from all member countries, responsible to the Secretary General. The Secretary General himself is responsible for promoting and directing the process of consultation within the Alliance. He may propose items for discussion. He has the authority to use his good offices at any time in cases of dispute between member countries, and with their consent, to initiate enquiries or mediation, conciliation or arbitration procedures. . . .

## CIVIL AND MILITARY STRUCTURE

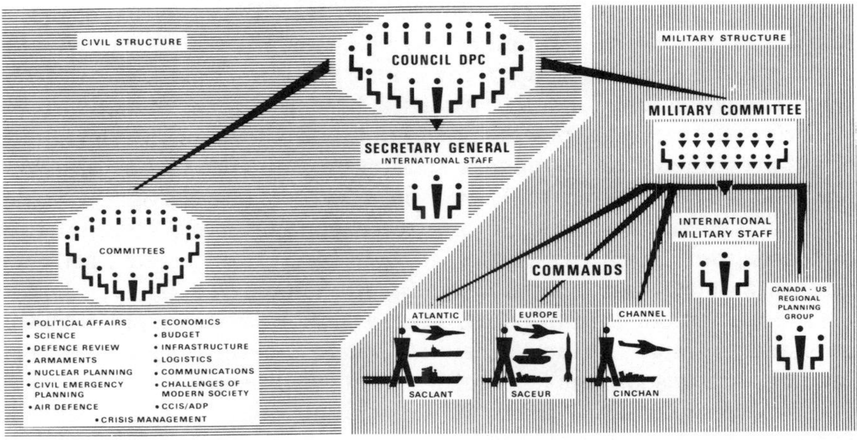

Figure 55.1

### The Military Committee

The Military Committee, the highest military body in the Alliance, is responsible for making recommendations to the Council and Defence Planning Committee on military matters and for supplying guidance on military questions to Allied Commanders and subordinate military authorities. It is composed of the Chiefs-of-Staff of all member countries, except France,* and Iceland (which has no military forces). The Chiefs-of-Staff normally meet three times a year—and whenever else it may be found necessary. However, to enable the Military Committee to function in permanent session with effective powers of decision, each Chief-of-Staff appoints a Permanent Military Representative. Liaison between the Military Committee and the French High Command is effected through the Chief of the French Military Mission to the Military Committee. . . .

### The International Military Staff

The Military Committee is assisted by an integrated International Military Staff (IMS) headed by a Director selected from one of the member nations. . . .

---

*Ed. note: France withdrew from NATO's integrated military command in 1966 but remains a member of the alliance.

## The NATO Commands

The strategic area covered by the North Atlantic Treaty is divided among three Commands: Allied Command Europe; Allied Command Atlantic; and Allied Command Channel. Plans for the defence of the North American area are developed by the Canada-United States Regional Planning Group, which makes recommendations to the Military Committee. It meets alternately in the United States and Canada.

The authority exercised by the Commands varies in accordance with geographical and political factors and with peace or wartime conditions.

Generally, the forces of member countries remain under national command in peacetime; however, some are placed under operational command or control of NATO, some are already assigned to NATO Commands and others are earmarked for these Commands.

The NATO Commanders are responsible for the development of defence plans for their respective areas, for the determination of force requirements and for the deployment and exercise of the forces under their Command.

The organisation of the Commands is flexible enough and the liaison between them close enough to allow for mutual support in the event of war, and the rapid movement of the necessary land, sea and air forces to meet any situation likely to confront the Alliance.

### The European Command

Allied Command Europe (ACE) covers the area extending from the North Cape to the Mediterranean and from the Atlantic to the eastern border of Turkey, excluding the United Kingdom and Portugal, the defence of which does not fall under any one major NATO Command. ACE is subdivided into a number of subordinate Commands.

ACE comes under the Supreme Allied Commander Europe (SACEUR), whose headquarters, near Mons in Belgium, are known as SHAPE (Supreme Headquarters Allied Powers Europe).

The ACE Mobile Force, also under SACEUR is composed of land and air force units supplied by different member countries. It can be ready for action at very short notice in any threatened area of ACE, particularly on the northern and southern flanks.

In peacetime SACEUR's main functions are to prepare and finalize defence plans for the area under his command, and ensure the combat efficiency of forces assigned to him in the event of war. SACEUR also makes recommendations to the Military Committee on matters likely to improve the organisation of his command.

In wartime SACEUR would control all land, sea and air operations in his area. Internal defence and defence of coastal waters remain the responsibility of the national authorities concerned, but SACEUR would have full authority to carry out such operations as he considered necessary for the defence of any part of the area under his Command.

Thirteen of the member countries maintain a National Military Representative (NMR) at SHAPE, providing military liaison with the Allied Chiefs-of-Staff. France has a military liaison mission at SHAPE.

SACEUR and his two Deputy Supreme Allied Commanders are assisted by political and scientific advisers in addition to their military staffs.

### The Atlantic Ocean Command

The Allied Command Atlantic (ACLANT) covers approximately 12 million square miles of the Atlantic Ocean. This area extends from the North Pole to the Tropic of Cancer and from the coastal waters of North America to the coasts of Europe and Africa, except for the Channel and the British Isles. ACLANT is subdivided into a number of subordinate Commands.

The Supreme Allied Commander Atlantic (SACLANT) has peacetime responsibility for preparing defence plans, conducting joint training exercises, establishing training standards and supplying the NATO authorities with information on his strategic requirements.

SACLANT's primary wartime task is to provide for the security of the Atlantic area by guarding the sea lanes and denying their use to an enemy in order to safeguard them for the reinforcement and resupply of NATO Europe with men and material.

The Standing Naval Force Atlantic (STANAVFORLANT), made up of ships from NATO navies normally operating in the Atlantic area is under the direct command of SACLANT. This force is the world's first permanent international naval squadron formed in peacetime and is assigned to SACLANT on a continuous basis. In addition, for training purposes and in the event of war, forces earmarked by the nations involved are assigned to SACLANT. Although these forces are predominantly naval, they also include ground forces and land-based air forces.

### The Channel Command

The Allied Command Channel (ACCHAN) covers the English Channel and the southern areas of the North Sea. Its mission is to control and protect merchant shipping in the area, co-operating with SACEUR in the air defence of the Channel. The forces earmarked for the Command are predominantly naval but include maritime air forces. The Allied Commander-in-Chief Channel (CINCHAN) has a Maritime Air Advisor who is also the Commander Allied Maritime Air Force Channel.

CINCHAN also has under his orders the NATO Standing Naval Force Channel (STANAVFORCHAN) which is a permanent force comprising mine counter-measure vessels of different NATO countries.

# Squaring Off Without the Bomb

*The New York Times*

In the following graphs, *The New York Times* contrasted the conventional military forces of NATO and the Warsaw Pact, showing how the balance shifted between 1965 and 1980. NATO personnel forces include more than 300,000 Americans, stationed primarily in Germany.

| | NATO | Warsaw Pact |
|---|---|---|
| **Military personnel\*** (in millions) | 1.096 | 1.216 |
| **Divisions \*** (includes West German territorial forces, three French divisions and others) | 32 | 50 |

\* derived from 1981–82 International Institute for Strategic Studies report

**Combat aircraft**

3,000
2,000 — Warsaw Pact
1,000 — NATO

'65 '70 '75 '80

**Main battle tanks**

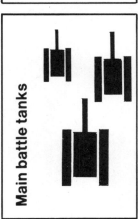

15,000 —
10,000 — Warsaw Pact
5,000 — NATO

'65 '70 '75 '80

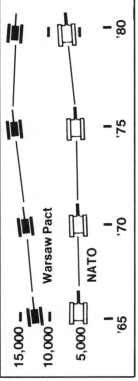

378

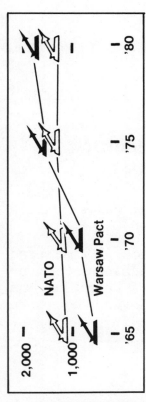

## Surface to air missile launchers

2,000 —

1,000 —

NATO

Warsaw Pact

'65　'70　'75　'80

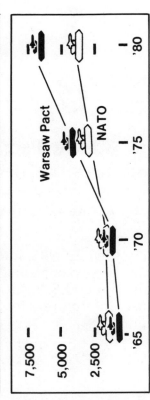

## Antitank guided missile launchers

7,500 —

5,000 —

2,500 —

Warsaw Pact

NATO

'65　'70　'75　'80

Source: U.S. Department of Defense

379

# NATO and Warsaw Pact Military Expenditures: 1978–1983

————— **International Institute for Strategic Studies** —————

These figures, compiled in 1983, indicate defense spending by the countries in the two opposing alliances. For many years, more than half of the U.S. military budget has been spent on NATO defense. Information for Soviet Union expenditures was not available.

| Country | $ million | | | $ per capita | | | % of government spending | | | % of GDP/GNP* | |
|---|---|---|---|---|---|---|---|---|---|---|---|
| | 1978 | 1981 | 1982 | 1978 | 1981 | 1982 | 1978 | 1981 | 1982 | 1978 | 1982 |
| **Warsaw Pact** | | | | | | | | | | | |
| Bulgaria | 432 | 1,245 | 1,287 | 49 | 140 | 144 | 6.2 | 5.6 | 5.7 | 2.3-3.0 | 2.2-2.9 |
| Czechoslovakia | 1,869 | 3,632 | 3,774 | 124 | 237 | 243 | 7.1 | 7.4 | 7.7 | 3.4-3.9 | 2.8-5.2 |
| GDR | 5,974 | 6,246 | 6,163 | 357 | 372 | 368 | 7.9 | 8.4 | 8.4 | 5.0-8.1 | 3.7-6.5 |
| Hungary | 790 | 1,237 | 1,318 | 74 | 115 | 123 | 3.8 | 3.9 | 4.0 | 2.4 | 2.4 |
| Poland | 3,369 | 5,532 | 6,254 | 96 | 153 | 173 | 8.6 | 5.2 | 7.1 | 3.0 | n.a. |
| Romania | 1,301 | 1,254 | 1,297 | 60 | 56 | 57 | 3.9 | 3.8 | 4.1 | 2.1 | 1.6 |
| Soviet Union | n.a. | n.a. | n.a. | n.a. | n.a. | n.a. | n.a. | n.a. | n.a. | n.a. | n.a. |
| **NATO** | | | | | | | | | | | |
| Belgium | 3,166 | 3,342 | 2,799 | 319 | 337 | 283 | 8.6 | 8.7 | 8.1 | 3.3 | 3.3 |
| Britain | 14,621 | 24,223 | 24,200 | 262 | 433 | 432 | 11.6 | 11.4 | 11.9 | 4.6 | 5.1 |
| Canada | 4,087 | 4,919 | 5,989 | 174 | 202 | 247 | 9.1 | 8.7 | 9.2 | 2.0 | 2.0 |
| Denmark | 1,315 | 1,434 | 1,122 | 256 | 279 | 219 | 6.4 | 7.0 | 5.5 | 2.3 | 2.0 |
| France | 18,874 | 23,545 | 21,969 | 354 | 438 | 408 | 18.6 | 18.9 | 17.5 | 4.0 | 4.1 |
| FRG | 26,851 | 29,047 | 28,453 | 438 | 471 | 461 | 27.4 | 28.2 | 27.9 | 4.2 | 4.3 |
| Greece | 2,119 | 2,273 | 2,574 | 228 | 237 | 265 | 27.3 | 21.4 | 23.5 | 6.7 | 6.7 |
| Italy | 6,246 | 8,681 | 8,924 | 110 | 152 | 156 | 6.6 | 6.4 | 5.6 | 2.5 | 2.6 |
| Luxembourg | 37 | 46 | 41 | 101 | 126 | 114 | 2.9 | 3.1 | 3.2 | 0.8 | 1.2 |
| Netherlands | 4,227 | 4,717 | 4,468 | 302 | 333 | 315 | 8.7 | 8.3 | 7.8 | 3.3 | 3.3 |
| Norway | 1,307 | 1,646 | 1,680 | 322 | 401 | 410 | 9.4 | 6.7 | 6.7 | 3.2 | 3.0 |
| Portugal | 623 | 840 | 778 | 64 | 83 | 79 | n.a. | 8.6 | 10.8 | 3.5 | 3.3 |
| Spain | 3,208 | 4,576 | 4,529 | 87 | 121 | 116 | 15.0 | 13.6 | 12.1 | 2.2 | 2.6 |
| Turkey | 2,728 | 2,306 | 2,755 | 63 | 50 | 59 | 20.2 | 20.7 | 21.7 | 5.2 | 5.2 |
| USA | 109,247 | 171,000 | 215,900 | 491 | 759 | 938 | 23.7 | 24.6 | 29.2 | 5.1 | 7.2 |

*Gross National Product

n.a. = not available

Source: The Military Balance 1983-84 (London: International Institute for Strategic Studies, 1983), pp. 125-126.

# Western Security: What Has Changed? What Should Be Done?

### Karl Kaiser, Winston Lord, ————————— Thierry de Montbrial, and David Watt —————————

The Research Institute of the German Association for Foreign Policy (Bonn), the Council on Foreign Relations (New York), the French Institute of International Relations (Paris), and the Royal Institute of International Affairs (London) are the leading non-governmental, yet establishment, foreign policy bodies in these countries. In early 1981, the directors of these institutions collaborated to prepare a report analyzing how the "formidable and often unprecedented" challenges facing the Western nations in the 1980s could best be met. In this chapter, the authors diagnose the factors which troubled relations between Western Europe and the United States at the decade's start.

## DIAGNOSIS

### Short-Term Factors

The current European-American tension finds its roots in historical and structural trends as well as in short-term, coincidental factors. To be sure, the latter have played an important role recently in exacerbating transatlantic quarrels and bringing them into the open. Poor management and policy errors by the American leadership in the past few years have clearly reduced European confidence in U.S. statesmanship. At the same time, Europeans were reluctant to act vigorously in the recent crises, thereby inducing impatience in the United States. Moreover, these factors have led at times to further tensions between the two sides of the Atlantic at the highest levels of government, thereby adding a "personal" element to an already strained relationship.

These short-term factors, however, fail to explain the magnitude and true nature of current transatlantic problems. It would be dangerously erroneous in particular to believe that once the international situation quiets down, the difficulties between Europe and America will disappear. They find their roots in deeper historical and structural trends.

## Historical and Structural Trends

Some of these elements have to do with wider societal developments in America and Europe, including the change of generations and the appearance of the new political elites. On the American side, there has been a gradual evolution of the United States away from a European-centered foreign policy, to a more global approach in which other regions (especially Asia and the Middle East) compete with Europe in U.S. preoccupations. To a certain extent this is paralleled by the gradual reduction in influence of a certain East coast, European-oriented elite which was highly knowledgeable and sensitive about European history and politics. Clearly, new American elites drawn from other regions (the South, the West) are, like the media, less concerned and informed about Europe. More important, perhaps, has been the emergence in the recent past of an increasingly nationalistic mood in the United States, born in part as a reaction to the decline of America's stature in the world since Vietnam. This new nationalism is reflected in a growing irritation and impatience with the Third World as a whole (particularly following the Iran hostage crisis) as well as with Soviet behaviour. A similar irritation has been noticeable toward the European allies, which are often perceived in the United States as "not doing enough" to fulfill their share of the collective Western burden.

A parallel evolution has been taking place in Europe. U.S. prestige has declined in the eyes of younger European elites, particularly as a result of the Vietnam war, and as European nations became stronger economically, Europeans have tried to assert their own voice in world affairs, at times in ways that conflict with U.S. policy, as in the case of the Venice initiative on the Middle East. At the same time, Europeans devoted increasing attention to Community matters (enlargement of the EEC, cooperation with African and Arab nations) and became more Euro-centered (in developing more political and economic relations with Eastern neighbours).

### The Transatlantic Balance of Power

This evolution is linked to the structural transformation of both the internal balance of power (between the U.S. and Europe) and the external balance of power (between the U.S. and the Soviet Union). The common denominator is the relative decline of U.S. power over the past decade and a half (in political and economic terms in the first instance, in military terms in the second).

Internally, the transformation of the balance of power between Europe and America has been most spectacular in the economic field. Here the American supremacy of the immediate post-war period has been replaced by a situation in which the European Community as a whole has become as rich as the U.S. and often more competitive on the world market. As a result, the ability of the United States to influence European policy in accordance with its own interests has sharply declined. Conversely, the Europeans have shown a greater willingness and ability to defend their own interests against those of the United States, where these have diverged. Examples are the German-American quarrel over the "locomotive theory" and the European-American controversy over nuclear energy and non-proliferation. In the monetary field, the creation of the European Monetary System was aimed to a large extent at shielding Europe from the consequences of the decline of the dollar-based international monetary system. Similarly, in November 1978, the Europeans obtained a direct influence on U.S. economic policy, as the United States was forced to defend the dollar following strong pressures from European central banks.

However, the growth of European economic power, relative to America's, has not been accompanied by a similar transformation of the security relationship between the Allies. Militarily, Europe as a whole remains dependent on the nuclear guarantee provided by the United States since the end of World War II. This dependence is modified in the case of Britain and France, both of which have independent nuclear forces. Nonetheless, it is the U.S. guarantee which safeguards the integrity of France's and Britain's neighbours. In that sense, the U.S. nuclear guarantee remains essential to the preservation of European security as a whole. Indeed, as Soviet military strength increased both in nuclear and conventional terms since the late 1960s, European dependence has in fact increased. This has sharpened the contradiction in a transatlantic relationship in which the protégé has become as rich as the protector and more reluctant to follow its lead, and yet does not assume the political and military responsibilities which come with its newly acquired economic might. So far, despite the existence of two nuclear powers in Western Europe, and of a strong German conventional army, the Europeans have not been willing or able since 1954 to move toward a more independent European defence posture. This failure has inhibited Europe's ability to play a more significant role in world affairs. In addition, there has been reluctance in some European nations to make an adequate defence contribution to NATO. Having been addicted to a regime of "security on the cheap" by being protected from the outside, certain European countries tend to resist serious efforts aimed at increasing their defence role and expenditures; indeed, when they have agreed to do so, it has more often been to placate the United States than to contribute to their own defence.

Politically, the development of the transatlantic relationship has been equally unbalanced. European political cooperation in the field of foreign policy has improved during the past decade, but Europe has yet to become a consistent actor in its own right on the world scene. Europe has often tended to criticize U.S. diplomatic moves without presenting a credible alternative, given its own military weakness and its internal divisions. The end result has been to damage political relations between the allies further, without reinforcing the stature of the West as a whole in world affairs.

In short, the relative decline of U.S. leadership has not been compensated by a substitute European leadership, and consequently Western power has been diluted. Small wonder that such an unbalanced transatlantic relationship, in which no clear leadership emerges, produces strains and frustrations on both sides.

### The Soviet-American Balance of Power

These tensions are magnified by the consequences of the other historical trend—namely, the change in the U.S.-Soviet balance of power. The key dimension is the growth of Soviet military strength. Its impact has been particularly painful in terms of transatlantic relations: increased Soviet pressures and leverage in Europe, as well as doubts about the credibility of the U.S. security guarantee, have led to even more tensions and strains among the allies.

In the security areas, the fragile "balance of imbalances" (whereby the Warsaw Pact's conventional superiority was to be compensated by Western superiority at the nuclear level) upon which NATO's flexible response posture has been based since the 1960s has been altered—some would say broken—by the magnitude of Soviet military expansion at every level over the past decade.

At the conventional level, the 1970s saw an aggravation of the military situation. As the military balance shifted further in favour of Soviet forces this was no longer offset by NATO's qualitative superiority. Indeed, in certain areas Soviet weapons are now superior (armoured vehicles, artillery), and in others (such as anti-tank weapons, tactical aviation) the gap is being closed.

At the theatre nuclear level, NATO's long-standing advantage in battlefield weapons has been eroded by obsolescence and the introduction of new Soviet systems. At the level of long-range theatre* systems, the Soviet advantage has been increased since the mid-1970s by the introduction of the long-range Backfire bombers and Mirved [Multiple Independent Re-entry Vehicle] MRBMs (the SS20).

At the strategic level, the Soviets have achieved "parity" in central systems since the early 1970s. Having deployed at least three new types of heavy ICBMs (the SS17, 18 and 19), they will, in theory, be in a position by the late 1980s to destroy most American ICBM silos in a first strike. This imbalance should, however, be corrected toward the end of the decade by the deployment on the U.S. side of new mobile MX ICBMs, as well as Trident II SLBMs, and possibly a new strategic bomber.

The combined impact of these factors has been to call into question the validity of NATO's strategy of flexible response. As the increased Soviet conventional superiority is no longer compensated by U.S. nuclear superiority at higher rungs of the escalation ladder, the Europeans may have in fact become even more dependent on U.S. first use of nuclear weapons. This "solution" could become less credible, given strategic nuclear parity and the absence, for some years, of an effective LRTNF [long range theatre nuclear force] on NATO's side. Nor is it very desirable for the Europeans to be excessively dependent on first use, since they would have to bear the consequences of "limited" nuclear exchanges on their continent.

This shifting military balance, and the resulting doubts about the credibility of the U.S. security guarantee, have also played an important role in worsening the climate of transatlantic relations as a whole. American leaders, while recognizing this problem, have called for greater European efforts on defence and a greater solidarity with the United States in checking Soviet expansion. To a certain extent, such American criticisms—to the effect that Europe does not carry its share of the defence burden—are unfair, as they ignore the fact that the European share in total NATO expenditure has risen from 22.7 per cent in 1969 to 41.6 per cent in 1979. Conversely, while Europeans have been accustomed to paying a political or economic price for their protection,

---

*Ed. note: Also variously referred to as intermediate- or medium-range theater nuclear weapons as distinct from intercontinental "strategic" weapons.

they have found that their protection has declined but that the price to be paid has increased. All these trends, if further developed, could increase the temptation in some European quarters, though in a minority, to envisage other types of security arrangements on the Continent.

## Detente, Arms Control and the Third World

Europeans have tended lately to give more emphasis to the other aspects of security, namely negotiations and arms control, in particular with respect to LRTNF and confidence-building measures. Their hope has been that the dialogue with the Soviet Union would be kept going and that such discussions would eventually check the growing imbalance of their defence posture. This renewed European interest in arms control talks, which is noticeable even in France, coming at the very time when the U.S. has become increasingly disenchanted with such negotiations, has caused further transatlantic strains, as with the failure to ratify the SALT II Treaty.

Similar tensions occurred in the political area, in the aftermath of the Soviet invasion of Afghanistan, with Americans and Europeans openly disagreeing as to the nature and future of detente. In contrast to Americans, for whom detente with the Soviet Union in recent years has been primarily a military and global geostrategic matter, detente has had a much more tangible and direct meaning for Europeans. For certain European nations, in particular Germany, detente translates into political relations, but also into economic and human day-to-day relations. In short, the United States has more of an option than the Europeans of discarding previous concepts of detente, playing down arms control and seeking alternative ways toward a stable relationship with the U.S.S.R., including an increase in the American defence budget. For most Europeans, however, the end of detente in Europe would result in a political, economic, human, and security price. Rightly or wrongly, most European governments and public opinions as a whole have thus far been reluctant to pay it.

The crisis triggered by the Soviet invasion of Afghanistan also served to highlight another set of transatlantic dissensions involving the whole question of how to respond to challenges to Western security arising in the Third World. Far from generating a new sense of cohesion within the Western Alliance in the face of a blatant military action by the Soviet Union in a country formerly non-aligned and situated close to a region vital to the West as a whole, Moscow's intervention in Kabul sharpened divisions and tensions within the West and forced them into the open. Not only did Afghanistan catch the West unprepared, but for several months after the invasion itself Western reactions to the crisis appeared to be chaotic and often contradictory. Initially, America and Europe, as well as Europeans themselves, were publicly divided on most counts: on the significance of the Soviet move itself; on its impact on East-West detente, particularly in Europe; on the type of response that was called for (economic sanctions, symbolic boycott of the Moscow Olympic Games, military presence in the Persian Gulf area).

To a certain extent, the Afghan crisis has served as a painful learning process for the Alliance. By the beginning of 1981, a certain degree of cohesion has been restored within the West. There is now a growing realisation of the seriousness of the security threat in the Persian Gulf region. The Soviet invasion of Afghanistan underlined the magnitude of Soviet military presence and capabilities in the immediate periphery of that area and the deficiencies of the Western military posture in a region vital for Western economic survival. The Soviet threat to Western interests compounds the local instabilities evidenced by the Islamic Revolution in Iran and by the Iran-Iraq war, both of which have a potential for increasing East-West confrontation in the region.

Nonetheless, strong differences remain between the United States and Europe, as well as among the Europeans themselves, on the political and military implications of security challenges arising in the Third World. At stake is the extent to which Europeans are to involve themselves militarily in the management of such threats. Politically, a key issue, yet to be answered, relates to the impact of Third World crises on European detente. Here, the problem of "divisibility of detente" is likely to create further tensions between the two sides of the Atlantic, as well as, perhaps, between major European nations.

### Policy Implications

The main conclusion to be drawn from the above analysis is that the crisis in American-European relations is the product of complex historical and structural trends, involving societal, political, economic and military dimensions. It will not go away by resorting to short cuts and other political or military "quick fixes".

Perhaps the most important policy implication therefore is that the days of the old "Atlantic" system, based on U.S. predominance and its corollary, European reluctance to take wider responsibilities, are over. Given today's international realities, neither the United States nor Europe can be expected to face the challenges of the 1980s on its own. This means that a new Alliance relationship has to be built and that it will have to be based on a more equal participation on both sides. In short, NATO must for the first time become a real alliance, not just one characterized by U.S. dominance and European passivity. Clearly, a great deal of skill and effort will be needed in order to establish a new framework of co-responsibility such as is proposed in this Report. For such a relationship implies that diversity—and at times disagreements—will occur. However, it is important to recognise at the outset that diversity can be reconciled with a modern alliance among democratic nations in the nuclear age. Indeed, diversity may also benefit the collectivity, as individual members provide their experience and special competence for the common good of the whole alliance.

In preparing for this new relationship, it is also important to be fully aware of the obstacles on both sides of the Atlantic. The quarrels of the past few years have left severe scars on both sides. This explains a tendency evident in Europe, as well as in America, to present the problem of the transatlantic relationship in conflictual and generally oversimplistic terms. It is particularly striking to note that the prevailing debate over the future of American-European relations (as well as East-West relations) revolves around two opposite nostalgias:

On the European side, it is the nostalgia for the far-reaching detente hoped for in the early 1970s, which would allow the Europeans to continue to enjoy the benefits of their peace whatever happens in the rest of the world, and whatever the Soviet Union does elsewhere. Hence, the temptation in some quarters in Europe to want to continue detente at any cost; to underestimate the Soviet military threat on the Continent; to play down events occurring in Third World regions; and to consider American reactions to Afghanistan as a short-lived sign of displeasure or as an overreaction to be shortly followed by a new era of U.S.-Soviet detente.

A similar phenomenon is at work in the United States. Here, a growing aspiration is to return to the era of U.S. supremacy and absolute leadership in world affairs. This is translated in the resurgent tendency to consider every event in the world in purely East-West terms, and the use of force as the panacea for most such issues. In this context, the behaviour of Europeans is viewed with increasing irritation as evidence that Europe is already sliding toward "appeasement", "finlandisation", or "self-neutralisation" with the Soviet Union. Given such perceptions, there is in some American circles the temptation to pressure Europe into action and, failing that, to leave it to its own fate.

There is a clear danger that such tendencies at work on both sides of the Atlantic, if left unchecked, could lead to a collision course. It is therefore urgently necessary to define common objectives and to coordinate the various Western policies with respect both to the Soviet Union and the Third World. At the same time, it is equally important to establish as soon as possible the new consultation and co-ordination mechanisms necessary to achieve these goals and implement these policies.

# 59

## The Theater Nuclear Weapons Debate

*The New York Times*

In 1977, the installation and modernization of Soviet bloc intermediate-range "theater" nuclear weapons in Eastern Europe prompted Helmut Schmidt, then Chancellor of West Germany, to urge the United States to deploy similar weapons for NATO's defense of Western Europe. After initial American reluctance, NATO announced in December 1979 the decision that the U.S. would begin to deploy Pershing II intermediate-range missile launchers in West Germany and cruise missiles in five Western European countries in December 1983 unless arms limitation talks to be conducted in the meanwhile between the U.S. and the U.S.S.R. in Geneva produced an agreement making the deployment unnecessary.

Popular opposition to the decision emerged in Europe when the United States rejected the SALT II agreement on long-range "strategic" nuclear weapons. After President Reagan proposed his "zero option" plan in November 1981, Paul H. Nitze and Yuli A. Kvitsinski, the American and Soviet negotiators at Geneva, proposed a compromise plan which neither government accepted. Yuri Andropov offered a different proposal when he assumed the leadership of the Soviet Union after the death of Leonid Brezhnev.

These *New York Times* charts outline the locations of the scheduled U.S. deployments and the basic features of the proposals and counter-proposals which proved only the beginning of an ongoing process.

## Where new U.S. missiles would go

Deployment is scheduled between Dec. 1983 and Dec. 1985 subject to progress of arms reduction talks and European approval.

| | Pershing 2 launchers* | Cruise missiles |
|---|---|---|
| West Germany | 108 | 96 |
| Britain | — | 160 |
| Italy (in Sicily) | — | 112 |
| Belgium | — | 48 |
| Netherlands | — | 48 |
| Total | 108 | 464 |

*Each launcher fires one missile, but could be reloaded with spare missiles.

## Proposals on medium-range missiles in Europe

| | U.S. | U.S.S.R. |
|---|---|---|
| **Reagan plan** (Nov. 1981) | U.S. to build 572 Pershing 2 and cruise missiles but not deploy them in Europe. | Soviet to dismantle all its approximately 340 modern SS-20's and 260 older SS-4 and SS-5 missiles. |
| **Andropov plan** (Dec. 1982) | U.S. will not deploy Pershing 2 and cruise missiles in Europe. | Soviet to keep 162 SS-20's aimed at Europe to match 162 French and British missiles. |
| **Nitze-Kvitsinsky aborted approach** (July 1982) | U.S. to deploy 75 cruise missiles with 4 warheads each in Europe. No Pershing 2 missiles allowed. 150 medium-range bombers. No formal counting of British and French missiles. | Soviet to deploy 75 SS-20's with 3 warheads each aimed at Europe. Freeze at about 90 SS-20's aimed at Asia. 150 medium-range bombers. |

# 60

## NATO and Nuclear Weapons:
## Reasons and Unreason

Stanley Hoffmann

Popular movements opposing nuclear armaments have emerged a number of times in Europe over the years as concern regarding the likelihood of a "hot war" has waxed and waned since World War II. In late 1981, Stanley Hoffmann analyzed the movement that was gathering strength at that time. These excerpts from his article in *Foreign Affairs* focus on the coalition of groups involved in the movement and the issues which made its impact dangerous for the NATO alliance.

---

The history of the Atlantic Alliance is a history of crises. But we must distinguish between the routine difficulties engendered by Western Europe's dependence on the United States for its security, as well as by the economic interdependence of the allies, and major breakdowns or misunderstandings which reveal not simply an inevitable divergence of interests but dramatically different views of the world and priorities. At the present time, complaints from West European leaders about the effects of high American interest rates on their economies, or about President Reagan's skeptical approach to North-South economic issues, belong in the first category. The current controversy in Europe over nuclear weapons belongs in the second, and now confronts the Alliance with one of its most dangerous tests.

On its face, that controversy revolves around NATO's double decision of December 1979 to deploy by 1983 new long-range nuclear forces in the European theater and to enter into arms control negotiations with the Soviets about such forces. It does not yet pit allied governments against our own. But the widespread West European popular movement opposed to the new deployments indicates both the existence in several nations of a broad politically destabilizing gap between government and a sizeable, mobilized section of the public, and a growing divorce of feelings and perceptions between the two sides of the Atlantic. Far more than technical questions of deterrence and strategy is at stake; these serve primarily as symptoms of fundamental issues.

The present popular movement in Western Europe is not the first of its kind. A vigorous campaign for nuclear disarmament attracted many Britons in the early 1960s; and we should not forget the strong opposition in West Germany to the development of nuclear energy in recent years. Nor is the current agitation evenly strong; the demonstration that took place in Paris on October 25 was organized and dominated by the Communist Party and one of its front organizations, and while the Rome demonstration on that same day went beyond the orbit of the Italian Communist Party and labor union, it did not offer the same agglomeration of forces as in the northern part of the continent.

Nevertheless, the current movement is new and formidable in several respects. It is a mass movement of continental dimension, which mobilizes and moves people across borders—something quite exceptional even in the partly integrated Western Europe of today. It entails the active participation of women and of a large number of religious movements and churches—predominantly but not exclusively Protestant—in countries where they have rarely taken part in big rallies. It is particularly strong in the country that has been, until now, the most reliable partner of the United States on the continent and the linchpin of NATO strategy: the Federal Republic of Germany. While it brings together people from a variety of parties, particularly in the Netherlands and Scandinavia, and is often led by well-known priests, intellectuals or politicians, the movement is largely a gathering of young people, a generational protest—the first since 1968. Above all, like the May 1968 movement in France, it is, in de Gaulle's word *"insaisissable"*—beyond grasp—for it represents a convergence of different concerns, fears and aspirations on a single issue, and offers more emotion and passion than hard-headed analysis. Hence the difficulty of finding an appropriate adjective that would define it.

Some—for instance those on the left wing of the British Labour Party—argue for the complete denuclearization of Europe and for unilateral action toward that goal; others want mutual arms reductions to be negotiated between Washington and Moscow. Some remain committed to NATO, minus the December 1979 decision; others dream of a neutral Europe. Many denounce both superpowers, described as brainless monsters, and attack the "policy of blocs" which keeps Europe divided and dependent; others concentrate their fire on the United States alone. Most seem to fear nuclear war above all; yet many are also moved by indignation about what they feel to be a mistaken emphasis on military approaches to international problems, and the excessive costs of defense at a time of high unemployment, cuts in social security and sometimes—as in England—severe industrial depression. Some are members of political parties, highly politicized and expert at manipulation. But many are almost defiantly un- or anti-political, in quest of a "concrete utopia," or convinced that in a world in which traditional power politics has failed to bring lasting peace or to remove the threat of nuclear destruction, spectacular gestures of renunciation could prove contagious; they believe that examples of self-abnegation, even by small nations, could shame the superpowers into respect or imitation. In the German movement, many are inspired by a determination to repudiate any form of policy that smacks of Germany's past—hence any reliance on force as a key instrument—and seek an identity that would be pure and blameless; others seem moved by a more resentful or ambitious nationalism.

Why has this complex movement arisen over the issue of long-range theater nuclear forces? Two questions are involved: why now? and why does it focus on this point?

There are profound differences between the mood of the late 1950s, when peace movements flourished in various places, and that of the present. Then, paradoxically, there was both general confidence in American nuclear superiority (hence relatively low fear of nuclear war) and general agreement that the Soviets were the bullies threatening to disrupt the peace in Europe. This was the era of the Berlin crises: what was feared in West Germany—and in West Berlin, whose mayor was Willy Brandt—was American softness. Now we find the opposite mix. There are serious doubts about the U.S. promise to preserve West European security through extended nuclear deterrence. In an age of nuclear parity, Washington seems unlikely to risk America's survival for the protection of Europe, despite ritual official reassurances. Given the new properties of nuclear weapons such as accuracy and mobility, nuclear strategy seems to point to war-fighting, as deterrence through the threat of massive city-busting is no longer wholly credible, and deterrence through the threat of a first strike against Soviet forces appears eroded by the loss of American superiority. . . .

Thus we encounter the first of many paradoxes. Instead of believing that the United States provides security and that the U.S.S.R. breeds insecurity, many young Europeans now feel the opposite. Insofar as they still understand that insecurity might come from the East, they react in a direction contrary to that of the United States. Here, the public mood, expressed by the election of President Reagan and by the new Congress, is one of restoring America's strength; in Western Europe, the public mood is one of fearing war, of believing that the accumulation of weapons can only lead to war, and of wanting the superpowers to deal with their differences in other ways, less dangerous to mankind. Hence the emphasis—by the governments themselves—on negotiations with the East, and the temptation—of the public—by various forms of escapism, from denuclearized zones to neutrality. The dramas of the 1970s have affected Americans and Europeans differently. Americans seem to want to "stop being pushed around" in the world and to turn to fundamentalist means for economic recovery: private enterprise and a reduced role for the state. West Europeans concentrate on their domestic troubles and, whatever their government's political orientation, rely on state initiatives and a mixed economy.

In recent years Americans and West Europeans, even at the official level, have diverged on three essential issues. Americans, in their relations with Moscow, have reverted to a view and to a policy in which hostility predominates; West Europeans have benefited from, and want to preserve, a mixed relationship. Americans, seeing a worldwide Soviet challenge, have nudged their allies toward a global alliance; the West Europeans have insisted on the geographical limitations of the Atlantic Alliance and resented Washington's attempts to present El Salvador as a test of Alliance solidarity, or to look at North-South issues from a cold war angle, or to give, in the Middle East, precedence to weaponry over diplomacy. Americans are convinced that the central problem of the age is the containment of Soviet imperialism, and that the military dangers posed by the U.S.S.R. are in many ways compounded by the huge weaknesses of the Soviet polity; West Europeans see these dangers, but think they are reduced, offset, or neutralized by those weaknesses, and by Soviet entanglements in Afghanistan and Poland. . . .

# Unit XIV

# The European Community

Hopes for the creation of a "United States of Europe," as enunciated by Winston Churchill in 1946, have not been realized. Nevertheless, the post-World War II impulse in Western Europe to transcend old animosities and cooperate for mutual benefit has overcome old rivalries to a remarkable degree, reflecting Europeans' recognition of their interdependence in today's world and of the strength that can be achieved through union. This unit traces the evolution of European cooperation since 1950 and examines the organizational framework and policies of the European Community,* which includes the European Coal and Steel Community, the European Economic Community, and the European Atomic Energy Community. Since 1958 these institutions have shared the European Parliament and Court of Justice, and in 1967 their individual councils and executive bodies were merged. Still, the ECSC, the EEC, and Euratom remain legally separate entities, and for this reason they are sometimes referred to as the "European Communities." While the term "European Community" generally pertains to all three bodies collectively, it is sometimes used to refer to the European Economic Community alone.

The readings in this unit highlight the Community's successes and failures and consider future prospects for cooperation as Europeans face the challenges of the 1980s. In "The

---

*The European Community has been in existence for more than thirty years. Its original member states consisted of Belgium, France, West Germany, Italy, Luxembourg, and the Netherlands, frequently referred to as the Six. After Britain, Denmark and Ireland joined the Community in 1973 the member states became collectively known as the Nine. Since 1981 when Greece was admitted to the Community, the states have been called the Ten.

Schuman Declaration," Howard Bliss introduces the key document which started Europe on the road to economic cooperation in 1950, and stresses the exceptional leadership and imagination demonstrated by its French authors. The declaration's call for placing French and German coal and steel production under a common "higher authority" met with immediate success, as Richard Mayne details in "Europe Responds: The ECSC." Within a year, a treaty establishing the European Coal and Steel Community was signed, and by 1952 the new institutions it called for were put into operation.

Although proposals to merge their armed forces in a European Defense Community (EDC) came to nothing, as did plans for a political union, by 1955 the foreign ministers of the six ECSC nations were sufficiently encouraged to make a statement that would prove to be as important as the Schuman Declaration in bringing about European cooperation. Howard Bliss quotes the opening paragraphs of the document that led to widespread economic unity in Europe in "The Messina Resolution." The next major step in establishing a European Community was the signing and ratification of the 1957 Treaties of Rome. "The European Community System," a compilation of materials published by the Commission of the European Communities, describes the new cooperative entities that the treaties set up—the European Economic Community and the European Atomic Energy Community; discusses the Community's history, goals, and organizational structure; reviews its policies; and evaluates its success.

The King of the Belgians pays tribute to the European Community in "Europe 25 Years After," a speech delivered at the official celebration of the 25th anniversary of the signing of the Treaties of Rome. While acknowledging that the Community has not yet attained all of its goals, King Baudouin points out that its successes have been commendable nonetheless. He goes on to urge the Community's ten member countries to renew their commitment to safeguarding peace both in Europe and elsewhere in the world through a "strengthening of the bonds" necessary to insure European solidarity.

The Commission of the European Communities summarizes the results of a 1981 public opinion poll revealing popular attitudes toward the European Community in "Towards European Union? A Public Opinion Poll." The poll shows how well the Community is accepted by the public, how people view its effects on individuals as well as on nations, and what they consider to be its prospects for the future.

# 61

## The Schuman Declaration

Howard Bliss

This declaration by French Foreign Minister Robert Schuman in 1950 led directly to the creation of the European Coal and Steel Community, the first building block in what political scientist Howard Bliss calls the "construction of Europe." Bliss prefaces the text of the declaration with comments on the roots of the European Community and the role of leadership in initiating its development.

The origins of the European Community are directly connected to audacious and innovative proposals of political leaders. Circumstances doubtless were favorable for the submission of these proposals to interested governments and a curious public: the impetus for European union in the Resistance movements of World War II, psychological trauma induced by the war and the realignment of the Great Powers caused by it, the intellectual tradition of the European idea, the growing challenge of a resurgent West German economy, disillusion with the organization of peace through the United Nations, and skepticism of real progress toward European unity ensuing from the high-sounding oratory of the Council of Europe's Strasbourg Assembly. Nonetheless, exceptional leadership was needed to grasp that circumstances were indeed propitious for a departure from the suspect but comfortable policies and diplomatic machinations of past decades. Initially, the necessary imagination and leadership was provided by Robert Schuman, French Foreign Minister in 1950, working in close collaboration with the astute, well-informed, and equally imaginative head of the French Planning Office, Jean Monnet. The result of this collaboration, the Schuman Declaration, . . . reversed a French policy toward Germany that had endured at least since the conclusion of World War I. More importantly, it marked the conversion of amorphous goals for European union into a concrete offer for positive action. The European Coal and Steel Community (ECSC), considered by Schuman a "first step toward European federation," was a direct outgrowth of the Declaration announced on May 9, 1950. . . .

The Schuman Declaration technically took the form of a communiqué to the press. It received no advance publicity nor was there formal consultation with leaders of the coal and steel industries prior to its release. The French Council of Ministers had hastily approved the text, ostensibly without full awareness of its implications. Both its contents and the timing of publication displayed the political acumen and, without overstatement, the diplomatic genius of Schuman and Jean Monnet. . . .

## THE SCHUMAN DECLARATION

World peace cannot be safeguarded without the making of constructive efforts proportionate to the dangers which threaten it.

The contribution which an organized and living Europe can bring to civilization is indispensable to the maintenance of peaceful relations. In taking upon herself for more than twenty years the rôle of champion of a united Europe, France has always had as her essential aim the service of peace. A united Europe was not achieved, and we had war.

Europe will not be made all at once, or according to a single, general plan. It will be built through concrete achievements, which first create a *de facto* solidarity. The gathering of the nations of Europe requires the elimination of the age-old opposition of France and Germany. The first concern in any action undertaken must be these two countries.

With this aim in view, the French Government proposes to take action immediately on one limited but decisive point. The French Government proposes to place Franco-German production of coal and steel under a common "higher authority," within the framework of an organization open to the participation of the other countries of Europe.

The pooling of coal and steel production will immediately provide for the setting-up of common bases for economic development as a first step in the federation of Europe, and will change the destinies of those regions which have long been devoted to the manufacture of munitions of war, of which they have been the most constant victims.

The solidarity in production thus established will make it plain that any war between France and Germany becomes, not merely unthinkable, but materially impossible. The setting-up of this powerful production unit, open to all countries willing to take part, and eventually capable of providing all the member countries with the basic elements of industrial production on the same terms, will lay the real foundations for their economic unification.

This production will be offered to the world as a whole without distinction or exception, with the aim of contributing to the raising of living standards and the promotion of peaceful achievements. Europe, with new means at her disposal, will be able to pursue the realization of one of her essential tasks, the development of the African continent.

In this way there will be realized, simply and speedily, that fusion of interests which is indispensable to the establishment of a common economic system; and that will be the leaven from which may grow a wider and deeper community between countries long opposed to one another by sanguinary divisions.

By pooling basic production and by setting up a new higher authority, whose decisions will be binding on France, Germany and other member countries, these proposals will build the first concrete foundation of the European Federation which is indispensable to the preservation of peace.

In order to promote the realization of the objectives it has thus defined, the French Government is ready to open negotiations on the following basis:

The task with which this common "higher authority" will be charged will be that of securing in the shortest possible time the modernization of production and the improvement of its quality; the supply of coal and steel on identical terms to the French and German markets, as well as to the markets of other member countries; the development in common of exports to other countries; and the equalization as well as improvement of the living conditions of the workers in these industries.

To achieve these objectives, starting from the very disparate condition in which the productions of the member countries are at present situated, certain transitional measures will have to be instituted, such as a production and investment plan, compensating machinery for equating prices, and an amortization fund to facilitate the rationalization of production. The movement of coal and steel between Member countries will immediately be freed of all Customs duties; it will not be permissible to apply differential transport rates to them. Conditions will gradually be created which will spontaneously ensure the most rational distribution of production at the highest level of productivity.

In contrast to international cartels, which aim at dividing up and exploiting the national markets by means of restrictive practices and the maintenance of high profits, the proposed organization will ensure the fusion of the markets and the expansion of production.

The principles and the essential undertakings defined above will be the subject of a treaty between the states to be submitted to Parliaments for ratification. The negotiations required to work out the details of implementation will be conducted with the assistance of a jointly designated arbiter. The latter's duty will be to see that the agreements conform with the principles and, in the event of final disagreement, to determine the solution to be adopted. The joint high authority charged with the operation of the entire system will be composed of independent personalities chosen on a basis of equality by the governments; a president will be chosen by the governments by common agreement; his decisions will be enforceable in France, Germany, and the other member countries. Appropriate measures will assure the necessary channels of appeal against the decisions of the high authority. A representative of the United Nations near the authority will be charged with making a public report to the United Nations twice a year on the functioning of the new organization, particularly with respect to protecting its peaceful aims.

The setting up of the high authority in no way prejudges the question of ownership of the enterprises. In the exercise of its mission, the joint high authority will take into account the powers conferred on the international Ruhr authority and the obligations of every kind imposed on Germany as long as they are in existence.

# 62

## Europe Responds: The ECSC

_____ **Richard Mayne** _____

In this excerpt from *The Community of Europe*, a former staff member of the Commission of the European Economic Community sketches the events following the Schuman Declaration, which, as he notes earlier in the book, Walter Lippmann considered "the most audacious and constructive initiative since the end of the war."

. . .The response to the Schuman Declaration was immediate. By the end of May, Belgium, Germany, Italy, Luxembourg, and the Netherlands had all agreed to consider the proposals; and although the Netherlands government had some reservations of principle about the "supranational" High Authority, negotiations were quickly under way. That they were not easy was to be expected, for there was considerable opposition to so unprecedented a step. Nevertheless, Schuman may not have been entirely mistaken when, looking back afterwards, he said: "The six delegations were in some sense allies, pooling their knowledge and their goodwill." At least four of the leaders of the countries in question were especially sympathetic to the project because they came from regions which had been the victims of successive wars. Schuman himself had been brought up in Alsace under German domination, and educated at a German school. Adenauer, Chancellor of the new German Republic, was a Rhinelander who as long ago as the 1920's had declared that "a lasting peace between France and Germany can only be attained through the establishment of a community of economic interests between the two countries". Alcide de Gasperi, the Italian Prime Minister, came from the Trentino, which had been under Austrian rule until 1918. Thus all three could incidentally converse in fluent German. A fourth important figure was the Belgian Socialist Paul-Henri Spaak, whose country had been invaded in two world wars, as had Luxembourg; while the Netherlands had similarly been overrun in World War II.

Under this leadership, and with a negotiating committee which included Jean Monnet and Walter Hallstein, the Treaty establishing the European Coal and Steel Community was drawn up within a year; signed on April 18, 1951, it was ratified by the summer of 1952. In contrast to the original Schuman proposals, it provided for a Common Assembly and a Council of Ministers as well as a High Authority and a Court; but its Preamble was practically a digest of the Schuman Declaration, including many of the same words and phrases. To implement it, the member states' Foreign Ministers met in Paris on July 23-25, 1952: on the principle that "the devil is in the details", what should have been a merely formal occasion developed into a debate about the Community's official languages and the site of its headquarters. France proposed respectively French and Saarbrücken; but after long discussion, French, German, Italian, and Dutch became the Community languages, Strasbourg the seat of the Common Assembly, and Luxembourg that of the High Authority and the Court of Justice. The latter decision, indeed, was not even "provisional", as is usually suggested: to avoid a late-night deadlock, the Ministers merely agreed to hold their next meeting in Luxembourg. Appointing the High Authority proved somewhat easier. Monnet became its first President, with Franz Etzel, later German Finance Minister, and Albert Coppé, former Belgian Economic Affairs Minister, as its two Vice-Presidents, although the Treaty only called for one. The other members were Dirk Spierenburg, head of the Dutch delegation to the O.E.E.C. and to the Schuman Treaty conference; Albert Wehrer, who had headed the Luxembourg delegation in the negotiations; Enzo Giacchero, a Vice-President of the Italian parliamentary Christian-Democrat party and an active federalist; Léon Daum, a French industrialist and coal-steel expert; and Heinz Potthoff, a former German steel worker who had been a member of the International Authority for the Ruhr. These eight members then co-opted a ninth, the Belgian Paul Finet, first president of the International Confederation of Free Trade Unions. So constituted, the High Authority held its first meeting in Luxembourg on August 10, 1952. . . .

# 63

## The Messina Resolution

Howard Bliss

The first three paragraphs of a longer document, adopted in June 1955 by the ministers of foreign affairs of the ECSC at Messina, Italy, summarize the goals of the Messina Resolution. Here, Bliss emphasizes the importance of this document.

. . . The Messina Resolution, which announced a new step forward in the "construction of Europe" in the economic domain, had less dramatic impact on foreign offices and public opinion than the Schuman Declaration, yet it was equally far-reaching in significance. Negotiations set in motion by the Messina Resolution subsequently led to the Treaties of Rome which established the European Economic Community (EEC or Common Market) and the European Atomic Energy Community (Euratom). . . .

### THE MESSINA RESOLUTION

The Governments of the Federal Republic, Belgium, France, Italy, Luxembourg and the Netherlands *believe that the time has come to make a fresh advance* towards the building of Europe. *They are of the opinion that this must be achieved, first of all, in the economic field.*

*They consider that it is necessary to work for the establishment of a united Europe by the development of common institutions, the progressive fusion of national economies, the creation of a common market and the progressive harmonisation of their social policies.*

*Such a policy seems to them indispensable if Europe is to maintain her position in the world, regain her influence and prestige and achieve a continuing increase in the standard of living of her population.* . . .

# 64

## The European Community System

———— Commission of the European Communities ————

The system of cooperation that took shape after the Treaties of Rome in 1957 incorporated the existing European Coal and Steel Community and used its institutions as models for a similar framework for the new components—the European Economic Community or Common Market and the European Atomic Energy Community. The following selection outlines the combined Communities' objectives, institutions, policies, and financial organization, as well as assessing their successes and failures in fulfilling expectations. The selection incorporates materials from a number of Commission publications, which do not necessarily reflect official views.

### THE TREATIES OF ROME

Europe's next step toward integration came when the Six resolved to extend to the whole economic field the methods that had already been used successfully by the ECSC, and to develop jointly the peaceful use of atomic energy.

In 1956 they decided to go ahead with negotiations aimed at drafting two treaties that would set up:

- a European Economic Community (EEC) to form a vast single market for all goods, with a wide measure of common economic policies. The EEC would constitute a powerful productive unit and generate steady expansion, greater stability and a more rapid rise in living standards;
- a European Atomic Energy Community (Euratom) to further the use of nuclear energy in Europe for peaceful purposes and to ensure that Europe did not lag behind in the energy revolution.

Less than a year later, on March 25, 1957, the Six signed in Rome the treaties setting up the European Economic Community and Euratom. Both treaties were ratified before the end of the year by the parliaments of all six member countries, with even greater majorities than the first treaty, which set up the ECSC. This was, in effect, a vote for the gradual merging of the separate economies of the six member states into a single economic area with much the same characteristics as an individual national market. A customs union was set up to remove obstacles that hindered the free movement of goods within the Community. This also affected the wider world: By merging the different national tariffs at the Community's external frontier, the customs union led to the establishment of uniform conditions under which imports from the rest of the world could enter the Community. At the same time, the Six enacted measures to ease the movement among their countries of people, firms, services and capital.

This merger of the separate national markets into a large, single market is being achieved gradually.

The Six recognized that their common market would have little chance of success if all its members continued to apply divergent economic policies. For this reason, the EEC Treaty specified that the common market would align national economic policies and apply common policies for the whole of the Community, particularly in the spheres of agriculture, anti-trust, transport and external trade. . . .

## THE INSTITUTIONS

Consisting initially of six countries, . . . joined on 1 January 1973 by Denmark, Ireland and the United Kingdom and on 1 January 1981 by Greece, The European Communities are managed by common institutions.

### The European Commission—Initiator and Executive

The Commission of the European Communities is composed of 14 Members—two British, two French, two German, two Italian and one from each of the other countries—appointed for a four-year period by mutual agreement of the governments of the ten countries. The Members of the European Commission act only in the interests of the Community; they may not receive instructions from any national government and are subject only to the supervision of the European Parliament which alone can force them collectively to resign their responsibilities. Commission decisions are taken collegiately, even though each Commissioner is directly responsible for one or more portfolios.

# THE INSTITUTIONS OF THE EUROPEAN COMMUNITY

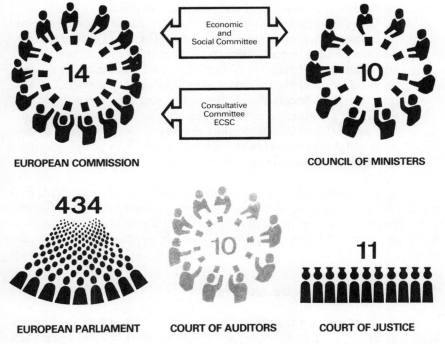

**Figure 64.1.**

The Commission's tasks are:

- to ensure that Community rules and the principles of the Common Market are respected. As guardian of the Treaties the Commission is responsible for seeing that they are observed and that decisions of the Community institutions deriving from the Treaties are correctly applied. . . .
- to propose to the Community's Council of Ministers all measures likely to advance Community policies (in the fields of agriculture, energy, industry, research, environment, social and regional problems, external trade, economic and monetary union, etc.). In 1981 the Commission transmitted 651 proposals to the Council of Ministers;
- to implement Community policies on the basis of Council decisions or derived directly from the provisions of the Treaties;

  - The Commission thereby has particularly extensive powers in the fields of coal and steel (investment coordination, price control, etc.), competition (control of monopolies and public aid), nuclear energy (supply of fissile materials, control of nuclear installations, etc.);

- In other cases the Commission operates upon a mandate from the Council, e.g. to negotiate trade agreements with third countries or to manage the agricultural markets;
- The Commission also administers the funds of the common programmes which account for most of the Community budget and which aim in particular to support and modernize agriculture (European Agricultural Guidance and Guarantee Fund), to encourage industrial, vocational and regional change (ECSC appropriations, Social Fund, European Regional Development Fund), to promote scientific research (the Joint Research Centres and other services employ 2,700 people), to affirm European solidarity towards the Third World (European Development Fund, food-aid programmes, etc.).

The Commission has an administrative staff—concentrated mostly in Brussels and, to a lesser extent, in Luxembourg—of about 9,000 officials. . . . One-third of the personnel is employed on linguistic work to ensure the equal recognition of the seven Community languages.

### Council of Ministers—Decision-Maker

The Community's Council of Ministers, which meets in Brussels and, less often, in Luxembourg, is composed of ministers from each Member State and decides on the principal Community policies. Each country acts as president of the council for a six-month period on a rotation basis. Attendance at meetings is determined by the agenda; national agriculture ministers, for example, deal with agricultural prices, economics and employment ministers deal with unemployment problems. The Ten's ministers for foreign affairs are responsible for coordinating the specialized work of their colleagues. The Council is assisted by:

- a Committee of Permanent Representatives (COREPER) which coordinates the preparatory work of Community decisions and is assisted by numerous working groups of senior officials from Member States;
- a general secretariat with a staff of some 1,900 people.

The European Councils which have met three times a year since 1975 (before this they were only occasional) bring together the Heads of State or Government and provide political guidance and impetus—a role which should not be underestimated even if the meetings do not directly produce legislative measures.

The Council of Ministers held 63 sessions in 1981. All the proposals it deals with come without exception from the Commission, and the Council can only reject them by a unanimous vote.

Unanimity in the Council is also required for certain important decisions. In practice it is frequently demanded by ministers even when not strictly necessary, which tends to slow down the Community's decision-making process. In recent times, there has been more frequent recourse to the use of the qualified majority vote—45 out of 63 votes— as instituted by the Treaties. France, Germany, Italy and the United Kingdom each have ten votes under this procedure. Belgium, Greece and the Netherlands have five, Denmark and Ireland three and Luxembourg two.

In the agriculture sector, procedures have been accelerated by the creation of 'Management Committees' composed of representatives from the Commission and national governments: Commission decisions have to be submitted for Council approval only if a qualified majority within the Committee disagree with them.

## Court of Justice and Community Law

The Community's Luxembourg-based Court of Justice is composed of eleven judges assisted by five advocates-general who are appointed for a six-year period by mutual agreement of Member States and who work independently of them. The Court's function is:

- to annul any measures taken by the Commission, the Council of Ministers, or national governments which are incompatible with the Treaties. This can be done at the request either of a Community institution, a Member State, or an individual directly concerned;
- to pass judgment at the request of national courts on the interpretation or the validity of the provisions of Community law. . . . Where a national court is the highest court of appeal it must submit an issue involving Community law to the Court of Justice for a ruling.

In 1981 the Court dealt with 323 cases . . . and passed 149 judgments. The Court can also be invited to give its opinion—which is then binding—on agreements which the Community envisages concluding with third countries.

Through its judgments and interpretations, the Court of Justice is contributing to the emergence of a veritable European law applicable to all: Community institutions, Member States, national courts and individuals. The authority of the Court's judgments in the field of Community law surpasses that of national courts. In cases of nonapplication of Community law by the Council, or Member States, the Court has been approached by individuals and upheld the direct applicability of principles contained in the Treaties relating to equal pay for men and women and the free exercise of the liberal professions throughout the Community.

### European Parliament and Participation

Since June 1979, the date of the first European elections, the European Parliament has been composed of members elected every five years through universal suffrage instead of members delegated from national parliaments. The European Parliament has 434 members: 81 from each of the countries with the largest populations, 25 from the Netherlands, 24 from Belgium, 24 from Greece, 16 from Denmark, 15 from Ireland and 6 from Luxembourg.

The members of the Parliament form political rather than national groups. [At the beginning of 1982,] the groups were as follows: 124 Socialists, 117 Christian Democrats of the European People's Party, 63 European Democrats (British Conservatives, etc.), 48 Communists and Allies, 39 Liberals and Democrats, 22 European Progressive Democrats (French Gaullists, Fianna Fáil, SNP), 11 independents, . . . and 10 non-attached members.

The European Parliament has a secretariat of some 2,900 officials based in Luxembourg. It has 18 parliamentary committees and its plenary and public sessions are held in Strasbourg or Luxembourg (though a vote gave preference to Strasbourg) in the presence of representatives from the European Commission and the Council of Ministers. This enables the Parliament to make fully-informed pronouncements on the problems of building Europe.

The European Parliament does not have the same legislative power as national assemblies. In the current Community system, it is the Commission which takes the initiatives and the council which passes most Community legislation. Nevertheless, the Parliament:

- has the power to remove the Commission by a two-thirds majority;
- supervises the Commission and the Council, and often addresses incisive written and oral questions to them (there were 2,946 in 1981);
- is called upon to give its opinion on Commission proposals before the Council can make its decision;
- has budgetary powers which enable it to participate in all major decisions involving expenditure. It is effectively the Parliament which accepts or rejects the draft budget prepared by the Commission and agreed by the Council following consultation procedures with the Council.

- For expenditure (mainly agricultural) arising from the Treaties and decisions taken as a consequence of these, the Council can reject the modifications introduced by the Parliament if it increases the total size of the budget;
- For non-obligatory expenditure, resulting in new developments in European construction, the Parliament has discretionary power over the limits of a margin of manoeuvre which is dependent on the economic situation in the Community and which can be modified by mutual agreement with the Council.

## The Economic and Social Committee and the Advisory Committee

Before a Commission proposal can be adopted by the Council it is sent for the opinion of not only the European Parliament but also, in most cases, of the Community's Economic and Social Committee—a consultative body composed of 156 representatives from employers, trade unions and other interested groups in the Ten such as farmers and consumers. For questions dealing with coal and steel there is the Advisory Committee composed of representatives of producers, traders, workers and consumers. The two committees adopted 120 opinions and resolutions in 1981, of which many were submitted on their own initiative.

Many specialized advisory bodies help associate professional and trade union interests in the development of the Community. The heads of their European federations set up in Brussels, and their experts, are frequently consulted by the Commission before it adopts proposals in their definitive form.

## The Court of Auditors

The operation of the [Community's] budget is supervised by a Court of Auditors. The Court is composed of ten members appointed by the mutual agreement of the Council of Ministers for a six-year period. The Court of Auditors has extensive powers to verify the legality and the regularity of Community revenue and expenditures. . . .

## EFFECTS OF THE INSTITUTIONS

Throughout the world there are a large number of international organizations to bring together the States that wish to cooperate with each other. The European Community goes much further than this:

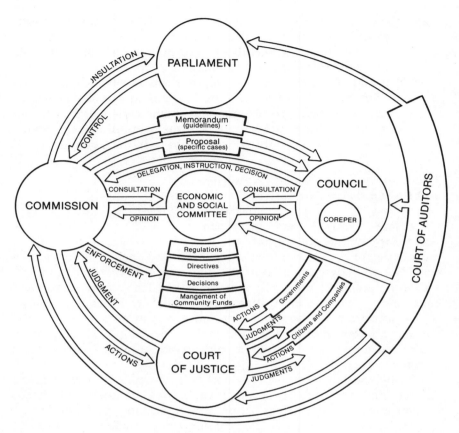

**Figure 64.2.** How the institutions of the European Community work (simplified diagram).

- in its aim: to build over a period of time a veritable European Union, the shape of which is still subject to considerable debate;
- in its methods: the operation of the Community is not purely intergovernmental—Community institutions have their own powers and the organization of their relationships aims to promote the general interest of Europeans;
- in its results: the Council of Ministers and the Commission, wherever it has autonomous decision-making powers, takes action with the force of law and which in many cases is applied directly to European citizens.

  Their actions are termed:

- regulations, which are applied directly;

- decisions, which are binding only on the Member States, companies or individuals to whom they are addressed;
- directives, which set down compulsory objectives but leave it to the discretion of Member States to translate them into their national legislation;
- recommendations and opinions which are not binding (except for recommendations in the ECSC sector where they are equivalent to directives). . . .

## POLICIES

The primary aim of the Treaties was to get rid of the economic barriers that divided member states as the first step toward removing the political ones. To achieve this, it was necessary to ensure the free movement within the Community of goods, people, services and capital.

By July 1968 the customs union for the original six members was completed, 18 months earlier than required by the Rome Treaty. Customs duties were eliminated and a common external tariff was established. The result was a massive increase in trade among the Six in intra-Community imports—from $6.8 billion in 1958 when the EC was set up, to $60 billion in 1972 just before the three new member states joined.

Since the 1973 enlargement, trade among the Nine has increased from around $111 billion to almost $192 billion in 1977 and $344 billion in 1980. The customs union for the Nine was completed at the end of 1977.

The Community is also gradually removing other barriers to the free movement of goods, such as differing technical standards traditionally applied by member states and differing taxation systems. It also ensures fair competition between manufacturers by controlling monopolies, cartels and state aids that favor a member state's manufacturing against competitors in other member states.

The creation of the customs union and the removal of other trade barriers has been to the advantage of both manufacturers and consumers. Manufacturers can benefit from the enlarged common market and can plan longer production runs of their goods, thereby keeping down unit costs. Lower costs are translated into lower prices for the consumer. The freer movement of goods has also offered the consumer a wider choice of goods, and the increased competition between manufacturers has helped keep down retail prices.

Community citizens can move about freely, whether they are traveling for pleasure or moving from one country to another to work. Since 1969, a citizen of one member state has been able to work in another member state by automatically obtaining a work permit. The Community also guarantees the same job security and social security benefits to EC migrant workers as to workers native to their host country.

A start has been made toward harmonizing the member states' qualifications for professional accreditations. Physicians are now able to practice wherever they choose in the Community and common qualifications have been agreed upon for lawyers, architects and other professions, and this right will be gradually extended. National laws governing banking, insurance and so on are being aligned so that companies can set up in business anywhere in the Community. Restrictions on individuals or companies of one member state investing capital in another are also being eliminated. The six original member states removed restrictions from most capital movements within the Community in 1960 and 1962. The three newer members had adopted these liberalization measures on currency exchanges and direct investments by 1978 and Greece will adopt them by 1986.

### Economic Policy

One of the principal goals of the Community is the creation of an economic and monetary union (EMU). Some progress toward this has been made since 1969. The member states generally have agreed on the coordination of short-term economic policies, and they have established Community reserve pools to give short-term and medium-term financial aid to member states in balance of payments difficulties.

Progress toward EMU was set back by the oil and raw material crises of the 1970s and the retreat from a fixed value for gold, which allowed the dollar, the world's leading currency, to float. EMU was relaunched in 1977 and 1978 by plans to create a zone of monetary stability within Europe that tied together the currencies of the Nine through a system of fixed but adjustable parities that would be supported by a large reserve fund. The core of the European Monetary System (EMS) is the European Currency Unit (ECU), the possible forerunner of a single Community currency.

In the Commission's view, progress toward economic and monetary union can make a decisive contribution to achieving the common national objectives of stability, growth and employment. It would strengthen the integration of the Community at a time when further enlargement to 12 is taking shape. It would be a decisive factor in restoring order within the international monetary system.

### Agriculture

A particularly successful area of integration has been agriculture, where more than 95 percent of agricultural production in the nine member states is governed at Community level. . . .

The common agricultural policy, one of the best developed and best known European policies, has five main aims:

- to increase productivity in the agricultural sector by promoting technical progress, ensuring a rational development of production and the optimum use of the factors of production, in particular labour;
- to ensure a fair standard of living for farmers;
- to stabilize markets;
- to ensure the availability of supplies;
- to ensure that supplies reach the consumer and the food industry at reasonable prices.

How are these objectives achieved? The various markets for agricultural products have been progressively organized following three basic principles:

- unity of the market: products must be able to circulate freely within the Community and agricultural markets must be organized according to common rules;
- Community preference: European products must be protected from low-cost imports and fluctuations on the world market;
- common financial responsibility: in order to strengthen solidarity between the various Community regions, the European Agricultural Guidance and Guarantee Fund finances, through its guarantee section, all public expenditure on common market organizations, and through its guidance section, the improvement of agricultural structures.

### The Need for Reform

In its Communication 'Guidelines for European agriculture' published on 23 October 1981, the European Commission notes that, despite certain drawbacks, the common agricultural policy has achieved its initial aims. Although these aims must be safeguarded, it is nevertheless necessary to adapt the policy to present-day realities, to the change in the economic situation and to developments within the agricultural sector itself. The modernization of the common agricultural policy is one of the key elements in the regeneration of the Community proposed by the Commission in response to the mandate assigned to it by the Council of Ministers on 30 May 1980. It is shortly to be the object of new discussions between ministers and heads of government of the Ten.

All countries, in some way or another, give agriculture a particular role and special treatment compared with other sectors of the economy. It is impossible to rely solely on world prices, which fluctuate wildly since they only apply to residual, and often very small quantities after domestic demand has been met. OECD figures show that public spending on agricultural price and income support varies considerably from one country to another. In 1977, the amount of expenditure in comparison with agricultural value added ranged from 7.5% in New Zealand to 21.4% in Norway and 27.3% in Switzerland. The Community figure of 11.9% was at the lower end of the scale, close to the United States (9.1%) and Austria (10.6%).

This does not, however, render reform of the common agricultural policy any the less necessary.

• The establishment of the common market and the extraordinary development of agricultural trade resulting from it have increased both the consumption and quality of foodstuffs; the Community has been protected from shortages; the European market has escaped the speculative movements affecting the world market; modernization of the agricultural sector has been stimulated. Nevertheless, this has in turn provoked a number of problems: the quantities produced have not always been matched to the needs of the market and, up until 1979, EAGGF spending increased faster than the Community's own resources.

• The common agricultural policy, which was conceived in a period of unprecedented economic growth, is now developing in the context of the energy crisis, a slowdown in growth, high unemployment, monetary instability and rising inflation. The crisis makes it hard for farmers to find alternative employment and imposes strict management of public spending.

• There are many factors behind the increase in Community agricultural spending: inflation, the increase in the level of self-sufficiency, extension of the area covered by the common agricultural policy (particularly in the fruit and vegetable and sheepmeat sectors), the granting of concessions to various trading partners, evolution of world market prices, the accession of Greece, etc. The rate of increase has not been regular: there was a sharp downturn between 1973 and 1974, followed by a steady growth until 1979 and then a marked slowdown between 1979 and 1982, largely thanks to action taken by the Community institutions. This action must be continued and expanded.

• Output of many agricultural products is forecast to continue to rise faster than consumption between now and 1988, without always sufficient export openings to absorb the surplus. It is worth noting that in 1980, Community farm exports represented 8% of world agricultural trade (while imports accounted for 17%). Given world food needs, it seems reasonable to plan a policy aimed at increasing European exports, so as at least to retain the Community's current share of world trade. This policy could include long-term supply contracts, particularly with developing countries, which took 51% of Europe's farm exports in 1980. But the fight against hunger in the world must primarily be carried on by developing the Third World's own food resources and the Community intends to contribute more and more to this. Indefinite increases in exports and food aid can no longer be counted upon. . . .

. . . The [European] Commission feels that the common agricultural policy must continue to play its three major roles: organization of the market, which ensures a stable economic framework for agriculture, structural aid, which assists farm modernization, and direct income aid in special cases. But through the fixing of production objectives and the implementation of measures designed to tax producers if these targets are exceeded, farmers will in future be obliged to take account of the realities of the market, which they have not always done in the past. This does not mean that artificial limits are put on farmers' output, but it does mean letting them know that guaranteed prices will not be the same for surplus products and that they will have to participate in the cost of disposing of them. Farmers will have to act more like businessmen. Community farm spending must cover only the quantities corresponding to the Community interest, taking account of domestic needs, international trade and the Community's role in the fight against world hunger. Farm spending will therefore continue to rise at least on average slower than the Community's own resources and this will allow more funds to be spent on other European policies.

## Fisheries

The Community is also developing a common fisheries policy under the influence of the recent changes at international level which saw territorial waters everywhere being extended.

To protect its fish stocks and the future of its industry, the Community declared a 200-mile limit at the beginning of 1977. At the same time, it opened negotiations on reciprocal rights with a number of third countries which had an interest in continuing to fish in Community waters. Parallel to these negotiations with third countries, the Community is working on an agreed level of fishing by its own boats.

## Industry

The Community is the world's most powerful industrial unit, a position it attained during its early years when its structure, size and cohesion enabled it to benefit fully from the favorable economic climate that then prevailed. The situation has now radically altered and almost 9 million people are unemployed in the Community, a third of them young people. Some of the problems industry faces are cyclical ones that could be solved with an upturn in the world economy. Others are structural and require long-term solutions.

Too many jobs in the Community depend on traditional industries such as steel, shipbuilding and textiles, which are in decline the world over. In addition, the Community is dangerously short of its own sources of raw materials and energy. Restructuring the traditional industries and concentrating new investment in growth industries is the task of the Community's industrial policy. The original Coal and Steel Community provided grants and loans for these two industries that have totalled over $7 billion thus far (1979). Low-interest loans for other industries are made by the European Investment Bank.

Through the "Ortoli Facility" or "New Community Instrument" the Commission can borrow up to $1.39 billion for the purpose of promoting investment in the Community. The EIB is responsible for handling the loans. The maximum amount of the loans through the "Ortoli Facility" is supposed to increase in the future to meet the needs. Three percent interest subsidies paid from the Community budget may be applied to selected loans from the EIB. These subsidized loans are to be concentrated on infra-structure projects in less prosperous countries fully participating in the European Monetary System, that is Ireland and Italy. These subsidies can total a maximum of $6.95 billion over the period 1979 to 1983.

The Community has also been in the vanguard of a movement to create a new relationship between the developing and developed countries. Stabilization of export earnings, technology transfers and financial aid to developing nations—all part of the Community's Third World policy as expressed in the Lomé Convention and other agreements—have helped to assure imports of raw materials.

### Energy

The Community is gradually developing a common energy policy. Its main aim is to reduce its dependence on imports, particularly of oil. It is trying to achieve this largely by developing its own alternative resources, although complete independence is not possible. Research in coal, solar, hydro and geothermal and nuclear energy are all part of the Community research emphasis. Nuclear capacity in the Community has more than doubled since 1973. The Community has a joint undertaking for nuclear fusion, which scientists believe can provide large quantities of pollution-free energy in the next century. Research is also being carried out on fast-breeder reactors.

Conservation is an important part of the Community's energy program, and the ten member states have a more successful record in this area than do other industrialized countries. To assure security of energy supply, member states are obliged to maintain a 90-day stock of oil against the contingency of another oil crisis. An oil sharing scheme has also been agreed.

In the development of a Community policy toward nuclear energy, safety and ecological issues are considered and "open debates" have been held so that ecologists, nuclear scientists, other experts and interested citizens may voice their concerns in a rational and informed way. Euratom safeguards exist to ensure that nuclear materials are not diverted for non-peaceful purposes.

## Transport

Common transport rules are important for a Community with such high levels of internal and external trade. Member states' transport regulations in roads, railways and inland waterways are gradually being harmonized, and new cooperation toward a common position on air and sea transport is proposed. The Community now participates as an entity in international negotiations on air and sea transport.

## Science and Research

The Community policy guidelines in science and research for 1977–80 set out four main objectives:

- secure supplies of energy, raw materials, food and water;
- protection of the environment;
- economic and industrial development;
- improvement of living and working conditions.

Research will continue in the traditional areas—coal and steel, agriculture, nuclear and non-nuclear energy, scientific and technical information, the environment, computers and aeronautics—and new projects will examine medicine and public health, urbanization, social matters, dwindling raw materials, water supplies and weather forecasting.

In the 1977–80 period, more than $1 billion has been spent for the science and research program. In addition to building a strong economy, which is essential to protect the livelihoods of its citizens, the Community constantly strives to improve their standard of living. It is developing a number of common policies toward this goal.

### Regional Policy

Balanced growth has been an aim of industrial policy, but disparities still exist between the industrial centers and the poorer agricultural areas. To help combat this situation, the Regional Fund was established in 1975 and from 1975 to 1978 $2 billion was spent to help finance industrial and infrastructural investments. $1.6 billion will be spent in 1981 alone. The Fund makes non-repayable grants to eligible investment projects. Money from the Fund is additional to national expenditure and cannot be used simply to reimburse national authorities. Italy, Ireland, Greece and the United Kingdom are the principal recipients of Regional Fund resources.

### Social Policy

The main instrument in achieving full and better employment has been the Social Fund, which spent $1.2 billion in 1981 to help finance training and retraining schemes to allow workers to keep pace with changing employment patterns. The Community is also trying to give workers a bigger say in the running of their companies and it has proposed measures to protect workers in the event of takeover or bankruptcy. Workers must be consulted if there is a prospect of lay-offs.

The Community has passed laws guaranteeing women equal pay for equal work and equal job and training opportunities. The member states have been directed to assure that men and women workers receive the same social security and pension benefits. Under the Social Fund, special funds are available to help the less well-organized sections of society—women, youth, the elderly and the handicapped—to take a more active part in working life. The Community is also turning its attention to the rights of migrants, particularly those from third countries.

The Community has common programs to promote the interests of consumers and to protect the environment. Common efforts are also being made to improve education, particularly to help youth enter the work force.

### THE BUDGET

The ECSC, through its production levy, enjoyed financial autonomy from the start. The Treaties of Rome provided for the EEC and Euratom to be financed initially by member state contributions on the basis of agreed percentages, but autonomous financing was planned eventually. In 1971 the Community began receiving a large portion of its budget revenues from agricultural levies and customs duties on imports into the Community. Since 1979 the Community also receives a maximum of 1 percent of an agreed assessment basis of the Value Added Tax, thereby financing the Community budget entirely from its own resources.

The Council and the Parliament determine the Community budget on the basis of the Commission's estimates of Community needs. The total budget for 1981 was almost $29 billion. The biggest budget item—just under 70 percent of the total—is agriculture expenditure. The remainder of the budget covers the social and regional sectors, research, energy, industry, transport and the development cooperation, information, administration and staff salaries. Compared to the member states' own budgets, the Community budget is pygmy-sized. It represents less than 1 percent of the Community's GDP, while member states' budgets represent, on average, 40 percent of their GDP.

# 65

## Europe 25 Years After

### Baudouin I, King of the Belgians

The official celebration of the 25th anniversary of the signing of the two treaties of Rome took place in Brussels, Belgium, on March 29, 1982. In this speech, one of five delivered at the ceremony, His Majesty the King of the Belgians reviews the original goals and objectives of the European Community, which was established in 1957 to bring about "a closer union among the peoples of Europe," summarizes the major accomplishments of the Community during its first 25 years, and calls for a "strengthening of the bonds" between its ten member countries.

. . . The official celebration of the 25th anniversary of the signature of the two Treaties took place on 29 March 1982 at the Palais des Académies in Brussels. [The] Prime Minister of Belgium, . . . Mr. Wilfried Martens, introduced . . . His Majesty the King of the Belgians . . . :

The celebration of the 25th anniversary of the Treaty of Rome must, first of all, be an occasion for taking stock of the results achieved and emphasizing their importance. They were the fruits of the initial enthusiasm and the impetus generated by the European Community.

Even if we are now confronted with worldwide problems of alarming proportions, and even if we regret that we have not attained all our European objectives, we must not underestimate what we have achieved and built up together over the past 25 years.

When the Treaty of Rome was signed we made a clear distinction between our long-term objectives and our immediate commitments. Our political aims were enshrined in the preamble to the Treaty of 25 March 1957: we declared our resolve to 'lay the foundations of an even closer union among the peoples of Europe'. But our legal commitments arose over a period of time, and proceeded from the articles of the Treaty: they provided for the creation of a common market in addition to the European Coal and Steel Community set up in 1953. When the phase of application of the Treaty of Rome commenced in 1970, each of our legal commitments had been fulfilled: tariff protection between the countries of Europe had been abolished, free movement of persons, services, capital and goods introduced, and the stability and security of agricultural production and trade ensured.

The political will developed to bring about economic, energy and monetary integration. The Community was enlarged to encompass nine and then ten countries. Now it is negotiating the accession of Spain and Portugal. It has established solid ties with 60 or so Third World countries, in a mutually advantageous association.

Even if we take account of only economic and commercial results, we can say that we have completely fulfilled the prediction made by Paul Hoffman, administrator of the Marshall Plan, when he said in 1950 that the Europeans could triple their national product if they created the common market.

Our Community commitments have therefore borne fruit: those who drafted and laid down the rules of operation were not wrong: with great sagacity they laid the foundations of the gradual development which has taken place.

As one of those who have witnessed the whole of this Community success story, allow me to pay homage to the distinguished group of statesmen, parliamentarians, Members of the Commission and the European Court of Justice and European officials who have contributed to it. On behalf of Belgium I thank them for what they have done for Europe.

By fulfilling the commitments of the Treaty we have accomplished some of the political aims which we set ourselves. By transferring part of their sovereign power to the European Community, in certain well-defined areas, our Member States have created a completely new model for political institutions, in which the degree of integration is in some respects greater than is generally the case in a confederation of States.

Thanks to the habit of working together which we have acquired, we have been able to go even further: a start has been made on the achievement of union in the economic, social, monetary and energy fields, and in the last ten years cooperation has gradually extended to essential sectors of external policy. Similarly, the European Parliament will henceforth be elected by universal suffrage and its budgetary powers will be extended.

An objective appraisal of what has been achieved by the Community in drawing the Member States closer together inevitably arouses two conflicting emotions: pride and dissatisfaction! We welcome the fact that we have overcome some of the excesses of the exaggerated nationalism of 19th-century Europe; but in a world which is already no longer the one which saw the beginning of the Community we have little time, as Louis Armand wrote as long ago as 1968, in which to construct a Europe which differs from the one we had foreseen and can meet the demands of the planetary age.

In 25 years the upsurge of life and youth in the world has rapidly moved towards the southern hemisphere: it is there that the most crying needs of humanity are concentrated, and we cannot ignore it. In this new situation the peoples of Europe will soon account for a percentage of the world's population no greater than the area which our territories occupy on the earth: barely 5%!

At the same time, the more the European economy has developed, the more its dependence on distant sources of supplies has grown.

Finally, in a world where the build-up of arms is a threat to the entire human race, questions of survival transcend each of the problems which the European Economic Community has to face. And the distinction between economic and external policy becomes blurred: all European questions are now highly political. They concern our security and our existence.

The independence of Europe is extremely relative. Its dependence is much more apparent. The important question is how to make ourselves interdependent in relation to the other major partners in the world.

Our security requires the links uniting us in an alliance with our friends and partners in North America to be maintained. But this common defence will be in jeopardy unless each partner shoulders its share of the burden and safeguards the individual interests of Europe and those of North America through continuous dialogue.

We must establish with the countries of the southern hemisphere a system of relations which favours those countries whose growth is the most hampered; our efforts at interdependence must lead us to establish with them a permanent pattern of relations which, while satisfying our own economies, are also a source of hope for those countries for years to come.

Finally, with respect to the States of Central and Eastern Europe, whatever the ideological differences dividing us, we must initiate negotiations in which the legitimate nature of our concern for the freedom of the seas is seen as a vital problem going beyond any defence problems since this is our only guarantee of security of our industrial supplies.

One last thought must override all the above considerations: The European Community developed during a respite from the tensions in a world which had become bipolar, whereas relations have now become multipolar and the entire world must seek new equilibria. In the meantime, tension is growing and Europe is not immune.

Are we together to join in the construction of a new world order? Can we not apply ourselves to organizing equitable relations on all sides which will safeguard peace in Europe as well as worldwide?

How can we face up to our duty in these respects without giving priority to the objectives and means of joint action which so many new circumstances require?

I believe that these new challenges can only be met by a common vision, jointly exercised diplomacy and European solidarity.

That is what the 1957 Treaty meant by 'an ever closer union'. And that is also what the Paris Summit had in mind in 1972 when it decided to complete 'European Union'. Ten years have gone by since then!

I am convinced that we can delay no longer. It is time for the Heads of State or Government of the ten member countries of the Community to provide a decisive impetus for a strengthening of the bonds in the face of these grave realities. The 25th anniversary of the signing of the Treaty of Rome provides the occasion for taking up this challenge.

# 66

# Towards European Union?
# A Public Opinion Poll

### Commission of the European Communities

Since 1973, the European Commission on Europe has sponsored twice-yearly surveys of European opinion on a number of topics. These excerpts from a 1981 poll focus on questions concerning European unity.

The construction of Europe will only make progress if it can count on the consent and active support of public opinion. What are the current attitudes of European citizens?

- The first question to be asked is whether they are generally in favour of or against the efforts being made to unify western Europe. The result of the poll is clear: 74% are in favour (against 69% in April 1981, 73% on average between 1975 and 1980), 13% against (compared to 16% in April, 11% on average between 1975 and 1980). Those in favour are clearly ahead in all countries (83% in Luxembourg—a record—65% in Greece, 64% in the United Kingdom, 62% in Ireland), though in Denmark they only represent 43% compared to 39% against. Neither sex nor age seem to have significant bearing on this generally supporting attitude. Only in Greece and in Denmark do those on the political right show a clear tendency to be more in favour. Those who we defined above as 'opinion leaders', who discuss politics the most and try to influence their contemporaries, are also more inclined to respond positively.

- Looking back, six Europeans in every ten think that relations between their country and their neighbours in western Europe are better than they were 25 years ago when the Treaties of Rome were signed. Two out of ten think the reverse is true. The age of the person interviewed has little bearing on these results. Even amongst those opposing integration, more than half of those questioned replied positively. The sceptics are only to be found in force in the United Kingdom (34%) and in Belgium (28%). In Greece, which has just joined the Community, the gap between the positive and negative viewpoints is largest (69 points). Next come Luxembourg, Germany and Ireland. . . .

• And the future? Faced with the economic crisis, will Community countries reinforce the links between them over the next ten years? Will they let them lapse? Or will cooperation continue very much as today? The continuation hypothesis is supported by 33% of Europeans whilst 30% are optimistic and 25% pessimistic. The optimistic hypothesis is most often supported in Italy and in the Netherlands; it is also predominant in France, Luxembourg, Ireland, Greece and, by a small margin, in Germany. By contrast, the more pessimistic assessment is subscribed to by more than a third of the Danes and the British. In general, there is a link between these responses and those given to the first question on the integration process. Those who support integration believe that links will be strengthened whilst those against it think that links will deteriorate.

• Is being a member of the Community a good or bad thing for my country? This question brought more of a response than the ones on European integration in general. It produced 53% positive responses (57% on average between 1974 and 1980, but 50% in April 1981: this could perhaps be the first indication of increasing popularity). Negative opinions were much less numerous: 14% (against 13% between 1974 and 1980, and 17% in April 1981). But opponents of the Community are ahead in the United Kingdom (by 41 to 27 whilst the score between 1974 and 1980 was 36 to 35 but 48 to 24 in April 1981). The two camps are roughly even in Denmark (around 30%). In Greece, the Community has 21% against it compared to 38% who support it, in Ireland 19% are opposed to it, compared to 49% in support. Finally, in the six founding countries, the Community's opponents only amount to 3% (Netherlands) to 7% (France) of public opinion. Supporters number more than 70% in Luxembourg, Netherlands and Italy. They amount to 55% in Germany, Belgium and France, where "don't knows" account for more than 20%. . . .

• What do people expect (or dread) from the Community? To answer this we must look at the opinion poll undertaken in April 1981 (this question was not posed in October). Amongst the favourable effects of the Community, the majority of Europeans mention the reduced risk of war and a better selection of goods in the shops. Next comes the role which their country can play in the world, the capacity to counter the world economic crisis more effectively, energy supplies, the functioning of democracy and export opportunities. By contrast, as far as prices, agriculture and jobs are concerned, the majority of Europeans attribute as many bad effects to the Community as good ones. If by refining this analysis we relate this trait to general feelings about the Community it is noticeable that this attitude is closely linked to the assessment of the Community's capacity to counter the economic crisis. However, the French and the Luxembourgers give priority to the role of their country in the world, the Germans highlight the choice of goods in their shops, and the Greeks stress the impact on their farming and the functioning of democracy in their country. . . .

# Unit XV

# The European Community _____ and the World _____

In studying Western Europe's relations with the rest of the world, it is important to make a clear distinction between the national policies of the individual countries and the policies of the ten European Community member states as a whole. We must also bear in mind that a real "European" foreign policy does not exist, although the EC does have certain treaty-making and diplomatic powers and indeed has made efforts to coordinate the foreign policies of its ten member states. While these efforts have been only moderately successful, it is nonetheless possible to discern something akin to a Europe-wide foreign policy in certain areas—for example, with respect to commerce with the United States and relations in general with the Third World.

Since its inception in 1957 the European Community has developed extensive commercial and political ties with countries throughout the world, many of them stemming from world interests built up by the individual member states over the past four or five centuries. Today, the nations of Western Europe, both separately and collectively are involved in relations with every industrialized country of the world, as well as with the developing countries of the Third World and the state-trading countries of Eastern Europe.

In this unit, a conscious decision was made to focus specifically on the policies of the European Community since these offer a provocative and interesting lens through which to view the many different aspects of European foreign policy. The readings explore the European Community's evolving policies toward the United States, the Soviet bloc, the Middle East, Latin America, and the Third World. They also consider

431

the ways in which the political choices and decisions made by the Western European governments in response to salient policy issues have affected their relationships with nations in other parts of the world. Incipient foreign policy differences between the United States and Western Europe, which at times have reached the level of disagreement, are also explored.

Werner J. Feld, in "An Emergent Power in World Politics?," questions whether the European Community could ever succeed in becoming a bona fide federal system, as many supporters of European unification hope it will. Because such an eventuality would require the Community's member states to surrender their precious national sovereignty in the area of foreign relations, Feld doubts such a transition of power could be achieved without considerable difficulty. Pointing out the inevitable conflicts involved in attempting to attain broad foreign policy goals through the use of national economic policy instruments, such as trade or commercial inducements, or the transfer of foreign policy-making powers from the national governments to the Community organs, Feld foresees little hope for a centralized foreign policy-making structure in the immediate future.

Kenneth J. Twitchett, in "The Common Market's External Relations," explains that while the Community resembles a federal system in that its functions and powers were established by its founding treaties, the actual governing processes of the Community are dominated by its constituent member states. He goes on to discuss the economic and political impact of the EEC on the international system as a whole, and points out that the organization's political influence in the international arena is not yet commensurate with its economic strength.

"The EEC's Relations With Developing Countries," excerpted from a "stocktaking" study prepared by the Economic and Social Committee of the European Communities, traces the growth of regularized efforts by the European Community to cooperate with and provide assistance to the less developed countries (LDCs) of the world, in keeping with one of the objectives set forth in the Treaty of Rome.

A report prepared by the Commission of the European Communities, "Europe and the United States," examines current relations between the European Community and the United States in such areas as trade, agriculture, monetary and investment policies, and manufacturing. While emphasizing the many interests, ideals, and values that Western Europe and the United States have in common, these excerpts also stress the fact that both areas are facing many of the same economic and social problems.

The president of the European Commission, Gaston Thorn, examines the state of European-American relations in "Europe and the U.S.: How Alike, How Different?," a speech delivered at a symposium on US-EEC relations held in the fall of 1981. Thorn calls for stronger communication and cooperation between "the two principal partners of the Western world" as part of an effort to achieve greater international stability.

# 67

## An Emergent Power in World Politics?

### Werner J. Feld

Should the European Community ever succeed in becoming a genuine federal system, as many supporters of European unification hope it will, foreign policy decisions would have to be made by the central government, a step that would require an important surrender of sovereignty by the member nations. In this brief excerpt from *The European Community in World Affairs*, author Werner J. Feld offers his perspective on the Community's chances of gaining exclusive decision-making power in the area of foreign policy. He warns of the inevitable difficulties involved in attempting to attain broad policy goals through the use of economic foreign policy instruments, such as trade or commercial agreements, or the transfer of foreign policy making powers from national governments to Community organs.

. . . [T]he formulation and execution of foreign policy are traditionally the most jealously guarded spheres of national sovereignty. Therefore, the bold but necessary step of the drafters of the Community Treaties to transfer certain, though rather limited, foreign policy making powers from the national governments to the Community organs has understandably created tensions and stress in the Community system. Conflicts are likely to arise when, in the view of member governments, the attainment of broad, important policy goals requires the use of economic foreign policy instruments such as trade or commercial agreements to offer or induce special concessions, and the availability of such instruments is found to be restricted by the obligatory transfer of certain segments of foreign policy making to the Community. Conflicts may also be generated by the difficulty of drawing a clear line between the area of economic policy and national security policy. Finally, if one considers that the establishment of the three Communities was in itself a manifestation of the foreign policies of the member governments in the pursuit of prominent, long-range national goals, one can readily realize the complexity of the interaction and coordination between the foreign policies of the member states and the development of a distinct economic "foreign" policy of the Community as a separate organization. . . .

# 68

## The Common Market's External Relations

### Kenneth J. Twitchett

In these excerpts from the preface of *Europe and the World*, Twitchett provides a brief description of the European Community—its structure, functions, and objectives—as a central representative of Community interests, and then discusses the economic and political impact of the EEC on the international system as a whole. Referring to the EEC's international activity as "external relations," as opposed to "foreign policy," the author notes that despite increasing pressures on the member states for collective international action, the organization's world political influence still is not commensurate with its collective economic strength.

The European Community is now an established feature of the international scene. . . .

This is not to say, however, that the Community has the characteristics of a new-style "super-state" along the lines of either the British unitary model or the American federal one. It does not fulfil the requirements of statehood as usually recognized under international law. The Community has no population and no territory apart from those of its nine member states. It can enter into relations with non-member states and other international bodies, but only with the consent of the Nine. While it resembles a federal system in that its functions and powers originate from those granted by the member states in its founding and subsequent treaties, the member states themselves dominate the Community's governmental processes. Although the Commission, representing the central Community interest, possesses a large degree of autonomous decision making capacity, in the final analysis it is subservient to the Council of Ministers, the organ representing the will of the member states.

Unlike the Covenant of the League of Nations, the Charter of the United Nations, and the North Atlantic Treaty, there are no procedures for withdrawal laid down in the Community treaties and the Community itself is regarded as being established for an unlimited period. But it is extremely unlikely that a member state would be forced to remain in the Community against its will. While there might be practical difficulties if one of the Nine wished to terminate its membership and in theory economic sanctions could be levied against a state which withdrew, there is no question of military force being employed against such a state. Among conventional federations there are often no such inhibitions, as shown in the cases of the coercion used against the South in the American civil war and Biafra in the Nigerian civil war.

Nevertheless, the Community is much more than just another international organization. Under international law it has a separate legal existence from that of its member states, and has been endowed with treaty making powers and the right to receive and to send diplomatic envoys. Although these characteristics are possessed by some other international organizations, the Community has been given an added legal dimension. . . . There is an embryonic but developing Community legal system in which EEC law can override national laws, and a number of Community decisions apply directly in the Nine without having to be embodied in national legislation. . . .

In fact its unique nature as an international organization added to the collective economic and political influence of the Nine gives the Community the characteristics of a civilian power: an international polity as yet possessing no military dimension, but able to exercise influence on states, global and regional organizations, international corporations, and other transnational bodies through diplomatic, economic and legal factors. To date the Community's response to the external demands made on it has been a regional rather than a global one. The Commission itself is organized to deal with three major problem areas: the industrialized world, including the United States, Japan and the old white Commonwealth; the developing countries of Africa, Asia, Latin America and the Middle East; and the state trading countries. The following percentage figures for 1973 demonstrate the relative importance of these three areas to the Community in terms of its trade with them: industrialized countries, 54 per cent; less developed countries, 38 per cent; state trading countries, 8 per cent. . . .

. . . [T]he nature of the EEC's international activity. . . is best described as external relations rather than foreign policy. The treaty and other bases of the Community's external relations . . . derive from commercial and economic requirements of the Rome Treaty and from the EEC's relations with the developing countries. . . . [T]here are numerous pressures on the Nine for collective international action, but . . . so far when acting together they have done so on a rather haphazard basis. In effect, in external relations the EEC does not exercise political influence commensurate with its collective economic strength. . . .

It should be constantly underlined that . . . '[t]he European Community is not a super-state. Rather it represents an attempt on the part of free countries to work out some important policies together, to make common decisions in such areas, and to implement these according to procedures laid down in the [Rome] Treaty and in Community decisions'.

This essential qualification, however, does not detract from the fact that the Europe of the Nine does have a very real political significance for and impact on contemporary global politics. In part, these stem from the world interests which the EEC members, particularly Britain and France, have built up over the past four or five centuries. The white domains of Australasia and the "new world" of the Americas sprang directly from the overseas adventures of the Western European states in the sixteenth, seventeenth and eighteenth centuries. Much of the recent history of the Third World is also that of Western Europe, whether in the negative sense of imperialism, colonial exploitation and bloody wars of independence or in the positive sense of shared historical experiences and mutual commercial interests. Western Europe's imperial splendour now belongs to the past, but residual economic interests and a heritage of mutual knowledge remain, as well as perhaps occasionally even understanding. . . .

# 69

# The EEC's Relations with Developing Countries

## Economic and Social Committee of the European Communities

Part of a "stocktaking" study of the EEC's external relations, these excerpts trace the growth of regularized efforts by the European Community to cooperate with and provide assistance to the world's less developed countries (LDCs), an objective envisioned in the Treaty of Rome. The EEC committee which published this study is composed of representatives from each of the ten member states.

## BACKGROUND

The Community can currently draw on an extensive battery of instruments for the purpose of implementing its development cooperation and aid policy. The Convention concluded with the African, Caribbean and Pacific (ACP) States and the Agreements with the Mediterranean countries are the contractual pillars of its operation in this area. The Generalized Preferences Scheme (GSP) is another specific instrument which has won widespread appreciation.

In addition to these three areas, the Community plays a prominent role within international organizations. It has participated in commodity negotiations, was one of the driving forces behind the North-South and Euro-Arab Dialogues, and is a party to numerous bilateral agreements with the LDCs. It also provides financial, food and emergency aid, loans to non-governmental organizations, and so on.

During the period immediately after the entry into force of the Treaty of Rome, the Community's development cooperation drive was channelled mainly through the Association provided for in Part IV of that Treaty. This Association was restricted to a number of former French colonies in Africa, the Italian trust territory of Somalialand, Netherlands, New Guinea, the Belgian Congo and Ruanda-Urundi.

Despite its circumscribed geographical area and the very modest funds available to it, the Association formed an efficiently structured core with its own institutions, which operated smoothly. In 1964, a fresh impetus was provided in the shape of the First Yaoundé Convention, though the Association's territorial scope remained limited. In 1967 the Community started to broaden its contractual ties with the African countries; the negotiations opened with Nigeria, Kenya, Uganda and Tanzania and culminated the following year in the Arusha Association Agreement (embracing only Kenya, Uganda and Tanzania). In 1969 the two Conventions were renewed and in 1973 Mauritius acceded to the Yaoundé Convention. 1973 saw the start of the talks that led to the conclusion of the first Lomé Convention in 1975. This Convention, encompassing 46 LDCs, was intended by the Contracting Parties to establish a new blueprint for relations between the industrialized and developing nations.

As the years went by, relations with the Mediterranean countries came to assume considerable importance. Following the conclusion of association agreements with Greece and Turkey in the early Sixties, the first agreements were concluded with the Maghreb States and exploratory talks got under way with Malta, the United Arab Republic and the Lebanon. Immediately afterwards, in 1970, agreements were signed with Israel and Spain, and negotiations with Cyprus and Portugal got off the ground.

As these contacts rapidly gathered momentum, the Community's relations with the Mediterranean countries gradually took shape, in mutual recognition of the de facto interdependence of all States in that region.

On a worldwide scale, the Community has been particularly active within the United Nations framework, and especially in UNCTAD (set up in 1961). In 1968 the Community took the lead in framing a Generalized Preferences Scheme (GSP) designed to aid the LDCs and played a decisive role in the establishment of this Scheme, to which other industrialized countries have subsequently acceded.

With the accession of the United Kingdom, Denmark and Ireland, the Community's external relations with all parts of the world, and especially certain East Asian countries (the ASEAN group) received a shot in the arm. Simultaneously, the prospect of opening negotiations with China started to become a reality.

The Paris Summit (1972) concluded that the various components of the Community's external relations policy should form part and parcel of a consistent, overall approach to the Community's specific international role. Applying this principle first to the Mediterranean countries, it was advocated that any existing or future agreements with them, would have to tie in with a balanced, general strategy.

It was clear from the Summit that the Member States needed to harmonize and coordinate their standpoints more effectively, both within international forums (particularly the United Nations) and for the purpose of framing a genuine Community development cooperation policy.

The political declaration made by the Nine at the Copenhagen Summit, in November 1973, paved the way for the Euro-Arab Dialogue. Later, in December 1975, the foundations for the North-South Dialogue were laid at the Paris Ministerial Conference on International Economic Cooperation.

Accordingly, at the time of the advent of the first oil crisis in 1973, the Community was able to conduct and develop its relations with developing countries all over the world on a number of fronts:

- active involvement in major UN and GATT negotiations;
- relations with the South and East Mediterranean countries;
- relations with the ACP States;
- negotiations with China;
- aid to non-associated LDCs;
- start of the Euro-Arab Dialogue;
- the launching of the "North-South Dialogue" in conjunction with other industrial nations.

Over the subsequent period, international economic relations have, needless to say, been severely strained by such pressures as the energy crisis, upheavals on the world money market and the deteriorating economic situation of many industrialized countries and, to an even worse extent, the LDCs.

The Community continues to press ahead with its external policies though the resources available are in no way commensurate with the serious problems that needed to be tackled. Nonetheless, the LDCs take a keen economic and political interest in such action; they recognize the importance of the Community keeping up its efforts in hard times like the present.

The signature of the Second Lomé Convention in 1979, the conclusion of the Tokyo Round Agreements, measures to assist the LDCs, commodity agreements, the Multifibre Agreement and food aid schemes, combined with the general expression of a firm political resolve to foster closer trade links between the Member States and the LDCs, are all milestones on the arduous uphill path to which the Community remains resolutely committed.

There are also some signs of progress as regards closer political cooperation among the Member States. Regular consultations (rooted in the 1973 Copenhagen declaration) have prompted the Nine to coordinate their stands more frequently, especially on their policies vis-à-vis the developing nations.

## GENERAL DEVELOPMENT POLICY INSTRUMENTS

### Generalized Tariff Preferences Scheme (GSP)

The Community deploys this autonomous instrument particularly in its relations with the non-associated LDCs. In theory, however, the GSP is designed for all LDCs and the Community compiles the list of beneficiaries. The experience acquired both by the Community and the developing countries in implementing the GSP have proved positive. The Community's offer has substantially increased since 1971, and especially after the United Kingdom joined the EEC in 1974. . . . On the other hand the developing countries' use of the GSP has not been entirely satisfactory. On average it was 60% for the year 1978, with very high rates of utilization for the most sensitive products (103%) and very low rates of utilization for non-sensitive or the least sensitive products (36.5%). The obvious explanation for this latter phenomenon is that the marginal gains from GSP are less than the administrative costs involved. Another conclusion to be drawn is that it is the most advanced beneficiaries that gain most from the GSP. These are South Korea and Taiwan (the two countries accounting for 25% of imports under the GSP for 1977), Hong-Kong, Yugoslavia and Brazil.

The wisdom of extending the GSP to China and Bulgaria as well as Romania has also been questioned.

The question to be asked therefore is whether the GSP actually fulfils the role the Community has always intended it to play, i.e. first and foremost to help countries whose needs are greatest, secondly to take into account the level of development achieved by individual beneficiary countries, and thirdly to show sensitivity to the economic and social problems of the Community itself.

There does seem to be some discordance between the aims of the GSP and actual achievements. This gap might be closed if the Community were able to return to normal GATT [,General Agreement on Tariffs and Trade,] rules for imports from developing countries which have reached a sufficiently high level of competitiveness, and if the Community were able to demand reciprocity in trade with such countries. Those developing countries which have not yet reached this level of competitiveness should, in their relations with the Community, behave in a manner that is in keeping with the agreements concluded and should ensure that there is healthy competition, especially with regard to prices, regularity of deliveries, terms of payment and access to markets.

Finally there is the case for insisting that beneficiaries under the GSP should observe minimum labour standards under ILO [International Labour Organization,] conventions and should respect basic human rights.

## International Conferences on Commodities

The great divide in all commodity negotiations is that between producers and consumers. The general issue, however, is further complicated by the fact that, although a few industrialized or developed countries are among the major producers of some commodities, in almost no case are their economies dependent on the export of any single commodity; whereas the economies of many developing countries are heavily dependent on the export of one or two commodities (though they are importers of others). Commodity issues therefore are not simple conflicts of interest between producers and consumers, but also play a major part in the North/South dialogue. This has led in recent years to efforts in UNCTAD [,United Nations Conference on Trade and Development] to promote commodity arrangements which deliberately favour developing producing countries at the expense of developed consuming countries.

The economic costs of such policies, if they were vigorously pursued over a wide range of commodities, would impose considerable burdens on consuming countries—at least in the short term; moreover there has been considerable debate over whether they would bring any real economic advantage to either producers or consumers in the longer term.

Ever since the UNCTAD IV Conference at Nairobi in 1976, however (at which the principles of a proposed "Integrated Programme" were worked out) there have been external pressures on the Community to achieve a "common" policy on Commodities. In this context the word "common" has two different meanings—viz. it can mean "common to all Member States or to the Community as a whole"; or it can mean "common to a whole range of commodities". In both senses of the word the Community enjoyed only limited success in achieving a "common" policy. Differences in approach between Member States still remain, together with difficulties in achieving a uniform approach to all commodity issues.

### The Difficulties in the Way of Achieving a
### Common Community Commodity Policy

With the major exception of sugar (of which the Community is the second largest exporter in the world), the Community is an importer of most of the commodities which are now the subject of international negotiation and consultation. . . .

On general commodity issues, Member States have tended until recently to negotiate individually rather than as members of the Community, and as far as their policies are concerned, these have been primarily dictated by their interests as consumers (sugar being the major exception). Recently, however, Member States and the Commission have agreed that there shall be a common approach to [a number of] commodity issues. . . .

## Conventions with ACP Countries

A new convention between the EEC and the ACP countries was signed in Lomé (capital of Togo) on 31 October 1979.

The specific features of the Lomé Convention are as follows:

- contractual relationships creating rights and obligations between two regional groups, which involve a series of cooperation instruments adaptable to the priorities of the individual countries (trade, Stabex,* aid, etc.)
- and which are based on a permanent dialogue through institutions provided for in the Convention (EEC-ACP Council of Ministers, Committee of Ambassadors, Consultative Assembly, consultations of economic and social circles).

The objectives of the Convention are to:

- promote trade between the ACP States and the Community and between the ACP States themselves;
- ensure greater stability in export earnings, economic viability and sustained growth of the economies of ACP States;
- support the economies of ACP States dependent on the mining industry;
- encourage EEC investments in the ACP States;
- promote industrial development in the ACP States;
- assist in resolving problems relating to rural development, including problems connected with agricultural production for domestic consumption;
- accord special treatment for least developed, landlocked and island ACP States;
- promote the economic and social development of the ACP States.

---

*Ed. note: Stabilization of export earnings.

Under the trade cooperation arrangements, manufactured goods and agricultural products that do not directly compete with products governed by the CAP, Common Agricultural Policy, enter the Community free of duty and quantitative restrictions. The ACP States thus enjoy preferential treatment compared with other third countries.

These concessions are not reciprocal. The ACP States have merely undertaken to give Member States the same advantages as the most favoured industrial nation. . . .

## Relations with the Arab Oil Producing Countries of the Middle East*

Economic relations between the Community and the Arab oil-producing countries of the Middle East have become a thorny issue since the energy crisis in 1973. These oil-exporting countries' large trade surplus, with the corresponding deficits of the Member States and the other Western countries, have given rise to complex economic and financial problems fraught with consequences, both direct and indirect, for international economic equilibrium.

In recent years, the Community has tried a regional approach by initiating the Euro-Arab dialogue. Since its inception, this dialogue has been confined to a limited range of subjects (oil matters were excluded), but it has got bogged down owing to the difficulties the Arab countries have in agreeing on a joint position. Thus the Community as such has not in fact been able to pursue a coordinated policy vis-à-vis this area, which is now (and will be even more in the future) facing problems of great importance for its development. There have been isolated, bilateral contacts between individual Member States and Arab oil-producing countries, when the latter have been prepared to conclude cooperation agreements with European countries. Overall, however, relations between the two areas remain confused, uncoordinated and difficult to grasp. The problems are serious and complex on both sides.

The Arab countries are asking for a larger contribution by Europe towards rapid industrialization and strengthening of their economies before their oil resources dwindle in the not so distant future. They are asking for technical cooperation, the transfer of technology and know-how, and cooperation in the sphere of management, training, etc. On the other hand, the Arab countries take for granted that their new industrial products should have free access to the Community market. . . .

---

*Saudi Arabia, Kuwait, Iraq, Bahrain, Quatar, United Arab Emirates, Oman.

## BILATERAL RELATIONS WITH THE NON-ASSOCIATED DEVELOPING COUNTRIES

### In Africa

On 4 November 1980 an agreement was signed (and is now in the process of being ratified) admitting Zimbabwe to the Lomé Convention. Angola and Mozambique are therefore the only developing countries in Africa not to be formally associated to the Community. The latter is a special case and in its policy on Namibia, the EEC is firmly convinced that it is necessary to go on supporting efforts to ensure that the United Nations plan is enforced in that country.

### In Asia

On 8 March 1980 the Community signed a co-operation agreement with the ASEAN countries [Association of South East Asian Nations: Indonesia, Malaysia, the Philippines, Singapore and Thailand]. The concordance of views of the two groups of countries on the Afghanistan and Cambodian crises gave much political impetus to the agreement in question.

The EEC-ASEAN agreement can be seen as an attempt to broaden the regional component (hitherto largely confined to Mediterranean LDCs and the ACP) of Community development-cooperation Policy. EEC-ASEAN trade is on a small scale (2.3% of EEC external trade in 1978), though it forged ahead in the Seventies. All five ASEAN States are attractive trade partners, either because of the level of development they have attained or because they are rich in natural resources.

It is clearly in the Community's interests to boost exports to ASEAN and to endeavour, through imports, to achieve greater security of supply as regards raw materials. Increased trade, however, might require greater Community willingness to buy manufactures from ASEAN. Singapore is already a vigorous exporter of manufactures but the other four ASEAN countries will soon also be able to flood the world market with cheap goods (textiles, electronics, etc.). This trend is also being fostered by Japanese firms in particular, which for several years now have been decentralizing and locating production in ASEAN countries. The price of greater access to ASEAN raw materials and closer EEC-ASEAN trade relations may be greater accessibility to the Community market for ASEAN manufactures in competition with EEC "lame-duck" manufactures. The ASEAN countries also have everything to gain from attracting investment from the Community, especially investment in industrialization schemes for the entire bloc, and from stepping up industrial and technological co-operation. . . .

## In Latin America

Trade with *Latin American* countries, which had been very limited for a long time, has developed relatively well over the last few years. . . . The Community's trade balance with the Latin American countries has always been in the red, although the deficit is not caused by oil imports from Mexico and Venezuela. As trading partners the 39 Latin American countries are more important than the 60 ACP states and come straight after the state-trading nations. Since the late 1960s the Community has made efforts to step up relations with the Latin American countries. . . .

The EEC's policy towards the Latin American countries is primarily influenced by the fact that it shares responsibility with the United States for the development of this sub-continent where some of the poorest people in the world live. The United States itself has traditionally considered aid to South American countries as falling within its own particular province. Secondly, the wealth of raw materials in this sub-continent, the potential size of its market, and the rapid economic expansion in some of the countries in this area, particularly Brazil and Mexico, unquestionably make Latin American countries attractive trading partners for the Community, although the problems they pose are not inconsiderable. Finally, Latin America has a wide variety of political regimes which frequently stray from the path of democracy. This makes it difficult to establish relations with the Community. . . .

# 70

## Europe and the United States

### Commission of the European Communities

This report from the Commission of the European Communities surveys current relations between the European Community and the United States in a number of areas, ranging from trade to agriculture to monetary relations, while emphasizing that Europe and the United States not only share many common interests, ideals, and living standards, they are also facing many of the same economic and social problems in the early 1980s.

---

The European Community and the United States of America are today the two principal pillars of the western political and economic systems. Their relations at all levels are particularly intense, and their world roles largely complementary. Both constitute great experiments in the democratic organization of society, the American idea having been inspired by the Revolution of 1776 and enshrined in the American Constitution, while the European idea, born out of the political vacuum, economic devastation and social upheavals of the years following the Second World War, is expressed in the basic Treaties of the Communities and promoted by the Community's institutions. Whereas the American nation is a union of fifty States within a federation, the European Community forms the foundation of an ultimate union between diverse historic nation States, a union whose final shape—whether federal, confederal or otherwise—has yet to be determined.

The European Community and the United States share many interests and ideals based on common or comparable political and cultural experience. The Community as a whole is the foremost economic partner and political ally of the United States. After the United States, the Community is the second industrial power in the world, but the combined gross national product of the Community is now somewhat higher than that of the United States. In many regions of the Community living standards are now comparable to American ones.

For more than thirty years the United States has provided considerable support for European unification, first through the Marshall Plan, which was a key to Europe's post-war economic recovery, then through active partnership with West European countries in the OECD (formerly the OEEC) and finally through active backing for the European Community and its subsequent enlargments.

At 270 million, the European Community's population is 50 million greater than that of the United States, although the Community's present area covers only one-sixth of the US land mass. As the West's major industrial powers, the Community and the United States face in the 1980s similar economic and social problems, especially in the areas of employment, prices, industrial policy, adaptation to new technology, energy, environmental and consumer protection, transportation, raw material supply and relations with developing countries. . . .

However, the coming to power in the United States of [an] administration that is fixedly wedded to the principles of free trade and hence frowns on any state intervention in economic affairs has led to a certain hardening of trade relations, particularly in respect of the common agricultural policy and the steel question. . . .

## POLITICAL FRAMEWORK

The European Community and the United States conduct their relations within the multilateral framework of the General Agreement on Tariffs and Trade (GATT), the OECD, the Conference on Security and Cooperation in Europe (CSCE) and other international bodies, and also at a bilateral level. The Community and its ten member countries have become the United States' principal western partner in practically all matters. Once a year the Heads of Government of the leading western industrialized countries, the United States, Japan, Canada, four member countries of the Community, namely France, the Federal Republic of Germany, Italy and the United Kingdom, together with the European Community as such (the latter represented by the President of the Commission), review their overall economic strategies at the so-called "Western economic summits". . . .

High-level consultations between the Commission and the US Administration are held twice yearly, in Brussels and Washington alternately, for the discussion of a vast range of bilateral and multilateral economic and trade issues, which are often highly complex. . . . Members of the European Parliament meet regularly with members of the US Congress. The 18th meeting was held in Washington from 18 to 22 May 1981 and the 19th in The Hague and Amsterdam from 6 to 10 January 1982.

The Community and the United States have long-term bilateral agreements covering fishing in US coastal waters (1977), the supply of nuclear fuels (1958) and cooperation in the field of peaceful use of

**TABLE 70.1  Comparative Table of Socioeconomic and Geographic Indicators**

| Country | Area 1,000 km² | Population (millions) 1978 | Population Density (per km²) 1979 | Population forecast (millions) | | Civilian Work-force (millions) 1980 | Unemployment % active population 1981 |
|---|---|---|---|---|---|---|---|
| | | | | 1985 | 1990 | | |
| _EC_ | | | | | | | |
| Belgium | 30.5 | 9.85 | 323 | 9.84 | 9.89 | 4.0 | 11.5 |
| Denmark | 43.1 | 5.12 | 119 | 5.17 | 5.21 | 2.6 | 8.2 |
| France | 544.0 | 53.48 | 98 | 54.83 | 56.08 | 22.6 | 7.8 |
| F. R. Germany | 248.6 | 61.36 | 247 | 59.61 | 58.59 | 26.1 | 4.9 |
| Ireland | 70.3 | 3.37 | 48 | 3.54 | 3.72 | 1.2 | 10.3 |
| Italy | 301.3 | 56.91 | 189 | 57.26 | 57.60 | 22.3 | 8.8 |
| Luxembourg | 2.6 | 0.36 | 140 | 0.36 | 0.36 | 0.2 | 1.0 |
| Netherlands | 41.2 | 14.04 | 341 | 14.25 | 14.65 | 5.2 | 7.3 |
| United Kingdom | 244.0 | 55.95 | 229 | 56.30 | 57.03 | 26.0 | 10.5 |
| Greece | 132.0 | 9.45 | 71 | 9.3 | 9.4 | n.c. | 1.1* |
| | 1,657.6 | 269.88 | 163 | 270.75 | 273.0 | 113.9 | |
| Portugal | 91.6 | 9.84 | 107 | 10.21 | 10.47 | 3.5 | 7.8* |
| Spain | 504.8 | 37.11 | 74 | 38.51 | 39.69 | 12.9 | 12.4* |
| United States | 9,363.1 | 220.58 | 24 | 232.88 | 243.51 | 104.7 | 7.6 |
| Canada | 9,976.1 | 23.69 | 2 | 25.49 | 26.83 | 11.5 | 7.5 |
| Japan | 370.0 | 115.81 | 307 | 119.73 | 122.77 | 56.5 | 2.2 |

*1980

n.c. = non-classified

_Source:_ Eurostat and _UN Monthly Bulletin._

450

atomic energy (1959). There has also been an exchange of letters on co-operation on environmental protection. The United States maintains a diplomatic mission to the European Communities in Brussels. The Commission, for its part, is served by a permanent Delegation in Washington, D.C.

## TRADE RELATIONS

### Multilateral Trade

The European Community was the main destination for US exports in 1980 (24%), followed by Canada (16%) and Japan (9%). It is the second biggest exporter to the United States (15%), after Canada (17%) and ahead of Japan (13%).

The Community has had a persistent trade deficit with the United States, which worsened until 1980 when it reached an all-time high of around $25 billion according to the accounts of the Statistical Office of the Communities or some $18 billion according to the US Department of Commerce. The discrepancy in these figures stems mainly from the way in which costs such as insurance and transport are entered in the accounts, which affects the statistics on goods according to whether they are imported or exported, as US export FOB (free on board) becoming a European import CIF (cost, insurance and freight). The figures available for 1981 show that the deficit was considerably reduced because of the continuing economic crisis and the strength of the dollar, which curbed US exports. . . .

### Tariffs

The Community's Common Customs Tariff was relatively low insofar as industrial products were concerned. In trade with its industrialized partners the Community's exports had continued to come up against tariff barriers which were often very high. Heavy import charges imposed on certain products and sometimes even on entire sectors provided effective protection because they were selective and had by and large remained intact despite successive tariff negotiations. Consequently, the Community sought the application of a formula which could be applied as generally as possible, and which while significantly reducing tariffs, would at the same time harmonize them. The US Trade Act gave the President extensive powers in relation to tariffs. He could abolish duties of 5% or less and reduce duties of over 5% by up to 60%. In September 1977 the Community and the United States agreed to apply tariff cuts in accordance with the "Swiss formula," under which high tariffs are cut proportionately more than low ones.

The proportion of US imports from the Community subject to duties over 10% was cut from 16.3% to 6%, while that of imports subject to duties over 20% dropped from 4.8% to 1.2%. After the negotiations were concluded only 185 headings, compared with the previous 756, remained above 20%. In the case of textiles the cut in the US tariff for Community goods was 27.5%. This reduction also applied to a number of very high duties which were making trade virtually impossible. In this sector the Community cut its duties vis-à-vis the US by 22.6%. As regards steel, where dutiable US imports from the Nine are four times imports from the US, the United States cut its duties on Community goods by 29.6%, apart from some legal exceptions concerning special steels. This reduction continued the process of harmonization in this sector which began under the Kennedy Round [(1964–67)]. In the paper sector, where there was strong US pressure for a substantial cut, the Community reduction vis-à-vis the United States was 28%. Where other sectors were concerned, the United States granted a substantial tariff reduction on machinery, transport equipment, ceramics and glass.

The tariff concessions were to be implemented in eight equal annual reductions starting in 1980, with a number of exceptions including textiles, steel and aircraft equipment. The agreement on aircraft took effect on 1 January 1980, while the concessions on textiles and steel were to be implemented in six annual reductions beginning in 1982. At the end of a preliminary stage of five years, the Community will examine whether it is able to pass on to the second three year stage. The other participants have also reserved their rights in this respect.

## Agriculture

Negotiations were pursued without calling into question the European Community's Common Agricultural Policy. Agreement was reached on multilateral arrangements for dairy products and beef. The arrangements provided for continuing consultation on developments in the world market for these products; the arrangement for dairy products contains minimum price agreements for milk and skimmed milk powder, butter, butteroil and cheese. The Community was able to win acceptance for the maintenance of the present provisions, including the possibility of applying export subsidies. The results of negotiations in this sector have made it possible to avoid any calling into question of the refund mechanism (hitherto sharply criticized in GATT).

In the negotiations with the United States, which is its largest agricultural customer, the Community's objective was to give priority to

**TABLE 70.2  External Trade of EC-10, 1980**

| | Imports | | Exports | | |
|---|---|---|---|---|---|
| | $ million | % | | $ million | % |
| 1. United States | 62,099 | 16.4 | United States | 37,280 | 11.8 |
| 2. Saudi Arabia | 34,927 | 9.2 | Switzerland | 31,042 | 9.8 |
| 3. Switzerland | 21,606 | 5.7 | Sweden | 16,262 | 5.2 |
| 4. Japan | 18,387 | 4.9 | Austria | 15,725 | 5.0 |
| 5. Sweden | 16,159 | 4.3 | Spain | 10,583 | 3.4 |
| 6. Soviet Union | 15,614 | 4.1 | Soviet Union | 10,558 | 3.3 |
| 7. Norway | 11,757 | 3.1 | Saudi Arabia | 10,424 | 3.3 |
| 8. Spain | 11,304 | 3.0 | Nigeria | 8,414 | 2.7 |
| 9. Iraq | 11,066 | 2.9 | Japan | 7,537 | 2.4 |
| 10. Nigeria | 10,962 | 2.9 | Norway | 7,157 | 2.3 |
| 11. Austria | 9,770 | 2.6 | South Africa | 7,024 | 2.2 |
| 12. Libya | 9,139 | 2.4 | Algeria | 6,619 | 2.1 |
| 13. Canada | 8,722 | 2.3 | Libya | 5,942 | 1.9 |
| 14. South Africa | 7,104 | 1.9 | Yugoslavia | 5,846 | 1.9 |
| 15. Finland | 6,270 | 1.7 | Iraq | 5,381 | 1.7 |
| 16. United Arab Emirates | 6,091 | 1.6 | Finland | 4,826 | 1.5 |
| 17. Brazil | 5,767 | 1.5 | Canada | 4,741 | 1.5 |
| 18. Kuwait | 5,622 | 1.5 | Iran | 4,572 | 1.5 |
| 19. Algeria | 5,607 | 1.5 | Egypt | 4,465 | 1.4 |
| 20. Hong Kong | 5,043 | 1.3 | Australia | 4,306 | 1.4 |

*Source:* Eurostat: Monthly Trade Bulletin, Special Number: 1958–1980

the question of the possible application by the United States of counter-vailing duties (which are a permanent threat to Community exports) and to examining the conditions governing the importation into the US of products exported by the Community. The Community obtained satisfaction on the majority of its requests and obtained major concessions on most of the principal subjects of discord that had arisen in the past. [See Table 70.2]. . .

**EC-US TRADE**

In the 1970s the European Community's trade with the United States was characterized by spectacular growth on the one hand and by a persistent and substantial trade deficit on the other. Indeed, since the Community's establishment in 1958, trade has developed at a brisk pace beneficial to both partners. The rising standard of living in the European Common [(EC)] Market and the abolition of virtually all customs barriers have made EC an attractive outlet for American products. Similarly, there has been substantial growth in Community exports to the United States.

The Community's common tariff was established as an average of the previously existing tariffs of the original six Member States. As a result of the enlargement of the Community through the entry of Denmark, Ireland and the United Kingdom in 1973, the previously existing tariffs of those countries were reduced as well since these tariffs were somewhat higher than the common external tariff which was effective before the enlargement. By 1 July 1977 all three countries, after a period of three years, had adopted the Community's external tariff. Furthermore, as a result of the GATT Multilateral Trade Negotiations [(MTN)] conducted between 1973 and 1979, the common external tariff of the European Community has been lowered even further.

With the implementation of the last stage of the tariff cuts only 10% of Community tariffs on industrial goods will exceed 10%, and 1.5% will exceed 15%. On the other hand 7% of US industrial tariffs will exceed 10%, 5% will exceed 15% and still 3% will exceed 20%. Only one out of a total of 2,100 dutiable tariff lines in the Community will remain subject to a tariff of more than 20% (22% on trucks). The average tariff on industrial products in the Community after implementation of the MTN agreement will be 3.9% whereas the US average tariff on all industrial products will be 4.7%.

US exports to the Community increased considerably in 1980 (from $47 billion to $62 billion) while imports from the Community only increased from $34.5 billion to $37.3 billion. In 1980 the Community's trade deficit with the United States reached an all-time high of $24.8 billion.

In 1980 the individual Member States of the Community all had a trade deficit with the United States. The United States' biggest customer is the United Kingdom, followed by the Federal Republic of Germany, France and Italy. The United States' leading supplier is the Federal Republic of Germany followed by the United Kingdom, France and Italy.

### Manufactures

In this sector bilateral relations have seriously deteriorated as a result of anti-dumping complaints lodged against European exporters by US steel producers. However, the difficulties facing the US steel industry are attributable more to the worsening economic situation in the United States, which has been particularly reflected by a spectacular fall in demand for steel on the US market. The decline in European steel sales on the US market in 1980 was considerably greater ( – 16%) than the reduction in production and consumption in the United States ( – 12%). This trend is borne out by the way in which the US market share held by European steel exports has developed.

In the automobile sector the Community share of US vehicle imports fell slightly in 1980 from 15% to 13%, while Canadian exports fell from 37% to 10% and Japanese exports leaped from 36% to 61%. Two out of three vehicles imported into the United States are Japanese. This led the United States Administration to exert pressure on Japan to limit its exports to the U.S. The EC Commission is closely following the effects of this agreement, to observe whether it leads to any diversion of Japanese exports towards the Community.

## Agriculture

The Community's agricultural trade deficit with the United States amounted to $6.8 billion in 1980. In fiscal 1981 the United States exported agricultural products totalling $45 billion (20% of exports) and imported $17 billion's worth (13% of imports). The European Community is by far the biggest market for US agricultural exports. Despite its leading position as an agricultural exporter the United States complains about the common agricultural policy, criticizing the exports refunds policy. The European Community, however, considers that it abides by the code on subsidies, adoption of which was one of the major objectives of the Tokyo Round negotiations [(1973–79)].

In the case of wheat, for instance, it should be pointed out that the United States at present exports some 60% of its production, compared with some 40% thirteen years ago. . . . With regard to other agricultural products, such as maize and soya bean products, which account for the bulk of US exports, the Community is the world's biggest importer because of new livestock feeding techniques.

The European Community and the United States are both exporters of poultry but their share of the world market has not changed significantly over the past few years, the United States accounting for 46% of the market in 1980 and the Community for 54%.

Sugar exports are also a source of difficulties between the United States and the European Community. On 1 July 1981 the Community set up a new market organization under which Community sugar producers are themselves to bear the cost of export when world prices are lower than Community prices.

The US Administration [has] accepted the US producers' complaints that their European competitors were receiving excessive subsidies for sugar, poultry, wheat and pasta products. The difficulties in this sector should, however, be viewed in its social context. Although the "green revolution" has helped rationalize and modernize the Community's agriculture in recent years, raising productivity in some areas and for some products to levels comparable to those in the United States, European farming is still by and large less efficient than its American counterpart. In 1978, for instance, 77% of farms in the Community were smaller than 20 hectares in area, whereas, the average American farm was 160 hectares (400 acres). . . .

## MONETARY RELATIONS

On 15 March 1979 the European Monetary System (EMS) came into operation after the European Council had, at Bremen on 7 July 1978, proposed that closer monetary cooperation be established between the Member States of the European Community. . . . The EMS is seen as a first and decisive step towards the Community's economic and monetary union; its long-term goal is to create a zone of monetary stability in Europe and to strengthen the international monetary system. Its more short-term objective—to stabilize the exchange rates between the currencies of the participant countries—has been largely successful in giving a real European dimension to markets.

It has been suggested in the United States that . . . the operation of a European Monetary Fund could rapidly and dangerously weaken the role of the dollar in international trade. The European Commission, however, has emphasized that, although a new reserve unit was created, its use will be strictly limited to transactions between the central banks of the Community. The Bremen agreement stated that "the EMS is and will remain fully compatible with the relevant articles of the International Monetary Fund agreement."

## INVESTMENT

Foreign investment from sources in the United States and the European Community represents by far the largest volume of direct foreign investment in the world today. Furthermore, American and European investors have the greatest share of foreign investment in the Community and the United States respectively.

### US Investment in the Community

. . . US capital investment in the early post-war years was an important element in the economic reconstruction of Western Europe. To-

**TABLE 70.3  EC–US Trade: EC Member Countries' Imports and Exports ($ billion)**

| | 1979 | 1980 |
|---|---|---|
| **Imports from USA (CIF)** | | |
| Germany | 10.4 | 13.5 |
| France | 7.2 | 10.8 |
| Italy | 5.3 | 7.0 |
| Netherlands | 5.7 | 6.8 |
| Belgium/Luxembourg | 4.0 | 5.5 |
| United Kingdom | 12.0 | 15.9 |
| Ireland | 0.8 | 0.9 |
| Denmark | 1.0 | 1.3 |
| Greece | 0.5 | 0.5 |
| **EC TOTAL** | 46.9 | 62.1 |
| **Exports to USA (FOB)** | | |
| Germany | 11.3 | 11.8 |
| France | 4.8 | 4.9 |
| Italy | 4.7 | 4.1 |
| Netherlands | 1.8 | 1.9 |
| Belgium/Luxembourg | 2.1 | 2.2 |
| United Kingdom | 8.6 | 10.8 |
| Ireland | 0.3 | 0.4 |
| Denmark | 0.7 | 0.8 |
| Greece | 0.2 | 0.3 |
| **EC TOTAL** | 34.5 | 37.3 |
| **Balance** | | |
| Germany | 0.9 | − 1.7 |
| France | − 2.4 | − 5.8 |
| Italy | − 0.6 | − 2.8 |
| Netherlands | − 3.9 | − 4.9 |
| Belgium/Luxembourg | − 2.0 | − 3.3 |
| United Kingdom | − 3.4 | − 5.1 |
| Ireland | − 0.5 | − 0.4 |
| Denmark | − 0.2 | − 0.5 |
| Greece | − 0.3 | − 0.2 |
| **EC TOTAL** | − 12.4 | − 24.8 |

*Source:* Eurostat

day it is a vital element in the kaleidoscope of Atlantic and international monetary relations. Since its establishment, the Community has been one of the fastest growing regions for US direct investment. The prospect of a large, more unified and affluent market encouraged many

US companies to establish manufacturing plants in Europe. In 1958 investment in the Community comprised only 7% of total US investment abroad. By 1971 the Community proportion had risen to 15.8% and by the end of 1980 this share had climbed to 35.9%.

The bulk of US investment in Europe, in contrast to that in most other areas, is in manufacturing industries, with the exception of North Sea oil. Particularly noteworthy is the concentration in the United Kingdom on the petroleum and manufacturing industries, in the Federal Republic on manufacturing; in each country especially in the machinery and transport equipment sectors. Although less marked, this breakdown also applies to France. . . .

More and more US products, from computers to detergents, which might formerly have been manufactured in the United States and exported to Europe are now being produced in Europe itself. This phenomenon is in direct contrast to that in other parts of the world, where output is often re-exported back to the United States. Such a development has of course had a big impact on the level of US exports to Europe. In 1976, the last year for which figures are available, the sales of US manufacturing subsidiaries located in the Community amounted to $171.5 billion. Thus, for 1976, the sales of these subsidiaries were nearly six and a half times the value of total US exports to the Community or more than eight and a half times the value of exports of non-agricultural goods.

### Community Investment in the United States

The community countries were the biggest direct investors in the United States at the end of 1980 (total value $37.85 billion), with the Netherlands in first place with $16.16 billion, the United Kingdom coming second with $11.4 billion and the Federal Republic of Germany in fourth place with $5.29 billion.

The US Administration's policy towards capital investment in the United States has traditionally been liberal. After a review of the official position in 1975 it was decided to take action to improve the system for collecting data on foreign investment, and to reach understanding with foreign governments to consult the Administration prior to making major official investments in the United States. A new inter-agency Committee on Foreign Investment was accordingly set up.

Investment from Community countries is concentrated in particular industries: $12 billion in manufacturing, $9.7 billion in petroleum, and $7.54 billion in trade.

# 71

# Europe and the U.S.: How Alike, How Different?

**Gaston Thorn**

In this speech delivered to a symposium on US-EEC relations in fall 1981, the president of the European Commission, Gaston Thorn, examines the current state of European/ American relations and calls for a "stronger Atlantic alliance and dialogue with the United States" as part of a Europe-wide effort to move toward greater international stability.

. . . Recent world events and threats to peace have underlined more strongly than ever the basic identity between our political and economic systems and our goals. How then can we explain the growing barrage of mutual criticism which is flying back and forth across the Atlantic?

The internal economic crisis goes on. The continuing everyday problems tempt both partners to become introspective and prompt politicians to indulge in strong words for internal consumption. The result is that suspicion and mistrust grow and doubts arise about the real intentions of the other partner. Differing specific interests may then become magnified out of all proportion. Europe is accused of being seduced by the siren song of neutralism while Europeans think they see a new form of isolationism arising in America. The Americans appear to be so intent on the East-West conflict that they tend not to see any other aspect of the problem.

At the beginning of my address, I asked whether the wind that was blowing was the wind of isolationism or one of greater unity of purpose between the two principal partners of the Western world.

As long ago as 1965, Henry Kissinger looked at the problems facing the Atlantic alliance at the beginning of the period of detente in his book "The Troubled Partnership". He concluded that the alliance, forged at a time when the United States was incontestably the dominant partner, had still not found a new balance to accommodate Europe's refound strength on the economic front at least, and even on the political front too.

Today, sixteen years later, this has still not been resolved. The European pillar of the "two-pillar partnership", in which Kennedy wished a united Europe and the United States to share, has still not been erected. In fact, a considerable section of European public opinion is challenging the need for a defence policy while, at the same time, the situation outside gives cause for concern. The Soviet Union's arms strength, events in Cambodia and the occupation of Afghanistan show that the Soviet Union's intentions are still expansionist. For a year Poland has lived under the permanent threat of foreign intervention which would deal the death blow to what is left of detente in Europe. The assassination of Anwar Sadat reminds us that the unresolved struggle in the Middle East is a constant threat to our own security.

In the face of this external challenge and the internal problems which confront us daily, I should like to propose that we put behind us the sterile wrangling over issues of minor importance and resolve to create a closer union between the Community and the United States.

To do this, we must make maximum use of the mechanisms which exist to deal with specific problems, especially those affecting trade, and we must reflect on the kind of dialogue which is required in other areas.

Let us try to concentrate on points of common interest rather than search for scapegoats.

Was that not how the Marshall Plan was conceived? That reflected common interests; democracy had to be safeguarded and defended in a large part of the Western world and American industry needed a "megamarket" which could absorb its enormous output when it switched production from the weapons of war to the goods of peace.

Now, rather than the two sides shouting louder and louder about American interest rates or the CAP, a more constructive approach would be for us to try to understand the reasons for our respective policies and seek ways of making them more consistent with both our common interests and those of each partner.

But, in reality, are our interests so different? I do not think so.

For example, neither the American public nor the Reagan Administration is pleased to see high interest rates, for they are an obstacle to economic recovery and they depress Wall Street. High interest rates are, however, a means to an end about which we are in agreement with America—the removal of the inflationary, and therefore destabilizing, elements which disrupt economic decisions both internally and internationally.

It is also probably true that high interest rates in the United States have pushed European rates above the level we would have wished.

This does not mean that we are pursuing contradictory policies but rather that our policy mix is slightly different.

The real reason for European concern over American interest rates is their impact on the exchange rates of our currencies resulting from the disproportionate influence of the dollar on financial markets.

But we must also recognize that the internal tensions of the EMS exacerbated the problems caused by high American interest rates and the dollar exchange rate until the realignment on 4 October. But after this realignment, and you will have observed for yourselves how smoothly it was done, the future trend of the dollar should be far less of a problem for the Community.

Disagreement across the Atlantic about the level of interest rates is perhaps only a reflection of the international monetary system. If we recognize this, we shall understand better what is happening and perhaps we shall be able to work to improve the system.

We must now consolidate what has been gained by the successive rounds of trade negotiations since the sixties by renewing efforts to remove barriers to invisible trade and giving fresh impetus to the movement for monetary reform which ran aground on the beaches of Jamaica five years ago.

The steps which the Community is about to take to consolidate and develop the EMS should contribute towards world monetary stability and give the Community a great say in international monetary cooperation.

For the second stage of the EMS, progress needs to be made and agreement rapidly reached on the following points: the nature, structure and responsibilities of the institutions responsible for managing the EMS; greater use of the ECU, particularly in transactions with the central banks; and the consolidation and development of Community credit systems managed by the EMF [(European Monetary Fund)].

All this will serve to strengthen the foundations of the monetary system and confirm the Community's determination to secure greater stability in international monetary relations.

The Common Market has been and still is a key factor in the management of the international trading system and its existence was indispensable to the opening of the Dillon Round, the Kennedy Round and the Tokyo Round which helped both to liberalize international trade and to buttress GATT against the often severe pressures favouring protectionism.

The liberalization of international trade cannot make progress unless there is order on the monetary front, not only at world level, but between the Community countries too.

The EMF is not only essential to monetary and economic negotiation and coordination at world level but a precondition for free trade and survival of the Common Market. It is a challenge which Europe cannot ignore in the interests of a greater Atlantic and international economic order.

The same argument could be applied to growing American concern about certain aspects of the Common Agricultural Policy.

Let us begin by recognizing that while systems may differ, agricultural markets are usually organized. The diversity of systems can be explained by numerous factors such as security of supply, income distribution, and the power wielded by lobbies on both sides of the Atlantic.

The need for changes in agricultural policy—particularly ours—cannot be denied. Difficult though it may be, it is a must if the Community's budget is to play its proper role, if expenditure is to be kept within reasonable limits.

This then is another area in which our interests coincide, an area in which disagreements used to be the order of the day. It would be unfortunate if our efforts to revamp our agricultural policy were to be impeded by a new "chicken war" or the like.

On the North-South issue, in other words on relations between developed and developing countries, I can see an Atlantic war of words looming. I can visualize Europe being accused of not importing enough from the developing countries and the United States being criticized for not providing enough in the way of development aid. The truth of the matter is that Europe does more on both points. But this is not the right way to approach the problem.

Any deadlock in North-South discussions resulting from a prolonged dispute between the United States and Europe could upset economic relations between the Atlantic powers in the long term.

What is to stop us endeavouring to improve on our performance in areas where our record is poor?

Why shouldn't the United States and the Community move ahead together, the United States on the aid front by giving more support to the IMF and mulitilateral development banks, the Community on the services front, banks and invisibles for example. Better still, why shouldn't we work together to futher energy cooperation with the Third World, to encourage and protect foreign investment in the developing countries. This was first advocated by the Commission in 1974 and the Reagan Administration is now looking into the possibilities.

Shouldn't we attach greater importance to devising a scheme for cooperation in new fields? I am thinking in particular of the various sectors of research and development which will shape tomorrow's world.

Perhaps this is the time to give cross-Atlantic cooperation on R and D a new lease of life with the ultimate aim of promoting our own economic growth and facilitating development in less fortunate countries.

A likely area could be joint research into new technologies for saving energy and exploiting new sources—geothermal energy, solar energy or biomass energy. If we were to succeed, we could lessen tensions associated with oil supplies and give a boost to the development of indigenous energy sources in the developing countries.

Similarly, more effective collaboration in coal or nuclear energy R and D should enable us to promote the technologies that will be so badly needed on both sides of the Atlantic. Scientific collaboration should not be confined to energy alone, although present difficulties make it an obvious choice. It should go much further to embrace all the scientific disciplines of the future, such as telematics, biotechnology, space and so on.

Nor should collaboration be confined, as so often in the past, to areas in which the public sector provides the bulk of the finance. We must devise mechanisms which would create a favourable climate for collaboration between our universities and our industries in the area of advanced technology.

The technologies of the future should make it possible for the men and women of tomorrow to evaluate and exploit our planet's resources more effectively and live in a better world. It is for us, the advanced industrialized nations of today, to work together to ensure that this technology is harnessed not merely to our particular needs but to those of the world as a whole.

The objective is undoubtedly an ambitious one. But it could be achieved if collaboration between the United States and Europe were organized in a coherent fashion. The idea merits reflection, because a lot is at stake.

I am aware, ladies and gentlemen, of the obstacles, the problems, the inertia which hinders all forms of progress. My aim today has been to plead for a more vital, a more active partnership between the United States and Europe.

I know that Europe does not always speak with one voice. I realize that in many cases it is difficult for the United States to seek Europe's opinion because it does not know who to ask, and consultations with only some of the member states is no way of solving the problems.

If we want a stronger Atlantic alliance and dialogue with the United States we must, as Henry Kissinger said a long time ago, strengthen the European pillar. The Commission of which I am President is doing everything in its power to do just this, because it is well aware that, without a strong Europe, all that has been achieved over the last few decades could be put in jeopardy.

But the United States and Europe together can take up the challenge of the future and move towards greater cohesion in the Western world and hence towards greater international stability.

# Bibliography

## Unit I: The Historical Background

Aron, Raymond. IN DEFENSE OF DECADENT EUROPE. South Bend, Indiana: Regnery-Gateway, 1979.

Barraclough, Geoffrey. AN INTRODUCTION TO CONTEMPORARY HISTORY. Baltimore: Penguin, 1968.

Laqueur, Walter. EUROPE SINCE HITLER: THE REBIRTH OF EUROPE. Baltimore: Pelican, 1972.

————. A CONTINENT ASTRAY: EUROPE, 1970–1978. London: Oxford University Press, 1979.

Mayne, Richard. POST-WAR: THE DAWN OF TODAY'S EUROPE. New York: Schocken Books, 1983.

————. THE RECOVERY OF EUROPE. New York: Harper and Row, 1970.

Meier, Charles. THE ORIGINS OF THE COLD WAR AND CONTEMPORARY EUROPE. New York: New Viewpoints, 1978.

Sampson, Anthony. ANATOMY OF EUROPE: A GUIDE TO THE WORKINGS, INSTITUTIONS AND CHARACTER OF CONTEMPORARY WESTERN EUROPE. New York: Harper and Row, 1969.

Unwin, Derek. WESTERN EUROPE SINCE 1945: A POLITICAL HISTORY. London: Longmans, 1968.

## Units II–VII

Much of the subject matter covered in Units II–VII is dealt with in detail in individual country texts. Additional readings for these areas are listed below according to country.

### Benelux (Belgium, Netherlands and Luxembourg)

Griffiths, R.T. THE ECONOMY AND POLITICS OF THE NETHERLANDS SINCE 1945. Boston: Kluwer, 1980.

Keefe, Eugene, *et al*. AREA HANDBOOK FOR BELGIUM. Washington: U.S. Government Printing Office, 1974.

Lijphart, Arend. THE POLITICS OF ACCOMMODATION: PLURALISM AND DEMOCRACY IN THE NETHERLANDS. Berkeley: University of California Press, 1975.

Weil, Gordon. THE BENELUX NATIONS: THE POLITICS OF SMALL COUNTRY DEMOCRACIES. New York: Holt, Rinehart and Winston, 1970.

## West Germany

Conradt, David. THE GERMAN POLITY. New York: McKay, 1982.

Dahrendorf, Ralf. SOCIETY AND DEMOCRACY IN GERMANY. New York: Doubleday, 1965.

Edinger, Lewis. POLITICS IN WEST GERMANY. Boston: Little, Brown, 1976.

Grosser, Alfred. GERMANY IN OUR TIME: A POLITICAL HISTORY OF THE POSTWAR YEARS. New York: Praeger, 1973.

Hartrich, Edwin. THE FOURTH AND RICHEST REICH. New York: Macmillan, 1980.

## France

Andrews, William and Hoffmann, Stanley, eds. THE IMPACT OF THE FIFTH REPUBLIC ON FRANCE. Albany: State University of New York Press, 1981.

Ardagh, John. THE NEW FRANCE: A SOCIETY IN TRANSITION. Baltimore: Penguin, 1973.

————. FRANCE IN THE 1980s. New York: Penguin, 1983.

Avril, Pierre. POLITICS IN FRANCE. London: Pelican, 1969.

Cerny, Philip. SOCIAL MOVEMENT AND PROTEST IN FRANCE. New York: St. Martin's, 1982.

———— and Schain, Martin. FRENCH POLITICS AND PUBLIC POLICY. New York: St. Martin's, 1980.

Crozier, Michel. THE STALLED SOCIETY. New York: Viking, 1973.

Duverger, Maurice. THE FRENCH POLITICAL SYSTEM. Chicago: University of Chicago Press, 1958 and 1975.

Ehrmann, Henry. POLITICS IN FRANCE. Boston: Little, Brown, 1976.

Hanley, D.L., Kerr, A.P., and Waites, N.H. CONTEMPORARY FRANCE: POLITICS AND SOCIETY SINCE 1945. Boston: Routledge and Kegan Paul, 1979.

Hayward, Kack. THE ONE AND INDIVISIBLE FRENCH REPUBLIC. New York: Norton, 1973.

Hoffmann, Stanley. DECLINE OR RENEWAL? FRANCE SINCE THE 1930s. New York: Viking, 1974.

Macrae, Duncan. PARLIAMENT, PARTIES AND SOCIETY IN FRANCE, 1946–1958. New York: St. Martin's, 1967.

Macridis, Roy. FRENCH POLITICS IN TRANSITION: THE YEARS AFTER DE GAULLE. Cambridge: Winthrop, 1975.

———— and Brown, Bernard. THE DE GAULLE REPUBLIC: QUEST FOR UNITY. Westport, Conn.: Greenwood, 1976.

Marceau, Jane. CLASS AND STATUS IN FRANCE: ECONOMIC CHANGE AND SOCIAL IMMOBILITY. New York: Clarendon, 1977.

Safran, William. THE FRENCH POLITY. New York: McKay, 1977.

Suleiman, Ezra. POWER AND BUREAUCRACY IN FRANCE: THE ADMINISTRATIVE ELITE. Princeton: Princeton University Press, 1974.

Vaughan, M.C. et al. SOCIAL CHANGE IN FRANCE. New York: St. Martin's, 1980.

Williams, Philip. CRISIS AND COMPROMISE: POLITICS IN THE FOURTH REPUBLIC. Garden City, N.Y.: Doubleday, Anchor, 1960.

————. POLITICS AND SOCIETY IN DE GAULLE'S REPUBLIC. Garden City: Doubleday, Anchor, 1973.

Zeldin, Theodore. THE FRENCH. New York: Pantheon, 1983.

### Italy

Allum, Percy. ITALY: REPUBLIC WITHOUT GOVERNMENT. New York: Norton, 1974.

Di Palma, Giuseppe. SURVIVING WITHOUT GOVERNING: THE ITALIAN PARTIES IN PARLIAMENT. Berkeley: University of California Press, 1977.

Zariski, Raphael. ITALY: THE POLITICS OF UNEVEN DEVELOPMENT. Hinsdale, Ill.: Dryden, 1972.

### Norway

Eckstein, Harry. DIVISION AND COHESION IN DEMOCRACY: A STUDY OF NORWAY. Princeton: Princeton University Press, 1966.

Kvavik, Robert. INTEREST GROUPS IN NORWEGIAN POLITICS. Oslo: Universitetsforlaget, 1976.

Martinussen, Willy. THE DISTANT DEMOCRACY: SOCIAL INEQUALITY, POLITICAL RESOURCES AND POLITICAL INFLUENCE IN NORWAY. New York: Wiley, 1977.

### Portugal

de Figueiredo, Antonio. PORTUGAL: FIFTY YEARS OF DICTATORSHIP. New York: Holmes and Meier, 1978.

Graham, Lawrence and Makler, H.M., eds. CONTEMPORARY PORTUGAL: THE REVOLUTION AND ITS ANTECEDENTS. Austin: University of Texas Press, 1979.

Payne, Stanley. A HISTORY OF SPAIN AND PORTUGAL. 2 vols. Madison: University of Wisconsin Press, 1973.

Robinson, A.H. CONTEMPORARY PORTUGAL: A HISTORY. Boston: Allen and Unwin, 1979.

### Spain

Alba, Victor. TRANSITION IN SPAIN. New Brunswick: Transaction, 1978.

Arango E. Ramon. THE SPANISH POLITICAL SYSTEM: FRANCO'S LEGACY. Boulder, Colorado: Westview, 1978.

Carr, Raymond and Fusi, Juan. SPAIN: DICTATORSHIP TO DEMOCRACY. London: Allen and Unwin, 1980.

Coverdale, John. THE POLITICAL TRANSFORMATION OF SPAIN AFTER FRANCO. New York: Praeger, 1979.

Thomas, Hugh. THE SPANISH CIVIL WAR. New York: Harper and Row, 1961.

### Sweden

Anton, Thomas. ADMINISTERED POLITICS: ELITE POLITICAL CULTURE IN SWEDEN. Boston: Nijhoff, 1980.

Childs, Marquis. SWEDEN: THE MIDDLE WAY ON TRIAL. New Haven: Yale University Press, 1980.

Hancock, M. Donald. SWEDEN: THE POLITICS OF POST-INDUSTRIAL CHANGE. Hinsdale, Ill.: Dryden, 1972.

Koblick, Steve, ed. SWEDEN'S DEVELOPMENT FROM POVERTY TO AFFLUENCE, 1750–1970. Minneapolis: University of Minnesota Press, 1975.

Korpi, Walter. THE WORKING CLASS IN WELFARE CAPITALISM: WORK, UNIONS AND POLITICS IN SWEDEN. London and Boston: Routledge and Kegan Paul, 1978.

### United Kingdom

Beer, Samuel. BRITISH POLITICS IN THE COLLECTIVIST AGE. New York: Knopf, 1965.

————. BRITAIN AGAINST ITSELF: THE POLITICAL CONTRADICTIONS OF COLLECTIVISM. New York: Norton, 1982.

Butler, David and Stokes, Richard. POLITICAL CHANGE IN BRITAIN. New York: St. Martin's, 1974.

Crossman, Richard. THE DIARIES OF A CABINET MINISTER (3 vols.). London: Jonathan Cape, 1978.

Jennings, Ivor. CABINET GOVERNMENT. New York: Cambridge University Press, 1959.

Mackintosh, J.P. THE BRITISH CABINET. London: Stevens, 1970.

Morrison, Herbert. GOVERNMENT AND PARLIAMENT. New York: Oxford University Press, 1960.

Nossiter, Bernard. BRITAIN: A FUTURE THAT WORKS. New York: Houghton Mifflin, 1978.

Pollard, Sidney. THE WASTING OF THE BRITISH ECONOMY. London: St. Martin's, 1982.

Rose, Richard. POLITICS IN ENGLAND. Boston: Little, Brown, 1974.

Sampson, Anthony. THE CHANGING ANATOMY OF BRITAIN. London: Hodder and Stoughton, 1982.

Wooton, Graham. PRESSURE POLITICS IN CONTEMPORARY BRITAIN. Lexington, Mass.: Lexington, 1978.

### Political Parties

There are a considerable number of useful monographs on political parties, especially of the left. Additional readings on this subject are, therefore, listed separately.

Barnes, Samuel and Kaase, Max. POLITICAL ACTION: MASS PARTICIPATION IN FIVE WESTERN DEMOCRACIES. Beverly Hills: Sage, 1979.

Brown, Bernard, ed. EUROCOMMUNISM AND EUROSOCIALISM: THE LEFT CONFRONTS MODERNITY. New York: Cyrco Press, 1979.

Carstairs, Andrew. A SHORT HISTORY OF ELECTORAL SYSTEMS IN WESTERN EUROPE. Boston: Allen and Unwin, 1980.

Castles, Francis. THE SOCIAL DEMOCRATIC IMAGE OF SOCIETY. London: Routledge and Kegan Paul, 1978.

Griffith, William. THE EUROPEAN LEFT: ITALY, FRANCE, AND SPAIN. Lexington, Mass.: Lexington Books, 1979.

Layton-Henry, Zig., ed. CONSERVATIVE POLITICS IN WESTERN EUROPE. New York: St. Martins, 1983.

Mackenzie, R.T. BRITISH POLITICAL PARTIES. London: Heineman, 1968.

Rasmussen, Jurgen. THE LIBERAL PARTY. London: Constable, 1965.

Rose, Richard. THE PROBLEM OF PARTY GOVERNMENT. Baltimore: Penguin, 1976.

## Unit VIII: The Economic Scene

Dahrendorf, Rolf, ed. EUROPE'S ECONOMY IN CRISIS. New York: Holmes and Meier, 1982.

Goldthorpe, John and Hirsch, Fred. THE POLITICAL ECONOMY OF INFLATION. London: Martin Robertson, 1978.

The best source for the economic climate in various European countries is the Country Studies published annually by the O.E.C.D.

Current economic data can be found in I.M.F. INTERNATIONAL FINANCIAL STATISTICS.

## Unit IX: Industrial Policy and Economic Nationalism

Bergsten, C. Fred. TRADE POLICY IN THE 1980'S. Washington: Institute for International Economics, 1982.

Howard, Jack and Narkiewicz, Olga. PLANNING IN EUROPE. New York: St. Martin's, 1978.

Johnson, Harry, Ed. THE NEW MERCANTILISM. New York: St. Martin's, 1978.

## Unit X: Social Welfare

Childs, Marquis W. SWEDEN: THE MIDDLE WAY ON TRIAL. New Haven: Yale University Press, 1980.

Einhorn, Eric and Logue, John. WELFARE STATES IN HARD TIMES: DENMARK AND SWEDEN IN THE 1970'S. Kent, Ohio: Popular Press, 1980.

Flora, Peter and Herden, Arnold L. THE DEVELOPMENT OF THE WELFARE STATES IN EUROPE AND AMERICA. New York: Transaction Books, 1981.

Fry, John, ed. LIMITS OF THE WELFARE STATE. Hampshire, England: Renouf, 1979.

Furniss, N. and Tiltan, T. THE CASE FOR THE WELFARE STATE. Indiana: Indiana University Press, 1979.

Korpi, Walter. THE WORKING CLASS IN WELFARE CAPITALISM. London: Routledge and Kegan Paul, 1978.

Lindbeck, Assar. SWEDISH ECONOMIC POLICY. Berkeley: University of California Press, 1973.

Ruinlinger, Gaston. WELFARE POLICY AND INDUSTRIALIZATION IN EUROPE. New York: Wiley, 1971.

Scase, Richard. SOCIAL DEMOCRACY IN CAPITALIST SOCIETY: WORKING-CLASS POLITICS IN BRITAIN AND SWEDEN. Totowa, N.J.: Rowman and Littlefield, 1977.

## Unit XI: Energy

DeCarmoy, Guy. ENERGY FOR EUROPE: ECONOMIC AND POLITICAL IMPLICATIONS. Washington: American Enterprise Institute, 1977.

Goodwin, Crandford D., ed. ENERGY POLICY IN PERSPECTIVE: TODAY'S PROBLEMS. Washington: Brookings Institution, 1981.

Kohl, Wilfrid L., ed. AFTER THE SECOND OIL CRISIS. ENERGY AND POLITICS IN EUROPE, AMERICA AND JAPAN. Lexington, Mass.: Lexington Books, 1982.

Stent, Angela. SOVIET ENERGY AND WESTERN EUROPE. New York: Praeger, 1982.

## Unit XII: Immigration

Bohning, Walter. THE MIGRATION OF WORKERS IN THE UNITED KINGDOM AND THE EUROPEAN COMMUNITY. New York: Oxford University Press, 1972.

Castles, Stephen and Kosack, Godula. IMMIGRANT WORKERS AND CLASS STRUCTURE IN WESTERN EUROPE. New York: Oxford University Press, 1973.

Freeman, Gary. IMMIGRANT LABOR AND RACIAL CONFLICT IN INDUSTRIAL SOCIETIES: THE FRENCH AND BRITISH EXPERIENCES. Princeton: Princeton University Press, 1979.

Kindelberger, Charles. MIGRATION, GROWTH AND DEVELOPMENT. Paris: Organisation for Economic Cooperation and Development, 1978.

Papademetriou, Demetrios. "European Labor Migration: Consequences for the Countries of Worker Origin," INTERNATIONAL STUDIES QUARTERLY, Vol. 22, No. 3, September 1978.

Power, Jonathan. MIGRANT WORKERS IN WESTERN EUROPE AND THE UNITED STATES. Oxford and New York: Pergamon, 1979.

Rist, Raymond. "Migration and Marginality: Guestworkers in Germany and France," DAEDELUS, Spring 1980.

## Unit XIII: Security

Boutwell, Jeffrey. "Politics and the Peace Movement in West Germany," INTERNATIONAL SECURITY, Spring 1983.

Hassner, Pierre. "The Shifting Foundations," FOREIGN POLICY, Fall 1982.

International Institute for Strategic Studies. DEFENSE AND CONSENSUS:

THE DOMESTIC ASPECTS OF WESTERN SECURITY, Adelphi Papers, Nos. 182, 183 and 184, London, 1983.

Mako, William. U.S. GROUND FORCES AND THE DEFENSE OF CENTRAL EUROPE. Washington: Brookings, 1983.

Schwartz, David. NATO'S NUCLEAR DILEMMAS. Washington: Brookings, 1983.

Steinbruner, John and Sigal, Leon, eds. ALLIANCE SECURITY: NATO AND THE NO-FIRST-USE QUESTION. Washington: Brookings, 1983.

Thompson, E.P. BEYOND THE COLD WAR: A NEW APPROACH TO THE ARMS RACE AND NUCLEAR ANNIHILATION. New York: Pantheon, 1982.


## Unit XIV: The European Community

Andrews, Stanley. AGRICULTURE AND THE COMMON MARKET. Ames: Iowa State University Press, 1973.

"The European Community After Twenty Years," THE ANNALS OF THE AMERICAN ACADEMY OF POLITICAL AND SOCIAL SCIENCE, Vol. 440, November 1978.

Graubard, Stephen. A NEW EUROPE? Boston: Houghton Mifflin, 1969.

Hallstein, Walter. EUROPE IN THE MAKING. New York: Norton, 1973.

Marsh, John and Swanney, Pamela. AGRICULTURE AND THE EUROPEAN COMMUNITY. London: Allen and Unwin, 1980.

Pryce, Roy. THE POLITICS OF THE EUROPEAN COMMUNITY. Totowa, N.J.: Rowman and Littlefield, 1973.

Scalingi, Paula. THE EUROPEAN PARLIAMENT: THE THREE-DECADE SEARCH FOR A UNITED EUROPE. Westport, Conn.: Greenwood, 1980.

Usher, John. EUROPEAN COMMUNITY LAW AND NATIONAL LAW: THE IRREVERSIBLE TRANSFER? London: Allen and Unwin, 1981.

Wallace, Helen. BUDGETARY POLITICS: THE FINANCES OF THE EUROPEAN COMMUNITIES. London: Allen and Unwin, 1980.

Wallace, Helen, Wallace, William and Webb, Carole, eds. POLICY MAKING IN THE EUROPEAN COMMUNITY. London: Wiley, 1983.


## Unit XV: The European Community and the World

Alting von Geusau, Frans. THE EXTERNAL RELATIONS OF THE EUROPEAN COMMUNITY. Lexington, Mass.: Lexington, 1974.

―――. THE LOME CONVENTION AND A NEW INTERNATIONAL ECONOMIC ORDER. Leyden: Sijthoff, 1977.

Chase, James and Ravenal, Earl. ATLANTIS LOST. New York: New York University Press, 1977.

Goldsborough, James. REBEL EUROPE: HOW AMERICA CAN LIVE WITH A CHANGING CONTINENT. New York: Macmillan, 1982.

Grosser, Alfred. THE WESTERN ALLIANCE: EUROPEAN-AMERICAN RELATIONS SINCE 1945. New York: Continuum, 1980.

Kaiser, Karl and Schwarz, H-P. AMERICA AND WESTERN EUROPE. Lexington, Mass.: Lexington, 1977.

Landes, David, ed. CRITICAL CHOICES FOR AMERICANS, Vol. 8: WESTERN EUROPE: THE TRIALS OF PARTNERSHIP. Lexington, Mass.: Lexington, 1976.

Long, Frank. THE POLITICAL ECONOMY OF EEC RELATIONS WITH AFRICAN, CARIBBEAN AND PACIFIC STATES. Oxford and New York: Pergamon, 1980.

Mathews, Jacqueline. THE ASSOCIATION SYSTEM OF THE EUROPEAN COMMUNITY. New York: Praeger, 1976.

Mowar, A.G. THE EUROPEAN COMMUNITY AND LATIN AMERICA: A CASE STUDY IN GLOBAL ROLE EXPANSION. Westport, Conn.: Greenwood, 1982.

Rosenthal, Glenda. THE MEDITERRANEAN BASIN: ITS POLITICAL ECONOMY AND CHANGING INTERNATIONAL RELATIONS. London: Butterworth, 1982.

Serfaty, Simon. THE FADING PARTNERSHIP. New York: Praeger, 1977.

Shlaim, Avi and Yannopoulos, George, eds. THE EUROPEAN ECONOMIC COMMUNITY AND EASTERN EUROPE. Cambridge: Cambridge University Press, 1978.

Stent, Angela. SOVIET ENERGY AND WESTERN EUROPE. New York: Praeger, 1982.

Taylor, Philip. WHEN EUROPE SPEAKS WITH ONE VOICE: THE EXTERNAL RELATIONS OF THE EUROPEAN COMMUNITY. Westport, Conn.: Greenwood, 1979.

Tucker, Robert and Wrigley, Linda. THE ATLANTIC ALLIANCE AND ITS CRITICS. New York: Praeger, 1983.

Zartman, William. POLITICS OF TRADE NEGOTIATIONS BETWEEN THE WEAK AND THE STRONG: AFRICA CONFRONTS THE EUROPEAN COMMUNITY. Princeton, N.J.: Princeton University Press, 1971.

# Glossary

**Capital flows**—Refers to the movement of money across international borders for investment or security reasons.

**Capital gains tax**—A tax on increases in the value of assets.

**Capital goods**—Goods that are used to facilitate further production.

**Capital intensive production**—Production techniques which use relatively large amounts of capital (machinery, industrial equipment) and small amounts of labor in producing a unit of output.

**Capital transfer tax**—Tax on assets (bonds, stocks, and real assets) transferred to another party.

**Capitalism**—An economic system based on private ownership of the means of production and distribution and reliance on the market to allocate resources.

**City-busting**—Refers to the targeting of cities and their destruction with nuclear weapons.

**Common external tariff**—All the members of the EEC apply identical tariffs on imported goods derived from centers within the community. This is known as a common external tariff.

**Confederal union**—Political union of independent nation-states.

**Constant prices**—A statistical "fiction" employed to eliminate the influence of price changes on, for example, the value of goods and services produced (gross national product). Thus in comparing two years, the assumption is made that the price level in one of ten years prevailed in both years. Observed changes in value can then be attributed exclusively to changes in volume of goods produced.

**Decartelize**—To break up an agreement by a group of businesses in the same industry limiting competition among them and regulating the market through such tools as price fixing and production control.

**Deflationary measures**—Any monetary or fiscal policy designed to reduce spending. Deflationary measures exert downward pressure on prices.

**Devaluation**—A reduction in the value of a nation's currency in terms of a foreign currency. The £ is devalued when the dollar price of the £ falls from $2.50 to $2.00.

**Devolution**—Decentralization of governmental authority to smaller administrative units.

**Direct taxes**—Includes taxes on income, property and wealth as contrasted with taxes on transactions (sales, excise, etc.) which are classified as indirect taxes.

**Economic liberalism**—Doctrine favoring reliance on market forces to allocate resources and opposed to government interference in economic matters.

473

**Elite**—The upper class, the most highly educated, or the most select group(s) in a society, a nation, or a profession.

**Embourgeoisement**—Process by which an individual or group acquires more "bourgeois" (or middle-class) values.

**European Free Trade Association (EFTA)**—Established in 1960 between Austria, Switzerland, the United Kingdom, and Denmark, with Finland joining in 1961. The U.K. and Denmark left EFTA when they joined the EEC in 1973. Goods traded between the members are not subject to customs duties.

**European integration**—Process by which the nations of Western Europe were gradually to integrate their economic and political activities with a view to the eventual formation of a United States of Europe.

**European Monetary Fund (EMF)**—A reserve system of the central banks of the EC.

**European Monetary System (EMS)**—Negotiated by the EC in 1978 and implemented in 1979. The objective was to establish a zone of currency stability within the European Community without, however, imposing an absolutely fixed exchange rate.

**European Payments Union (EPU)**—Functioned between 1950 and 1958 as the organ which facilitated the restriction of convertibility of European currencies.

**Fixed but adjustable parities**—A system of currency valuation in which there is an agreed upon ratio of exchange between currencies but in which exchange ratio can be altered if changes are necessary to maintain balance of payments equilibrium.

**Flexible response**—NATO policy providing for limited but graduated retaliation from conventional to theater nuclear to strategic strikes in response to various levels of offense activity by the Warsaw Pact. Flexible response replaced massive retaliation.

**Floating exchange rate**—A currency regime in which the value of currencies fluctuate in response to the forces of supply and demand in the foreign exchange market.

**Gaullist**—Nationalistically oriented foreign policies characteristic of those pursued by Charles de Gaulle, French President from 1958-1969.

**General Agreement on Tariffs and Trade (GATT)**—Created in 1947 to work toward free trade. GATT promotes non-discrimination and reciprocity in trade and endeavors to eliminate quantitative restrictions to trade, such as quotas. Also provides for a forum for multilateral trade negotiations.

**General Preference System (GPS)**—An agreement by ten advanced industrial countries to permit certain manufactured inputs from the less developed countries to enter at lower tariff rates than those applied to similar inputs from other countries. This system was designed to help promote economic development in the less developed countries.

**Indirect taxes**—Taxes on transactions—sales taxes, excise taxes, purchase taxes, etc.—rather than on income or wealth.

**Labor intensive production**—Production techniques which use little capital but large amounts of labor to produce a unit of output.

**Laissez-faire**—Economic policy based on the belief that government should pursue a "hands-off" policy with respect to economic activity.

**"Lame-duck" manufacturers**—Refers to those firms or industries which are no longer profitable, or have become too expensive to subsidize.

**Landed gentry**—In England, the class immediately below the nobility whose wealth was based on the ownership of large amounts of land.

**North Atlantic Treaty Organization (NATO)**—Collective self-defense pact signed April 4, 1949 by the U.S., Britain, France, Belgium, the Netherlands, Luxembourg, Canada, Italy, Iceland, Denmark, Norway and Portugal. Greece and Turkey were invited to join in 1951 and West Germany entered in 1955. Spain became a member in 1982.

**North-South dialogue**—On-going debate between the advanced and the less-developed countries regarding the responsibilities and obligations of the two for the economic and political development of the less developed countries.

**North-South issues**—Problems especially relating to trade and development between the developed and industrialized countries of the Northern hemisphere and the underdeveloped or developing countries of the southern hemisphere.

**Protectionism**—Policy limiting competition by foreign firms by restricting imports of goods through tariffs, quotas, and the erection of non-tariff barriers to trade.

**Provincialism**—Maintenance of local customs, traditions, and values.

**Supply-side economics**—A theory popularized by President Reagan which emphasizes the importance of incentives as the key to economic growth and prosperity.

**Trade deficit**—The excess of the value of imports over the value of exports.

**Transnational organization**—An organization or body which conducts or governs activity in more than one country (usually several).

**Value-added tax (VAT)**—An indirect tax imposed at each stage in production and distribution on the value that has been added to the product by processing costs.

**Venice initiative on the Middle East**—Communiqué issued in Venice in June 1980 by the Heads of State of the member countries of the European Community. For the first time the notions of Palestinian self-determination and the need for negotiations with the Palestine Liberation Organization were directly mentioned.

**Voluntary export restraints**—The imposition of export quotas by the exporters. These quotas are usually imposed to avoid the imposition of more restrictive quotas by the importers.

# About the Contributors

Jens Alber  is a research fellow at the European University Institute in Florence and a university assistant at the University of Cologne.

P.A. Allum is a lecturer in politics at the University of Reading in Great Britain.

King Baudouin I has been the king of Belgium since 1951.

A.H. Birch is professor of political science at the University of Victoria, British Columbia. He is president of the Political Studies Association of the United Kingdom and author of *Political Integration and Disintegration in the British Isles*.

Howard Bliss was professor of political science at Vassar College until his retirement several years ago.

David Brand is a correspondent for the *Wall Street Journal*.

John H. Burnett is a professor of political science at Texas Tech University.

Francis G. Castles is a political scientist specializing in Scandinavian politics. He is the author of *The Social Democratic Image of Society* and coauthor of *Immigrant Workers and Class Structure in Western Europe*.

Karl W. Deutsch is Stanfield Professor of International Peace at Harvard University and director of the International Institute for Comparative Social Research in West Berlin. He was Fulbright Professor at the Goethe University in Frankfurt in 1968 and received Guggenheim Fellowships in 1954 and 1971 and the German Prize of Culture in 1977. He writes extensively on nationalism, international law, and political affairs.

Juergen B. Donges is professor of economics at the University of Kiel in West Germany, where he is head of the Development Economics Department, or Institut für Weltwirtschaft. He is a member of the Advisory Council of the Federal Ministry of Economic Cooperation, Federal Republic of West Germany.

Lewis J. Edinger is professor of political science at Columbia University and author of several books, including *Politics in West Germany.*

Barnaby J. Feder is a correspondent for *The New York Times*.

Werner J. Feld is chairman of the political science department at the University of New Orleans. He writes on international trade and industry, law, and politics. His most recent work is *Multinational Corporations and UN Politics*, published in 1980.

Peter Flora is professor of sociology at the University of Cologne and at the European University Institute in Florence. His publications include *Quantitative Historical Sociology* and *State, Economy, and Society in Western Europe*.

483

Milton Friedman is a Nobel laureate in economics and Paul Snowden Russell Distinguished Service Professor of Economics at the University of Chicago. He has been a Senior Research Fellow at the Hoover Institution at Stanford University since 1976 and a contributing editor to *Newsweek* since 1966. He is the author of numerous books and articles, including *Free to Choose*, which was published in 1980.

Harry K. Girvetz was chairman of the Department of Philosophy at the University of California, Santa Barbara, from 1958 to 1965. His works include *From Wealth to Welfare* and *Evolution of Liberalism*. He died in 1974.

Wyn Grant teaches at the University of Warwick in Great Britain.

Godfrey Hodgson has been a reporter for the *Sunday Times* of London since 1967. He is also a television reporter in Britain specializing in American politics and race relations. He is the author of *America in Our Time: From World War II to Nixon—What Happened and Why.*

Stanley Hoffmann is a professor of government at Harvard University. Educated in France, he writes extensively on international relations, law, and the French political system.

Sir Geoffrey Howe served as Britain's solicitor general from 1970 to 1972 and then as chancellor of the exchequer under Margaret Thatcher from 1979 to 1983. In mid-1983 he was appointed foreign minister. He is perhaps best known for his political activities in the areas of racial and sexual discrimination and social welfare.

Karl Kaiser is director of the Research Institute, German Institute of Foreign Relations and author of *German Foreign Policy in Transition*.

Britta Kellgren is a Swedish writer and journalist who concentrates on social issues in Sweden.

Jürgen Kohl is assistant for social policy in the sociology department at the University of Bielefeld in West Germany. He was educated in Germany and is a frequent contributor to German scholarly journals.

William L. Langer was formerly professor emeritus at Harvard University, where he held the Coolidge professorship in history from 1936 until 1964. He worked at various times for the Central Intelligence Agency and was also a member of the President's Foreign Intelligence Advisory Board. He died in 1977.

Walter Laqueur is director of the Institute of Contemporary History in London. He is also head of the Wiener Library in London and chairman of the Research Council for the Center of Strategic International Studies in Washington, D.C. He has edited numerous books including *The Reader's Guide to Contemporary History* and *Fascism: A Reader's Guide*.

Winston Lord, currently president of the Council on Foreign Relations, has had extensive experience in government service. He served as the director of the policy planning staff of the U.S. State Department from 1973 to 1977 and worked as special assistant to the Assistant to the President for National Security Affairs from 1970 to 1973. He was also a National Security Council Staff member from 1969 until 1973.

Roy C. Macridis is professor of political science at Brandeis University and was chairman of the department from 1968 to 1974. He was awarded a Guggenheim Fellowship in 1971, Rockefeller grants in 1956, 1958, and 1961, and a Ford Foundation Fellowship in 1950. He was also Fulbright Professor at the University of Paris in 1961–1962. He specializes in French politics.

Lawrence C. Mayer is professor of political science at Texas Tech University.

Richard Mayne is a Special Advisor to the European Economic Community Commission. He frequently writes on European history and politics.

Janice McCormick is an assistant professor in the graduate school of business administration at Harvard University.

Colin Mellors is the author of *The British MP: A Socio-economic Study of the House of Commons*.

Thierry de Montbrial is director of the French Institute of International Relations.

William H. Overholt is a research associate at the Research Institute on International Change at Columbia University and is editor of the Institute's quarterly journal, *Global Political Assessment*. He specializes in foreign, especially Asian, politics.

B. Guy Peters is professor of political science at Tulane University in New Orleans.

Sylvia Poggioli is an Italian writer, free-lance journalist, and broadcaster for National Public Radio in Rome.

Jonathan Power has been a columnist for the *International Herald Tribune* and is a frequent contributor to the British Broadcasting Company. A filmmaker, Power has worked in diverse fields and settings, including a stint with Martin Luther King during his civil rights campaign.

R.M. Punnett is a senior lecturer in politics at the University of Strathlyde. He was a visiting professor at McMaster University in Ontario from 1976 to 1977. He is the author of *The Prime Minister in Canadian Government and Politics*.

Steven Rattner, an investment broker, was formerly a correspondent for *The New York Times*.

Ray C. Rist is Deputy Director of Program Evaluation at the Government Accounting Office in Washington, D.C. He has taught in the College of Human Ecology at Cornell University and has been a consultant to the U.S. Commission on Civil Rights and the National Institute of Education. He is a frequent contributor to *Harvard Education Review* and is the editor of the *Northwest Journal of African and Black American Studies*.

Charles L. Robertson is a professor of government at Smith College and has been a frequent lecturer at the University of Massachusetts and at Amherst

College. The author of numerous articles and books, including *International Politics Since World War II*, he is currently involved in research on the politics of international economic relations.

Tim Robinson is a lecturer in sociology at Sheffield University in Britain and a lecturer in journalism at The City University in London. He writes on social deviance, medicine, and welfare politics.

John E. Rodes has taught at Occidental College in Los Angeles since 1950. He was a Fulbright Lecturer at the University of the Saarland in West Germany from 1974 until 1975 and is the author of *Quest For Unity.*

William Safran is professor of political science at the University of Colorado, Boulder.

D. Brent Smith is a political scientist specializing in West German politics. He is the author of *The Opposition to Ostpolitik: Foreign Policy as an Issue in West German Politics, 1969–1972.*

T. Alexander Smith teaches at the University of Tennessee.

Ezra N. Suleiman is professor of political science at Princeton University. He was a visiting professor at the University of Grenoble in 1973 and at the Sorbonne, University of Paris in 1973–1974. He is the recipient of numerous awards, including the Fulbright senior scholar in France in 1977, a Guggenheim Fellowship in 1977–1978, and a German Marshall Fund Fellowship in 1978–1979. His publications include *Comparative Politics* and *The Transformation of French Society in the Post-War Period.*

Gaston Thorn is president of the EEC Executive Commission in Brussels. He was a member of the European Parliament from 1959 to 1969 and has served as Luxembourg's prime minister since 1977. In 1975, he served as president of the 30th General Assembly of the United Nations.

Kenneth J. Twitchett has taught at the University of Aberdeen and at the London School of Economics. He specializes in international politics and European integration.

Robert E. Ward, previously professor of political science at the University of Michigan and an associate at the University's Center for Japanese Studies, is currently director of the Center for Research in International Studies at Stanford University. He is also a member of the Comparative Politics Committee of the Social Science Research Council.

David Watt, a British journalist and international affairs specialist, was director of the Royal Institute of International Affairs in London until January 1984. He has been a columnist for *The Times* since 1981.

# About the Editors

GLENDA G. ROSENTHAL is currently assistant professor of political science at Columbia University. She holds a Diploma in European Studies from the College of Europe in Bruges, Belgium, a master's degree in modern history from Oxford University, and a Ph.D. in political science from Columbia University. Dr. Rosenthal, who is also Co-Chair of the Council for European Studies, has taught at Vassar College, Rutgers University, the City University of New York, and New York University. She has published numerous articles in both European and American scholarly journals and is the author of *The Mediterranean Basin: Its Political Economy and Changing International Relations* and *The Man Behind the Decisions: Cases In European Policy Making*. Her current research activities include a comparative study of the roles of the United States, Canada, and the European Community in the political and economic development of the Caribbean Basin.

ELLIOT ZUPNICK is Director of the Institute on Western Europe at Columbia University, where he is also professor of international economics. Dr. Zupnick holds both a master's degree and a Ph.D. in economics from Columbia University. He has held teaching positions at the City University of New York, where he was also Dean of Graduate Studies from 1959 to 1973, and has been a visiting professor at Cornell University. Dr. Zupnick has published numerous reviews and articles on international economics in both scholarly and professional journals and is the author of four books, including *Britain's Postwar Dollar Problem*, *United States Foreign Economic Policy*, *Understanding the International Monetary System*, and most recently, *Direct Foreign Investment in the U.S.: Costs and Benefits*.

RITVA POOM is currently a Research Staff Associate at the Institute on Western Europe at Columbia University. Ms. Poom, who holds a bachelor's degree from Tufts University and a master's degree from Columbia University, received a Finnish Ministry of Education Fellowship to Helsinki in 1981–1982 and a grant from the New York State Council on the Arts in 1983–1984. She has worked as a consultant in the design of intercultural programs and in the development of outreach programs. Her translations from the Finno-Ugric languages have appeared in the *Literary Review*, *The Drama Review*, *Cross-Cultural Communications*, and *The Scandinavian Review*.

LINDA WOOD, a free-lance writer, has been an editorial consultant at University Extension, University of California, San Diego, since 1979. She is currently editorial director of print materials for two audio/print courses developed by the Global Understanding Project at National Public Radio. Ms. Wood holds both a bachelor's degree and a master's degree from the University of California, Berkeley, and a diploma in French civilization from the Sorbonne. Her publications include *The Psychology Primer*, the *Reader/Study Guide* and *Viewer's Guide* for Carl Sagan's "Cosmos," *A Land Called California*, *Working: Changes and Choices*, and *Understanding Space and Time*. She is also the coauthor of an award-winning children's book, *Windows in Space*, published in 1982.